Transformation
in Psychotherapy

Transformation
in Psychotherapy

Corrective Experiences Across Cognitive Behavioral, Humanistic, and Psychodynamic Approaches

Edited by **LOUIS G. CASTONGUAY** and **CLARA E. HILL**

American Psychological Association • Washington, DC

Published by
American Psychological Association
750 First Street, NE
Washington, DC 20002
www.apa.org

To order
APA Order Department
P.O. Box 92984
Washington, DC 20090-2984
Tel: (800) 374-2721; Direct: (202) 336-5510
Fax: (202) 336-5502; TDD/TTY: (202) 336-6123
Online: www.apa.org/pubs/books
E-mail: order@apa.org

In the U.K., Europe, Africa, and the Middle East, copies may be ordered from
American Psychological Association
3 Henrietta Street
Covent Garden, London
WC2E 8LU England

Typeset in Goudy by Circle Graphics, Inc., Columbia, MD

Printer: Edwards Brothers, Inc., Ann Arbor, MI
Cover Designer: Naylor Design, Inc., Washington, DC

The opinions and statements published are the responsibility of the authors, and such opinions and statements do not necessarily represent the policies of the American Psychological Association.

Library of Congress Cataloging-in-Publication Data

Transformation in psychotherapy : corrective experiences across cognitive behavioral, humanistic, and psychodynamic approaches / edited by Louis G. Castonguay and Clara E. Hill.
    p. cm.
  Includes index.
  ISBN 978-1-4338-1159-3—ISBN 1-4338-1159-6 1. Psychotherapy. 2. Cognitive therapy. 3. Psychodynamic psychotherapy. I. Castonguay, Louis Georges. II. Hill, Clara E., 1948-.
  RC475.T73 2012
  616.89'1425—dc23
                              2011053042

British Library Cataloguing-in-Publication Data
A CIP record is available from the British Library.

Printed in the United States of America
First Edition

DOI: 10.1037/13747-000

To Marvin Goldfried and Charles Gelso,
for their inspiration and friendship.

CONTENTS

CONTRIBUTORS

Timothy Anderson, PhD, Ohio University, Athens
Lynne E. Angus, PhD, York University, Toronto, Ontario, Canada
Jacques P. Barber, PhD, ABPP, Adelphi University, Garden City, NY
J. Gayle Beck, PhD, University of Memphis, Memphis, TN
Thomas Berger, PhD, University of Bern, Bern, Switzerland
Margit I. Berman, PhD, Dartmouth Medical School, Hanover, NH
Arthur C. Bohart, PhD, California State University, Dominguez Hills
Thomas D. Borkovec, PhD, Penn State University, University Park
James F. Boswell, PhD, Boston University, Boston, MA
Alan W. Burkard, PhD, Marquette University, Milwaukee, WI
Franz Caspar, PhD, University of Bern, Bern, Switzerland
Louis G. Castonguay, PhD, Penn State University, University Park
Christopher Christian, PhD, The New School for Social Research and
     Beth Israel Medical Center, New York, NY
Michael J. Constantino, PhD, University of Massachusetts Amherst
Rachel E. Crook-Lyon, PhD, Brigham Young University, Provo, UT
Robert Elliott, PhD, University of Strathclyde, Glasgow, United Kingdom
Barry A. Farber, PhD, Teachers College, Columbia University, New York, NY

Christoph Flückiger, PhD, University of Zurich and University of Bern, Zurich, Switzerland

Myrna L. Friedlander, PhD, University at Albany, State University of New York

Marvin R. Goldfried, PhD, Stony Brook University, Stony Brook, NY

Leslie S. Greenberg, PhD, York University, Toronto, Ontario, Canada

Martin Grosse Holtforth, PhD, University of Zurich, Zurich, Switzerland

Adele M. Hayes, PhD, University of Delaware, Newark

Jeffrey A. Hayes, PhD, Penn State University, University Park

Laurie Heatherington, PhD, Williams College, Williamstown, MA

Bernadette D. Heckman, PhD, Ohio University, Athens

Shirley A. Hess, PhD, Shippensburg University, Shippensburg, PA

Clara E. Hill, PhD, University of Maryland, College Park

Arpana G. Inman, PhD, Lehigh University, Bethlehem, PA

John Jackson, BS, University of Maryland, College Park

Sarah Knox, PhD, Marquette University, Milwaukee, WI

Nicholas Ladany, PhD, Loyola Marymount University, Los Angeles, CA

Kenneth N. Levy, PhD, Penn State University, University Park

Jingqing Liu, BS, University of Maryland, College Park

Peter MacFarlane, MS, Ohio University, Athens

Andrew A. McAleavey, MS, Penn State University, University Park

Stanley B. Messer, PhD, Rutgers University, Piscataway, NJ

J. Christopher Muran, PhD, Adelphi University and Beth Israel Medical Center, New York, NY

Dana L. Nelson, PhD, University of Delaware, Newark

Michelle G. Newman, PhD, Penn State University, University Park

Samuel S. Nordberg, MS, Penn State University, University Park

Elizabeth Nutt Williams, PhD, St. Mary's College of Maryland, St. Mary's City

Benjamin M. Ogles, PhD, Brigham Young University, Provo, UT

Jeremy D. Safran, PhD, The New School for Social Research and Beth Israel Medical Center, New York, NY

Brian A. Sharpless, PhD, Penn State University, University Park

Wonjin Sim, PhD, University of Maryland, College Park

Patricia Spangler, PhD, University of Maryland, College Park

William B. Stiles, PhD, Miami University, Oxford, OH

Barbara J. Thompson, PhD, Independent Practice, Ellicott City, MD

Jessica A. Walker, PhD, Hefner VA Medical Center, Salisbury, NC

Henny A. Westra, PhD, York University, Toronto, Ontario, Canada

Carly Yasinski, BA, University of Delaware, Newark

ACKNOWLEDGMENTS

This book is based on the work that was accomplished during and after three conferences at Penn State University in the spring of 2007, 2009, and 2011. We are grateful for the support of Dr. Mel Mark, the head of Penn State's Department of Psychology, and especially for the help and financial commitment that Dr. Brian Rabian has provided us on behalf of the university's psychology clinic.

We also express our gratitude to our colleagues and friends who participated in the Penn State meetings and wrote outstanding chapters about corrective experiences (CEs) in psychotherapy. We also thank many of our current and past graduate students and postdoctoral fellows (some of whom participated in the meetings) for their collaborative spirit, hard work, and insights. Furthermore, much of what we learned about CEs and psychotherapy came from our work with our clients—we are grateful to them for sharing so much of what happened in their lives with us.

As with our previous books, it has been a great pleasure to work with Susan Reynolds, senior acquisitions editor at the American Psychological Association. Her expertise, guidance, and collaborative nature have greatly facilitated our work. This work also would not have been possible without the love and support of our respective spouses—heartfelt thanks go to Michelle and to Jim.

Finally, we also express our deepest gratitude to our mentors, who have facilitated and provided the stage so that our journeys (as researchers, teachers, and clinicians) were actualizing (and at times even corrective) experiences.

Transformation
in Psychotherapy

1

CORRECTIVE EXPERIENCES IN PSYCHOTHERAPY: AN INTRODUCTION

LOUIS G. CASTONGUAY AND CLARA E. HILL

We open this volume with an example of a corrective experience from the first author's college days:

> I chose very carefully the college I attended. I had not been a good student in high school and seriously feared that I would not be able to complete an undergraduate degree. So, when it came time to choose between the two universities that accepted me into their psychology program, I said to myself, "Well, University of Montreal accepted more than 90 students, while University of Sherbrooke took less than 30. It will be no big deal for a university to throw out one student out of 90 because he can't make it, but getting rid of one student when there is only 30 accepted the program, that would be huge—that is much less likely to happen. So Sherbrooke it is!"
>
> The fear of being kicked out of school came back with a vengeance when I wrote my first paper, and even more so when I got it back. Glued to my desk, I slowly turned the seven to eight pages that I wrote, feeling a mixture of nausea, shame, anxiety, and depression while staring at the comments throughout the paper. I swear that I stopped breathing when I got to the end and saw the full page and a half of written text. I felt assailed and devastated by the heavy red ink and underlined comments

that were jumping out from the sheets of paper. "I knew it. I just knew it. I can't believe this.... I failed. Oh, f—... I am so out of here."

How long I stayed at my desk, I don't know. I know that I failed to notice that all of the other students had left the classroom, and I startled when the faculty member approached my desk and said, "You seem dismayed by my feedback." "But I worked so hard," I replied. "Yes, and it shows," he said. "But you have no idea how hard I worked on this," I pursued. "Yes, yes, yes, I know that. Listen, you did well, very well. You got the highest grade in the class.... There, at the end of my comments, see, I gave you 19 out of 20 points," he said. "Oh ... but, but this is a long comment you wrote, I mean it's a very long comment," I bemoaned. "Well, if you read it," he replied, "you will see that what I am saying is that you presented a very good behavioral analysis of human functioning. Your analysis is perfectly correct; there is nothing false about it. In fact, you presented classical and operant conditioning more clearly than I ever could. You will write one day, I am sure of that. I just disagree with the assumptions of this approach, and I was trying to articulate my Rogerian position regarding them. I'd be curious to know what you think about it."

"What do you mean by 'I will write one day?'" came out of my mouth while I was saying to myself, "Sh—, he obviously thinks that I don't know how to write, and unless I pick this up, I will be thrown out." "Well, I mean writing, publishing," he replied. "Hmm, but I have no intention of becoming a journalist," I said. "No, no, I mean scientific stuff. I predict that you will be writing articles and other types of professional publications later in your career," he clarified.

I do not remember anything more of this event other than feeling totally shocked and relieved by this unexpected feedback and (I must admit) very proud. Obviously, it took more than this event for me to decide to go into academia, including the steady and nurturing guidance and support from this faculty member throughout my undergraduate program. To this day, however, I am convinced that it opened my mind to a career direction that I had never thought about before, increased my confidence toward completing college and setting ambitious goals beyond it, and certainly fueled energy toward my reading (and writing about) psychology. Of course, I will never know how much of an impact this event has had on my career. One thing that I am sure of, however, is that it is directly linked to one of my publications that is most meaningful to me: Twenty-five years later, and after keeping up with my published work, this mentor (Yves Saint-Arnaud) asked me to write the preface to the last book he wrote before retiring from academia. The resonance of this event has been long lasting.

Although they may not all be as transformative as this example, events that challenge one's fear or expectations and lead to new outcomes often take place in psychotherapy. In fact, many therapists across a variety of theoretical orientations hope that their clients will achieve such corrective experiences (CEs). Unfortunately, limited attention has been given (by scholars and researchers alike) to the definition of CEs, to the delineation of their nature, to what facilitates them, and to their therapeutic consequences. The goal of this book is to address these gaps in knowledge by providing conceptual, clinical, and empirical descriptions of CEs as they manifest themselves in different approaches of psychotherapy.

ORIGINS OF THIS BOOK

This book is based on a series of three conferences held at Penn State University (PSU). As with a previous set of PSU conferences that led to a book on insight in psychotherapy (Castonguay & Hill, 2006), this series of meetings involved psychotherapy researchers from a variety of theoretical orientations and a range of methodological (quantitative and qualitative) backgrounds. All participants were internationally known for their empirical contributions to psychotherapy and, with very few exceptions, lived within driving distance of PSU (needless to say, we had to restrict the number of people we wanted to invite, both to provide optimal conditions for group work and for financial reasons).

We agreed ahead of time that we would focus on CEs in psychotherapy. We were particularly interested in CEs because we wanted to examine common factors across theoretical orientations to further understandings of the mechanisms of change in psychotherapy.

DEFINITION OF CORRECTIVE EXPERIENCES

The origins of the term CE go back to Alexander and French (1946), who coined the term *corrective emotional experiences* to describe such events within the context of psychoanalytic therapy (see Chapter 3, this volume, for more history about this construct). To broaden the term, however, and make it more applicable to experiences that occur in different types of psychotherapies, we use the term CEs here. In this way, we followed Goldfried (1980), who considered CEs to be a common curative factor across all psychotherapy approaches.

On the basis of 12 hours of open discussions and observations of CEs in videotaped sessions, the first PSU meeting led to a consensus about the definition of CEs: CEs are ones in which a person comes to understand or experience affectively an event or relationship in a different and unexpected way. Note that this definition allows for events that are emotional, relational, behavioral, or cognitive. This definition stresses, however, that such events are not just typical helpful events in therapy but that they are surprising or disconfirming of past experiences and often have a profound effect.

ORGANIZATION OF THE BOOK

As mentioned above, our goal was to shed theoretical, empirical, and clinical light on CEs. Hence, the first section of the current book provides a number of conceptual contributions about CEs. In the second section, we present several empirical investigations. In both of these sections, the authors include clinical materials not only to show the clinical relevance of their concepts or findings but also to offer guidelines that may improve practitioners' ability to foster CEs and promote change. In the final chapter, we summarize what we have learned.

Theoretical and Conceptual Background

The first section begins with Chapter 2, by Goldfried, who more than 30 years ago identified CEs as a common factor in psychotherapy. He expands on his thinking and argues that, as a principle of change, CEs play a crucial role in the general process of helping clients move from states of unconscious incompetence, to conscious incompetence, to conscious competence, and finally to unconscious competence. The next two chapters review the role of CEs in psychoanalytic psychotherapy, providing a historical perspective of how the construct has changed over time. Reflecting CEs' complexity, Sharpless and Barber (Chapter 3) identify 12 components within Alexander and French's (1946) perspective on CEs. In addition to differentiating CEs from other major constructs (e.g., alliance, transference), they describe several of the controversies that this construct triggered within the psychoanalytic tradition, especially regarding the role of insight versus the relationship in therapeutic change. Christian, Safran, and Muran (Chapter 4) then focus on how CEs fit within relational psychoanalysis. Specifically, they discuss how Alexander and French's emphasis on interpersonal components (i.e., the therapeutic value of experiencing a new type of relationship) has been echoed in some of the contemporary (interpersonal and relational) psychodynamic models. On the basis of their own research, they show how Alexander and French's view of CEs is highly consistent with the therapeutic benefit that can be derived from the exploration and resolution of alliance ruptures.

Interestingly, Hayes, Beck, and Yasinski, in Chapter 5, also argue that Alexander and French's (1946) view resonates strongly with several principles of change underlying cognitive behavior therapy (CBT). They highlight such theoretical convergence by showing how exposure and cognitive techniques (including setting up behavioral experiments to test thoughts and expectations) are aimed at activating maladaptive patterns of reaction, exposing clients to (and helping them process) new information, and learning and consolidating more adaptive patterns. Involved in this process of change are the activation of emotion and the construction of new meaning, which according to Hayes et al. are not only consistent with Alexander and French's view of CEs but also congruent with other theoretical orientations.

Humanistic and experiential perspectives about CEs are the focus of the next two chapters. After delineating the conceptions of CEs that are central to some of the most influential approaches of the "third" movement of psychology, Greenberg and Elliott (Chapter 6) describe two forms of CEs (intrapersonal and interpersonal) that they espouse in emotion-focused therapy. Both forms of CEs involve the conscious access of emotions (persistent and maladaptive; overlooked and adaptive) and rest on facilitative conditions provided by the therapeutic relationship. Another crucial approach of the humanistic tradition, the person-centered therapy, is the focus of Chapter 7, by Farber, Bohart, and Stiles. These authors identify three manifestations of CEs (e.g., disconfirmation of "conditions of worth" that can result from the therapist's unconditional positive regard) that emerged in the work of Carl Rogers and Eugene Gendlin. They then describe how these different strands of CEs played an important role in the well-known brief session that Rogers had with "Gloria."

In contrast with the previous chapters, the last two chapters of this section present perspectives of CEs that are not tied to a particular approach or tradition in psychotherapy. In their expectancy-based model, Constantino and Westra (Chapter 8) define CEs as revisions of the client's view (working model) of self and others, and they argue that such revisions frequently involve different levels of functioning (interpersonal, cognitive, and affective). Their integrative view incorporates constructs from psychodynamic, interpersonal, cognitive behavior, and humanistic theories, as well as from basic social and developmental psychology. Basic psychological research is also the foundation of Chapter 9, by Caspar and Berger, who take on the challenge of demonstrating how we can advance our thinking about CEs by paying attention to recent advances in cognitive and neuropsychological sciences. They illustrate how CEs develop and help to change brain structures.

Each of the chapters described above provides a sophisticated understanding of the complex theoretical issues related to CEs. Each of them also presents case materials to illustrate subtle clinical processes related to these constructs. As a whole, they offer a broad and multifaceted view of CEs. This view, however, is further enriched by the new, and much needed, empirical investigations presented in the second section of the book.

Empirical Investigations of Corrective Experiences in Psychotherapy

The first two chapters in this section provide what may be the first window on how clients experience CEs. Based on a multisite collaboration, Heatherington, Constantino, Friedlander, Angus, and Messer (Chapter 10) content analyzed responses provided by 76 clients after every four sessions to open-ended questions aimed at assessing changes in therapy and how such changes took place. In the Chapter 11, Knox, Hess, Hill, Burkard, and Crook-Lyon provide qualitative analyses of interviews conducted with 12 clients—therapists themselves—regarding corrective relational experiences during their own psychotherapies.

Chapters 12 through 15 describe studies examining CEs in specific forms of therapy or treatment settings. Berman et al. (Chapter 12) qualitatively focus on relational events (making judgments about whether these were corrective) in three cases of acceptance and commitment therapy (a recent approach in CBT) for anorexia nervosa. In Chapter 13, Castonguay et al. use comprehensive process analyses to examine CEs for one anxious client who participated in both CBT and interpersonal/experiential therapy. Qualitative analyses are also presented in Chapter 14, by Anderson, Ogles, Heckman, and MacFarlane, who intensively analyzed the in-session process of CEs identified by clients in posttherapy interviews. Finally, Grosse Holtforth and Flückiger (Chapter 15) describe the results of a quantitative study on CEs. Within the context of a CBT-based treatment, they investigate which of two forms of CEs (those that are built gradually, i.e., micro events, or those that occur as a singular, macro, event) is most predictive of client's improvement. This section ends with Chapter 16, a qualitative study of CEs in supervision. Ladany et al. analyze interviews with 15 doctoral trainees to assess what types of CEs occur in supervision and the impact of such events on the trainees, their clients, and the supervision process.

From a scientific perspective, all of these studies were conducted rigorously. In addition, they all have great clinical relevance. With the interest of clinicians in mind, the authors provide examples and practical implications that anchor their findings in clinical reality.

Summary Chapter

Chapter 17, the final chapter of book, reflects a collective effort to describe what we have learned and what should be done to better understand CEs. This chapter is based on the third and final PSU meeting, which was aimed at getting consensus among our group of researchers (in terms of both what we agreed on and disagreed on) with respect to four major questions: What is the nature of CEs? What facilitates them? What are their effects?

And what are some of the future directions (with regard to theory, research, and practical implications) that can be recommended to the field in order to further clarify and more effectively foster CEs? Considering the breadth of the conceptual, methodological, and clinical knowledge represented by the authors in this volume, we believe that this chapter offers a good glimpse of what is currently known about CEs, as well as potentially fruitful suggestions to address some of what still needs to be known about them.

REFERENCES

Alexander, F., & French, F. (1946). *Psychoanalytic therapy: Principles and application.* New York, NY: Ronald Press.

Castonguay, L. G., & Hill, C. E. (Eds.). (2006). *Insight in psychotherapy.* Washington, DC: American Psychological Association.

Goldfried, M. R. (1980). Toward the delineation of therapeutic change principles. *American Psychologist, 35,* 991–999. doi:10.1037/0003-066X.35.11.991

I

THEORETICAL PERSPECTIVES ON CORRECTIVE EXPERIENCES

2

THE CORRECTIVE EXPERIENCE: A CORE PRINCIPLE FOR THERAPEUTIC CHANGE

MARVIN R. GOLDFRIED

The patient needs an experience, not an explanation.
—Frieda Fromm-Reichmann

You must do the things you think you cannot do.
—Eleanor Roosevelt

The corrective experience (CE) occupies a central role in the therapy change process. Although the therapy relationship and specific techniques have been acknowledged by many as being essential to therapeutic change, far less attention has been paid to how CEs contribute to change. In this chapter, I highlight the importance of CEs, a concept that originated in psychoanalytic circles but has clear relevance to all orientations. Indeed, CEs cut across all therapies, perhaps representing the core principle of change (Goldfried, 1980).

I begin by clarifying the concept of the CE, as it at times is not thoroughly understood. I then discuss of the role of CEs, their relationship to other principles of change, the importance of helping clients process their CEs once they occur, and how both facilitation and processing of CEs may be accomplished therapeutically. I conclude by highlighting some issues related to CEs that are in need of empirical investigation.

WHAT ARE CORRECTIVE EXPERIENCES?

Franz Alexander and Thomas French were two psychoanalysts who were very much ahead of their time. Writing in the 1930s and 1940s, they departed from Freud's drive theory to view the therapy change process as involving more of a new learning than a resolution of old conflicts (Goldfried, Pachankis, & Bell, 2005). In 1946, they introduced the somewhat radical concept of the *corrective emotional experience*. This concept suggests that clients' ability to interact with a therapist in a way that is different from how they interacted with earlier significant figures in their lives could, in itself, produce therapeutic change. What was most radical about this notion was the basic assumption that the therapeutic change process could take place without insight into the past or resolution of earlier conflicts. Although they referred to these new interpersonal encounters as corrective *emotional* experiences, such transformative experiences also involved a shift in cognition and behavior. Rather than labeling this principle of change as *corrective–emotional–cognitive–behavioral experience*, it might be simpler to call it the *corrective experience* but recognize its complexity.

It is of particular interest that the concept of the CE has been discussed in the literature in a variety of different ways, without using the term as such. Fenichel (1941), in his book *Problems of Psychoanalytic Technique*, predated Alexander and French in suggesting that fears may be reduced with repeated contact alone, without the need for insight or conflict resolution, noting:

> When a person is afraid but experiences a situation in which what was feared occurs without any harm resulting, he will not immediately trust the outcome of his new experience; however, the second time he will have a little less fear, the third time still less. (p. 83)

Bandura (1969) reached this same conclusion in his classic volume *Principles of Behavior Modification*, in which he discussed the use of exposure to treat phobias: "Extinction of avoidance behavior is achieved by repeated exposure to subjectively threatening stimuli under conditions designed to ensure that neither the avoidance responses nor the anticipated adverse consequences occur" (p. 414). And in a 1980 special issue of the journal *Cognitive Therapy and Research*, a number of prominent therapists representing different theoretical orientations were questioned about general change principles associated with their particular approach. One of the questions asked of them was "What is the role played by new experiences provided to the patient/client in facilitating change?" They consistently viewed new experiences as being at the very core of the change process, describing them as "critical," "essential," "crucial," and "basic" (Brady et al., 1980; see Exhibit 2.1).

EXHIBIT 2.1
Prominent Therapists' Responses to the Question "What Is the Role Played by New Experiences Provided to the Patient or Client in Facilitating Change?"

"I regard new experiences, that is, experiences of the patient since treatment was initiated, as crucial to favorable change. It is only by behaving differently, trying out new responses to old situations, that the patient can hope to alter habitual maladaptive ways of responding" (p. 273). —John Paul Brady

"I have absolutely no doubt that this factor is absolutely crucial for therapeutic change and that, indeed, it cuts across all therapy orientations. The subtle questions have to do with the nature of new experiences, as well as with the way such experiences are brought about" (p. 273). —Gerald C. Davison

"In psychoanalysis and psychoanalytic psychotherapy, new experience plays a crucial role in facilitating change" (p. 274). —Paul A. Dewald

"Without new experiences, there is no change. I wish it was my canny wisdom, understanding, and clarity that makes the differences. However, it is only after the client does something that is novel, something outside of therapy, that the insubstantial excitement of understanding is transformed into lasting change" (p. 275). —James Fadiman

"In a sense, all psychotherapy is a new experience in that it provides the patient with a relationship with a helping figure that differs from previous ones and uses procedures that are not part of daily living" (p. 275). —Jerome D. Frank

"There is little doubt that the therapist's personality and his manner of relating can often provide the patient with a new and beneficial interpersonal experience" (p. 276). —Merton M. Gill and Irwin Hoffman

"By definition, without 'new experiences' there can be no change. There are data demonstrating that therapeutic change usually follows methods that are performance-based. Purely cognitive or verbal methods are often less effective" (p. 277). —Arnold A. Lazarus

"Almost everything I do in therapy consists of trying to provide the client with new experiences so that he can gain new perspectives on himself and on himself in relation to significant others" (p. 277). —Victor Raimy

"While insight into the origins of behavior or insight into the future consequences of behavior can be highly significant for some patients, it seems reasonable that it is important for all patients to try out new behaviors in their present life circumstances and to discover for themselves whether or not they are more adaptive" (p. 278). —Julian B. Rotter

"Basic to all forms of psychotherapy, whether or not it is acknowledged by the theory to which the therapist subscribes is the patient's experience with a human being who . . . modifies basic aspects of the patient's patterns of relatedness in ways that are called therapeutic" (p. 279). —Hans H. Strupp

Note. Quotes are from "Some Views on Effective Principles of Psychotherapy," by J. P. Brady, G. C. Davison, P. A. Dewald, G. Egan, J. Fadiman, J. D. Frank, . . . H. H. Strupp, 1980, *Cognitive Therapy and Research, 4,* pp. 273–279. Copyright 1980 by Springer Publishing. Reprinted with permission.

According to the Penn State definition, "CEs are ones in which a person comes to understand or experience affectively an event or relationship in a different and unexpected way" (p. 5, Chapter 1, this volume). In this definition, there are numerous aspects of an individual's functioning that operate, including one's thoughts, emotions, expectations, and consequences within the context of a particular situational event or interaction. What is not clearly specified, however, is the behavior that accompanies all these other components of functioning. CEs involve a certain amount of risk taking, in that individuals do things differently from how they would usually behave and, much to their relief and satisfaction, are surprised when they realize that nothing bad has happened. In this regard, one may think of the CE as involving both a principle of change and an indication that change has occurred.

To further clarify my own conceptualization of the CE, the acronym STAIRCaSE—which refers to situation, thought, affect, intention, response, consequence, and self-evaluation—may be helpful. For example, a CE may be said to have occurred when a given situation (S) elicits negative expectations (T) and affect (A) in individuals, and in which they have an intention (I) and respond (R) in a way consistent with what they want, which results in a positive instead of negative consequence (C), and (a) their self-evaluation (SE) of how well they did.

Although there may be a consensus regarding the importance of CEs from different theoretical orientations, it is important to recognize that the way this general principle of change is implemented clinically may vary from orientation to orientation. When Alexander and French (1946) first proposed the concept of the corrective emotional experience, it primarily referred to the corrective power of the therapeutic relationship. An example from within a contemporary psychodynamic orientation is given by Levenson (1995), who suggested that the CE "emphasizes change through doing" (p. 41). She illustrated this concept in the case of a passive client who learned to interact with his therapist in a more self-assertive way. Thus, in the context of the therapy relationship, the client

> has the opportunity actively to try out new behaviors in therapy, to see how they feel, and to notice how the therapist responds. This information then shapes the client's interpersonal schemata of what can be expected from self and others. (p. 41)

Alexander and French also acknowledged that the corrective emotional experience could take place in the client's daily life, a view that tends to be more the focus with cognitive behavior therapy than psychodynamic therapy. Thus, within a cognitive behavioral orientation, the between-sessions CEs often take the form of the client's exposure to anxiety-inducing situations. This exposure can very closely parallel the CE illustrated by Levenson (1995), except that it occurs outside of therapy instead of in the therapeutic relationship. I would hasten to add, however, that even though one's theory of change may not acknowledge that the CE can be implemented in ways other than those specified by their orientation, it nonetheless may still occur, even without the therapist's deliberate intervention or even awareness. Thus, cognitive behavior therapists, by virtue of their very interaction with their clients, may unwittingly produce therapeutic change, when working with clients having a history of attachment problems, and psychodynamic therapists may indirectly encourage their clients to take risks and confront their fears. And although therapists often play an important role in facilitating CEs, it is certainly possible for clients to have such experiences in areas of the lives in which the therapist has played no role, such as change resulting from ongoing interactions with a partner.

WHAT IS THE ROLE OF CORRECTIVE EXPERIENCES IN THERAPY?

To better understand the nature of CEs and the ways they may be facilitated during the course of therapy, a general overview of the therapeutic process may prove to be helpful. Therapists of all orientations generally agree that clients' need for therapy is based on the fact that their current cognitive–emotional–behavioral patterns of dealing with various events and the world result in negative consequences. In addition to constitutional and genetic factors, early learning history may not have adequately prepared them to function competently at a later point in their lives. Although these earlier experiences may have helped clients adapt to the demands of their life at the time, their learned methods of coping may not be effective in dealing with their current life situations. It is the role of therapy to assist them in changing these ineffective cognitive–emotional–intentional–behavioral patterns.

Phases of Change

In the most general sense, we may characterize clients who arrive for treatment as not being competent in dealing with the events of their lives and being unaware as to the nature or origin of their incompetence. For example, they may be depressed and not functioning well, but they may not understand the factors associated with their mood and functioning. Thus, they may be characterized as being in a state of *unconscious incompetence*.

During the course of therapy, clients begin to gain a better understanding of the source and nature of their incompetent functioning, as might be the case with clients who are depressed because their standards are so unrealistically high that they are never satisfied with what they do, or because they lack the interpersonal skills to get what they need. By gaining an understanding of the reasons they are depressed, they consequently move from a state of unconscious incompetence to *conscious incompetence*.

Although they may understand why their lives are not working as well as they would like, clients may still be unaware of what to do to make things better. To improve their functioning, they would have to learn more effective ways of thinking, feeling, and acting. In the case of clients who are depressed because of their unrealistically high standards, they would need to reevaluate the standards they use in evaluating their accomplishments. Other depressed individuals may need to improve their interpersonal communication skills, learning to ask for what they need from others. Changing standards for self-evaluation or learning more effective communication skills would require deliberate and conscious efforts—the stage of *conscious competence*.

Changing one's thinking, emotions, and behaviors takes time and ongoing effort, with the goal being to have new cognitive–emotional–behavioral patterns that are less effortful and more automatic. If and when this occurs, clients reach the final phase of change, *unconscious competence*, as repeated engagement in CEs serve to make the new behavior occur without any conscious effort.

This depiction of the therapeutic change process is indeed general, but in being so, it is able to capture how change occurs in varying approaches to treatment. Although it may be the case that important changes occur as a result of the interaction between client and therapist, the place where CEs typically occur outside the therapy relationship is probably at the move from stage two to stage three. It is here that clients use their better understanding of the factors associated with their incompetence to address the question, "Now that I understand why I'm having these problems (conscious incompetence), what can I do to change things?" The answer is that they need to take deliberate risks to behave more competently so as to change not only their behavior but also their thinking and emotion—that is, to become involved in conscious competence. The place of CEs in the change process can become even clearer by placing them in the context of general principles that are associated with therapeutic change.

Principles of Change

As Exhibit 2.2 shows, principles of change may be thought of as falling at a level of abstraction somewhere between the theoretical orientation of a therapeutic approach and the specific clinical procedures it uses. In the

Theoretic orientation (e.g., psychodynamic, experiential, cognitive behavior)

General principle (e.g., increasing awareness)

Clinical procedure (e.g., interpretation, reflection, self-monitoring)

example provided in this exhibit, methods of interpretation, reflection, and self-monitoring are different interventions used in different theoretical orientations but may all be seen as reflecting a common principle of increasing awareness for the client. And although different theoretical orientations may specify the theory-specific techniques that help move clients from unconscious incompetence to unconscious competence, a consensus across orientations is more likely to be obtained by examining the principles at this middle level of abstraction. These principles involve the role of positive expectations and client motivation, the presence of an adequate therapeutic alliance, increasing client awareness, and the CE.

Enhancing Positive Expectations and Client Motivation

Regardless of the therapist's theoretical orientation, it is important for clients entering therapy to have some positive expectation that treatment will help and at least a minimal level of motivation to change. Clients who have read about the effectiveness of therapy, or have been referred by someone who has benefited from it, are more likely to have positive expectations than someone whose past therapy experiences have been negative. And, for example, someone experiencing panic attacks is more likely to be more motivated to change than an adolescent who has been sent to therapy by a parent. When positive expectations and motivation are less than optimal, therapists need to intervene to help increase these important prerequisites to change.

Facilitating the Therapeutic Alliance

Another important principle of change that is common to different forms of therapy is the *therapeutic alliance*: a bond between client and therapist—in which clients trust that the therapist is competent and interested in their welfare—and a mutual agreement on the goals of therapy and the ways that these goals may be accomplished. The nature of the therapeutic alliance will clearly vary as a function of the client and the competence of the therapist. Extra effort and clinical skill are needed to create a good alliance with a pessimistic and unmotivated client or with a client whose anger is at times directed toward the therapist. The therapeutic alliance is not only the glue that keeps clients in treatment but also a factor that can motivate them to engage in the change process.

Increasing Client Awareness

Much of the work of therapy, as practiced from different orientations, involves increasing clients' awareness—such as helping them to move from unconscious incompetence to conscious incompetence. The nature of the awareness that is required therapeutically varies considerably from client to client and from clinical problem to clinical problem. Some clients may be unaware of how their thinking is influencing their feelings, others may be unaware of how their emotional reaction results in behavior, and still others how their behavior negatively impacts on others. Thus, individuals who are unaware of their anger, and also their tendency to withdraw when angry, may be unaware of how this emotion–action link adversely affects their relationships with others. There are numerous issues associated with increasing client awareness, such as timing, frequency, and certainly the nature of the thoughts, feelings, and behaviors—all of which may be thought of as the important parameters of the principle of increasing awareness. Moreover, the development of a clear case formulation is needed for therapists to understand the determinants and dynamics of any given case, providing them with the necessary guideline for assisting clients in becoming more aware of what it is that is creating problems in their life.

Facilitating Corrective Experiences

In many respects, having positive expectations about the therapeutic process, being motivated to change, working within a good therapeutic alliance, and becoming aware of those factors associated with one's problem all set the stage for the next and most essential principle of change—the CE. Here clients need to take the risk of behaving differently, often in the presence of some skepticism and apprehension. By experiencing a positive outcome, thinking (e.g., expectations that something bad will happen) and emotion (e.g., anxiety) will start to change as well. An interesting marker that a CE has occurred during the course of therapy is when clients report a between-sessions experience with the tone of surprise in their voice—either because they behaved in a way that was different for them or because of the unexpected positive consequences that followed what they did. At other times, the CEs may be less salient but nonetheless impactful, as may result from ongoing interaction with a supportive and affirming therapist.

It is important to recognize that there is both a subjective and an objective vantage point associated with CEs. Although the term *experience* is clearly subjective in connotation, CEs typically take place when a person behaves in a way that is counter to his or her typical actions. Thus, what one may externally observe as novel, risk-taking behavior on the part of clients may afford them with important subjective experiences. The subjective and behavioral components of a CE are nicely summarized in Rogers's (1961) discussion of how the therapy relationship can produce change. From the subjective view of the client, Rogers presented it as follows:

> I can even tell him just how I'm feeling toward him at any given moment and instead of this killing the relationship, as I used to fear, it seems to deepen it. Do you suppose I could be my feelings with other people too? Perhaps that wouldn't be too dangerous either. (p. 68)

The quote from Rogers (1961) nicely reflects the nature of the CE within the context of the therapy relationship. In contrast to the negative reaction that others in the past may have had toward the client under such circumstances (e.g., "I don't care what you think. Do what you're told!"), the therapist accepts and validates what the client has to say. From a learning point of view, this may be thought of as involving both positive and negative reinforcement. The positive reinforcement results from the therapist's acceptance and validation; the negative reinforcement, from the reduction of the client's apprehension associated with the anticipation of negative consequences. Although Alexander and French (1946) never used these concepts in the discussion of the corrective emotional experience, they nonetheless believed that some sort of learning was definitely involved.

As a result of their CEs, clients begin to update their view of reality, recognizing that things are now different. However, this shift in their personal sense of reality—especially about how they view themselves—may need to be ongoing, requiring the processing of repeated CEs.

PROCESSING CORRECTIVE EXPERIENCES: ONGOING REALITY TESTING

There are often times when having CEs is not enough, and they may need to be processed afterward, particularly when clients fail to detect, accept, or recall their success experiences. This need may be manifested clinically in a number of ways, such as by failing to report them during a session, mentioning it as a "by the way" at the end of the session, or negating it with a "yes, but." As observers of clients, we as therapists may be clearer than clients in recognizing when they begin to change and function in more competent ways. The tendency for clients to overlook or minimize their successes can be very frustrating to therapists, unless therapists understand that because the CEs are schema inconsistent, this lack of awareness is to be expected.

The schemas individuals have about themselves and others can play an important role in processing information. When clients enter therapy, their self-schemas are often negative, based on a history of unconscious incompetence. As clients start to change and become more competent, these new experiences go counter to their views of themselves. Although changes occur, the anachronistic, negative self-schemas may make it difficult to recognize, store, and retrieve these more recent counterschematic CEs.

Self-schemas are notoriously difficult to change, and therapists need to take specific steps to help their clients recognize, recall, and make use of CEs that hopefully will lead to more efficacious self-schemas. In short, clients need to make use of their newfound CEs to alter their negative views of themselves. The need for changing how they view themselves is particularly important because research has shown that an individual's sense of self-efficacy is an important predictor of future behavior (Bandura, 1986). For therapeutic change to maintain over time, then, positive efficacy expectations, a reflection of a more positive self-schema, are an important therapeutic objective.

To counteract the natural tendency to maintain one's self-schema in light of contradictory evidence, deliberate therapeutic efforts are required. Goldfried and Robins (1983) suggested that performance-based changes associated with CEs require having clients (a) discriminate between their present and past functioning; (b) view the changes in their lives from both an objective and subjective vantage point; (c) retrieve their recent CEs; and (d) align their expectancies, anticipatory emotions, behaviors, consequences, and subsequent self-evaluation.

Discriminating Between Present and Past

Because it is the nature of schemas to detect consistent experiences but to overlook those that are schema inconsistent, clients may fail to recognize that they are changing. As a way to help them to recognize that a change—however small—has occurred, therapists can deliberately inquire about clients' experiences during the course of the week, hoping to uncover those instances that might consist of CEs, such as behaving in a novel way, having had more adaptive thoughts, or feeling better. Specifically asking clients whether what happened was different from the way they would have reacted in the past in similar situations can counteract typical "yes, buts" that can serve to discount this schema-inconsistent experience. If it represents only a small step, clients may claim, "Yes, but I have so much more to do." Because the change may have occurred in only one aspect of the person's life, they may state, "Yes, but I can't do that in other situations." And if they compare themselves with others, their schematic discounting can take the form of "Yes, but other people are so much better than me." The therapeutic strategy is to help clients use the metric of comparing the present with the past as the means of detecting change.

Adding an Objective Vantage Point to the Client's Subjective Outlook

Because clients' views of themselves are typically schema based and often not accurate, there is a discrepancy between how they view themselves (i.e., schema based and often general) as compared with how they currently are functioning (i.e., reality based and specific). Although they may have had a CE (e.g., being self-assertive in a given situation), clients may nonetheless view themselves as unassertive (e.g., "I can never ask for what I need."). Thus, they need to be helped to become aware that their schema-driven, negative self-evaluation about their assertiveness is not consistent with their recent CE. The following transcript from Goldfried and Robins (1983, p. 62) illustrates one of the ways responding to this discrepancy:

Client: I just feel that I'm always being taken advantage of, and get caught up in things that I really dislike.

Therapist: Such as?

Client: Like at work, I always seem to end up with the dirty work. When I look at other people, they don't seem to have the same problems. Like Lisa, for example . . . she handles herself much better than I ever can.

Therapist: What can she do that you can't?

Client: Well, she's not overburdened the way I am. She doesn't let other people take advantage of her.

Therapist: Can you give me some examples?

Client:	If the boss comes in and there's extra work to be done, and she feels she's too busy with what she has to do, she's able to say something about it. I always go along with it.
Therapist:	So, like Lisa, you'd like to be better able to refuse to do extra work when it's inconvenient for you.
Client:	Yes.
Therapist:	Such as telling your boss that it's inconvenient for you to work late on given day [which the client had reported earlier in the session]?
Client:	[Visibly embarrassed.] Uh . . . Well . . . But that was different.
Therapist:	How so?
Client:	[Pause.] I see what you're getting at. I guess it's just hard for me to see myself that way. But it's true; I was able to stand up for my rights in that situation.

In essence, what is happening therapeutically is that clients learn to become observers of, as well as participants in, their newly acquired CEs. This awareness is not accomplished in the abstract but rather in the context of specific experiences and preferably what is happening at the time.

Retrieving Past Successes

The natural tendency for clients to recall their more plentiful past failures than their fewer recent successes can be counteracted by having them keep records of their CEs and by encouraging them to use these to more accurately predict what they can do. This is illustrated in the following transcript from Goldfried and Robins (1983, pp. 64–65):

Therapist:	Because you've had difficulty in asserting yourself for so long in the past, it's sometimes hard to keep in mind the changes that have been happening to you.
Client:	I know. And it feels kind of different, almost as if it's not me that's doing it.
Therapist:	That's certainly a natural part of the change process, which will probably continue until you start to build up more of a backlog of positive experiences. With each new situation you handle well, it should get a little bit easier. As a way of helping you to change, it's also important for you to remember the successes you have had.
Client:	I do think of them sometimes.

Therapist: That's good, because there is a natural tendency to think of the more typical way you've reacted in the past—which is to not assert yourself—and that's why it's so important for you to really focus in on what seems to be a new pattern of handling situations on your part.

Client: Yes.

Therapist: In fact, when you think about your past successes, it can often help you to continue along those lines in the future. For example, when you finally speak to that friend of yours who is always showing up late, you might keep in mind successful instances of assertiveness you've experienced in the past. Before speaking to this friend, you might say to yourself something like, "I was able to say what was on my mind in these past situations, and I can do the same here as well." It doesn't have to be in those exact words; any way that you can remind yourself of past successes will help you in new situations where you want to stand up for your rights.

This clinical vignette illustrates the need to have clients make use of their more recent CEs in predicting how well they will handle difficult situations in the future. Although the immediate pessimism and apprehension they may be experiencing can lead them to conclude that they will function incompetently, the recollection of their past successful experiences—even in situations in which they may have been pessimistic and apprehensive—can be a better predictor of their efficacy.

Aligning Expectancies, Feelings, Behavior, Consequences, and Self-Evaluation

In helping clients process their CEs, the acronym STAIRCaSE, described earlier, can be clinically useful in helping them become aware of how each component of their functioning is involved when having a CE. In this regard, the ongoing reality testing involved in reviewing clients' CEs continues to enhance their awareness of their functioning associated with such experiences.

When clients first arrive at therapy, a STAIRCaSE assessment is likely to reveal a consistency among the components of their functioning. For example, when confronted with a situation in which they need to be self-assertive (S), they have negative anticipations about doing so (T), are apprehensive (A), are intent in not displeasing another person (I), respond by acquiescing (R), experience the consequence of being inconvenienced and feeling badly (C), and are displeased with themselves (SE). As they move from conscious incompetence to conscious competence by engaging in CEs, they may begin to function in more successful ways and experience positive consequences but may do so with remaining initial negative expectations and apprehension, may not feel positive about how they handled the situation, or both. In such instances, the therapeutic task is to encourage clients to have CEs and process them in session, so that this ongoing reality testing can help them align the different components of their functioning.

The processing of CEs represents the point in therapy at which the goal is to move the client from conscious competence to unconscious competence. Unlike what might occur early in therapy, namely, the exploration of the reasons why the client is not functioning effectively, the therapeutic guideline changes so as to identify and solidify what the client is doing differently and more effectively. The role of this ongoing reality testing, in which CE after CE is processed, is to help clients realize the specific ways in which they are changing. In doing so, the objective is to help them become more consistent in their thinking, feelings, and actions once again—but this time to reflect their unconscious competence.

WHAT FACILITATES CORRECTIVE EXPERIENCES?

As noted earlier, the therapy relationship can provide an important context within which CEs occur. If the clinical problem in the client's life involves relational issues, having positive interactions with the therapist often can itself be therapeutic, particularly if the therapist is validating and supportive when this has not been part of the client's past experiences. Indeed, in those instances in which therapists inadvertently are invalidating or rejecting, the interaction may serve only to repeat the unpleasant interactions clients have had in the past, often resulting in adverse therapeutic effects (Castonguay, Boswell, Constantino, Goldfried, & Hill, 2010).

Beyond affording a venue in which new interpersonal patterns can be learned, the therapy relationship can play another major role in facilitating CEs. Although different therapeutic schools tend to be thought of as being composed of different techniques, much of what goes on in all approaches consists of talk therapy, and only on occasion the use of specific techniques. And although talk therapy can help to create positive expectations, increased motivation, provide a greater awareness, and foster a good therapeutic alliance, it also serves as a context within which clients are encouraged to engage in CEs.

In an early article describing the key elements of behavior therapy, Kanfer and Phillips (1966) described the way that behavior therapists could use techniques to prepare clients to behave differently in their lives (e.g., using role play for purposes of behavior rehearsal). Perhaps what is less well known about the foundation of behavior therapy is the very important role of the relationship as a means of influencing clients—especially to encourage them to take the kinds of risks that are needed to produce change. Referring to this as *instigation therapy*, Kanfer and Phillips indicated that this aspect of the change process involves the "use of the therapeutic relationship for joint planning of the program, which the client executes in his daily environment in the absence of the therapist" (p. 117). Using learning principle language, they emphasized that "the natural occurrence of reinforcement consequent to adequate client behavior in the outside situation is used to enhance the likelihood of a change" (p. 117). With continued practice, the client proceeds toward the development of conscious competence.

Although behavior therapists and cognitive behavior therapists may be explicit and structured in providing such between-session instigations, I would suggest that all forms of treatment involve an interpersonal influence in one way or another. In this regard, a useful overview of how "homework" is used from within different theoretical orientations can be found in Nelson, Castonguay, and Barwick (2006). Thus, the therapist who seemingly is only "exploring" a given issue with clients may indirectly and somewhat subtly be encouraging them to do something differently. Asking a client, "Have you ever thought of moving out of your parents' house?" is not simple an inquiry, but may be thought of as "planting a seed" that eventually could bring about behavior change—and hopefully a CE. Indeed, those clients with an internal locus of control who resist being directly told what to do may be best approached with this more indirect method.

There are numerous specific ways in which therapists can encourage clients to engage in CEs, such as the use of graded tasks. For example, individuals who tend to put the needs of others above their own can be encouraged to gradually take risks in situations in which they verbalize what they want, starting with those interpersonal interactions that may be relatively easy (e.g., making a request to a salesclerk) and moving on to those that are more difficult (e.g., telling a friend you would rather go to a different restaurant). For some clients, simply giving permission to take such risks may be sufficient. In other instances, a detailed discussion, rehearsal, or both, during the session may make it easier for a client to carry out new ways of functioning in real-life situations.

CONCLUDING COMMENT

Much of what is known about the role of CEs in the process of change comes from theory and clinical experience, with little in the way of research having been carried out on this most important principle of change. Based on what is currently known about the CE, a number of researchable questions may be raised. Although one may assume that more than a single CE is needed to bring about lasting change, there are no empirically based guidelines about the number of experiences that are needed with different kinds of clients. Related to this is whether the critical mass of necessary CEs depends on the aspects of the client's functioning in need of change—thoughts, emotions intentions, actions, or self-evaluation. Another related question is whether the number of necessary experiences is a function of the breadth or narrowness of the class of situations that is the focus of the therapy, which can range from interpersonal relations in general to self-assertiveness in intimate interactions. Also unknown is the extent to which the processing of CEs is required above and beyond simply having them, and whether this depends on whether the CEs involve major or minor changes within the client. These are but some of the parameters researchers need to investigate to make better use of CEs in bringing about change.

REFERENCES

Alexander, F., & French, F. (1946). *Psychoanalytic therapy: Principles and application.* New York, NY: Ronald Press.

Bandura, A. (1969). *Principles of behavior modification.* New York, NY: Holt, Rinehart, & Winston.

Bandura, A. (1986). *Social foundations of thought and action.* Englewood Cliffs, NJ: Prentice-Hall.

Brady, J. P., Davison, G. C., Dewald, P. A., Egan, G., Fadiman, J., Frank, J. D., . . . Strupp, H. H. (1980). Some views on effective principles of psychotherapy. *Cognitive Therapy and Research, 4,* 271–306.

Castonguay, L. G., Boswell, J. F., Constantino, M. J., Goldfried, M. R., & Hill, C. E. (2010). Training implications of harmful effects of psychological treatments. *American Psychologist, 65,* 34–49. doi:10.1037/a0017330

Fenichel, O. (1941). *Problems of psychoanalytic technique.* Albany, NY: Psychoanalytic Quarterly.

Goldfried, M. R. (1980). Toward the delineation of therapeutic change principles. *American Psychologist, 35,* 991–999. doi:10.1037/0003-066X.35.11.991

Goldfried, M. R., Pachankis, J. E., & Bell, A. C. (2005). A history of psychotherapy integration. In J. C. Norcross & M. R. Goldfried (Eds.), *Handbook of psychotherapy integration* (2nd ed., pp. 24–60). New York, NY: Oxford University Press.

Goldfried, M. R., & Robins, C. (1983). *Self-schema, cognitive bias, and the processing of therapeutic experiences.* In P. C. Kendall (Ed.), *Advances in cognitive-behavioral research and therapy* (Vol. 2, pp. 330–380). New York, NY: Academic Press.

Kanfer, F. H., & Phillips, J. S. (1966). Behavior therapy: A panacea for all ills or a passing fancy? *Archives of General Psychiatry, 15,* 114–128. doi:10.1001/archpsyc.1966.01730140002002

Levenson, H. (1995). *Time-limited dynamic psychotherapy: A guide to clinical practice.* New York, NY: Basic Books.

Nelson, D. L., Castonguay, L. G., & Barwick, F. (2006). Directions for the integration of homework in psychotherapy practice: Conceptual and clinical consensus toward the benefits and implementation of between-sessions activities. In N. Kazantis & L. L'Abate (Eds.), *Handbook of homework assignments in psychotherapy: research, practice, and prevention* (pp. 425–444). New York, NY: Springer.

Rogers, C. R. (1961). *On becoming a person.* Boston, MA: Houghton Mifflin.

3

CORRECTIVE EMOTIONAL EXPERIENCES FROM A PSYCHODYNAMIC PERSPECTIVE

BRIAN A. SHARPLESS AND JACQUES P. BARBER

Psychoanalysis could rightfully lay claim to being the earliest example of an organized and secular talk therapy oriented toward the alleviation of human suffering. It has been practiced for more than a century, and in that time has witnessed expansive amounts of theoretical evolution, the development of alternatives to established clinical orthodoxy, and many theoretical accommodations (e.g., see Greenberg & Mitchell, 1983, for an overview). It is not surprising that some of this literature has been devoted to finding out how (and whether) it works (i.e., mechanisms of change, or *therapeutic actions*). And although empirical exploration of these concepts has progressed at a much slower pace than theoretical and clinical speculation, this wealth of ideas has eventuated in a number of possibilities for researchers to pursue. One of these constructs is the corrective emotional experience (CEE), first discussed by Franz Alexander and Thomas French (1946). To situate CEEs in a historical context, we briefly discuss some earlier therapeutic actions elaborated by Menninger (1958, p. 126).

At least six mechanisms of change are described in the early analytic literature. The earliest mechanism (Breuer & Freud, 1893/1955) was thought to arise from the clear (and full) recollection of half-remembered traumatic experiences. Another (abreaction) involved the riddance of pockets of toxic emotion. Subsequently, abandoning fixations, reducing an overly harsh superego, and expanding the domain of the observing ego were also discussed. In the years before Alexander and French's (1946) conceptualization of the CEE, however, insight held predominance. This took various forms, such as "making the unconscious conscious" (via expressive techniques) and providing "mutative interpretations" (Strachey, 1934), which integrate affect and cognition.

As we further demonstrate, Alexander and French's (1946) conception of the CEE as a main agent of therapeutic change differed markedly from previous explanations. In fact, it is difficult to imagine a construct in psychoanalytic writings with a more checkered and controversial past than the CEE (e.g., Wallerstein, 1990). Even some of the more provocative psychoanalytic notions that elicited reactions from the lay public (e.g., infantile sexuality, polymorphous perversity, the primacy of unconscious life) have been more or less uniformly accepted by analysts and many psychodynamic therapists.

In contrast, the initial presentation of the CEE, although in many ways an intuitive concept, caused tremors throughout the analytic community. A main reason for this upheaval arose from a fear that therapists were, in effect, manipulating clients by deliberately assuming particular roles or attitudes (i.e., abandoning technical neutrality) for the purpose of directly refuting clients' transferential expectations and facilitating a different and reparative emotional response. Thus, CEEs as therapeutic change agents were perceived by some psychoanalytic scholars to be an adulterated and baser alloy of the "pure gold" of psychoanalytic work proper (i.e., transference interpretation and resolution), with the ultimate result being to circumvent the complete and successful analysis of the client. We discuss these viewpoints in more detail below, but it should be noted that in recent years acceptance of CEEs in psychoanalysis and in other orientations has increased, and we believe that this important concept warrants additional clinical consideration and conceptual analysis.

Our purpose in this chapter is fivefold. First, we discuss the genesis of the concept of the CEE from historical precursors to Alexander and French's (1946) formulations. Second, we discuss several of the major critiques of CEEs as they relate to psychoanalytic treatment goals and techniques. Third, we reflect on the concept of CEEs more generally (also considering the Pennsylvania State University Conference consensus definition of *corrective experiences* [CEs; see Chapter 1, this volume]) and attempt to define boundaries for the concept. Fourth, we speculate on factors that may facilitate CEEs. And, finally, we discuss some possible clinical consequences of CEEs for both clients and therapists.

CORRECTIVE EMOTIONAL EXPERIENCES IN HISTORICAL PERSPECTIVE

CEEs were originally defined as "reexperiencing the old, unsettled conflict but with a new ending" (Alexander & French, 1946, p. 338). However, we argue that the idea of CEEs has an extensive prehistory and seems to be an intuitive and exceedingly human concept. The following two theorists clearly anticipated aspects of Alexander and French's (1946) CEE.

Kierkegaard (1844/1980, p. 56) described a technique for alleviating human suffering that is consonant with certain aspects of the later conceptualization of CEEs and that bears a more general relevance in the history of clinical psychology (Sharpless, 2012). Specifically, he discussed how one can use intimate knowledge of a suffering individual and his or her emotional state to bring about psychological relief. These emotional states are imitated and presented to the suffering individual at a higher level of emotional intensity. Kierkegaard did not elaborate on the exact mechanism that causes relief. Regardless, the self-conscious adoption, and use, of intimate knowledge about a person for the purpose of relieving suffering (see next section) is in keeping with Alexander and French's (1946) descriptions of CEEs.

Another early anticipator of CEEs was Sándor Ferenczi, a key member of the early psychoanalytic community. He suggested that analysts may sometimes have to "cool down a too impetuous transference by something of reserve, or to make some advances to the shy . . . to establish the 'optimum temperature' of the relations between doctor and patient" (Ferenczi, 1920/1953, p. 216). Going further, Ferenczi and Rank (1924/1925) stated that

> it is not the task of the analysis to bring happiness to the patient by tender and friendly treatment . . . but to repeat under favorable conditions the reactions of the patient to frustration . . . and to correct the disturbance in development which can be reconstructed historically. (p. 225)

This statement comes closest to Alexander and French's (1946) subsequent thinking. However, in contrast to Alexander and French, Ferenczi and Rank (1924/1925) did not seem to suggest an intervention or explicit manipulation that would significantly deviate from psychoanalytic technique proper beyond the creation of favorable circumstances.

ALEXANDER AND FRENCH'S CORRECTIVE EMOTIONAL EXPERIENCES AND THEIR CONSTITUENT PARTS

Returning to Alexander and French (1946), it is clear that their brief formulation is complex and contains at least the following 12 individual components and specifications:

1. The client must have experienced traumatic events (construed fairly broadly) or events that caused a traumatic influence which were not successfully or adaptively dealt with in the past. (p. 66)
2. The client must be reexposed to these emotional situations that were not successfully/adaptively dealt with. (p. 66)
3. This reexposure must occur in more favorable circumstances than the original situation allowed. (p. 66)
4. The client must be able and willing to face the reexposure (implied in definition).
5. This reexposure does not necessarily need to take place with the therapist or within typical session confines. (p. 66)
6. The therapist (or another person in the client's life) must assume or express an attitude different from that of the individual or individuals involved in the original traumatic event. (p. 66)
7. Building on Item 6, with CEEs specifically involving the therapist, the therapist may or may not self-consciously assume a particular role or attitude (or, similar to Kierkegaard [1844/1980], facilitate a particular emotional atmosphere) to elicit the emotional situation (i.e., manipulation may be present, but not necessarily; Alexander, 1961; Alexander & Selesnick, 1966). (p. 66–67)
8. The client must handle or react to this novel situation (Item 6) in a manner different from before. (p. 67)
9. Such a result often takes repetition of the conflicts before a new ending occurs (i.e., it seems unlikely that CEEs occur with a single reexposure). (p. 67)
10. Patient insight into these patterns may accompany a CEE but is neither necessary nor sufficient to cause the CEE, and the experiential component holds predominance. (p. 67)
11. As a result of the above, the trauma becomes "repaired" in some way. (p. 66)
12. The results of the CEE should generalize to other situations and experiences (implied).

As we demonstrate in subsequent sections of this chapter, several of Alexander and French's (1946) formulations (especially 5–7, 10) aroused controversy and require additional conceptual inquiry. This is particularly the case regarding manipulation of a client's expectations/transference by the therapist, and it appears that Alexander and French emphasized self-conscious manipulation more in this formulation than Alexander did later (e.g., Alexander & Selesnick, 1966). We argue that these various factors were primarily responsible for the negative reception of CEEs in early psychoanalytic circles.

Alexander and French's Critics and Their Positions

On publication, Alexander and French's (1946) writings on the CEE were met with an obstreperous reception (Wallerstein, 1990). Given that this occurred when ego psychology was predominant and insight held primacy of place among putative therapeutic actions, this may not be surprising. Critics levied at least four key charges against them, discussed in the respective sections below.

Corrective Emotional Experiences Are Not "Analytic"

Some critics felt that CEEs were anathema to analysis proper, as they deemphasize insight and self-understanding (i.e., expressive techniques) as agents of change and instead emphasize the more experiential aspects of psychoanalysis. For example, Stone (1957) took umbrage with the manipulative cast of CEEs mentioned above (i.e., the deliberate and manipulative adoption of attitudes to facilitate CEEs). Although Bibring's (1954) classic article codified the many possible techniques available to analytic practitioners, manipulation (combined with abreaction) was seen as fairly low on the hierarchy of established techniques and was indeed considered to be most appropriate in supportive psychotherapies where the prospects for more expressive analytic work were limited.

The origin of this particular discomfort also seems to be related to the fact that any manipulation of the transference (by the therapist purposefully contradicting the patient's transferential expectations) circumvents the possibility of bringing to bear the supposedly active ingredient of change in analytic therapy (i.e., analysis and resolution of the transference neurosis). CEEs, in effect, serve to take the "analysis" out of psychoanalysis, as emerging therapeutic elements (e.g., resistance, transference) are not explored (Horner, 1991). Instead, an interpersonal response (i.e., an action) is substituted for intrapsychic scrutiny, with the result being that clients are not provided with the same opportunity to recognize, understand, and learn from their resistances (e.g., Greenson, 1965). It is interesting to note that these early critics believed that an alteration of psychic structure was possible with CEEs but were fairly unanimous that such therapeutic actions ruined or corrupted the analytic climate and other (possibly more robust) possibilities for change (e.g., Brenner, 1979).

Considering this "nonanalytic" charge further, one wonders whether critics found the facilitation of CEEs to be unacceptable because, at least in some ways, any manipulative, nonneutral action reduces client autonomy. For instance, instead of having clients begin to understand their responses through traditional expressive work, therapists facilitating CEEs make a decision for the client by self-consciously adopting stances that may, for lack of a better term, "force" a nonstandard response or reaction through this therapist manipulation. The majority of modern analysts would be more apt to recognize that the process of psychotherapy ineluctably involves some degree of manipulation or influence, as any commentary on the process of client-generated material serves to direct the client to certain content while minimizing other possibilities (e.g., Sartre, 1943/2003). Similarly, interpretations provide the client with specific and implicit instructions on ways of thinking that are consonant with the treatment as construed by the therapist. Granted, this is quite different from the therapist adopting a particular role for the client, but it seems to be a difference of degree, not of kind.

Psychoanalysis, as Practiced, Is Already a Corrective Emotional Experience

Whereas the authors cited above have argued that this "addition" to standard analytic therapy is harmful to the analytic process, others would say that the facilitation of CEEs is nothing new, but has always been a de facto part of analysis. Namely, the analytic stance, and the analytic process itself, are both believed to be vehicles for facilitating CEEs (e.g., Dewald, 1976; Gill, 1954). If therapists adhere to what is often termed the *therapeutic frame*, a CEE will, all things being equal, usually result.

The therapeutic frame in analysis consists of many elements that are not often present in everyday life. For instance, few people in clients' lives are curious about them, focused solely on the client for 45 to 50 minutes at a time, and in possession of a reality-oriented empathic attunement. Furthermore, few nonanalysts attempt to maintain therapeutic neutrality (e.g., Gill, 1954). *Neutrality* can sometimes be confused with therapeutic abstinence (i.e., limiting gratifications); it refers instead (in structural parlance) to the therapist adopting a position equidistant from ego, id, and superego. In other words, analysts do not side with any aspect of the conflict (e.g., neither societal norms nor drive impulses). Furthermore, the frame allows for the integration of new experiences, which takes place in the context of repetitions of archaic negative experiences (e.g., transference), and this is crucial for both psychoanalytic process in general (e.g., Dewald, 1976) and the possible facilitation of CEEs in particular.

On reflection, most therapists can remember instances in which their typical way of conducting therapy facilitated a CEE (sometimes inadvertently). For instance, when the first author worked with a woman possessing an extensive trauma history at the hands of men, a typical therapeutic stance led her to think and feel that it was possible to have a healthy relationship with a man whom she felt was trustworthy and safe. Therefore, theorists adopting this conception of CEEs would argue that the analytic stance itself differs sufficiently from the stances of others such that CEEs can occur without entailing the risks inherent when assuming particular roles based on client history, a criticism often levied at Alexander and French. In fact, Alexander (e.g., 1961) agreed with this possibility for what could be termed a "business as usual" CEEs as well.

Corrective Emotional Experiences Confuse the Means for the End

Another counterpoint made by critics is that Alexander essentially confuses the means of therapy for the end. For example, H. C. Curtis (1979) argued that there is a danger to viewing the relational aspects of therapy (especially a desire to have the client experience a new and corrective object relationship in terms of a discrete event or course of therapy) as a treatment goal instead of as the environmental precondition and context under which resistances and transference phenomena arise, are analyzed, and are scrutinized. And, consonant with the first criticism discussed above (i.e., CEEs are not analytic), all clinical material should be thoroughly scrutinized (presumably CEEs as well).

Can Corrective Emotional Experiences Be Facilitated in Actual Clinical Practice?

Another concern expressed by Wallerstein (1990) relates to the practical problem of how psychoanalytic therapists can even facilitate an Alexanderian CEE. To counteract a client's transferential expectation with a therapeutic response or CE (or what could be termed an experiential "antidote" or a complementary response, as in interpersonal theory), a therapist would have to have an exquisitely sophisticated understanding of the client. In many cases, therapists do indeed possess this knowledge. However, making the matter more complex, clients may have a limited understanding of their own history (traumatic or otherwise) or could be engaging in unconscious subterfuge (e.g., vivid screen memories instead of a real parental interaction). And although words can certainly convey a great deal of intrapsychic meaning, some elements of human interactions have an ineffable quality or may defy verbalization. From our perspective, these factors make the correct assessment of what is needed for certain very sophisticated and therapist manipulation-based CEEs relatively less likely. However, there are clearly many other clients (and CEEs) that may be much less complicated, and obviously, as described in more detail below, the more accidental facilitation of CEEs is always possible. Relatedly, can therapists realistically plan CEEs in advance, or is it more likely that they can merely set the stage for CEEs respond to their aftermath (be it positive or negative), or both? Put differently, to what degree can CEEs be consciously executed, or do they occur indirectly because therapists are supportive and display regard in ways that other figures important to the clients do not?

Putting these questions together, one wonders whether the unexpected, fortuitous, and somewhat haphazard nature of CEEs may explain some of the discomfort seen in certain psychoanalytic circles. As therapists, we have an implicit but not unassailable belief that we are largely responsible for the client's positive therapeutic changes. Although diligence, technical ability, and a strong alliance may be useful, CEEs by their very nature are often at least partially instigated by elements incidental to the therapy hour, which may be both elusive and difficult to formalize. In summary, CEEs often occur without the clear intentional planning of the therapist.

Furthermore, it is clear that events or actions expected to result in a CEE may often occur in clients' lives without engendering either a CEE or significant insight. For example, a client who was abandoned by his parents yet currently is not abandoned by a spouse, the therapist, or both, may still retain pronounced abandonment fears despite having experienced the interpersonal "antidote" numerous times. This fact leads to an important clinical question: Why did these potentially mutative events not lead to the more dramatic CEE?

In summary, a number of conceptual questions are clearly associated with CEEs, but before discussing them, we first consider the Penn State consensus definition. In ending this section, however, we note that several more recent analytic theorists and schools are much less critical of CEEs as the agent of therapeutic change (e.g., Kohut, 1977; Sifneos, 1992) but that discomfort with role-playing remains. From our review of the literature, however, little development in terms of refining the definitions of CEEs has taken place apart from different theorists emphasizing certain aspects of CEEs over others. Bearing this in mind, we now discuss a recent consensus definition in light of the psychodynamic perspectives on CEEs described above.

The Penn State University Consensus Definition of Corrective Experiences

Whereas the above considerations indicate conceptual difficulties and uncertainties with CEEs as traditionally stated, other non-Alexanderian (and transtheoretical) formulations have been put forth. For instance, the Penn State University workgroup's initial definition of CEs is as follows: "CEs are ones in which a person comes to understand or experience affectively an event or relationship in a different and unexpected way" (Chapter 1, this volume, p. 5). Clearly, this definition is different from Alexander and French's (1946) in at least five ways.

First, there is no explicit requirement that the CE take place in an interpersonal context. Second, there is no direct indication that the therapist needs to behave in a way different from normal procedure. Thus, in contrast to some of Alexander and French's (e.g., 1946) writings, no direct manipulation of the therapeutic encounter deviating from standard psychoanalytic procedures is required. In fact, a therapist or other individual need not be required at all. Third, and likely apparent because of the other contributors to this edited volume, there is no implicit requirement that CEs take place within the confines of psychoanalysis, psychoanalytic psychotherapy, or any type of psychotherapy. Fourth, there appears to be no requirement that the client has been unable to handle a past conflict or difficulty. What seems to be changed is an understanding or experience, and the consensus definition does not require a previous incapacity or lack of understanding (i.e., a repair need not take place). Finally, and perhaps most fundamentally, CEs are not necessarily limited to emotional content but could consist of behavioral, cognitive, or relational experiences. For example, if a client is worried that his friend is indifferent, then later learns that the friend was merely preoccupied with other matters, this change within the client would presumably fall under the rubric of a CE.

From our perspective, there appears to be some vagaries in this definition, which may limit its usefulness. As we further demonstrate in the next section, one of the primary difficulties with CEEs is their breadth. This breadth mushrooms with the revised definition of CEs and more clearly impinges upon other therapeutic constructs. Whereas the definition of CEs includes all CEEs, it also encompasses many other interventions or constructs. In strictly psychodynamic terms, it appears to encompass a diverse array of therapeutic actions related to insight (see Boswell et al., 2011), such as understanding and resolving intrapsychic and interpersonal conflicts, better understanding defensive operations, exploring and understanding object relations and relatedness (including the transference), and changing personal narratives. In general, we question the utility of such a broadly construed concept, as the lumping of conceptually and clinically distinct constructs may in effect muddy the already somewhat murky waters surrounding core psychodynamic constructs.

Now that we have discussed two definitions, we next evaluate them. We hope to more firmly delineate their conceptual boundaries.

WHAT IS, AND WHAT IS NOT, A CORRECTIVE EMOTIONAL EXPERIENCE, FROM A PSYCHODYNAMIC PERSPECTIVE

One of the primary impediments to a fuller clinical appreciation of CEEs is the clear lack of conceptual demarcation, and the broader definition of CEs makes this concern even more acute. Although this charge is somewhat lessened for CEEs, it is a matter of degree, not kind. For example, descriptions of CEEs in the analytic literature have ranged from relatively circumscribed events (little CEEs?) to the course of a multiyear analysis (big CEEs?). Wallerstein (2000) noted that CEEs have been invoked to explain almost all mutative changes in the supportive psychotherapies.

This expansive nature of CEEs may be partially due to their attractive nature. We believe that CEEs are compelling and appealing because they certainly speak to a wish that many of us in the helping professions clearly take for granted (i.e., that there can be a profoundly healing power to human relationships). However, despite its appeal, the lack of boundaries is troubling, as CEEs risk being construed as meaning "everything" (thus, meaning nothing) and losing real explanatory power. Given this risk, we attempt to differentiate CEEs from other closely related or overlapping terms, and we explore the crucial questions about CEEs' boundaries in the hope that CEEs can become both more clearly circumscribed and operationally definable.

The Working Alliance and Positive Dependent Transference

One of the primary difficulties involved in the demarcation of CEEs involves their relation to several of the common factors of therapy. As one example, the predictive value of the working alliance and its association with outcome have been often discussed in the literature (e.g., Barber, 2009; Barber, Khalsa, & Sharpless, 2010). Similarly, the concept of a positive dependent transference (which allows clients to continue analytic therapy in spite of frustrations engendered by the therapist's abstinence) has also been seen as an agent of change. These above-mentioned constructs seem to differ from CEEs in several respects, although they clearly possess a similarly relational nature.

First, they appear to be more generic factors of (good?) therapy process and not specifically linked to the more personal historic material involved in CEEs (although one could easily argue that historic factors contribute to client ability to attach to a therapist). Second, they seem less likely to be CEEs on their own and more likely to be considered to be facilitative of CEEs. For example, it seems reasonable to assume that a strong alliance may allow clients to feel safer and more explorative in their possible reactions or their descriptions of their reactions; thus, they may be more amenable to CEEs (see the next section). However, both the alliance and positive dependent transference seem to be neither necessary nor sufficient causes, for CEEs can just as likely occur outside of the therapy hour. Thus, they are not necessarily a direct product of therapy but may be much more fortuitous or arbitrary.

Transference, Countertransference, and Projective Identification

The relation between CEEs and transference is fairly complex. The transference may reflect the origin of the experience, which has yet to be understood or experienced in a new way, as clients come to new or ambiguous situations with (usually unconscious) preconceptions and scripts for behavior. In fact, clients often interpret ambiguous situations in a manner consonant with these transference phenomena. Thus, as with the alliance, a client's transference is another means of setting the stage for the possibility of a CEE.

Therapist countertransference (in either the more general or specific sense of the term) also bears a potential relationship with CEEs (e.g., Renik, 1993). In general, therapists clearly react to client behaviors and session content, and therefore experience a number of pushes and pulls to behave or respond in certain ways (e.g., Benjamin & Friedrich, 1991). It is not surprising that some of these therapist responses may be counterproductive (i.e., if related to the therapist's unresolved issues), may not lead to CEEs, and may engender negative consequences. However, therapists who are able to observe, understand, and disentangle themselves from such patterns and enactments retain the possibility to turn these patterns to their (and their clients') advantage.

We should also note that unresolved therapist issues may still lead to CEEs, albeit inadvertently, and it is interesting to consider the relative proportion of consciously formulated versus unwitting CEEs. These inadvertent CEEs may occur when a therapist's countertransference-influenced behavior is incongruous with the client's expectations. For instance, a therapist may be incorrectly attuned to, or overly identify with, a client, or may be unable to disconnect from their own unresolved issues. This misalignment would obviously manifest in any number of his or her (e.g., jarring and inappropriate interpretations, poor empathy). In such an unfortunate environment, which seems to be so mired down with problems that its very effectiveness is in question, possibilities for CEEs remain if the participants remain open to them.

In one clinical scenario, this sense of misalignment may be familiar and distressing to the client, but confronting another person is fraught with anxiety and fears of rejection. As a result, the client usually acquiesces rather than face another's anger. However, the peculiarity of the therapeutic relationship may allow the client to take a chance and correct the therapist's misunderstandings. Contrary to the client's expectations, the therapist may then both recognize and acknowledge the mistake and take pains to warmly remedy the situation, thus possibly facilitating a CEE.

In general, countertransference reactions can be used to facilitate CEEs. In Alexander's (1961) formulations, he remained steadfast that CEEs were not the result of therapists' acting out but were often based on a nuanced and profound knowledge of particular clients' histories and needs. However, these two alternatives need not be mutually exclusive.

Similarly, the construct of projective identification can be distinguished from, and situated in relation to, CEEs. *Projective identification* is a psychological defense in which a client projects unconscious beliefs or attributions to another. However, in contrast to typical projection, what is expulsed outward is often not just an impulse but a part of the self. Furthermore, the projector modifies his or her behavior in such a way as to actually elicit confirmatory (i.e., projection-congruent) behavior in the other. There are attempts to elicit the projected behavior in the receiver of the projected material (in this case, the therapist) and validate the projections. Like a self-fulfilling prophecy, it attempts to elicit disavowed feared or desired behaviors in others while keeping them out of consciousness. But how can this relate to CEEs? As in countertransference, clients may provoke a multitude of reactions, but occasional instances will occur in which behaviors incongruent with the projective identifications will manifest. Such deviations from unconscious expectation may lead to CEEs, and this seems to be one possible example of a consciously and deliberately planned CEE.

What Is Corrective in Corrective Emotional Experiences?

A fundamental question is whether CEEs correct anything at all. As there is not yet evidence on this point, we take it for granted that CEEs can either be a source of clinical change in their own right or serve as a catalyst for subsequent clinical changes (see the sections below). Miller (1990) argued that what CEEs appear to correct are negative object attachments and the distressing affects associated with them. These affects, specifically, must be experienced at an optimal level of intensity (similar to Kierkegaard, 1844/1980, and Ferenczi, 1920/1953) for them to contribute to the correction. We view this assessment of CEEs as certainly plausible in many cases. We also include the fact that experiencing a CEE may cause flexibility to enter a rigid and calcified system. This may eventuate, in some cases, in an altered (emotional?) worldview.

One way to conceptualize CEEs that we have found useful, fairly transtheoretical, and not incompatible with Alexander and French's (1946) formulations is in terms of Popperian refutations (Popper, 1959). Sir Karl Popper, whose philosophy of science had an enormous influence on science in general, and psychological research in particular, discussed how theories can never be proven correct but can be reasonably falsified through *modus tollens*. So, for instance, a crucial experiment or proposition A can be deduced from theory X. If A does not pan out, and is therefore rejected, X is rejected as well (if X, then A; ~A, then ~X). We put forth that a parallel process may be occurring in CEEs. A client comes to therapy with particular interpersonal expectations, intrapsychic expectations, or both, and in effect, holds these as a theory. When a crucial expectation derived from this theory of human interaction is violated, the possibility for either rejecting or significantly modifying the theory (through ad hoc arguments) exists. In the latter case, when too many ad hoc arguments have accrued, the theory itself may be rejected, leading to a CEE.

This idea is consonant with Lakatos and Musgrave's (1970) writings on scientific research programs and, especially, those research programs that are not characterized by growth and flexibility (i.e., degenerating programs). Presumably, a CEE would occur when enough anomalies have accrued that ad hoc arguments cannot protect the hard core of the theory or worldview, and this core must be rejected in favor of an alternative (whether this results in a new object relatedness, insight, or some other factor likely varies across individuals and situations). Of course, the process of experiencing a CEE is likely to be much less rational and much more subterranean than we describe here, but this conception may be helpful nonetheless. This may also explain why one refutation is often insufficient, in the same way that one rarely rejects a scientific theory because of one anomalous observation. Thus, psychotherapy's characteristic repetition and working through may provide the repeated refutations of pathological beliefs or experiences (e.g., J. T. Curtis, Silberschats, Sampson, & Weiss, 1994) not encountered in real life.

Regardless of the particular mechanism or correction that occurs, that which changes is clearly something endogenous to the client. External circumstances (e.g., the reactions of others, chance, positive and negative therapist behaviors) are facilitators of CEEs, but the actual CEE itself is reliant on modifications of crucial aspects of emotional experience.

WHAT VARIABLES MAY EITHER FACILITATE OR INHIBIT CEES?

Although there are little to no data on this question, it may be useful to reflect on hypothetical factors that, from an a priori psychodynamic perspective, may be related to the genesis of CEEs. We organize the factors into those specific to the client, therapist, and process.

There appear to be at least five client factors likely related to the possibilities for CEEs, although this number will obviously be modified as research accrues. First, an overall flexibility and openness to the possibility for novel experiences may be an important prerequisite. Unless a client is amenable to such events, it seems unlikely that CEEs will take place. Therefore, clients with particularly rigid characterological disturbances or entrenched behavioral repertoires may not be as able to benefit from CEEs as quickly as others. However, they would presumably be as effective, as they might serve to insert elasticity into even the most intransigent client's life.

Second, and related to the above, a willingness to be action-oriented, experimental, and take risks (e.g., interpersonal, emotional) would likely eventuate in more CEE possibilities. This risk taking may be reflected in a willingness to disclose, confront others (including therapists), or even just behave in ways that feel outside the norm (or possibly dangerous) to the client. It seems to us that qualities such as these are more likely to eventuate in a wide range of responses from others (and the self) than would occur in those who are less action oriented and daring.

Third, the presence of a rich network of important people in a client's life will provide more opportunities for extratherapeutic CEEs. Such a heightened degree of complex interpersonal interactions (with people possessing different worldviews and typical ways of interacting with others) would presumably lead to greater possibilities for receiving novel responses from others, and these may be related to difficult past situations. On the other end of the continuum, a paucity of relationships would seemingly relegate the possibilities for CEEs to session time and interactions with the therapist. Thus, any increases in a client's social network (brought about either through symptom reduction or a general dampening of interpersonal fears) might serve to better harness CEEs as an additional agent of therapeutic change.

Fourth, what is really important is not only a willingness to act but also clients' willingness to speak about their experiences aloud and in their interactions with therapists and significant others. We surmise that context is important and that without discussion with a therapist or significant other, the refutation is less likely to facilitate a CEE.

Finally, a client's reflective functioning capacity may be related to CEEs. Level of reflective functioning may not facilitate the occurrence of CEEs in a direct fashion but would likely come into play after the CEE. Namely, higher levels of reflective functioning may serve to facilitate generalization of the results of CEEs.

We also identify three therapist factors likely related to CEEs. First, an openness to both experience and experimentation in session on the part of the therapist likely facilitates CEEs. In the writings of Alexander and French (1946; and earlier, the writings of Ferenczi & Rank, 1924/1925), this was clearly present, with radical departures from analytic orthodoxy often taking place.

Second, a therapist's own psychological health as well as emotional attunement and awareness (including reflective functioning) may facilitate CEEs. These capacities assist in recognizing and resisting characteristic client pulls to act in ways that may be damaging at worst or nontherapeutic at best. Understanding a client's mental states allows a therapist to discern what is experientially needed to facilitate or execute a CEE. This does not necessarily demand the transgression of boundaries, modification of the range of the therapist's typical reactions, or deviations from the standard frame. However, an awareness of both the client's and the therapist's internal mental states and needs may serve to limit possibilities for abuse.

Finally, a therapist's overall level of competence (Sharpless & Barber, 2009) is likely related to CEEs. We believe that the judicious use of all aspects of the therapeutic process as well as flexibility in the face of the often unexpected vicissitudes of clinical work can lead to many opportunities for client CEEs. It is interesting to note that one can also foresee instances in which therapist incompetence (as either a state or a trait) may facilitate CEEs as well. For instance, a therapist's thoughtless or careless remark may indeed set the stage for any number of relevant CEEs, but in this case it may require the client's taking more initiative for their genesis. And, of course, this scenario presumes that the therapist can recognize and competently respond to his or her error in a way that maximizes clinical impact.

We have already noted four process factors that may be facilitative of CEEs (i.e., alliance, transference, countertransference, and projective identification) and do not discuss them further here. However, we note two other potentially relevant process variables. First, one can speak of what has been termed *fusion of horizons*. Specifically, some hermeneutic thinkers (e.g., Bernstein, 1983; Gadamer, 1960/1975) speak of horizons that, for our purposes, can be considered to encompass an individual's worldview (*Weltanschauung*) and way of experiencing the world. Each worldview contains a number of (often tacit) prejudgments and prejudices favoring particular views and ways of engaging the world. These prejudgments or assumptions could be considered to be blind when not articulated or not consciously considered and thus do not serve to enlarge one's horizon. However, when they are discussed and carefully considered in a dialectical manner (as often occurs in therapy), they shift to being enabling prejudices and, like a Venn diagram of two intersecting circles, the shared space between the two expands. This fusion of horizons creates the possibility for both greater understanding of other people and novel approaches toward experiencing the world, and such events likely facilitate CEEs by enlarging a client's repertoire of interpersonal and intrapersonal understanding. Second, chance often plays a part in CEEs. It seems to us that any underestimation of the role of chance (related to either the client's external world or the therapist's inability to determine in advance what may be corrective) would limit an understanding of the occurrence of CEEs.

WHAT ARE THE POSSIBLE CONSEQUENCES OF CORRECTIVE EMOTIONAL EXPERIENCES?

Another important question worth reflecting on (but on which significant data are lacking) are the consequences of CEEs. We briefly outline five hypothetical consequences for clients. First, symptom reduction is an obvious possibility. This may be in a fairly circumscribed domain (e.g., reduction in obsessive defenses following a CEE involving anger) or as a more general reduction. Second, positive interpersonal changes could result such that formerly rigid or maladaptive interchanges are now more fluid and satisfactory. This seems as likely to occur with intratherapeutic as with extratherapeutic CEEs. Third, greater self-awareness may result such that pre- and post-CEE behaviors can be compared, contrasted, and evaluated. In combination with the second consequence, there may be an increased level of reflective functioning insofar as the client is better able to reflect on his or her own and others' internal motivations. Fourth, CEEs could remove therapeutic stalemates, or blockages. Therapists have all had experiences in treatment in which a client's progress appears to have reached a plateau or become stagnant. CEEs, by their very refutational nature, can be very dramatic and unexpected and may energize the treatment or serve as a catalyst for additional change, additional CEEs, or both. Thus, CEEs may foster subsequent therapeutic change. Finally, there could be increases or intensifications of the process variables discussed above. For example, a strengthening of the alliance might be a sequela of CEEs, especially those CEEs that occurred largely as a result of interactions with the therapist.

CEEs may also evoke certain consequences for the therapist. First, both CEEs and clients' responses to CEEs provide information about clients' intrapsychic worlds. Such knowledge may lead to a better responsiveness to emerging client needs. Second, having clients benefit from CEEs, whether directly associated with treatment or not, will only help to retain clients in therapy and prompt them to build upon gains.

CONCLUSION

CEEs as a psychodynamic construct have had quite a checkered past. However, the very human nature of the concept as well as the fact that it retains an *élan vital* in many schools of dynamic thought (as well as in non-dynamic therapies) warrants attention. We have attempted to clarify some of the ambiguities that hamper a fuller exposition of CEEs, but more work is required to better demarcate boundaries for this ever broadening concept, as the definition remains complex and somewhat problematic. However, CEEs, particularly in a more strictly Alexanderian sense (and divorced of overt manipulations, such as self-consciously and inauthentically assuming a role to facilitating a CEE) are interesting constructs to explore both clinically and in traditional psychotherapy research. We also believe that the Alexanderian CEE, possessing as it does an irremovable interpersonal context, may be useful in avoiding certain vagaries, which are increasingly likely with more expansive definitions.

One important question we have struggled with in the writing of this chapter is whether CEEs are best conceptualized as (a) interventions a therapist or other person applies, (b) changes that occur within a client (i.e., as a mechanism of change), or (c) both. Given the broad nature of CEEs, we are uncertain whether clarity can be gained through separate analysis of these options, as the choice of focus likely depends on particular perspectives and research questions. However, as we did throughout this chapter, it may be useful for the time being to reserve the phrase *facilitating a CEE* for the intervention and retain *CEE* as the descriptor of the change or correction occurring within the client.

REFERENCES

Alexander, F. (1961). *The scope of psychoanalysis*. New York, NY: Basic Books.

Alexander, F., & French, T. M. (1946). *Psychoanalytic therapy: Principles and application*. New York, NY: Ronald Press.

Alexander, F. G., & Selesnick, S. T. (1966). *The history of psychiatry: An evaluation of psychiatric thought and practice from prehistoric times to the present*. New York, NY: Harper & Row.

Barber, J. P. (2009). Toward a working through of some core conflicts in psychotherapy research. *Psychotherapy Research, 19*, 1–12. doi:10.1080/10503300802609680

Barber, J. P., Khalsa, S.-R., & Sharpless, B. A. (2010). The validity of the alliance as a predictor of psychotherapy outcome. In J. C. Muran & J. P. Barber (Eds.), *The therapeutic alliance: An evidence-based approach to practice & training* (pp. 29–43). New York, NY: Guilford Press.

Benjamin, L. S., & Friedrich, F. (1991). Contributions of structural analysis of social behavior (SASB) to the bridge between cognitive science and a science of object relations. In M. J. Horowitz (Ed.), *Person schemas and maladaptive interpersonal patterns* (pp. 379–412). Chicago, IL: University of Chicago Press.

Bernstein, R. (1983). *Beyond objectivism and relativism*. Philadelphia, PA: University of Pennsylvania Press.

Bibring, E. (1954). Psychoanalysis and the dynamic psychotherapies. *Journal of the American Psychoanalytic Association, 2,* 745–770.

Boswell, J. F., Sharpless, B. A., Greenberg, L. G., Heatherington, L., Huppert, J. D., Barber, J. P., … Castonguay, L. G. (2011). Schools of psychotherapy and the beginnings of a scientific approach. In D. H. Barlow (Ed.), *The Oxford handbook of clinical psychology* (pp. 98–127). New York, NY: Oxford University Press.

Brenner, C. (1979). Working alliance, therapeutic alliance, and transference. *Journal of the American Psychoanalytic Association, 27,* 137–157.

Breuer, J., & Freud, S. (1955). On the psychical mechanism of hysterical phenomena: Preliminary communication. In J. Strachey (Ed.), *The standard edition of the complete psychological works of Sigmund Freud* (Vol. 2, pp. 1–17). London, England: Hogarth Press. (Original work published 1893)

Curtis, H. C. (1979). The concept of therapeutic alliance: Implications for the "widening scope." *Journal of the American Psychoanalytic Association, 27,* 159–192.

Curtis, J. T., Silberschats, G., Sampson, H., & Weiss, J. (1994). The plan formulation method. *Psychotherapy Research, 4,* 197–207. doi:10.1080/10503309412331334032

Dewald, P. A. (1976). Transference regression and real experience in the psychoanalytic process. *The Psychoanalytic Quarterly, 45,* 213–230.

Ferenczi, S. (1953). The further development of an active therapy in psychoanalysis. In *The selected papers of Sándor Ferenczi: Vol. 2. The theory and technique of psychoanalysis* (pp. 198–216). New York, NY: Basic Books. (Original work published 1920)

Ferenczi, S., & Rank, O. (1925). *The development of psychoanalysis* (C. Newton, Trans.). New York, NY: Nervous and Mental Disease Pub. (Original work published 1924) doi:10.1037/10664-000

Gadamer, H. G. (1975). *Truth and method* (J. Weinsheimer & D. G. Marshall, Trans.). New York, NY: Continuum. (Original work published 1960)

Gill, M. M. (1954). Psychoanalysis and exploratory psychotherapy. *Journal of the American Psychoanalytic Association, 2,* 771–797. doi:10.1177/000306515400200413

Greenberg, J. R., & Mitchell, S. A. (1983). *Object relations in psychoanalytic theory.* Cambridge, MA: Harvard University Press.

Greenson, R. R. (1965). The working alliance and the transference neurosis. In R. R. Greenson (Ed.), *Explorations in psychoanalysis* (pp. 199–224). New York, NY: International University Press.

Horner, A. J. (1991). *Psychoanalytic object relations therapy.* Northvale, NJ: Aronson.

Kierkegaard, S. A. (1980). *The concept of anxiety* (R. Thompte, Trans.). Princeton, NJ: Princeton University Press. (Original work published 1844)

Kohut, H. (1977). *The restoration of the self.* New York, NY: International Universities Press.

Lakatos, I., & Musgrave, A. (Eds.). (1970). *Criticism and the growth of knowledge: Vol. 4. Proceedings of the international colloquium in the philosophy of science.* New York, NY: Cambridge University Press.

Menninger, K. (1958). *Theory of psychoanalytic technique.* New York, NY: Basic Books. doi:10.1037/10843-000

Miller, J. P., Jr. (1990). The corrective emotional experience: Reflections in retrospect. *Psychoanalytic Inquiry, 10,* 373–388. doi:10.1080/07351690.1990.10399612

Popper, K. R. (1959). *The logic of scientific discovery.* New York, NY: Basic Books.

Renik, O. (1993). Analytic interaction: Conceputalizing technique in light of the analyst's irreducible subjectivity. *The Psychoanalytic Quarterly, 62,* 553–571.

Sartre, J. P. (2003). *Being and nothingness* (2nd ed., H. E. Barns, Trans.). New York, NY: Routledge Press. (Original work published 1943).

Sharpless, B. A. (2012). *Kierkegaard's conception of psychology.* Department of Psychology, Pennsylvania State University. Manuscript in preparation.

Sharpless, B. A., & Barber, J. P. (2009). A conceptual and empirical review of the meaning, measurement, development, and teaching of intervention competence in clinical psychology. *Clinical Psychology Review, 29,* 47–56. doi:10.1016/j.cpr.2008.09.008

Sifneos, P. E. (1992). *Short-term anxiety provoking psychotherapy.* New York, NY: Basic Books.

Stone, L. (1957). [Review of the book *Psychoanalysis and psychotherapy: Developments in theory, technique, and training,* by F. Alexander.] *The Psychoanalytic Quarterly, 26,* 397–405.

Strachey, J. (1934). The nature of the therapeutic action of psychoanalysis. *The International Journal of Psychanalysis, 15,* 127–159.

Wallerstein, R. S. (1990). The corrective emotional experience: Is reconsideration due? *Psychoanalytic Inquiry, 10,* 288–324. doi:10.1080/07351690.1990.10399609

Wallerstein, R. S. (2000). *Forty-two lives in treatment: A study of psychoanalysis and psychotherapy.* New York, NY: The Analytic Press.

4

THE CORRECTIVE EMOTIONAL EXPERIENCE: A RELATIONAL PERSPECTIVE AND CRITIQUE

CHRISTOPHER CHRISTIAN, JEREMY D. SAFRAN,
AND J. CHRISTOPHER MURAN

It has become a commonplace assumption in many psychotherapy traditions that a corrective emotional experience (CEE; Alexander, 1950; Alexander & French, 1946) is an important mechanism of therapeutic action (Goldfried, 1980). In this chapter, we present a contemporary relational perspective on the CEE (Aron, 1996; Bromberg, 1998, 2006; Mitchell, 1988, 1993, 1997). We also present Safran and Muran's (2003) model of therapeutic alliance rupture and repair as an example of an empirical research program that has been informed by the relational perspective on the CEE. We begin by outlining Franz Alexander's original conceptualization of the CEE, and the theoretical controversies that it engendered. We also provide a retrospective account of some sociopolitical factors that led to its marginalization within mainstream psychoanalysis at the time. We then proceed to discuss a more contemporary psychoanalytic perspective on the CEE, with a particular emphasis on relational thinking.

FRANZ ALEXANDER AND THE HISTORY OF THE CORRECTIVE EMOTIONAL EXPERIENCE

At the age of 30, Franz Alexander was the first graduate of the Berlin Psychoanalytic Institute. He was also the founder of the second oldest psychoanalytic institute in the United States—the Chicago Institute for Psychoanalysis, established only 5 months after the New York Psychoanalytic Institute. Freud considered Alexander to be one of the more "promising of the younger generations of analysts" (Marmor, n.d., p. 5), and he wrote of the young Alexander in a letter (Freud, 1925) to Ferenczi: "The boy is certainly something extraordinarily good." Indeed, with the development of the CEE, Alexander advanced one of the most disputed ideas in psychoanalytic theorizing.

His influential article of 1950, "Analysis of the Therapeutic Factors in Psychoanalytic Treatment," stood as a critical reevaluation of how psychoanalysis was thought to achieve its clinical aims. This important article explored methods of shortening the duration of therapy and developing specific techniques that would keep treatments from drifting into what Alexander and French (1946) deemed "interminable analyses" and "insoluble transference neuroses." Alexander began his controversial treatise with questions about the process that takes place in psychoanalysis that accounts for meaningful change. Are the changes observed in protracted treatments the product of intellectual insight, expression of emotions, feelings in relation to the therapist, or simply due to the passage of time as events in a person's life transpire over the course of a long psychotherapy?

Before his 1950 article, Alexander had used the term *corrective emotional experience* in a talk delivered to the American Society for Research in Psychosomatic Problems in 1945 and then, a year later, in the article "Individual Psychotherapy" in the Journal of Psychosomatic Medicine (1946). In this seldomly cited work, drawing on Freud's (1912/1953) ideas about the role that transference plays in treatment, Alexander (1946) argued that the "revival of the original conflicts in the transference situation gives the ego a new opportunity to grapple with the unresolved conflicts of the past" (p. 112). In relationship with the therapist, the client could now reexperience the thoughts, desires, and impulses that existed earlier in life in relation to his or her parents that, for a variety of reasons, had been repressed. Treatment offered the client an opportunity to bring the repressed material in line with an ego that in its present time was more mature and less easily overwhelmed than it was at the time of repression. It entailed what Alexander (1946) described as an "emotional training" that gave the ego "an opportunity to face again and again, in smaller or larger doses, formerly unbearable emotional situations and to deal with them in a different manner than in the past" (p. 115).

According to Alexander (1946), several features make transference usable. One is that the intensity of the repressed material itself is diminished when reexperienced in the transference as compared with when repression was initially mobilized. Furthermore, the therapist represents a less frightening object in the present than the parents did to the client's less resourceful ego at the time of repression. In the course of analysis, and in relationship with the less dangerous therapist, the client has the chance to confirm or disconfirm his or her fears regarding the consequences of expressing what had hitherto been repressed or otherwise defended against. In this process, Alexander (1946) believed that "intellectual insight alone is not sufficient" (p. 115). Only the actual experiencing of a new outcome, an outcome that was the exact opposite of the client's expectation, could "give the patient the conviction that a new solution is possible and induces him to give up the old neurotic patterns" (p. 115). For this new experience to be curative, the therapist's response needed to be deliberately aimed at correcting the pathogenic effects of the parental attitudes; They should reverse "the adverse influences in the patient's past" (Alexander, 1950, p. 500).

Although the term *corrective emotional experience* was introduced in 1946, the basic ideas underlying this construct had been spelled out by Alexander (1925) in a much earlier article, "A Metapsychological Description of the Process of Cure." Here, Alexander maintained that "the task of all future psycho-analytic therapy" (p. 32) was to analyze and dissipate the tyrannical superego as it became experienced in relation to the therapist. His focus on undoing the effects of the introjected "educational code" from the parents and taming the harshness of the superego would be themes taken up a decade later by Strachey (1934) in his classic article "The Nature of the Therapeutic Action of Psychoanalysis," one in which Strachey credited Alexander's influence. However, different from Strachey, Alexander (1946) argued that it was not enough for the therapist to assume a neutral stance that would throw into sharp relief the distortion between the client's expectations of the therapist (i.e., transference) and the therapist's actual behavior. For Alexander, what was required was an active assumption of a role designed to lean in the exact opposite direction of the client's expectations. Alexander (1946) wrote:

> The intimidating influence of a tyrannical father can frequently be corrected in a relatively short time by the consistently permissive and pronounced encouraging attitude of the therapist but only after the patient has transferred to the therapist his typical emotional reactions originally directed towards the father. (p. 114)

Alexander (1946, 1950) disagreed with the main tenets of ego psychology by recommending a type of analytic action or activity to be assumed by the therapist that could be characterized as concrete demonstrations rather than the insight achieved through the type of interpretation on which ego psychology traditionally relied. In Alexander's (1950) model, the client is awakened from his or her transference-induced somber, not just, or even mainly, by an interpretation, but by the therapist's overt attitude crafted as if to say, "Look, I'm different from the father or the mother that you expected." This new experience leads to a type of learning that could not have occurred outside the treatment setting. After all, it's unlikely that every past object in the client's life should have behaved in exactly the same distressing way as his or her parents. Only a therapist, by virtue of the transference with which he or she is invested, was now in a position to both inhabit the parent's role and undo the parent's iatrogenic impact. Furthermore, and herein lies a second highly contentious issue, this active stance of the therapist would lead, Alexander (1950) believed, to "speedy" results, bypassing the process, considered critical in classical psychoanalysis, of *working through*—a process that entails repeatedly applying psychoanalytically obtained insight across multiple situations over an extended period of time.

THE CRITIQUE FROM THE PSYCHOANALYTIC MAINSTREAM: THE CENTRAL ROLE OF INSIGHT

From the perspective of ego psychology, the dominant psychoanalytic tradition in North America during Alexander's lifetime (and until the 1980s), the concept of the CEE threatened "the very heart of the psychoanalytic enterprise" (Wallerstein, 1995, p. 55), challenging the mutative primacy of interpretation and insight. As Blum (1979) put it, "insight is the sine qua non of psychoanalysis" (p. 43) and "interpretation leading to insight is the specific and most powerful agent of the psychoanalytic curative process" (p. 43). The reliance on interpretation as opposed to the therapeutic relationship and the emphasis on insight in the context of heightened affect were fundamental tenets that defined psychoanalysis and distinguished it from other forms of therapy. Loewenstein (1951), commenting on Alexander's (1950) ideas shortly after they were published, asserted that the notion of a CEE was "a devaluation of what is specifically psychoanalytic: i.e., of the dynamic of changes produced by insight gained from interpretations" (p. 3).

Alexander's (1950) recommendation that the therapist assume a role that was designed to counter that of the parents raised concerns among mainstream therapists that he was attempting to change the client through the intentional use of the therapeutic relationship, considered by some as a form of technical manipulation, rather than through the process of showing the client the nature of his or her intrapsychic conflicts and the corresponding attempts at solutions. Why was this considered so controversial? When Freud first began developing his approach at the turn of the century, he had used hypnosis to help his clients recover repressed memories (and associated emotions) of traumatic events. After a few years, Freud abandoned the use of hypnosis, because of its unreliability as a method, but more important, because he came to distrust the reliability of the recovered memories themselves. Over time, Freud (1916) and the early therapists came to believe that it was vital to make a clear distinction between psychoanalysis and the tradition of hypnosis out of which it had emerged. Although it was common in the early 20th century for both charismatic healers and many members of the medical profession to use hypnosis and various forms of suggestion to treat psychological and psychosomatic problems, hypnosis had not yet completely shed its public image as a form of quackery. Freud and his colleagues were thus eager to establish psychoanalysis as a treatment that, unlike hypnosis, was based on true scientific principles (Safran, 2011). By doing so, Freud sought to dispel the accusation put forth by critics who charged that changes in psychoanalysis were nothing more than the result of suggestion and manipulation. Henceforth, a belief in the value of autonomy as a therapeutic goal and a disciplined effort to avoid imposing personal influence of any kind that would compromise the client's growth in an autonomous direction became a central tenet of psychoanalysis—one that Alexander's (1946, 1950) approach seemed to challenge as he proposed the use of the therapeutic relationship to bring about change.

CHALLENGING THE PSYCHOANALYST'S IDENTITY: PSYCHOANALYSIS VERSUS PSYCHOTHERAPY

To some, Alexander's (1950) recommendations were radical alterations to standard analytic method: the shortening of treatment, the use of overt action in place of interpretation to achieve therapeutic change, and a re-assessment of the value of working through. Despite the magnitude of these changes, some argued that the intense opposition to Alexander's recommendations had much less to do with his specific clinical suggestions than with the impression, perhaps an accurate one, that psychoanalysis as an enterprise was being undermined with the promise of briefer, alternative forms of treatment, the likes of which threatened to erode the boundary between psychoanalysis and psychotherapy.

Alexander, the most promising of the young generation of analysts, had managed to unsettle the psychoanalytic establishment, and in response to a perceived threat, the psychoanalytic establishment became more rigid. Eisold (2005) pointed out that the notion of "parameters" introduced by Eissler in 1953 was meant to draw the line between what was acceptable, standard technique in response to Alexander's (1950) "flexibility" (p. 500): "I define the parameter of a technique as the deviation, both quantitative and qualitative, from the basic model technique, that is to say, from a technique which requires interpretation as the exclusive tool" (Eissler, 1953, p. 110).

A CEE was considered by many as an alloyed version of the true gold of psychoanalysis, diluted, as Freud (1919/1953) described it, "with the copper of direct suggestion" (p. 168) and fated to become part of the cadre of supportive and brief psychotherapies. Leading figures in ego psychology, including Rangell (1954), argued that although the maneuvers of a CEE may occasionally be indicated, they "distinctly constitute dynamic psychotherapy in contrast to psychoanalysis" (p. 743). Similarly, Gill (1954) stated that analysis "results in the development of a regressive transference neurosis and the ultimate resolution of this neurosis by technique of interpretation alone" (p. 775). Wallerstein (1989) concluded that the CEE would be deemed appropriate in supportive therapies, along with advice giving, and reeducation, but serve as a clear contrast to "interpretation leading to insight as the central mechanism in the expressive psychotherapeutic approaches" (p. 138).

CORRECTIVE EMOTIONAL EXPERIENCE AS ACTION

Paralleling the valuing of insight in psychoanalysis was a concurrent devaluing of action. Traditionally, action was discussed on the part of the client and deemed anathema to the goals of psychoanalysis, which emphasized the suppression of action in the service of recollection. Roughton (1996) noted that "from the very beginning of 'the talking cure,' there has been a strong tendency to exclude action, both in fact and in theory, from this mostly verbal process" (p. 130). The client was thought to "act out" that which he or she wished not to remember. If psychoanalysis was to be a successful form of treatment, it was necessary that the client be capable of refraining from action in favor of thinking and remembering. Freud (1914/1953) wrote that the client repeats "without, of course, knowing that he is repeating it" (p. 150). Action serves both to communicate what cannot be recalled and to avoid full recollection by acting out.

These ambivalent views of action and of the action-prone client also applied to the therapist. If treatment was to be considered psychoanalytic, the therapist's action needed to be limited to interpretation. The ego psychologist's aim was to help the client move from privileging and valuing action to a more cognitive place that privileged the value of insight and the client's ego capacity for refraining from action and discharge, in favor of reasoning.[1]

---

[1]For an incisive look at the ways in which psychoanalysis is grounded in the Enlightenment, see Eagle (2011).

To Alexander's (1946) refrain that intellectual insight alone was not enough, ego psychologists would rejoin that emotional experience without insight was without therapeutic value at best and counterproductive at worst—counterproductive, that is, to the extent that action served as a resistance to self-knowledge, the true aim of psychoanalysis. By the mid 1970s, the fate of Alexander's CEE was all but sealed.

THE SPLINTERING OF MAINSTREAM PSYCHOANALYSIS AND THE RESURGENCE OF INTEREST IN THE CORRECTIVE EMOTIONAL EXPERIENCE

By the 1980s, the unified psychoanalytic mainstream in North America was beginning to splinter into different factions, and a new era of psychoanalytic pluralism was beginning to emerge (Wallerstein, 2002). There were many factors responsible for this, but certainly one of the more important ones was the growing influence of Heinz Kohut's (1971, 1977) self psychology. Kohut, who had established solid credentials as a psychoanalytic insider, gradually developed a psychoanalytic approach that increasingly came to diverge in fundamental ways from the mainstream. Central to his thinking was the pivotal role that empathic mirroring plays in helping the individual develop a cohesive sense of self, as well as the role that working through empathic failures plays in the change process.

Although interpretation always remained a critically important therapeutic tool for Kohut, he increasingly came to emphasize the role of the therapeutic relationship as a central mechanism of change in and of itself. From his perspective, the critical turning points in treatment occur when inevitable periods of misattunement take place between the therapist and client, and when the therapist and client are able to work through these potentially traumatic experiences in a constructive fashion. Without going into the details of Kohut's (1984) thinking about the precise mechanisms through which these periods of relational miscoordination and repair lead to change, suffice to say that there is something about a constructive relational experience at play here.

Kohut's (1984) emphasis on the importance of working through potentially traumatic events in the therapeutic relationship, or therapeutic impasses, had been prefigured in the psychoanalytic literature as early as the 1930s by Freud's close colleague Sándor Ferenczi. Although ultimately marginalized by the psychoanalytic mainstream, the influence of Ferenczi's thinking operated as an underground current that influenced the thinking of many subsequent psychoanalysts, including contemporary relational psychoanalysts.

In some essential respects, Alexander's ideas about the role of the therapeutic relationship were no different from what Kohut would in time propose. In fact, the language that Kohut and Alexander used to describe the relational aspects of treatment was often indistinguishable. Kohut (1984), for instance, asserted that the therapist's protracted and consistent endeavor to understand the client leads to results that are analogous to the outcome of childhood development. The client comes to realize that "contrary to his experience in childhood, the sustaining echo of empathic resonance is available in this world" (p. 78). Note that here Kohut is not emphasizing change that occurs as a consequence of interpretation and ensuing insight, but rather, a change that occurs in response to an analytic attitude. Kohut concurred with Alexander that the working through in psychoanalysis is a process by which the client revisits old conflicts with a more mature psyche, and in 1968, Kohut granted that on certain occasions, with certain clients,

> the analyst must indulge a transference wish of the analysand; specifically, that the client had not received the necessary emotional echo or approval from the depressive mother, and that the analyst must now give it to her in order to provide a "corrective emotional experience." (p. 111)

Early on, Kohut (1968) envisioned the use of a CEE as an auxiliary element of treatment but not the predicate of therapeutic change, and he was quick to add that the "true analytic aim is not indulgence but mastery based on insight, achieved in a setting of (tolerable) analytic abstinence" (p. 111).

Yet, in time, Kohut's (1984) views about the role of insight shifted, falling more in line with that of Alexander, who relegated insight to a general category of factors that accounted for change in treatment but was not the principal factor as ego psychology insisted. By 1984, in his last book, anticipating obvious comparisons to Alexander, Kohut responded that if the charge is that "I both believe in the curative effect of the 'corrective emotional experience' and equate such experience with analysis, I could only reply: so be it" (p. 78). The defensive tone of Kohut's statement attests to the level of controversy that had accrued around the concept of a CEE.

THE RELATIONALIST AND INTERPERSONALIST CRITIQUE: ENACTMENTS AND THE THERAPIST'S AUTHORITY

With the emergence of the interpersonal and relational perspectives in North America, Alexander's ideas would find some support in the challenge that they represented to the preeminent status afforded to insight in the analytic process. Few analysts disagree with Alexander's (1946) premise that insight is not enough and that therapeutic change relies on relational elements of psychoanalysis. Aron (1990), for example, asserted that "for relational model theorists, relationship along with insight are thought to be the central therapeutic factors" (p. 443). Yet, despite areas of overlap, specifically as it pertains to Alexander elevating the mutative role of the analytic relationship, interpersonalists and relationists disagree with Alexander's views on the nature of the relationship as Alexander envisioned, by virtue of how Alexander privileges the therapist's authority as the one who supposedly knows precisely what type of experience is, in fact, corrective. Cooper (2007) stated, "More than any other writer/analyst I have encountered, [Alexander] believes in the value and power of the analyst's ability to be objective and neutral" (p. 1091). From a relational perspective, there are two interdependent issues at the heart of the disagreement with Alexander's (1950) position. The first concerns the relational critique of the classical psychoanalytic perspective, which assumes that the therapist has a privileged perspective on reality and on what the client needs. This critique is related to the relational position on analytic authority and the emphasis on deconstructing the role of power in the therapeutic relationship (Safran, 2011). The second issue is the relational assumption that the therapist is always part of a bipersonal field constituted by the therapist–client relationship, and a related skepticism about the therapist's ability to ever step completely outside of this field and look at the client with some degree of objectivity. This, in turn, is related to the relational perspective on the process through which any type of corrective experience (more broadly defined) can actually take place in the treatment.

Many relationists contend that it is inevitable that clients and therapists will become embedded in repetitive relational scenarios that reflect the unconscious contributions of both client and therapist. These repetitive, bipersonal scenarios, referred to as *enactments*, are viewed as both one of the most challenging aspects of working with more difficult clients and an important potential source of understanding about the client and an opportunity for change. Through the process of participating in these inevitable enactments, the therapist is able to develop a lived sense of what it is like to be part of the client's relational world. By reflecting on the nature of his or her participation in these enactments, the therapist is ultimately able to disembed himself or herself and begin acting in a different way. This process is the relational equivalent of a CEE; that is, the process of disembedding and finding a new way of being with the client, which will hopefully provide the client with a relational experience that is sufficiently different from the repetitive and unreflected-on scenarios that the client consistently enacts in his relationships with others. With these new experiences, the client's view of what might actually be possible in the interpersonal realm begins to change (Aron, 1996; Bromberg, 1998, 2006; Mitchell, 1988, 1993). The contemporary relational perspective is thus very much in harmony with Alexander's emphasis on the relational and experiential aspect of treatment. Where it differs, however, is in its sense of (a) whether the therapist is capable of determining in advance what type of relational stance on his or her part might be desirable and (b) whether it is desirable to intentionally play a certain role with the client, even if it were possible.

THE CORRECTIVE EMOTIONAL EXPERIENCE AND THE CONCEPT OF ENACTMENTS

Alexander's (1950) view of how the relationship was curative would, in time, clash with the emphasis that relational thinking places on the unconscious nature of enactments. Sandler (1976), for example, clearly articulated how the therapist responds to the client's demands and how this role responsiveness develops both interpersonally and outside of conscious awareness of both participants. This is in sharp contrast with Alexander's (1950) purposeful therapeutic strategy, which Aron (1992) described as a curative "role-playing" (p. 494), one that would inevitably taint the therapist's responses to the client with an element of disingenuousness. For relationists and interpersonalists, it was critical that the therapist's response to the client not be deliberate or staged. Enactments, as Lionells (1995) aptly pointed out, are only "potent when they occur spontaneously so they may be studied as emerging, unconscious interpersonal paradigms" (p. 229). Similarly, Sandler (1976) wrote,

> very often the irrational response of the analyst, which his professional conscience leads him to see entirely as a blind spot of his own, may sometimes be usefully regarded as a compromise-formation between his own tendencies and his reflexive acceptance of the role which the patient is forcing on him. (p. 46)

It is the unintended quality of the enactment that is important in the client–therapist relationship to the extent that it creates a space for the unconscious processes emanating from both participants to be analyzed. Katz (1998) labeled the process as the *enacted dimension of psychoanalysis*, which he believed

> occurs naturally and inevitably, without conscious awareness or intention. It exists alongside, and in concert with, the treatment's verbally symbolized content, an ongoing and evolving realm of analytic process with features unique to each analytic dyad. In these terms, the therapeutic action of psychoanalysis may be considered a function of two interwoven and inextricable treatment processes: transference experienced enactively and insight symbolized verbally. (p. 1132)

In the wake of the controversies attendant to Alexander's (1950) ideas about the role of action in psychoanalysis and the role of the person of the therapist as an agent of change, insight became increasingly pitted against the analytic relationship. Although this argument is largely recognized as a straw man by most analysts today, who would readily agree that insight is only transformative in the context of an affectively charged and meaningful relationship with the therapist, the question becomes an empirical one. After all, the real challenge that a CEE poses to classical psychoanalysis is the idea that meaningful change can occur in treatment irrespective of the development of insight as traditionally defined, that is, in terms of semantic knowledge. Many of the arguments for and against Alexander's (1946, 1950) model have been made on theoretical grounds.

A line of research that has some bearing on contemporary views of the CEE has been carried out by Safran and Muran (1990, 1996, 2003; Safran, Muran, & Eubancks-Carter, 2011; Safran, Muran, Wallner Samstag, & Stevens, 2001) on the negotiation of the therapeutic alliance and rupture resolutions strategies in psychotherapy. Drawing on the recognized importance of a therapeutic alliance in the treatment process, Safran and Muran (2003) proposed a method for assessing how clients respond to ruptures in the alliance that can aid our understanding of how and why such ruptures emerge, and the means by which they are repaired. The relational theoretical perspective on which this line of research rests converges in some important respects with Alexander and French's (1946) notion of the corrective emotional experience.

A CORRECTIVE EMOTIONAL EXPERIENCE: THE THERAPEUTIC ALLIANCE, ITS RUPTURES, AND ITS REPAIRS

Over the past 2 decades, Safran and colleagues (Safran, 1993; Safran, Crocker, McMain, & Murray, 1990; Safran & Muran, 1996, 2003) have placed particular emphasis on the role that repairing ruptures in the therapeutic alliance can play in facilitating a CEE. Building on developmental research on affect miscoordination and repair (e.g., Tronick, 2007), Safran et al. (1990) suggested that the process of repairing ruptures in the therapeutic alliance may help clients to develop a representation of self as capable of reestablishing interpersonal connection and the other as potentially available, even in the face of life's inevitable disruptions in interpersonal relatedness. Safran (1993) explicitly linked the mechanism of change associated with repairing alliance ruptures to Alexander's (1946) notion of the CEE, and traced the origins of this line of thinking back to the early influence of Ferenczi (1933/1980) and the subsequent influence of his protégé Michael

Balint (1968). Safran and Muran (2003) conceptualized the therapeutic alliance as a process of ongoing negotiation between therapist and client, which can provide the client with a vital opportunity to learn to negotiate the dialectical tension between his or her own needs for agency versus relatedness.

In their research program, Safran and Muran (2003) have found it useful to identify ruptures in the alliance in terms of specific client behaviors or communication and have organized these ruptures into two general subtypes: withdrawal and confrontation. In ruptures marked by withdrawal, the client withdraws or partially disengages from the therapist, his or her own emotions, or some aspect of the therapeutic process. In confrontation-type ruptures, the client directly expresses anger, resentment, or dissatisfaction with the therapist or some aspect of the therapy, with variations in terms of how directly or indirectly the confrontation is initially expressed. Withdrawal and confrontation reflect different ways of coping with the dialectical tension between the needs for agency and relatedness. In withdrawal ruptures, the client strives for relatedness at the cost of the need for agency or self-definition. In confrontation ruptures, the client negotiates the conflict by favoring the need for agency or self-definition over the need for relatedness.

Working through alliance ruptures involves a process of clarifying both underlying needs that are dissociated and tacit fears and expectations that lead clients to dissociate these needs. If the therapist is able to maintain a curious and nondefensive stance, a CEE takes place in which clients learn that the relevant fears are unwarranted and that it is safe to express dissociated needs and wishes in the therapeutic relationship.

The process of working through withdrawal ruptures in a constructive way thus constitutes a form of CEE through the process of helping clients learn that they can express dissociated needs for self-assertion or agency without destroying relationships. The process of working through confrontation ruptures can provide clients with a type of CEE by virtue of the fact that (a) clients can learn that the therapist can tolerate and survive their aggression and (b) dissociated needs for dependency and nurturance are safe to express.

Consistent with a contemporary relational perspective, Safran and Muran (2006) do not believe that clients have one core maladaptive schema that is activated in therapy and then challenged by an intentional effort by the therapist to assume an interpersonal stance that challenges this schema. Instead, they conceptualized the therapeutic process as an ongoing cycle of *mutual enactment* and *disembedding*. Therapists unwittingly become partners in enactments, or interpersonal dances, that reflect the unique intersection of unconscious aspects of both clients' and therapists' subjectivities. It is only through the process of collaboratively exploring what is taking place at such times that both therapists and clients can begin to understand the nature of the enactments that are taking place. This process of developing an experientially based awareness of what is taking place helps the client and therapist to disembed, or unhook, from the dance in which they are trapped. This process of disembedding functions as a CEE insofar as it challenges the client's stereotypes expectations of the way relationships will play out.

For example, a therapist gradually becomes aware that he has been feeling frustrated and angry with his client and unconsciously expressing aggressive feelings toward him. By acknowledging and exploring this aspect of his contribution to the interaction, the therapist is able to reposition himself into a more genuinely sympathetic role vis-à-vis the client's experience of being a persecuted victim and the therapist's recognition of his participation in a role-responsive enactment. This process in turn paves the way for the client to begin the process of becoming aware of the way in which his expectations that others will exploit him lead him to act in a passive–aggressive fashion that elicits sadistic responses from others. It is critical to emphasize that this process of collaboratively making sense of what is taking place in the therapeutic relationship constitutes a contemporary version of a CEE— one that stresses the unconscious dimensions that determine the therapist's and client's participation in the enacted dimension of treatment that can potentially render, once recognized and explored, the relational process in treatment as a clinically significant mechanism of change.

CONCLUSION

Today, when the concept of a CEE is invoked in psychoanalytic thinking, it tends to be stripped of the elements that made the original concept so controversial. The idea that the therapist should manipulate the transference so as to overtly behave in a way that is opposite to that of the client's past objects has virtually disappeared from most discussions of a CEE for reasons that we elucidated in this chapter. Instead, what has been preserved in the current usage of the term is the idea that there is something curative about the relationship with the therapist that works alongside interpretation and insight, and by now, this idea has become an unobjectionable and, in fact, widely accepted tenet across theoretical orientations.

What remains controversial among psychoanalysts is the question of the particular mechanisms through which CEEs contribute to the change process. Is some form of conceptual understanding on the client's part necessary for significant therapeutic change to occur in therapy, or is there something about the experience with the therapist that, in and of itself, suffices to bring about meaningful change? Can insight encompass or be defined by learning that occurs at a procedural, implicit, or subsymbolic level, which is not dependent on its verbal expression for it to have lasting therapeutic effects? Or does verbalization allow for a mode of processing and representing experience that is indispensable for real change, anchoring insight in a different mode of experience, or by virtue of perhaps addressing the motivations that keep procedural or relational insight from being made verbally explicit? Questions of this type can breathe new life into the field of psychoanalysis and psychotherapy in general, as they are explored from different angles, including psychotherapy research and insights gleaned from mother–infant developmental research.

REFERENCES

Alexander, F. (1925). A metapsychological description of the process of cure. *The International Journal of Psycho-Analysis*, 6, 13–34.

Alexander, F. (1946). Individual psychotherapy. *Psychosomatic Medicine*, 8, 110–115.

Alexander, F. (1950). Analysis of the therapeutic factors in psychoanalytic treatment. *The Psychoanalytic Quarterly*, 19, 482–500.

Alexander, F., & French, T. (1946). *Psychoanalytic therapy: Principles and Application.* New York, NY: Ronald Press.

Aron, L. (1990). Free association and changing models of mind. *Journal of the American Academy of Psychoanalysis*, 18, 439–459.

Aron, L. (1992). Interpretation as expression of the analyst's subjectivity. *Psychoanalytic Dialogues*, 2, 475–507. doi:10.1080/10481889209538947

Aron, L. (1996). *A meeting of minds: Mutuality in psychoanalysis.* Hillsdale, NJ: Analytic Press.

Balint, M. (1968). *The basic fault.* London, England: Tavistock.

Blum, H. P. (1979). The curative and creative aspects of insight. *Journal of the American Psychoanalytic Association*, 27, 41–69.

Bromberg, P. M. (1998). *Standing in the spaces: Essays on clinical process, trauma, and dissociation.* Hillsdale, NJ: Analytic Press.

Bromberg, P. M. (2006). *Awakening the dreamer: Clinical journeys.* Hillsdale, NJ: Analytic Press.

Cooper, S. H. (2007). Alexander's corrective emotional experience: An objectivist turn in psychoanalysis. *The Psychoanalytic Quarterly*, 76, 1085–1102.

Eagle, M. (2011). Classical theory, the Enlightenment vision, and contemporary psychoanalysis. In M. J. Diamond & C. Christian (Eds.), *The second century of psychoanalysis: Evolving perspectives on therapeutic action* (pp. 41–67). London, England: Karnac.

Eisold, K. (2005). Psychoanalysis and psychotherapy: A long and troubled relationship. *The International Journal of Psychoanalysis*, 86, 1175–1195. doi:10.1516/8RMN-4EQF-LG1E-JG03

Eissler, K. R. (1953). The effect of the structure of the ego on psychoanalytic technique. *Journal of the American Psychoanalytic Association, 1*, 104–143. doi:10.1177/000306515300100107

Ferenczi, S. (1980). Confusion of tongues between the adult and the child. In M. Balint (Ed.) & E. Mosbacher (Trans.), *Final contributions to the problems and methods of psychoanalysis* (pp. 156–167). London, England: Karnac Books. (Original work published 1933)

Freud, S. (1916). The history of the psychoanalytic movement. *Psychoanalytic Review, 3*, 406–454.

Freud, S. (1925, October 18). Letter from Sigmund Freud to Sándor Ferenczi. In Falzeder & E. Brabant (Eds.) & P. Hoffer (Trans.), *The correspondence of Sigmund Freud and Sándor Ferenczi, Vol. 3, 1920–1933* (pp. 231–233). Cambridge, MA: Harvard Press.

Freud, S. (1953). The dynamics of transference. In J. Strachey (Ed. & Trans.), *The standard edition of the complete psychological works of Sigmund Freud: Vol. 12. The case of Schreber, papers on technique, and other works* (pp. 97–108). London, England: Hogarth Press and the Institute for Psychoanalysis. (Original work published 1912)

Freud, S. (1953). Lines of advance in psycho-analytic therapy. In J. Strachey (Ed. & Trans.), *The standard edition of the complete psychological works of Sigmund Freud: Vol. 12. The case of Schreber, papers on technique, and other works* (pp. 157–168). London, England: Hogarth Press and the Institute for Psychoanalysis. (Original work published 1919)

Freud, S. (1953). Remembering, repeating, and working-through (further recommendations on the technique of psychoanalysis II). In J. Strachey (Ed. & Trans.), *The standard edition of the complete psychological works of Sigmund Freud: Vol. 12. The case of Schreber, papers on technique, and other works* (pp. 145–156). London, England: Hogarth Press and the Institute for Psychoanalysis. (Original work published 1914)

Gill, M. M. (1954). Psychoanalysis and exploratory psychotherapy. *Journal of the American Psychoanalytic Association, 2*, 771–797. doi:10.1177/000306515400200413

Goldfried, M. (1980). Toward the delineation of therapeutic change principles. *American Psychologist, 35*, 991–999. doi:10.1037/0003-066X.35.11.991

Katz, G. A. (1998). Where the action is: The enacted dimension of analytic process. *Journal of the American Psychoanalytic Association, 46*, 1129–1167. doi:10.1177/00030651980460040801

Kohut, H. (1968). The psychoanalytic treatment of narcissistic personality disorders: Outline of a systematic approach. *The Psychoanalytic Study of the Child, 23*, 86–113.

Kohut, H. (1971). *The analysis of the self: A systematic approach to the psychoanalytic treatment of narcissistic personality disorders.* New York, NY: International Universities Press.

Kohut, H. (1977). *The restoration of the self*. New York, NY: International Universities Press.

Kohut, H. (1984). *How does analysis cure?* (A. Goldberg & P. Stepansky, Eds.). Chicago, IL: University of Chicago Press.

Lionells, M. (1995). Interpersonal–relational psychoanalysis: An introduction and overview. *International Forum of Psychoanalysis, 4*, 223–230. doi:10.1080/08037069508409552

Loewenstein, R. M. (1951). The problem of interpretation. *The Psychoanalytic Quarterly, 20*, 1–14.

Marmor, J. (n.d.). *The contributions of Franz Alexander to modern psychotherapy*. Nutley, NJ: Roche Laboratories.

Mitchell, S. A. (1988). *Relational concepts in psychoanalysis*. Cambridge, MA: Harvard University Press.

Mitchell, S. A. (1993). *Hope and dread in psychoanalysis*. New York, NY: Basic Books.

Mitchell, S. A. (1997). *Influence and autonomy in psychoanalysis*. Hillsdale, NJ: Analytic Press.

Rangell, L. (1954). Similarities and differences between psychoanalysis and dynamic psychotherapy. *Journal of the American Psychoanalytic Association, 2*, 734–744. doi:10.1177/000306515400200411

Roughton, R. E. (1996). Action and acting out. In B. E. Moore (Ed.), *Psychoanalysis: The major concepts* (pp. 130–145). New Haven, CT: Yale University Press.

Safran, J. (1993). Breaches in the therapeutic alliance: An arena for negotiating authentic relatedness. *Psychotherapy, 30*, 11–24. doi:10.1037/0033-3204.30.1.11

Safran, J. D. (2011). *Psychoanalysis and psychoanalytic therapies*. Washington, DC: American Psychological Association.

Safran, J. D., Crocker, P., McMain, S., & Murray, P. (1990). The therapeutic alliance rupture as a therapy event for empirical investigation. *Psychotherapy, 27*, 154–165. doi:10.1037/0033-3204.27.2.154

Safran, J. D., & Muran, J. C. (1996). The resolution of ruptures in the therapeutic alliance. *Journal of Consulting and Clinical Psychology, 64*, 447–458. doi:10.1037/0022-006X.64.3.447

Safran, J. D., & Muran, J. C. (2003). *Negotiating the therapeutic alliance: A relational treatment guide*. New York, NY: Guilford Press.

Safran, J. D., & Muran, J. C. (2006). Has the concept of the therapeutic alliance outlived its usefulness? *Psychotherapy: Theory, Research, & Practice, 43*, 286–291. doi:10.1037/0033-3204.43.3.286

Safran, J. D., Muran, J. C., & Eubancks-Carter, C. (2011) Repairing alliance ruptures. In J. C. Norcross (Ed.), *Psychotherapy relationships that work* (2nd ed., pp. 224–238). New York, NY: Oxford University Press.

Safran, J. D., Muran, J. C., Wallner Samstag, L., & Stevens, C. (2001). Repairing therapeutic alliance ruptures. *Psychotherapy, 38*, 406–412.

Sandler, J. (1976). Countertransference and role-responsiveness. *The International Journal of Psychoanalysis, 3*, 43–47.

Strachey, J. (1934). The nature of the therapeutic action of psychoanalysis. *The International Journal of Psychoanalysis, 15*, 127–159.

Tronick, E. (2007). *The neurobehavioral and social–emotional development of infants and children.* New York, NY: Norton.

Wallerstein, R. S. (1989). The psychotherapy research project of the Menninger Foundation: An overview. *Journal of Consulting and Clinical Psychology, 57*, 195–205. doi:10.1037/0022-006X.57.2.195

Wallerstein, R. S. (1995). *The talking cures: The psychoanalyses and the psychotherapies.* New Haven, CT: Yale University Press.

5

A COGNITIVE BEHAVIORAL PERSPECTIVE ON CORRECTIVE EXPERIENCES

ADELE M. HAYES, J. GAYLE BECK, AND CARLY YASINSKI

The concept of corrective experiences (CEs) has a long history and an important place in theories of change in psychotherapy. This concept has its roots in psychoanalytic and psychodynamic traditions. As early as 1946, Alexander and French conceptualized the corrective emotional experience as a common therapeutic principle:

> In all forms of etiological psychotherapy, the basic therapeutic principle is the same: to reexpose the client, under more favourable circumstances, to emotional situations which he could not handle in the past. The client, in order to be helped, must undergo a corrective emotional experience suitable to repair the traumatic influence of previous experiences. It is of secondary importance whether this corrective experience takes place during treatment in the transference relationship or parallel with the treatment in the daily life of the client. (p. 66)

In a later discussion of CEs in the context of learning theory, Alexander (1963/2004) described these experiences as involving the disruption of habitual maladaptive patterns and the development of new patterns. In this account, the original negative experience is activated, brought into the client's awareness, and the therapist's response is different from what the client expects

69

based on his or her history. Alexander emphasized the importance of repetition so that the new reaction can become more automatic and consolidated. These descriptions of CEs suggest that they are experiential and affectively charged, involve a shift in meaning, and require repetition to solidify the new patterns of responding.

As highlighted by Goldfried and Davila (2005) and Grosse Holtforth et al. (2007), the CE describes a principle of therapeutic change that transcends theoretical orientation. Alexander and French's (1946) early ideas come from a psychoanalytic tradition, yet the principles described in their account of CEs sound strikingly similar to principles that underlie modern exposure and learning-based interventions. We present a cognitive behavioral perspective on CEs and illustrate that although the language and therapeutic techniques differ, the concept of the CE seems central to the process of change in both orientations.

A COGNITIVE BEHAVIORAL PERSPECTIVE
ON CORRECTIVE EXPERIENCES

In a review of the historical and philosophical roots of the cognitive behavior therapy (CBT) perspective, Dobson and Dozois (2010) described the basic tenets of this therapeutic approach. First, this approach assumes that most behavioral disorders can be treated by teaching individuals new skills. For example, individuals who are struggling with depression might be taught skills to challenge negative thoughts and increase the frequency of pleasant interactions with others. Second, within a CBT framework, the therapist is regarded more as a coach than as an individual who imparts interpretations or clinical observations. The therapist–client relationship is explicitly situated in a learning relationship. The therapist's role is to identify areas in which the client could benefit from new skills and perspectives and to facilitate the learning of these and one's sense of efficacy (Bandura, 1977, 1982). Third, a CBT perspective does not conceptualize behavior as motivated by unconscious needs or desires; rather, this approach postulates that environmental contingencies, cognitions, and biological inputs interact to influence behavioral disorders. Specific problem behaviors are conceptualized as composed of cognitive, affective, behavioral, and physiological elements, each of which can be a legitimate target for intervention.

From a cognitive behavioral perspective, a CE is often facilitated by repeated exposure to new information and experiences that violate negative expectancies and disrupt negative behavior cycles, a definition that is wholly consistent with the Penn State consensus definition. These CEs create dissonance and facilitate a change in meaning and affective response (Carey,

2011; Foa & Kozak, 1986; Goldfried & Davila, 2005; Safran & Segal, 1990; Tryan & Misurell, 2008). It is through exposure to novel information, as well as continued processing of these experiences, that lasting change can occur (Foa & Kozak, 1986; Goldfried & Davila, 2005). The challenges that facilitate CEs can target specific problematic behaviors or well-entrenched patterns that contribute to and maintain psychopathology.

As we describe below, the process of change can be turbulent, as the old ways are challenged through exposure exercises, behavioral experiments, and cognitive restructuring techniques. Alexander and French (1946) noted that challenges that facilitate CEs can occur within the therapy setting or outside of it, in the person's everyday life. Consistent with Alexander and French's emphasis on repetition, changes in meaning and affective response in CBT are thought to come with multiple challenges or repeated exposure, as single experiences might not be potent enough to produce lasting change. The new learning that emerges from these CEs is fragile, so these therapies include specific exercises to solidify and generalize the new changes to other aspects of the client's life.

From a cognitive behavioral perspective, a CE need not be interpersonal in nature; these experiences can be generated to reduce a range of maladaptive patterns related to psychopathology. We focus in this chapter on one type of CE—that which occurs in the interpersonal domain—to facilitate discussion across theoretical orientations.

WHAT FACILITATES CORRECTIVE EXPERIENCES IN COGNITIVE BEHAVIOR THERAPIES?

Cognitive, behavioral, and cognitive behavioral approaches have in common a view of therapy as a means of facilitating new learning. Designing experiences that challenge and correct old maladaptive patterns is central to these therapies. CBT includes direct, planned challenges to facilitate a CE. As with most therapies, it is important to increase the client's readiness for change by addressing factors that maintain current maladaptive patterns and inhibit change. We describe below some CBT principles and techniques that can facilitate CEs.

Preparation for Change

From a cognitive behavioral perspective, people settle into patterns that are influenced by biological factors and by situational learning that has occurred over the course of one's life. These patterns are reinforced over time and can be maintained by processes such as behavioral avoidance, biased perceptions, and avoidance. These processes can prevent challenges from becoming key learning experiences and, thus, maintain dysfunctional patterns. An important early goal of therapy, then, is to reduce these barriers to change. Without addressing such inhibitors, efforts to expose the person to new experiences are likely to be deflected or weakened.

Strategies to address inhibitors of learning and to increase the client's readiness for change across orientations include those that aim to reduce avoidance, increase resources, and foster a strong therapeutic alliance (Castonguay & Beutler, 2006; Goldfried & Davila, 2005; Prochaska & Prochaska, 1999). In most forms of CBT, clients are taught general emotion regulation skills, such as problem-solving skills, breathing retraining and relaxation, and active coping, all of which can facilitate healthy engagement with emotions and a sense of self-efficacy (Bandura, 1977, 1982; Dobson & Dozois, 2010; Goldfried & Davison, 1994). Specific CBT strategies have been developed to both increase motivation and foster the therapeutic relationship. For instance, Miller and Rollnick (2002) described interventions designed to help clients examine the costs and benefits of maintaining current behavioral patterns and to help therapists work with rather than against client resistance. Grosse Holtforth and Castonguay (2005) described specific strategies that can be used in CBT to reduce avoidance and increase approach behaviors. Activation of the approach system theoretically opens the person to new information and to the experience of positive emotions. They describe ways to align the client's motivational goals and the therapist's interventions, thereby fostering the therapeutic alliance. Change of entrenched patterns of pathology is difficult, and cognitive behavior therapists have increasingly recognized the importance of concentrated effort on developing and maintaining a solid working alliance and preparing the client to undergo the process of change (Prochaska & Prochaska, 1999; Safran & Segal, 1990; Waddington, 2002).

With some energy and openness, challenges to maladaptive patterns can be introduced. For interpersonal difficulties, exercises can be designed to expose the client to interactions and have them act or respond in different ways. Exposure exercises also can be used to foster hypothesis testing and to challenge one's view of self, others, and one's future. The therapeutic relationship can be an important vehicle of change when addressing interpersonal dysfunction (Beck, Freeman, & Davis, 2004; Safran & Segal, 1990; Young, Klosko, & Weishaar, 2003). In the next section, we describe exposure and other behavioral techniques, hypothesis-testing strategies, and the use of the therapeutic relationship to facilitate CEs.

The Process of Change

A particularly potent way to challenge and destabilize pathological patterns is exposure, which is designed to facilitate CEs. Exposure can take many forms, but its essence involves (a) activating the maladaptive pattern or patterns related to the person's psychopathology; (b) creating inconsistencies by introducing corrective information; and (c) focusing the client's attention on these inconsistencies to facilitate a reorganization and movement toward new patterns of thinking, feeling, and behaving (Carey, 2011; Foa, Huppert, & Cahill, 2006; Foa & Kozak, 1986). This dissonance induction (Tryon & Misurell, 2008) is destabilizing and uncomfortable, but it is thought to be critical so that new information is not simply assimilated into the old patterns, and instead new patterns can emerge. Defined in this way, the concept of exposure can apply beyond the anxiety disorders and have broad application across forms of behavior and emotional disorders.

For instance, Hayes and colleagues (Hayes, Beevers, Feldman, Laurenceau, & Perlman, 2005; Hayes et al., 2007) applied the principles of exposure to the treatment of depression. Clients were first taught strategies to decrease avoidance and rumination, which maintain maladaptive patterns. Core cognitive, affective, behavioral, and somatic patterns related to clients' depression were then activated, and in the context of affective engagement, corrective information was introduced to facilitate emotional processing of previously avoided material. Similarly, schema-focused treatment of personality disorders (Beck et al., 2004; Young et al., 2003) involves activating and disrupting deeply entrenched patterns of cognition, affect, and behavior ("early maladaptive schemas"), which are related to early life experiences. Challenges related to these core patterns are often met with resistance and avoidance, as these patterns are particularly stable (Beck et al., 2004; Safran & Segal, 1990).

Alexander and French's (1946) early presentation of the CE concept also postulated that exposing the client to new experiences could facilitate the unlearning of old patterns and learning of new ones. Thus, the principles of exposure and emotional processing can provide a useful framework for understanding the CE construct from a cognitive behavioral and learning perspective.

There is converging evidence across theoretical orientations that in-session activation of relevant emotions is important, if the level of arousal is moderate and emotional engagement is coupled with cognitive processing that involves conscious reflection and the construction of new meaning (Carey, 2011; Whelton, 2004). This combination of change in meaning and affective responses has been referred to as *emotional processing* (Foa & Kozak, 1986; Lang & Cuthbert, 1984; Teasdale, 1999), *experiencing* (Greenberg, 2002; Klein, Mathieu-Coughlan, & Kiesler, 1986), *cognitive–emotional processing* (Hayes et al., 2007; Rachman, 2001), and *emotional insight* (Alexander, 1963/2004). Whatever the label, processing is the goal of the exposure, and dissonance induction is thought to be part of CEs. CEs, as conceptualized by

Alexander and French (1946) and Alexander (1963/2004), also involve the activation of old patterns, affective arousal, exposure to inconsistent information, and processing. Processing then allows room for the development of new interpersonal patterns that solidify with repetition.

Other types of behavioral exercises can be used to encourage the client to engage in novel ways of interacting with the world and can generate material for hypothesis-testing exercises. Within the CBT framework, homework (or practice outside of the therapy session) plays a central role. Homework is thought to help clients refine newly acquired skills and to practice them in the context of their ongoing experiences. Homework can include behavioral exercises and strategies, such as the social skills taught in CBT treatments for social anxiety disorder (e.g., Turk, Heimberg, & Hope, 2001). Cognitive aspects of dysfunctional patterns also can be the target of homework by having clients maintain daily records of negative thoughts or engage in structured exercises that help them explicitly test specific expectations. These types of exercises reinforce the notion that thoughts need to be approached as hypotheses, not as reality, a stand that often helps clients increase awareness of their cognitive distortions and longstanding negative expectations. Homework also can be oriented toward helping the client to understand the links between specific cognitions (e.g., "my voice sounds stupid" and "I am boring"), emotions (e.g., embarrassment, anxiety), and behavior (e.g., avoidance, awkward interactions).

Also consistent with the spirit of exposure, cognitive theorists emphasize the importance of fully activating the cognitive, affective, behavioral, and somatic components of the problematic associative network, increasing tolerance of avoided emotions and thoughts, and increasing exposure to corrective information to facilitate cognitive restructuring and emotional processing (e.g., Beck et al., 2004; Hayes et al., 2005; Power & Brewin, 1997; Samoilov & Goldfried, 2000; Teasdale, 1999; Young et al., 2003). Imagery exercises and other affectively charged interventions are thought to be particularly potent ways to increase the accessibility of problematic patterns and to facilitate new learning through hypothesis testing and corrective information (Samoilov & Goldfried, 2000).

Recent developments in human and animal research suggest that learning is context dependent and that it is critical for learning to occur in multiple contexts if the new learning is to consolidate in long-term memory and help prevent relapse (Bouton, 2002; Foa et al., 2006). Most current CBT approaches encourage learning in multiple contexts, especially outside of the therapy room. This cross-situation learning can not only solidify the new learning but also increase the accessibility of the new patterns, which will be weaker than the pathological patterns. It is interesting to note that practicing new patterns across different contexts was also highlighted by Alexander and French

(1946), suggesting some theoretical convergence. CBTs are based on learning theories and therefore include a number of strategies to enhance retrieval, such as flash cards and computerized reminders (Dobson & Dozois, 2010).

All of these interventions can be used in the context of the therapeutic relationship, which can be used as a vehicle for interpersonal change in CBT (Waddington, 2002). Safran and colleagues (Safran & Muran, 2002; Safran & Segal, 1990) have illustrated how the therapeutic relationship and its disturbance can be used to identify and challenge problematic patterns of relating to others. The CBT therapist can use the therapeutic relationship to help the client challenge entrenched and problematic interpersonal patterns and develop and practice new ways of interacting. Goldfried and Davila (2005) highlighted how the therapeutic relationship can be used across theoretical orientations to facilitate important principles of change, including CEs. For instance, cognitive therapy for personality disorders (Beck et al., 2004; Young et al., 2003) includes specific strategies for accessing early maladaptive schemas related to attachment experiences, linking them with current patterns of relating, and using the therapeutic relationship and alliance ruptures as therapeutic tools. Even more traditional behavioral approaches have recognized the importance of the therapeutic relationship as a potent way to work in vivo with interpersonal difficulties (e.g., Lejuez, Hopko, Levine, Gholkar, & Collins, 2005).

Case Example

We illustrate how exposure, other behavioral interventions, and cognitive therapy techniques can be combined to facilitate the new learning that occurs with CEs. This example is drawn from a trial of exposure-based cognitive therapy (EBCT) for depression developed by the first author (Hayes et al., 2005, 2007). We also use this case to describe the kinds of changes associated with CEs in the next section. As mentioned before, CEs from a cognitive behavioral perspective need not be interpersonal in nature, but to facilitate comparisons with other perspectives presented in this book, we focus on those CEs that occurred in the context of important relationships. In this case, EBCT targeted the cognitive, affective, and behavioral components of the client's problematic interpersonal patterns.

Laura was a 34-year-old African American divorced woman with two children. She was employed as a teacher's aide and was living in poverty. She never knew her father, and her mother had been addicted to alcohol and crack cocaine for as long as Laura could remember. Her mother neglected the children and constantly told Laura that she was worthless and would not amount to anything. Since the age of 14, Laura raised herself and her younger sister, and reported chronic feelings of defectiveness, abandonment, and betrayal. She learned that she could count on no one. There was also no room for her emotions or distress because she was caring for everyone else. Laura presented with major depressive disorder and reported four previous episodes. She had been prescribed antidepressants but was still clinically depressed.

Laura's most recent depressive episode was precipitated by her divorce from her husband of 10 years. Her husband began smoking crack with Laura's mother, and he also became addicted. This reactivated her feelings of abandonment and betrayal. Laura also criticized herself for repeating the pattern by marrying an addict, and she again felt defective and unlovable. She was left alone to care for her children, with little money to support them.

Laura coped with these chronic feelings of defectiveness, abandonment, and betrayal by avoiding these feelings and pushing others away. In the 3 years since her divorce, several men expressed interest in dating her, but she quickly pushed them away to avoid getting hurt again. It is not surprising that Laura was difficult to engage in therapy, as she was quite guarded and had adopted an angry and defensive demeanor to protect herself. The therapist maintained a stable, nonjudgmental stance and provided support and a safe environment, something Laura had never known. The alliance was strengthened in the first phase of therapy, which focused on improving coping, problem solving, and healthy lifestyle habits (e.g., healthy exercise, diet, sleep). This first phase of EBCT is designed to prepare the client for change by increasing stability and the resources for change and decreasing avoidance and rumination. This phase of therapy was associated with an improvement in her symptoms of depression.

The next phase of therapy involved activating the core patterns associated with her depression and introducing corrective information to challenge these patterns. During this exposure and activation phase, Laura was able to access her feelings of loss and abandonment when she lost her mother to the fog of drug addiction. She recalled how her mother would be kind at one moment and then, the next moment, betray her or tell her that she was worthless and a burden to bear. Laura accessed the emotions associated with these early experiences and became aware of the emptiness and pain that she had felt and had warded off by avoiding emotions and close relationships. She then fled from therapy for several weeks.

The therapist called the client consistently to send the message that she was not going to abandon her and that she would be available when Laura was ready to come back. After the fifth call, Laura said that she was ready to return to therapy. She said that she was afraid to be so vulnerable and feared that the therapist would not be there for her. The therapist's calls were inconsistent with this view, and it became clear to her that she actually could count on the therapist. The outcome was different from what she had come to expect. The therapist and Laura examined this alliance rupture and the expectancies that were activated, and then they discussed the connection between this reaction and Laura's abandonment and defectiveness schemata and other relationships in her life.

One of the men she had rejected, James, was a leader in her church and had been expressing interest in her for more than a year. Laura kept pushing him away, but an assessment of the relationship potential suggested that he might be worth dating. As this topic was approached, Laura had another surge of anxiety as she faced the possibility of hope and of getting hurt. However, James had pursued her respectfully for an entire year. A therapeutic task was to engage with him as a friend. Laura and the therapist designed specific and gradual behavioral tasks and experiments to challenge her expectation of rejection and betrayal. As intimacy increased, she experienced a wave of panic, which she now could link to her early experiences with her mother and her ex-husband. She was taught to work through her urges to run or sabotage the relationship. James provided another CE, as no matter how hard she pushed him away, he was there. She felt the steadiness and that she was loved. Through gradual exposure and working through her fears, Laura was eventually able to feel safe and begin an intimate relationship. She experienced a series of CEs with the therapist and with James. As Alexander and French (1946) noted, these experiences can occur both inside and outside of the therapeutic relationship. With repeated exercises as part of therapy and practice interacting in new ways, these positive experiences generalized to other relationships, including those with her children, sister, and even her mother.

In addition, more traditional cognitive strategies were used to examine her deeply held belief that she was defective, worthless, and a bad mother, just as her mother had been. By exploring the historical roots of these interpersonally oriented beliefs, she was able to see that she had been abandoned by her parents and told by her mother that she was no good and that no one would ever love her. Laura was able to see how as a child, she could have incorporated this view but that her mother was incapable of parenting and was abusive. These feelings of defectiveness and worthlessness were very painful and therefore had been avoided. They also contributed to her avoidance of close relationships. If these feelings were triggered by an environmental event or interaction, they came flooding out in much the same way that a trauma would. Imaginal exposure techniques were used in therapy to have her approach this distress, recall the associated memories, and process them in a safe environment and with more ability to tolerate this distress. Graded exposure was used outside of therapy to put her in contact with interpersonal situations that activated her depressive cognitions, emotions, and memories of loss and betrayal.

These challenges, together with the stress management skills taught in the first phase of treatment, helped Laura to increase her distress tolerance without avoiding or getting consumed by her emotions. She was also able to process the old interpersonal experiences related to her current depressive patterns and develop new ways of perceiving relationships and new ways of behaving. She also realized that she was strong, that she had gotten herself and her sister out of this cycle of addiction and abuse, and that she had raised two healthy children and taken very good care of them. Laura and the therapist developed exercises to strengthen and consolidate these new perspectives and ways of interacting. She wrote a story about this side of herself—the survivor—and also came up with slogans and reminders to use when she lost sight of this new perspective.

This case illustrates the use of exposure exercises, other behavioral tasks, and cognitive hypothesis-testing strategies to facilitate and process CEs related to Laura's early relationships. The therapist also helped her to generalize these experiences to consolidate the new learning. Laura no longer met criteria for depression at the end of treatment and maintained the gains at the 1-year follow-up. She was in a stable romantic relationship with James; enrolled in college; and able to get a higher paying job to support her children, both of whom were also interested in attending college. We next use this same case to discuss the types of changes that can come from CEs.

THE CONSEQUENCES OF CORRECTIVE EXPERIENCES

Potent CEs not only involve a perspective shift and change in affective response but also generalize to the person's life and are manifested in actual behavior change. With repeated practice, the person is also more likely to be able to recognize old patterns and change them so that he or she can react in a different and more adaptive way.

CEs associated with core interpersonal patterns are likely to facilitate multimodal changes in cognitions, emotions, and behaviors. The changes, although positive, can also be frightening. Thus, new learning must be practiced and elaborated so that it is encoded in long-term memory and more easily activated. In the case described above, the consequences were captured in the client's weekly essays about her depression. After a CE with the therapist and significant processing of earlier interpersonal experiences of abandonment, Laura's new expectancies began to generalize, as she began to open to a romantic relationship with James. Laura was able to step back from the automaticity of her depressive patterns and began to feel a sense of efficacy and hope. At the same time, she experienced a spike in fear, as old expectations that everything would be taken away were activated. Part of the treatment involved writing about the thoughts and feelings of depression each week over the course of therapy. In the week after the CEs described above, Laura wrote:

> I believe I have learned and am still learning not to let my depression get me down. I am able to see that when I get overwhelmed I tend to get discouraged, which leads to depression and stress for me. But I have learned how to take a step back and look at what is bothering me and think about positive ways to fix things. I have learned how to stop blaming myself for everything. I can control what I can, so that's good for me. I have been talking to James a lot and we are supposed to go to the movies. I have been reading a book called *How to Make Love Work*. It's interesting, but I'm not sure about a relationship yet. This week hasn't been too bad but seems like I am waiting for something to happen. I guess because things seem too perfect . . . it scares me. I am used to failure.

As the therapist assigned behavioral exercises to challenge the client's avoidance of romantic relationships and to facilitate generalization from the therapy experiences, Laura noted the connection between her early interpersonal experiences and her self-blame and fear of relationships. She reported systemwide change in her thoughts about herself, future, and others, and she reported more positive emotions and significant behavioral changes:

> I feel I have come a long way. I am able to deal with the fact that my mother treated me bad when I was a child and that my sister was treated better, but I realize that I have no control of her actions or anyone else's. I can sit and think about my past relationships without taking the total blame. I realize what's done is done and that I have to learn from my mistakes. I am glad I can see a positive outcome to all the madness in my life. I am even dating, which I thought I would never do again. I am also more able to be with my kids. The good news is that I take one day at a time and realize this is a process. I think because of my depression and stress, things tend to get me down when I can't fix a problem immediately. I feel helpless or like I have no control and that comes from when I was younger trying to fix things in my life that I had no control over, like my mother's addiction. I know I am a good mother. I do all I can to keep my children safe and happy, so I am holding on to that. James [new boyfriend] has been so good to talk to about the problems I am having with my ex. He makes me feel so much better. I feel calm and peaceful. I have someone I can talk to and be open and honest with. Except for God, I didn't have that growing up. I think if I did, my depression and stress would not have been so bad. I'm learning to trust now and that doesn't seem so bad.

CONSIDERATIONS IN FUTURE RESEARCH ON CORRECTIVE EXPERIENCES

Within a CBT framework, CEs involve a challenge to expectations that are based on prior experiences, an increase in dissonance and affective arousal, and a new perspective and change in affective responses that often manifests in behavioral changes in the person's life. As noted throughout this chapter, many of these elements have also been identified within a psychodynamic perspective, albeit with different nomenclature. A task in research on CEs is to identify points in the course of therapy at which these experiences occur. Because CEs are hypothesized to occur during periods of affective arousal and dissonance, discontinuities and periods of increased variability can serve as important markers to isolate where in the course of therapy CEs might be occurring (Hayes et al., 2007). Such discontinuities can be identified by tracking affective arousal or symptom ratings across sessions.

For instance, Hayes et al. (2007) used this method to identify transient spikes in depressive symptoms in EBCT. It was during this period of increased turbulence that they isolated instances of cognitive—emotional processing, which in turn predicted treatment outcome. Because CEs are also thought to occur in an affectively charged environment and to be associated with the disturbance of old patterns, this method might also be a useful way to identify and study CEs.

CEs are hypothesized to influence functioning in a number of domains of functioning, so it will be important to assess not only changes in expectations but also the affective, behavioral, and perhaps somatic components of the CE. Assessments of the multimodal impact of CEs would be most useful. Theoretical accounts of CEs focus on changing old patterns and developing new ones, which calls for methods to quantify and study both the pathological and the more adaptive patterns that emerge over the course of therapy. For instance, in a follow-up to the Hayes et al. (2007) study, we found that cognitive—emotional processing in EBCT is associated with more disturbance or variability in depressive patterns (with cognitive, affective, behavioral, somatic elements) and also with the emergence of more positive and adaptive patterns after this disturbance (Hayes, Yasinski, Ready, & Feldman, 2011). The patterns are quantified by coding client narratives for cognitive—emotional processing and for positive and negative cognitions (view of self, hope, and others), affect, behaviors, and somatic functioning, using the Change and Growth Experience coding system (Hayes, Feldman, & Goldfried, 2006). This is only one example of how researchers might capture the multimodal structure of maladaptive patterns and the multimodal changes that can follow CEs. Assessment of these kinds of patterns seems crucial to our understanding of what facilitates CEs and their consequences.

The CE was described by Alexander and French (1946) decades ago in the context of psychodynamic therapy. The theoretical base and intervention strategies of CBT are different, but we come to very similar places. Such convergence and applicability over time often highlight important principles of change. Facilitating the CE seems to be one of those general principles of therapeutic change.

REFERENCES

Alexander, F. (2004). A classic in psychotherapy integration revisited: The dynamics of psychotherapy in the light of learning theory. *Journal of Psychotherapy Integration, 14,* 347–359. doi:10.1037/1053-0479.14.4.347 (Original work published 1963)

Alexander, F., & French, T. M. (1946). *Psychoanalytic therapy: Principles and application.* New York, NY: Ronald Press.

Bandura, A. (1977). Self-efficacy: Toward a unifying theory of behavioral change. *Psychological Review, 84,* 191–215. doi:10.1037/0033-295X.84.2.191

Bandura, A. (1982). Self-efficacy mechanism in human agency. *American Psychologist, 37,* 122–147. doi:10.1037/0003-066X.37.2.122

Beck, A. T., Freeman, A., & Davis, D. D. (2004). *Cognitive therapy of personality disorders* (2nd ed.). New York, NY: Guilford Press.

Bouton, M. E. (2002). Context, ambiguity, and unlearning: Sources of relapse after behavioral extinction. *Biological Psychiatry, 52,* 976–986. doi:10.1016/S0006-3223(02)01546-9

Carey, T. A. (2011). Exposure and reorganization: The what and how of effective psychotherapy. *Clinical Psychology Review, 31,* 236–248. doi:10.1016/j.cpr.2010.04.004

Castonguay, L. G., & Beutler, L. E. (2006). Principles of therapeutic change: A task force on participants, relationships, and techniques factors. *Journal of Clinical Psychology, 62,* 631–638. doi:10.1002/jclp.20256

Dobson, K. S., & Dozois, D. J. A. (2010). *Historical and philosophical bases of the cognitive-behavioral therapies.* New York, NY: Guilford Press.

Foa, E. B., Huppert, J. D., & Cahill, S. P. (2006). Emotional processing theory: An update. In B. O. Rothbaum (Ed.), *Pathological anxiety: Emotional processing in etiology and treatment* (pp. 3–24). New York, NY: Guilford Press.

Foa, E. B., & Kozak, M. J. (1986). Emotional processing of fear: Exposure to corrective information. *Psychological Bulletin, 99,* 20–35. doi:10.1037/0033-2909.99.1.20

Goldfried, M. R., & Davila, J. (2005). The role of relationship and technique in therapeutic change. *Psychotherapy: Theory, Research, Practice, Training, 42,* 421–430. doi:10.1037/0033-3204.42.4.421

Goldfried, M. R., & Davison, G. C. (1994). *Clinical behavior therapy* (Expanded ed.). New York, NY: Wiley.

Greenberg, L. S. (2002). Integrating an emotion-focused approach to treatment into psychotherapy integration. *Journal of Psychotherapy Integration, 12*, 154–189. doi:10.1037/1053-0479.12.2.154

Grosse Holtforth, M., & Castonguay, L. G. (2005). Relationship and techniques in cognitive–behavioral therapy—A motivational approach. *Psychotherapy: Theory, Research, Practice, Training, 42*, 443–455. doi:10.1037/0033-3204.42.4.443

Hayes, A. M., Beevers, C. G., Feldman, G. C., Laurenceau, J., & Perlman, C. (2005). Avoidance and processing as predictors of symptom change and positive growth in an integrative therapy for depression. *International Journal of Behavioral Medicine, 12*, 111–122. doi:10.1207/s15327558ijbm1202_9

Hayes, A. M., Feldman, G. C., Beevers, C. G., Laurenceau, J., Cardaciotto, L., & Lewis-Smith, J. (2007). Discontinuities and cognitive changes in an exposure-based cognitive therapy for depression. *Journal of Consulting and Clinical Psychology, 75*, 409–421. doi:10.1037/0022-006X.75.3.409

Hayes, A. M., Feldman, G. C., & Goldfried, M. R. (2006). The Change and Growth Experiences Scale: A measure of insight and emotional processing. In L. G. Castonguay, & C. Hill (Eds.), *Insight in psychotherapy* (pp. 231–253). Washington, DC: American Psychological Association. doi:10.1037/11532-011

Hayes, A. M., Yasinski, C., Ready, C. B., & Feldman, G. C. (2011). *Disturbance and associative network change in an exposure-based cognitive therapy for depression.* Manuscript submitted for publication, University of Delaware.

Klein, M. H., Mathieu-Coughlan, P., & Kiesler, D. J. (1986). *The Experiencing Scales.* New York, NY: Guilford Press.

Lang, P. J., & Cuthbert, B. N. (1984). Affective information processing and the assessment of anxiety. *Journal of Behavioral Assessment, 6*, 369–395. doi:10.1007/BF01321326

Lejuez, C. W., Hopko, D. R., Levine, S., Gholkar, R., & Collins, L. M. (2005). The therapeutic alliance in behavior therapy. *Psychotherapy: Theory. Research, Practice, Training, 42*, 456–468. doi:10.1037/0033-3204.42.4.456

Miller, W. R., & Rollnick, S. (2002). *Motivational interviewing: Preparing people for change* (2nd ed.). New York, NY: Guilford Press.

Power, M. J., & Brewin, C. R. (Eds.). (1997). *The transformation of meaning in psychological therapies: Integrating theory and practice.* Hoboken, NJ: Wiley.

Prochaska, J. O., & Prochaska, J. M. (1999). Why don't continents move? Why don't people change? *Journal of Psychotherapy Integration, 9*, 83–102. doi:10.1023/A:1023210911909

Rachman, S. (2001). Emotional processing, with special reference to posttraumatic stress disorder. *International Review of Psychiatry, 13*, 164–171. doi:10.1080/09540260120074028

Safran, J. D., & Muran, J. C. (2002). Intervention strategies: Impasses and transformations. *NYS Psychologist, 14*, 2–4.

Safran, J. D., & Segal, Z. V. (1990). *Interpersonal process in cognitive therapy*. Lanham, MD: Aronson.

Samoilov, A., & Goldfried, M. R. (2000). Role of emotion in cognitive–behavior therapy. *Clinical Psychology: Science and Practice, 7*, 373–385. doi:10.1093/clipsy.7.4.373

Teasdale, J. D. (1999). Emotional processing, three modes of mind and the prevention of relapse in depression. *Behaviour Research and Therapy, 37(Suppl. 1)*, 53–77. doi:10.1016/S0005-7967(99)00050-9

Turk, C. L., Heimberg, R. G., & Hope, D. A. (2001). Social anxiety disorder. In D. H. Barlow (Ed.), *Clinical handbook of psychological disorders: A step-by-step treatment manual* (3rd. ed., pp. 114–153). New York, NY: Guilford Press

Tryon, W. W., & Misurell, J. R. (2008). Dissonance induction and reduction: A possible principle and connectionist mechanism for why therapies are effective. *Clinical Psychology Review, 28*, 1297–1309. doi:10.1016/j.cpr.2008.06.003

Waddington, L. (2002). The therapy relationship in cognitive therapy: A review. *Behavioural and Cognitive Psychotherapy, 30*, 179–192. doi:10.1017/S1352465802002059

Whelton, W. J. (2004). Emotional processes in psychotherapy: Evidence across therapeutic modalities. *Clinical Psychology & Psychotherapy, 11*, 58–71. doi:10.1002/cpp.392

Young, J. E., Klosko, J. S., & Weishaar, M. E. (2003). *Schema therapy: A practitioner's guide*. New York, NY: Guilford Press.

6

CORRECTIVE EXPERIENCE FROM A HUMANISTIC–EXPERIENTIAL PERSPECTIVE

LESLIE S. GREENBERG AND ROBERT ELLIOTT

In this chapter, we describe the corrective experience (CE), and more specifically, the corrective emotional experience (CEE), and related constructs from a humanistic–experiential therapeutic perspective, beginning with a review of classical formulations. We describe emotion-focused therapy (EFT) and its formulation of the central role played by emotion in CEEs. We refer to the latter as CEEs. In particular, we look at how CEEs involve changing maladaptive or stuck emotions associated with previous painful or traumatic situations—first, by helping clients access the maladaptive emotions in the safety of the therapeutic relationship, and second, by helping them access other, more adaptive but previously overlooked emotions. In particular, we describe the two major forms of CEEs: intrapersonal CEEs, in which therapists help their clients work with their own processes; and interpersonal CEEs, in which the relationship with the therapist is the vehicle of corrective emotional experience.

DIFFERENT HUMANISTIC–EXPERIENTIAL PERSPECTIVES

In general, humanistic–experiential theorists have viewed CEEs as coming from participating in a genuinely empathic and positively regarding relationship, as well as from the reowning of previously avoided, often dreaded or painful, experiences. Thus, new emotional experience and increased awareness rather than behavioral change are seen as corrective. EFT has added another key component of CEEs: experiencing a new adaptive emotion that alters an old maladaptive emotion, suggesting the importance of changing how people feel, which in turn changes how they react and think. We begin by discussing views of CEEs within several important humanistic–experiential therapy approaches.

Person-Centered Therapy

In Rogers's (1959) view, client-centered therapy is effective because the therapeutic relationship provides an antidote to the introjected conditions of worth, and clients have the CEE of being seen as they are (empathy) and being genuinely (or congruently) accepted without conditions (unconditional positive regard). Rogers theorized that this gives rise to an intrapersonal CEE for the client: self-acceptance of their previously unacknowledged organismic experience.

What became apparent from process-outcome research in client-centered therapy was that clients' reference to their internal experience was of central importance in client change (e.g., Gendlin, Jenney, & Shlien, 1960). Beginning with his article "A Process Conception of Psychotherapy," Rogers (1958) emphasized that therapy was made up of a series of moments of movement that were characterized by experiencing something different in the relationship. He described clients as moving along a continuum from fixity to flexibility, from rigid structure to flow, from stasis to process. This idea was later developed into the seven-stage Client Experiencing Scale by Klein, Mathieu, Gendlin, and Kiesler (1969). The research that came out of this revealed that what is important in therapy is facilitating a new mode of experiencing in the client, which increasingly involves directing attention to current experiencing, followed by loosening of the previous rigid structures for symbolizing organismic experiencing. Thus, expressing and experiencing feelings in the present came to be viewed as the key moment of CEEs, as in statements such as "As I think of this, I just feel so sad" or "It's just like being kicked in the stomach." The view that emerged in the 1950s from the work of Rogers, Gendlin, and others at the University of Chicago Counseling Center was that CEEs took place when the client felt received by the therapist and that such reception led to a deepening of experiencing in the client.

Rogers's (1959) concept of the CEE evolved to also emphasize interpersonal CEEs, illustrated by a later example of a key moment of change described by Rogers (cf. Farber & Raskin, 1996). This moment can be seen in a transcript of a session with Jim, a withdrawn, psychiatrically hospitalized client who, when he begins to feel hopeless, says he wants to end the session. Rogers then responds with, "You want to go because you just don't care about yourself," followed after a pause by, "I care about you." After 30 seconds, Jim bursts into tears and unintelligible sobs, and Rogers's comments that this "makes all the feeling pour out." Jim later responds, sobbing, "I wish I could die," and Rogers, laying his hand gently on Jim's arm, reflects, "You just wish you could die, don't you, when you just feel so awful you wish you could perish." In his commentary, Rogers offers this as an example of a moment of change.

Thus, according to Rogers (1959), not only does one accept into one's self-concept previously disavowed material, providing a new and different experience of self, but opening oneself to another's acceptance also itself provides a CEE (Greenberg, Rice, & Elliott, 1993). Disclosure to another person and acceptance by the other also provide a CEE by breaking a sense of isolation and often can produce connection and a sense of intimacy—a new and unexpected experience. Revealing previously private aspects of oneself and being seen, validated, and accepted are seen as healing. In addition, given that disclosing of fears is not easy, taking risks, being open, and expressing are also important aspects of a CEE, as they can lead to different or novel experiences. Thus CEEs occur both interpersonally in the therapeutic relationship through unconditional positive regard and also intrapersonally within the client by the process of accepting new experience into awareness. (See also Chapter 7, this volume.)

Focusing

As mentioned above, Klein et al. (1969) developed the Client Experiencing Scale, which measured the extent to which the individual is remote from or engaged with their experiencing and became one of the sources of the focusing method. In the first stage of the client process continuum measured by it, clients are seen as talking about external events and as being unwilling to communicate anything of themselves. In the second stage, there is more reference to self, but in a rather external way. At higher levels, there is a focus on a bodily felt sense in a descriptive and associative manner; feelings in the present moment are freely expressed, and there is a strong tendency toward differentiation of feelings and meanings.

Gendlin (1962) started from the premise that people are in essence processes of experiencing and that excessive stability or rigid experiencing, based on inadequate symbolization of bodily felt experience, is the major cause of disturbance. He argued that optimal self-functioning involves an ever-increasing use of experiencing as a process in which felt meanings interact with verbal symbols to produce explicit meaning. In this view, CEEs involve the ongoing creation of new meaning from a bodily felt sense, a move away from more structural, denial or incongruence models to a process view of functioning. Blocking of the experiencing process is seen as the cause of dysfunction: When the experiencing process becomes stuck and people are unable to carry forward their experience, they either distort it or impose past perceptions on present experience.

Therefore, in Gendlin's (1962) view, it was not so much change in the content of the perception that was the CEE but rather change in the manner of experiencing. CEEs involve changing one's manner of experiencing from one that is structure-bound and patterned to one that is an immediate response to a present event. Facilitation of this type of CEE in therapy then involves turning clients' attention to their present experience, to affect both physiology and meaning creation. This process of unblocking became known as *focusing*. (See Chapter 7, this volume.)

Focusing involves checking words against experience and finding a fit that generates the feeling of certainty, of "yes, that captures it." The "yes" is a small but definite CEE. The new symbolization of what is experienced captures something new or unexpected and moves people forward step by step, moment by moment, toward new meaning. An important tenet is that the felt sense can be articulated in a variety of ways, but it is not a matter of anything goes. The felt sense is vague in that there are as yet no words for it, but it is quite precise in that only certain words will fit it (Gendlin, 1996). There is an interaction between the continuing feeling process and the attention people bring to it to create new meaning. This interaction generates a specifiable feeling, a "this is what I feel," that is the CEE of moving forward.

Making the implicit explicit now becomes the process goal of treatment and the experience of something new and unexpected according to Gendlin (1996) would constitute a CEE—albeit a mini-CEE—in that it involves the creation of new meaning. In this view, language then is seen as creating meanings rather than as acquiring meanings through corresponding to, reflecting, or being congruent with a nonlinguistic reality. Symbolization thus is not seen as a simple congruence between symbols and experience or as owning the disowned but instead is also a CEE in which new experience is constructed or organized into a new form or configuration. In this view, a CEE can be seen as being built from, and as typically occurring after, several steps of symbolizing the bodily felt sense, when these crystallize into a new and often highly unexpected or novel view.

For example, one of our clients, "Carol," had severe social anxiety that led her to spend much of her time hiding in her bed. In Session 4, focusing enabled her to symbolize her social anxiety as a harsh, staccato quality that she symbolized with a rapid, horizontal movement of her hand and the sound "zuzzy." In Session 6, she said she wanted to feel free of the social anxiety, and the therapist helped her focus on her internal felt sense of this desired freedom. In doing so, she was surprised to discover a fluid, wavy, resilient feeling in her chest. On her postsession form, she described the most helpful event in the session as

> focusing on what being "free" felt like. I actually had a deep and real feeling of being free inside—of being fluid and flowing, and I'm thinking now that I've been searching for and working for and trying to find a "freedom" that's been inside me all along.

In this case, the CEE involved a movement from the rigid, jerky stuckness of social anxiety to the different and unexpected feeling of being fluid and free—a key step in Carol's journey of recovery.

Gestalt Therapy

Similar to Rogers (1959), Perls (1969) held that the source of many difficulties is located in the conflict between an image (introjected self-concept) that the person is trying to adopt and what in gestalt theory is called the *self-actualizing tendency* (similar to Rogers's *organismic experiencing*). Introjects (similar to Rogers's conditions of worth) were seen as interfering with self-actualization through people trying to manipulate their self to behave and experience in accord with the dictates of their introjects. Health involves the owning of emerging experience, whereas dysfunction involves the automatic disowning, alienation, or lack of awareness of this experience. Change, and by implication a CEE, thus involves changing to "be who you are, not who you are not"—although who you are is now a different and unexpected experience of self and is thus a CEE. Some form of agency in the personality ("I") is seen as either identifying with, or alienating itself from, aspects of spontaneous, preverbal level of experiencing to form a "me" (James, 1890). Awareness of the process of identification and alienation of experience is seen as the road to CEEs because one encounters new and different aspects of self as one becomes aware. Awareness of functioning provides people with the option to choose if and when to own experience and act on it (Perls, Hefferline, & Goodman, 1951). Therapy, then, offers clients the opportunity to experiment and make deliberate their awareness to promote the experience of being an active agent in experience, which allows the person to begin to have the new and different experience that "I am thinking, feeling, or doing this" (Perls et al., 1951).

One of the most basic premises in gestalt therapy is to make everything immediate and here and now, or what Perls (1969) referred to as *presentness*. The revivification of experience brings the client a sense of presence that may be generally lacking in his or her life. Because it offers new ways of being, this wake-up call to be more present for oneself in everyday experiencing can be a CEE. Most existential approaches view the present as the only reality; that is, all forces are seen to be acting now, in this immediate moment. The past exists here and now as memories, regrets, and sources of shame or pride. The future exists here and now as anticipation, hope, rehearsing, and dread. CEEs involve seeing clearly how the past is alive in the present in the form of unfinished business. This view generates a new experience of self and a new view of others. As wounds heal and unfinished business is completed, the person unexpectedly opens again to new experience.

One of the reasons gestalt therapy is powerful in helping people change neurotic patterns is that the process involves experiencing the past (e.g., age regression to a childhood trauma) or the future (e.g., rehearsing an upcoming anxiety-provoking confrontation) as an experience in the present. Experiencing meaning and purpose in life in the here and now is associated with satisfactory life experiences and positive future expectations. A common outcome of a CEE in therapy thus is one of experiencing life fully in the present moment.

Gestalt therapy introduced the method of a dialogue between a critical or controlling "top dog" and a more subservient "underdog" as a method for helping clients learn to take responsibility in the present for their self-critical processes. For example, in Session 4 of her therapy, Carol, the client referred to earlier, was helped to enact a dialogue between the socially anxious part of herself and a socially shaming, critical part of herself. In the description she later wrote about the most helpful part of the session, she clearly described this work as a CEE in classically gestalt terms:

> Realizing that it's "me" that's giving "me" a hard time! I'm the one who criticizes, etc. It's "me" who says that everything I think of doing, I'll get wrong. It's got me thinking about watching out for the kind of things I say to myself.

Carol's statement certainly sounds like a new and unexpected CEE.

Emotion-Focused Therapy

EFT, as well as incorporating the above views of CEEs from client-centered therapy, focusing, and gestalt therapy, reframes these as CEEs, that is, experiences in which a person has a new emotional response to an old situation. For example, a CEE occurs when a man who is prone to depression is able, in therapy, first to access shame and fear connected to the treatment he suffered by his abusive father and then to generate new emotional responses to the old situation, such as adaptive anger at violation, sadness at loss, or compassion for the pain he suffered when younger. A CEE such as this results in an expansion in the person's emotional response repertoire. In this process, core emotional memories are accessed in therapy within their original framework of abuse, but now in the novel environment of a warm, accepting, genuine therapist who is empathically attuned to affect; this new relational environment induces a new feeling of calm and relaxation rather than the old feelings of fear and shame.

In addition, the therapist offers the client opportunities to turn his or her attention to previously unattended-to aspects of experience, such as the anger at violation and the sadness of loss, so new responses become possible; this reowning of experience also helps people respond in new ways to the old situation, promoting change in internal emotion organization (emotion schemes). With the help of the therapist, the cues activating the old response are disattended to and new cues are focused on, thereby attenuating the old habitual response. The client thus is encouraged to exert mental effort to both interrupt the old maladaptive response and to attend to new cues in self and situation, thereby allowing the new emotional response to be generated. The therapist thus guides clients to change in an adaptive direction by helping them access new possibilities in their experience. To do this, therapy needs to provide safety and novelty, to create momentary situations that encourage new adaptive responses.

The most fundamental process of the CEE in EFT involves the transformation of one emotion into another (Greenberg, 2002, 2010). The principle is discussed here, and clinical examples that flesh out these processes are provided in the next sections, where this process is discussed more extensively. Probably the most important way of dealing with maladaptive emotion in therapy involves not mere exposure to the maladaptive emotion, nor its regulation, but its transformation by other emotions. This process of transformation applies most specifically to primary maladaptive emotions, those old familiar bad feelings that occur repeatedly but do not change. Access to, and contact with, more adaptive emotions can lead to a CEE. We suggest that maladaptive emotional states such as chronic fear and shame, and the accompanying sadness of lonely abandonment, are best transformed by undoing them through activating other more adaptive emotional states, such as empowering anger or the sadness of grief. In EFT, an important objective is to arrive at a maladaptive emotion, not for its value as information and source of motivation, but to make it accessible to transformation. In time the coactivation of the more adaptive emotion, along with or in response to the maladaptive emotion, helps transform the maladaptive emotion.

As Hebb (1949) so aptly noted, neurons that fire together wire together and continue to fire together; thus, at a neurological level coactivation produces a synthesis of prior experience and the formation of a new higher level schematic structure. In addition, recent memory reconsolidation research (Nadel & Moscovitch 1997; Schiller et al., 2010) suggests that this type of emotional transformation results from the updating of prior emotional memories through a process of reconsolidation that incorporates new emotional experiences that occur in the present. This change process involves activating old memories, creating a window (lasting of 10 minutes or longer but less than 6 hours; Schiller et al., 2010) during which new emotional experiences can be incorporated into reconsolidated memories. CEEs thus occur by activating old memories and their associated emotions, introducing new emotional experiences in therapy while the old memories are activated to enable new emotional elements to become incorporated into that memory trace when it is stored through reconsolidation (Greenberg, 2010).

The paradox of the path to emotional change, however, is that it needs to start with not trying to change emotion but with fully accepting the painful emotion. Emotions need to be fully felt and their information used before they are accessible to new input from other emotions. Only when the painful, maladaptive emotion has been fully accessed and acknowledged is there room for other, more adaptive emotional experiences to enter. A major premise guiding intervention in EFT is that if one does not accept oneself as one is, one cannot make oneself available for transformation. Thus, one needs to arrive at a place before one can leave it, and so it is for emotion; even those aspects of oneself one truly wants to change must first be accepted before they can be changed. Self-transformation thus requires self-acceptance.

In an interesting line of investigation, positive emotions have been found to undo lingering negative emotions (Fredrickson, 2001). The basic observation is that key components of positive emotions are incompatible with negative emotions. Fredrickson (2001) suggested that broadening a person's momentary thought or action repertoire with a positive emotion may loosen the hold that a negative emotion has on his or her mind. Joy and contentment produced faster cardiovascular recovery from negative emotions than did a neutral experience. Furthermore, Fredrickson, Mancuso, Branigan, and Tugade (2000) found that resilient individuals coped by recruiting positive emotions to regulate negative emotional experiences. They found that these individuals manifested a physiological bounce back that helped them to return to their cardiovascular baseline more quickly.

Another study by Whelton and Greenberg (2005) demonstrated that emotion changes emotion. They found that people who were more vulnerable to depression showed more contempt and were also less resilient in response to self-criticism than people less vulnerable to depression. The less vulnerable people were able to recruit positive emotional resources, such as self-assertive pride and anger, to combat and transform depressogenic contempt and the attendant negative cognitions. In other words, after a distressing experience, resilient people appear to generate a positive feeling, often through imagery or memory, to soothe themselves; they are then better able to combat negative feelings and views of self in this more resilient state. Accessing a positive emotional state therefore helps them counteract the effect of a negative emotional state.

Davidson (2000) suggested that the right hemispheric withdrawal–related negative affect system can be transformed by activation of the approach system in the left prefrontal cortex. He defined *resilience* as the maintenance of high levels of positive affect and well-being in the face of adversity and highlighted that resilient people do feel negative affect but the negative affect does not persist. Levenson (1992) also reviewed research indicating that specific emotions were associated with specific patterns of autonomic nervous system activity, providing evidence that different emotions express themselves differentially in one's physiology. In addition, LeDoux and Gorman (2001) showed that the fear response of freezing (withdrawal, avoidance, emotional paralysis, and despondency) is incompatible with the motor response of taking action.

Furthermore, introducing new present experience into currently activated memories of past events has been shown to lead to memory transformation by the assimilation of new material into past memories (Nadel & Bohbot, 2001; Schiller et al., 2010). When activated in the present, the old memories (e.g., trauma-related fear) are restructured both by the new experience of being in the context of a safe relationship and also by the coactivation of more adaptive emotional responses (e.g., primary anger or sadness) and new adult resources (e.g., self-soothing and self-reflection) and understandings to cope with the old situation. The memories are thus reconsolidated in a new way by incorporating these new elements. The past, in fact, can be changed—or rather, the memories of it can be.

The process of changing emotion with emotion goes beyond limited ideas of catharsis or completion, exposure, extinction, or habituation in that the maladaptive feeling is not purged, nor does it simply attenuate from the person feeling it. Transformation involves more than simply feeling or facing the feeling leading to some kind of extinction process. Instead, a different, more adaptive feeling is used to transform or undo a feeling that no longer fits the situation. Although exposure to emotion can be helpful for overcoming affect phobia (McCullough Vaillant, 1997), in our view change occurs primarily because one emotion is transformed by another emotion rather than through a mechanical process of attenuation. In these instances, a CEE occurs by the activation of an incompatible, more adaptive, experience that undoes or transforms the old maladaptive response.

Clinical observation of and research on the process of change suggest that CEEs occur by a process of dialectical synthesis of opposing emotion schemes (Elliott, Watson, Goldman, & Greenberg, 2002, 2004). When opposing schemes are coactivated, they synthesize compatible elements from the coactivated schemes to form new, higher level schemes, just as in development when a toddler's schemes for standing and falling are dynamically synthesized into a higher level scheme for walking (Greenberg & Pascual-Leone, 1995; J. Pascual-Leone, 1991). Similarly, schemes of different emotional states are synthesized to form new integrations. Thus, for example, in therapy, maladaptive fear, once aroused, can be transformed into security by the more boundary-establishing emotions of adaptive anger or disgust, or by evoking the softer, connecting feelings of compassion or forgiveness. Similarly, maladaptive anger can be undone by the adaptive sadness of grieving for loss. Maladaptive shame can be transformed into self-acceptance by accessing both anger at violation and self-comforting feelings, together with pride and self-worth. Thus, the tendency to shrink into the ground in shame is transformed by the thrusting forward tendency in newly accessed anger at violation. Withdrawal emotions from one side of the brain are replaced with approach emotions from another part of the brain or vice versa (Davidson, 2000). Once the alternate emotion has been accessed, it transforms or undoes the original state and a new state is forged, constituting a CEE. The experience of the socially anxious client, Carol, in which she accessed a fluid, wavy sense of resilient strength that led to a transformation of the static-y feeling of social anxiety into a sense of freedom, is a clear example of this process of changing emotion with emotion.

CORRECTIVE EMOTIONAL EXPERIENCES IN THERAPY

CEEs in humanistic–experiential therapies and, more specifically, in EFT come in two main forms: those in which the primary action involves different parts of the self, and those in which the primary action is in the client–therapist interaction. We discuss these two processes in the rest of the chapter.

Intrapersonal Corrective Emotional Experiences

On the basis of both clinical theory and practice, a model of intrapersonal CEEs, which involves changing emotion with emotion by moving from secondary emotions through primary maladaptive emotions to primary adaptive emotions, has been proposed and tested (Greenberg & Paivio, 1997; Hermann & Greenberg, 2008; A. Pascual-Leone & Greenberg, 2007). We elaborate on this process in this section. Transformation of distressed feelings begins with attending to the aroused bad feelings, such as secondary hopelessness or anxiety, followed by exploring the cognitive–affective sequences that generated the bad feelings. Eventually, this leads to the activation of some core maladaptive emotion schematic self-organizations often based on fear and sadness about abandonment or shame related to inadequacy. At this point in the transformation process, a CEE involves accessing self-organizations linked to emotion schemes, such as adaptive sadness at loss or pride at accomplishment.

When clients in states of global distress begin to elaborate and differentiate their thoughts and feelings, they subsequently move in one of two directions: (a) into a core maladaptive self-organization based on maladaptive emotion schemes of fear, stuck sadness of lonely abandonment, or shame; or (b) into some form of secondary expression, often of hopelessness or rejecting anger (A. Pascual-Leone & Greenberg, 2007). More resourceful clients often move directly from secondary emotions directly to assertive anger or sadness but more wounded clients often need first to work through their core maladaptive emotions of fear, shame, and abandonment sadness (Greenberg 2002; Greenberg & Paivio, 1997; Greenberg & Watson 2006). Transformation occurs when these maladaptive states are differentiated into adaptive needs, which act to refute core negative evaluations about the self that are embedded in their core maladaptive schemes.

The essence of this process is that the core needs (to be connected and validated) embedded in the maladaptive fear, shame, or sadness, when mobilized and validated, act to access more adaptive emotions and to refute that the person is not deserving of love, respect, and connection. The inherent opposition of these two experiences, "I am not worthy or lovable" and "I deserve to be loved or respected," supported by adaptive anger or sadness, in response to the same evoking situation, overcomes the maladaptive state by access to new self-experience and the creation of new meaning in which a new, more positive evaluation of the self emerges. The path to resolution leads to the expression of the adaptive grief and to empowering anger or self-soothing, which then facilitate a sense of self-acceptance and agency. A refined model of this core change process was recently empirically validated (A. Pascual-Leone & Greenberg, 2007).

One particular type of intrapersonal CEE involves helping the client transform past experiences, effectively rewriting episodic and schematic memories of important relationships. Alexander and French (1946) claimed that reexperiencing the old, unsettled difficulties but with a new ending is the secret of all penetrating therapeutic results. The actual lived experience of a new solution to old problematic patterns convinces people that new solutions are possible, inducing them to replace their old patterns. Through repetition, these corrected reactions gradually become automatic and evolve into a new higher level pattern of functioning. Children who have experienced trauma had few alternatives available to them in response to the traumatic situation. In returning to reexperience the early traumatic moments in therapy, however, individuals have much more perspective and many more resources available to them with which to respond to and understand what occurred. People bring with them an expanded repertoire of possible emotional responses. The client also has the therapist alongside, to guide the reexperiencing and to promote the development of a new ending. In addition, although the threat system is activated in reexperiencing, the help of the therapist provides a containing, calming, and compassionate presence, reducing fear and shame to tolerable levels so that the client can work effectively with these dreaded feelings to create a difference.

Fundamentally, transformation takes place in the body. The therapist helps clients focus their attention on their emotional and bodily experience, using questions such as "What emotions are you feeling?" "Where do you feel that in your body?" "What is the sensation?" "What do you need?" Helping people become aware of and label body experiences can aid in providing a clear path to follow back to the source trauma and gives access to adaptive emotions that could not originally be expressed in the situation. An important aspect of the CEE is for clients to access, symbolize in narrative form, and act on their expanded emotional repertoire while compassionately recognizing their pain, without blaming the self for the choices made at the time.

As we noted in the EFT section, a key method of promoting a CEE involves the transformation of an unwanted maladaptive emotion with an adaptive emotion. The method rests on the premise that a person cannot experience two incongruent emotional states simultaneously without a sense of tension and without the emotions affecting each other. For example, if while experiencing an unwanted negative state (e.g., shame), the client exerts effort to access a resource state by shifting focused attention or accessing and asserting a need (e.g., deserving to feel validated and loved), the dominance of the unwanted state is supplanted. Similarly, if while in the presence of imagined previously distressing stimuli (e.g., a humiliating situation), one can focus attention on some alternate stimuli (e.g., a comforting idealized parent), the person can evoke an alternate emotional state. Therefore, the person needs to access an adaptive state that is incongruent with the unwanted dysfunctional state. As access to a new state is experienced repeatedly, the process becomes more and more automatic. Critically, transformation occurs best when the person initially is in the problematic emotional state.

CEEs of this type allow individuals to experience a difference between the way it was for them originally and the way they are now able to experience it. To experience this new state, however, people need to experience appropriate and healthy support. If internal support (self-soothing) is not available at the moment of reexperiencing a traumatic childhood event, therapists must provide the support so the client's child aspect can have a CEE of being supported. That support can come in the form of imagining one of the adults in the child's life at the time (e.g., grandmother, teacher, policeman, older sibling) or alternatively, a make-believe substitute, spiritual connection, or even the client's own adult self. A preferred option is for the age-regressed person to experience in fantasy a supportive adult who was actually in the child's life at the time, coming into the traumatic scene to provide safety, nurturing, and bonding. In this way the individual's child state experiences healthy re-parenting in a manner that comes closest to real life and requires the least suspension of disbelief.

For example, a client had been berated and shamed at age 4 for spilling a glass of milk on the kitchen floor, and the age-regressed 4-year-old boy believed what his father had yelled at him: "You are clumsy, and no good." As a little boy, the client needed, at the time, to have an appropriately loving and compassionate authority validate that all little boys spill things and his accident did not diminish his value as a person. The therapist therefore might ask the regressed client, "Who in your life at age 4 could come into the kitchen with you and help you feel safe?" and thereby promote a CEE of feeling supported in this virtual reality, changing the emotion schematic memory of the past situation.

In our view, enduring emotional change in maladaptive emotional responses occurs by generating new emotional responses, not through a process of insight or understanding but by generating new emotional responses to old situations (CEEs), revising the meaning of specific episodic memories, incorporating these into schematic memory, and thus developing new narratives. As we have said, EFT works on the basic principle that people must first arrive at a place before they can leave it. When maladaptive emotion schematic memories of past childhood losses and traumas are activated in the therapy session, they become available to be changed by memory reconstruction.

Interpersonal Corrective Emotional Experiences

Interpersonal damage often is healed by new interpersonal experience. When there has been consistently unrepaired misattunement in a person's experience growing up, the result is disruption in an ability to enter and maintain healthy close relationships. This generally results in difficulties in forming intimate relationships as an adult. Fortunately, close relationships later in life can compensate for earlier deprivation. New lived experiences with another person (often the therapist) are especially important in providing an interpersonal CEE. Experiences that provide interpersonal soothing, disconfirm pathogenic beliefs, or offer new success experiences can correct interpersonal patterns set down in earlier times. Interpersonal CEEs commonly occur over the course of therapy, whenever the client experiences the therapist as someone who is attuned to and validates the client's inner world. The empathic relationship with the therapist is a major curative element of psychotherapy. Empathic attunement, experienced in the unique setting and structure of psychotherapy, has been shown to be a critical predictor of successful outcome (Elliott, Bohart, Watson, & Greenberg, 2011).

The goal of EFT is for clients to experience mastery by reexperiencing and transforming emotions they could not handle in the past, with the help of the more favorable circumstances provided by therapy. The client then undergoes an interpersonal CEE that repairs the damaging influence of previous painful relational experiences. Overall, the consistency of the genuine relationship between the patient and the therapist is a CEE. Thus, an experience in which a client faces shame in a therapeutic context while experiencing genuine acceptance (rather than the expected contempt or denigration) has the power to change the feeling of shame. Having one's anger accepted, rather than rejected, by the therapist can lead to new ways of being.

The therapist facilitates CEEs by creating an environment that is safely contained. The therapist helps the client modulate the intensity of long-buried feelings as they emerge by proposing useful and appropriate methods of doing so, or the therapist suggests a time out when the client begins to feel overwhelmed. The CEE comes from the therapist effectively providing what the client needs now and needed originally, namely, genuine empathic attunement, acceptance, support, and help with modulating the client's activation and expression of previously threatening emotional material. The latter requires that the therapist be able to distinguish between productive, contained reexperiencing versus flashback and retraumatization, and to promote the former and modulate the latter. Providing CEEs to repair traumatic shock requires slow and steady reconnection with the client's inner resources. With sufficient safety and corrective attachment experiences, the client's shock can be modulated over time.

The types of interpersonal CEEs in individual EFT occur predominantly in the therapeutic relationship, although it is generally recognized that successful experiences in the world enabled by taking risks and engaging in new interpersonal experiences also provide important CEEs. For example, having one's feelings accepted by an intimate partner in life or in couples therapy is a deeply CEE (Greenberg & Goldman, 2008).

CONCLUSION

Humanistic views on CEEs presented in this chapter are consistent with the core components of the consensus definition that "CEs are ones in which a person comes to understand or experience affectively an event or relationship in a different and unexpected way" (Chapter 1, this volume). These humanistic–experiential views, however, do not hold that the differences are always cognitively mediated or unexpected in any conscious manner. Instead, the humanistic–experiential perspective emphasizes and elaborates the affective component of the definition.

Specifically, from a humanistic–experiential perspective, CEEs involve having new and different lived emotional experiences that undo old emotional experiences by providing new emotional responses to old situations or to current interpersonal situations. CEEs occur by first reenacting old situations in the virtual reality created in therapy, often by psychodramatic enactments, but now responding freshly to the old situations by adding different responses that provide new endings. By means of the process of memory reconsolidation, people can incorporate present CEE into past memory, thereby changing their memories of the experience of the old situation. In addition, experiencing new and possibly unexpected feelings in the reality of the current relationship also serves to change old feelings. Humanistic–experiential therapies work in these ways to promote both intra- and interpersonal CEEs.

REFERENCES

Alexander, F., & French, T. M. (1946). *Psychoanalytic therapy: Principles and application.* New York, NY: Ronald Press.

Davidson, R. J. (2000). Affective style, psychopathology, and resilience: Brain mechanisms and plasticity. *American Psychologist, 55,* 1196–1214.

Elliott, R., Bohart, A. C., Watson, J. C., & Greenberg, L. S. (2011). Empathy. *Psychotherapy, 48,* 43–49. doi:10.1037/a0022187

Elliott, R., Watson, J. E., Goldman, R. N., & Greenberg, L. S. (2004). *Learning emotion-focused therapy: The process–experiential approach to change.* Washington, DC: American Psychological Association. doi:10.1037/10725-000

Farber, B., & Raskin, P. (1996). *The psychotherapy of Carl Rogers: Cases and commentary.* New York, NY: Guilford Press.

Fredrickson, B. L. (2001). The role of positive emotions in positive psychology: The broaden-and-build theory of positive emotions. *American Psychologist, 56,* 218–226. doi:10.1037/0003-066X.56.3.218

Fredrickson, B. L., Mancuso, R. A., Branigan, C., & Tugade, M. M. (2000). The undoing effect of positive emotions. *Motivation and Emotion, 24,* 237–258. doi:10.1023/A:1010796329158

Gendlin, E. T. (1962). *Experiencing and the creation of meaning.* New York, NY: Free Press.

Gendlin, E. T. (1996). *Focusing-oriented psychotherapy: A manual of the experiential method.* New York, NY: Guilford Press.

Gendlin, E. T., Jenney, R. H., & Shlien, J. M. (1960). Counselor ratings of process and outcome in client-centered therapy. *Journal of Clinical Psychology, 16*, 210–213. doi:10.1002/1097-4679(196004)16:2<210::AID-JCLP2270160228>3.0.CO;2-J

Greenberg, L. S. (2002). *Emotion-focused therapy: Coaching clients to work through their feelings.* Washington, DC: American Psychological Association. doi:10.1037/10447-000

Greenberg, L. S. (2010). *Emotion-focused therapy: Theory and practice.* Washington, DC: American Psychological Association.

Greenberg, L. S., & Goldman, R. N. (2008). *Emotion-focused couples therapy: The dynamics of emotion, love, and power.* Washington, DC: American Psychological Association. doi:10.1037/11750-000

Greenberg, L. S., & Paivio, S. C. (1997). *Working with emotions in psychotherapy.* New York, NY: Guilford Press.

Greenberg, L. S., & Pascual-Leone, J. (1995). A dialectical constructivist approach to experiential change. In R. A. Neimeyer & M. J. Mahoney (Eds.), *Constructivism in psychotherapy* (pp. 169–191). Washington, DC: American Psychological Association. doi:10.1037/10170-008

Greenberg, L. S., Rice, L., & Elliott, R. (1993). *Facilitating emotional change.* New York, NY: Guilford Press.

Greenberg, L. S., & Watson, J. C. (2006). *Emotion-focused therapy for depression.* Washington, DC: American Psychological Association. doi:10.1037/11286-000

Hebb, D. (1949). *The organization of behavior.* New York, NY: Wiley.

Herrmann, I., & Greenberg, L. (2008). Emotion types and sequences in emotion-focused therapy. *European Psychotherapy, 7*, 41–60.

James, W. (1890). *The principles of psychology.* Oxford, England: Holt. doi:10.1037/11059-000

Klein, M. H., Mathieu, P. L., Gendlin, E. T., & Kiesler, D. J. (1969). *The Experiencing Scale: A research and training manual* (Vol. 1). Madison: Wisconsin Psychiatric Institute.

LeDoux, J. E., & Gorman, J. (2001). A call to action: Overcoming anxiety through active coping. *The American Journal of Psychiatry, 158*, 1953–1955.

Levenson, R. (1992). Autonomic nervous system differences among emotions. *Psychological Science, 3*, 23–27. doi:10.1111/j.1467-9280.1992.tb00251.x doi:10.1176/appi.ajp.158.12.1953

McCullough Vaillant, L. (1997). *Changing character: Short-term anxiety-regulating psychotherapy for restructuring defenses, affects, and attachments.* New York, NY: Basic Books.

Nadel, L., & Bohbot, V. (2001). Consolidation of memory. *Hippocampus, 11*, 56–60. doi:10.1002/1098-1063(2001)11:1<56::AID-HIPO1020>3.0.CO;2-O

Nadel, L., & Moscovitch, M. (1997). Memory consolidation, retrograde amnesia and the hippocampal complex. *Current Opinion in Neurobiology, 7*, 217–227. doi:10.1016/S0959-4388(97)80010-4

Pascual-Leone, A., & Greenberg, L. (2007). Emotional processing in experiential therapy: Why "the only way out is through." *Journal of Consulting and Clinical Psychology, 75*, 875–887. doi:10.1037/0022-006X.75.6.875

Pascual-Leone, J. (1991). Emotions, development, and psychotherapy: A dialectical constructivist perspective. In J. Safran & L. Greenberg (Eds.), *Emotion, psychotherapy and change* (pp. 302–335). New York, NY: Guilford Press.

Perls, F. (1969). *Gestalt therapy verbatim*. Moab, UT: Real People Press.

Perls, F., Hefferline, R. F., & Goodman, P. (1951). *Gestalt therapy*. New York, NY: Dell.

Rogers, C. R. (1958). The process conception of psychotherapy. *American Psychologist, 13*, 142–149. doi:10.1037/h0042129

Rogers, C. R. (1959). A theory of therapy, personality, and interpersonal relationships, as developed in the client-centered framework. In S. Koch (Ed.), *Psychology: A study of a science* (Vol. 3, pp. 184–256). New York, NY: McGraw-Hill.

Schiller, D., Monfils, M.-H., Raio, C. M., Johnson, D. C., LeDoux, J. E., & Phelps, E. A. (2010). Preventing the return of fear in humans using reconsolidation update mechanisms. *Nature, 463*, 49–53. doi:10.1038/nature08637

Whelton, W., & Greenberg, L. (2005). Emotion in self-criticism. *Personality and Individual Differences, 38*, 1583–1595. doi:10.1016/j.paid.2004.09.024

7

CORRECTIVE (EMOTIONAL) EXPERIENCE IN PERSON-CENTERED THERAPY: CARL ROGERS AND GLORIA REDUX

BARRY A. FARBER, ARTHUR C. BOHART, AND WILLIAM B. STILES

> Only connect! That was the whole of her sermon. Only connect the prose and the passion and both will be exalted, and human love will be seen at its height. Live in fragments no longer.
>
> —E. M. Forster, *Howard's End*

Although some now regard Franz Alexander as a clinical maverick, his original definition of *corrective emotional experience* appropriated the metapsychology of the dominant psychoanalytic tradition of that time: "reexperiencing the unsettled old conflict but with a new ending" (Alexander, 1946, p. 67). That is, whereas Alexander advanced the then-contentious notions that insight was insufficient to effect change and that the power of corrective experience (CE) lay within the transferential relationship, his definition, with "conflict" at its core, was framed in a way that makes it an imperfect fit for contemporary, relationally oriented psychotherapeutic models, such as person-centered therapy. These perspectives emphasize changes in clients' sense of self and/or relational patterns reenacted and reexperienced with the therapist. New experiences with the therapist—new ways of thinking, feeling, speaking, and/or behaving—may transform clients' ways of seeing themselves and being with others. These changes include alterations in clients' feelings of self-worth, sense of identity, trust in others, connection to others, self-disclosure patterns, internal voices, bodily experiences, and ability to accept and/or modify problems in interpersonal relationships.

To achieve a consensus definition, members of the Penn State University (PSU) conference dropped the word *emotional*: "CEs are ones in which a person comes to understand or experience affectively an event or relationship in a different and unexpected way" (see Chapter 1, this volume, p. 5). Although this definition avoids some of the metapsychological baggage of Alexander's (1946) psychoanalytically oriented definition, from our person-centered perspective it seems vague and overinclusive. For example, by this definition, a client's intellectual acceptance of a therapist's interpretation would be a CE. In addition, this definition omits aspects we regard as important, such as the expectation that significant change experiences occur in the context of a meaningful relationship.

In a person-centered approach, the clients, rather than the therapists or third parties, are responsible for evaluating the correctness of experiences. It may be clearer to speak of experiences that lead to change or growth rather than experiences that correct. Nevertheless, we are content to speak of them here as CEs.

In that spirit, here is what Rogers said about CEs in his spoken preamble to his 30-minute filmed interview with Gloria (Shostrom, 1965), which served to introduce to the audience the basic tenets of his approach:[1]

> Suppose I am fortunate and that I do experience some of these attitudes [genuineness, prizing, and empathic understanding] in the relationship, what then? Well, then a variety of things are likely to happen. . . . She'll explore some of her feelings and attitudes more deeply. She is likely to discover some hidden aspects of herself that she wasn't aware of previously. Feeling herself prized by me, it is quite possible she'll come to prize herself more. Feeling that some of her meanings are understood by me, then she can more readily perhaps listen to herself, listen to what is going on within her own experience, listen to some of the meanings she hasn't been able to catch before. And perhaps if she senses realness in me, she'll be able to be a little more real within herself. I suspect there will be a change in the manner of her expression, at least this has been my experience in other instances. From being rather remote from her experiencing, remote from what is going on within her, it's possible that she'll move toward more immediacy of experiencing, that she will be able to sense and explore what is going on in her in the immediate moment. From being disapproving of herself, it is quite possible she'll move toward a greater degree of acceptance of herself. From somewhat of a fear of relating, she may move toward being able to relate more directly and to encounter me more directly. From construing life in somewhat rigid black and white patterns, she may move toward more tentative ways of construing her experience and of seeing meanings in it. From a locus of evaluation which is outside of herself, it is quite possible she will move toward recognizing a greater capacity within herself

Excerpts of dialogue from the film *Three Approaches to Psychotherapy* (Shostrom, 1965) are reprinted here with permission of Psychological and Educational Films, Inc.

for making judgments and drawing conclusions. So those are some of the changes that we have tended to find and I think that they are all of them changes that are characteristic of the process of therapy or of therapeutic movement.

Rogers here articulated some key themes in person-centered theory and therapy: CEs are indeed emotional experiences and are an inextricable part of the therapeutic process. The relational attitudes consistently offered by the person-centered therapist are intended specifically to facilitate the kinds of immediate and enduring changes that have been called CEs.

In the following sections, we review three strands of classical person-centered understandings of CEs, using Rogers's case of Gloria (Shostrom, 1965) as illustrative material. We then offer two examples of more recent work advancing a person-centered understanding of change experiences. We conclude our chapter by comparing person-centered approaches to CEs with those of contemporary psychoanalytic theorists.

CORRECTIVE EXPERIENCE IN CLASSICAL PERSON-CENTERED THEORY: THREE STRANDS

The classical person-centered literature contains at least three somewhat different—although overlapping—accounts of CEs: conditions of worth, the process theory, and unblocking.

Corrective Experience and Conditions of Worth

The conditions-of-worth account (Rogers, 1959), like the psychodynamic account, suggests that people's problems trace to early experiences with parents who impose conditions of worth on their children. Children learn that they are valuable (i.e., have worth) only if they hold certain beliefs or behave in certain ways (e.g., never expressing anger). They develop a rigid self-concept that does not allow for discrepant experiences. Incongruence between the self-concept and the inevitable discrepant experiences results in psychopathology. These ideas are consistent with Winnicott's (1960) contemporaneous notions about the development of the false self.

The mechanism of correction in the conditions-of-worth account is the therapist's unconditional positive regard, which is meant to counter the experience of conditional positive regard—the client's experience that he or she is valuable only if he or she behaves, thinks, or feels in a certain way. Experiencing unconditional positive regard from the therapist allows the client to become more accepting of experiences and feelings that are discrepant with the self-concept laid down in childhood. Echoing the preamble to the Gloria interview, Gendlin and Rogers (1967) wrote,

> As the client finds himself prized, in all the facets and aspects of himself which he is able to expose and express, he begins to prize himself, and to value his feelings and reactions. He commences to place more confidence in his own basic responses to situations. (p. 12)

In support, a recent meta-analysis found a significant association between therapists' provision of positive regard and positive therapeutic outcome (Farber & Doolin, 2011).

The other two necessary and sufficient conditions for therapeutic change provided by the therapist—empathy and genuineness (Rogers, 1957)—also play a role in this process. To quote Gendlin and Rogers (1967) again:

> As the client finds himself understood by someone who seems to "stand in the client's place" in his understanding, he begins to take a more acceptantly understanding attitude toward his own reactions. He desires to know more of himself; he begins to regard the process of understanding his basic feelings as a worthwhile undertaking. As he recognizes the realness of the therapist, and the fact that the therapist is close to his own experiencing, able in the relationship to express and be his real feelings without fear, he (the client) is increasingly able to live in a closer relationship to his own experiencing, to what is going on within his own skin. He is able to express his feelings more accurately and with less fear. He discovers that his experiencing is a referent to which he may turn in guiding his behavior. (p. 12)

Although this account superficially resembles cognitive–behavioral accounts of correcting dysfunctional beliefs, traditional psychodynamic accounts of CE in the transference, and even contemporary psychodynamic efforts to reconfigure maladaptive attachment patterns, there is a subtle but important difference: The client, rather than the therapist or the theory, evaluates the correctness of the emergent alternative. Unconditional positive regard replaces the client's experience of conditional positive regard as the criterion for self-evaluation. It is important to note that the view that "I am valuable only if I live, think, or feel in a certain way" is altered by creating a different, more accepting sense of self, not by suggesting a rational alternative valuing system or an accurate interpretation. The person moves from being afraid to listen to his or her experience to trusting experience as a valuable source of information. The person relates to himself or herself differently and processes discrepant information differently, both information from the world and information from his or her own experiencing process.

Corrective Experience and the Process Theory

A second account of the CE is associated with the process theory, which was central in two critical works of person-centered theory: *The Therapeutic Relationship and Its Impact* (Rogers, Gendlin, Kiesler, & Truax, 1967; The Wisconsin Schizophrenia Project) and *New Directions in Client-Centered Therapy* (Hart & Tomlinson, 1970). The process theory describes therapeutic change as a developmental sequence. The following version of the process theory comes from the Gendlin and Rogers (1967) chapter that opens the Wisconsin Schizophrenia book:

> [In response to the therapeutic conditions, the client] begins to show certain characteristic changes. . . . He shows a change in the manner of his experiencing of his feelings, moving from a remoteness from what is going on in his organism to an ability to experience feelings and personal meanings with immediacy. He changes in the way he construes experience, from rigid constructs which are thought of as fixed facts to a recognition that he is the creator of these constructs and that they are best held tentatively and are subject to checking. He changes in his manner of relating to his problems, from viewing them as entirely outside himself to accepting his own contributions to his problems and the degree of his responsibility for them. He changes in his manner of relating to others, from avoiding any close or expressive relationships to living openly and freely in such relationships. (pp. 12–13)

This process theory, which draws heavily on Gendlin's (e.g., 1961, 1966) work on experiencing, is compatible with the conditions-of-worth theory but assumes a broader perspective on etiology and change. First, it does not restrict the source of fixity and rigidity to early primary relationships. Rigid patterns of thoughts, feelings, or behaviors could result from adult episodes of trauma or high levels of threat, or they could develop over time, as when a scientist refuses to believe data that contradict a long-held theory. Conditions of worth, then, become only one way that fixity may develop.

Second, change is not restricted to reconciling the self-concept with experience but may involve many or all of a person's concepts. The person moves from holding constructs rigidly (any constructs, including theoretical ones in science) toward a hypothesis-testing, being-in-touch-with-experience way of functioning. This aspect of person-centered theory evolved into Rogers's (1961, 1980) view of the fully functioning person. Thus, therapy can produce change in a person's overall way of being. Clients move from feeling distant from their experience and holding constructs rigidly toward feeling open to experience and holding constructs flexibly. In this view of CE, therapy corrects the manner of relating to oneself and to information. Stated somewhat differently, the process theory shifted emphasis from healing the split between self-concept and experience to changing the person's way of being.

The process theory also shifted emphasis to the therapist's way of being with the client. Unconditional positive regard did not lose its importance, but in the process theory, the curative factor is not healing the split because of conditions of worth so much as learning to be different through being in relationship with a prizing, understanding, and real therapist. Through being listened to empathically, clients learn to listen to themselves. Through relating to a congruent, real therapist, clients learn to be open and congruent. The therapeutic relationship is a CE in which clients learn to hold constructs openly and move toward a more process-oriented way of living.

Corrective Experience as Unblocking

The unblocking account of the CE is a variant of the process theory that appeared in Gendlin and Rogers's (1967) chapter on working with people with schizophrenia in the Wisconsin Schizophrenia volume. Problems occur because the ongoing, self-correcting, self-healing process of the organism is blocked; the person cannot refer inwardly, focus on feelings, or articulate felt meanings. This may happen because the person adheres to a rigid self-concept that does not allow experience in or because he or she never learned the skill of inwardly referring that facilitates the carrying forward process.

Blocking may also occur when a person experiences heavy stress from conflicting personal or work-related demands and has no one who will listen in a way that facilitates the self-evolutionary process. He or she therefore does not have the support for the experiencing or carrying forward process. Such circumstances may be deeply destabilizing and distressing whether or not they involve conditions of worth. Without an empathic listener to help get unstuck, the person's capacities for self-healing may be overwhelmed.

This account resembles that of some systems therapists (e.g., Watzlawick, Weakland, & Fisch, 1974) who have argued that people get stuck by holding their basic beliefs without question, assuming they are real or the only truth. They try to solve problems within those premises (first-order change) when what is needed is a revision in the premises (second-order change). Empathic listening within the therapeutic relationship opens the premises to reexamination and thus unblocks or frees up the person's creative potential, including his or her self-healing process.

GLORIA'S CORRECTIVE EXPERIENCES

To illustrate these traditional person-centered ways of understanding CEs, we focus on Gloria, surely Rogers's most famous case (Shostrom, 1965). Rogers's work with Gloria demonstrated how the necessary and sufficient conditions of therapeutic change (i.e., the therapist's ability to be genuine, positively regarding; Rogers, 1957) facilitate the expression of the strands of CE described in previous sections. We begin with a summary of this interview.

Rogers's 30-minute session was one in a series of filmed interviews with Gloria (a former client of Shostrom's, the producer of this series) that were conducted by therapists representing three different theoretical orientations: Ellis (rational–emotive therapy), Perls (gestalt therapy), and Rogers. All interviews were done on the same day; the interview with Rogers was the first in the series. This summary is based on one by Rosenzweig (in Farber, Brink, & Raskin, 1996); the full transcript of this interview can be found in Rogers and Wood (1974).

Rogers begins by saying, "Good morning, I'm Dr. Rogers; you must be Gloria" and offers that although they only have a half hour to talk, he hopes that they can make something of their time together. He follows with, "I'll be glad to know whatever concerns you." Gloria, smiling, responds that she had been nervous but feels more comfortable now because of the sound of his voice ("the way you're talking") and adds, "I don't feel like you'll be so harsh on me." She tells Rogers the "main thing" she'd like to discuss is that she's newly divorced and now has to adjust to her single life. More specifically, she explains that she's concerned about how her 9-year-old daughter, Pammy, is being affected by her (Gloria's) lying to her about whether she'd had sexual relations with any of the men she's brought to the house. She tells Rogers that she wants him to tell her if being truthful would in fact damage her daughter. She acknowledges feeling torn between being truthful and fearing the consequences. Rogers responds: "I sure wish I could give you the answer as to what you should tell her . . . 'cause what you really want is an answer."

Gloria acknowledges that she does want more from Rogers and fears that he'd just let her "stew" in her feelings. Rogers replies:

> No, I don't want to let you just stew in your feelings, but on the other hand, I also feel that this is the kind of very private thing that I couldn't possibly answer for you, but I sure as anything will try to help you work toward your own answer. I don't know whether that makes any sense to you, but I mean it.

They discuss the bind she feels herself in—between her sense of responsibility as a mother and her acknowledgment that she has sexual needs. Still, she does not want to be responsible for causing any of her children any trauma. To this, Rogers says, "I guess that's what I meant what I said life was risky . . . it's a hell of a responsibility . . . a very frightening one." A few minutes later, continuing their discussion of the choice she feels she must make between lying to her children and following her own desires, Rogers says, "I guess, judging from the tone of your voice, you sound as though you hate yourself more when you lie than you do in terms of things you disapprove of in your behavior." Gloria then offers the following: "I feel like that is solved, and I didn't even solve the thing. But I feel relief." She then tells him that she senses that he is backing her up, giving her permission to follow her instincts. He responds, "I guess the way I sense it is you've been telling me that you know what you want to do, and yes, I do believe in backing up people in what they want to do."

Gloria then speaks of knowing for sure that she made the right decision in leaving her husband, and that such moments of following her true feelings are a form of "utopia." Rogers responds, "I sense that in those utopian moments, you really feel kind of whole, you feel all in one piece." To which Gloria replies, "It gives me a choked-up feeling when you say that because I don't get that as often as I like." Rogers "suspects" that "none of us" gets that feeling as often as we would like. There is a pause, and Gloria's eyes well up. She then responds by saying she was also thinking about how nice it is to talk to him. She says she misses that her father did not talk to her like Rogers does. "I mean, I'd like to say, 'Gee, I'd like you for my father.'" Rogers responds, "You look to me like a pretty nice daughter. 'Cause you really do miss the fact that you couldn't be open with your own dad."

They then speak for a few moments about Gloria's relationship with her father. She says that he did not listen to her and that the relationship between them was another hopeless situation. She has tried working on it, but she feels it is just one more thing she has to accept. Rogers describes Gloria's feeling this way: "'Well, I'm permanently cheated.'" Gloria says this is the reason she likes substitutes. She values talking to Rogers and other men she can respect. She describes a feeling she keeps "underneath" that "we are real close, you know, like a substitute father." Rogers says, "I don't feel that's pretending," and Gloria says, "But you're not really my father." He replies, "No. I meant about the real close business." Gloria says she does feel it is pretending. She cannot expect him to feel that close to her because he does not know her that well. Rogers finishes the filmed portion of the interview by saying, "Well, all I can know is what I am feeling, that is, I feel close to you in this moment."

Despite some occasional lapses in maintaining his focus on Gloria's subjective state (Zimring, 1996), Rogers's behavior and demeanor throughout the interview indicate a close adherence to the essential principles of person-centered therapy. Moreover, Gloria's shifts by the end of the interview—her feelings of closeness to Rogers, her greater acceptance of self, and her sense of resolution of her stated conflict (despite the actual lack of a resolution)—all suggest the presence of some powerful healing moments. Indeed, although one could argue that specific instances near the end (i.e., the moments surrounding Gloria's statement about how nice it was to talk to Rogers and how she'd like him for a father; the moments a little later when Rogers expressed his sense of feeling close to her in that moment) constitute CEs, one could make an equally good case for considering the entire interview a CE.

More specifically, though, how do the powerful moments in this interview accord with the different strands of CEs in traditional person-centered therapy that we have outlined? We offer some examples below, although in a fashion analogous to distinguishing among genuineness, empathy, and positive regard, these three types of CEs tend to overlap in actual sessions.

In his postinterview comments, Rogers analyzed the interaction with Gloria in terms of the process theory. He pointed out that she began the interaction talking about herself somewhat distantly, and moved, by the end, to expressing her feelings with immediacy. For example, in the interchange near the end of the interview about utopian moments (noted above), Gloria allows that she now has a "choked up feeling" because she does not have such experiences as often as she would like. Indeed, one senses in watching this film that she experiences this feeling deeply in this moment. There is another powerful scene, and arguably a CE, near the end of this interview when Gloria's attention switches to her relationship with Rogers and she speaks about how free she felt talking with him in comparison with talking with her father. Here, her words express her sense of unblocking, apparently associated with experiencing Rogers's empathy and unconditional positive regard.

> Yeah, and you know what else I was just thinking? I, I feel dumb saying it uh, that all of a sudden while I was talking to you I thought, "Gee, how nice I can talk to you and I want you to approve of me and I respect you, but I miss that my father couldn't talk to me like you are." [Touches her chin.] I mean, I'd like to say, "Gee, I'd like you for my father. I don't even know why that came to me. [Smiles.]

To which Rogers responds:

> You look to me like a pretty nice daughter. [Pauses; Gloria looks down.] But you really do miss the fact that you, you couldn't be open with your own dad.

Gloria then describes what appear to be conditions of worth imposed by her father:

> Yeah, I couldn't be open, but I, I wanna blame it on him. I think I'm more open than he'd allow me. He would never listen to me talk like you are and not disapprove, not lower me down. I thought of this the other day. Why do I always have to be so perfect? I know why. He always wanted me to be perfect. I always had to be better [touches her lips] and uh . . . yeah, I miss that.

We believe that multiple healing processes occurred during this sequence. We suggest that Gloria was experiencing Rogers as accepting and was moving toward feeling more open and less defensive. Then, in seemingly rapid fashion, her attention shifted, and she simultaneously became aware of how open (unblocked) she was feeling with Rogers and how she had not felt that with her father. She became tearful. Suddenly, this all bubbled up (a favorite metaphor of Rogers) into awareness. By then a change had already occurred: Gloria was already in this open, active, receptive, organismic state. The contrast between Rogers's unconditional positive regard and her father's conditions of worth catalyzed this CE.

Another example of the unblocking process in Rogers's work with Gloria arose when she wondered whether it was okay to have sex outside of marriage. She struggled with trying to figure out what was "really her." By listening empathically, Rogers gave her a chance to face the internal conflict and find a way out. Rogers says:

> I am sure this will sound evasive to you, but it seems to me that perhaps the person you are not being uh fully honest with is you? [Gloria: Sure.] Because I was very much struck by the fact that you were saying, "If I feel all right about what I have done, whether it's going to bed with a man or what, if I really feel all right about it, then I do not have any concern about what I would tell Pam or my relationship with her."

To which Gloria responds movingly:

> Right. All right. Now I hear what you are sayin'. [sighs and shifts back and forth in chair.] Then all right, then I want to work on . . . [Rogers: It's kind of tough, huh?], I wanna work on accepting me, then. I want to work on feeling all right about it.

A few moments later, Gloria acknowledged in her own way that something has been unblocked as a result of Rogers' empathy, genuineness, and support.

> And I would like, at least, to be able to tell her that I remember lying and I am sorry I lied and it has been driving me bugs because I did. [pauses.] I do. Now I feel like, now that's solved, and I didn't even solve a thing, but I feel relieved. [Rogers: Mhm, mhm.] I uh, I do feel like you have been saying to me—you're not say, giving me advice—but I do feel like you are saying, "You really wanna, you know what pattern you want to follow Gloria, and go ahead and follow it." I sort of feel a backing up from you.

Such changes appear to take place prior to—or even without—the person thinking, recognizing, accepting, or engaging in the cognitive processing postulated by theorists who describe insight or corrected thinking as psychotherapy's mutative ingredients. Moreover, the shift in whole-body receptivity needn't even be large to make a significant difference in an individual's effective functioning or profound sense of being understood fully and accepted entirely in the moment.

CONTEMPORARY ELABORATIONS

Person-centered understandings of CEs continue to develop. Here we review two contemporary elaborations.

The Client as Active Self-Healer

From a person-centered perspective, CEs are inextricably linked to the idea of the client as active self-healer. That is, it is clients who make therapy work. Bohart and Tallman (2010) argued that research supports the hypothesis that clients are the major self-healing force in psychotherapy, that clients often interpret events in therapy in their own ways to facilitate their own growth. The events clients see as helpful may be ones that their therapists had not intended to be especially helpful or even noticed. Indeed, clients may interpret apparently neutral events, or even therapeutic blunders, as CEs.

At least twice in the film, Gloria actively interpreted the therapeutic process in ways that made it a CE for her. In one instance, as we previously discussed, she spontaneously identified a discrepancy between how Rogers treated her and how her father treated her. Nowhere previously in the interview had her father been mentioned. Instead, her own synthetic efforts turned the interview into a potential CE vis-à-vis her relationship with her father.

In a second instance, Gloria told Rogers that she felt he had been telling her all along that she should be honest with her daughter. Rogers denied that he had been saying this. That is, Gloria actively interpreted Rogers as having said this. She then used this to help herself make a decision that appeared, at least to us, to be what she wanted to do in terms of her deeply held value of honesty.

Corrective Experience as Building Meaning Bridges

A series of intensive case studies has suggested that the therapeutic movement toward greater openness to experience involves the construction of meaning bridges between the conflicting internal parts of a person (Brinegar, Salvi, Stiles, & Greenberg, 2006; Mosher, Goldsmith, Stiles, &

Greenberg, 2008; Stiles, 2011; Stiles & Glick, 2002). Rice (1984; Rice & Saperia, 1984) introduced the term *meaning bridge* to describe clients' new (corrective) understanding of some seemingly problematic inner reaction to a situation. Work in the assimilation model, which can be regarded as an elaboration of Rogers's process model (Stiles et al., 1990), has generalized this to encompass any semiotic constructions (e.g., narratives, terms, gestures, images) that allow smooth communication between—and eventually joint action by—the conflicting parts of the person, which are described metaphorically as internal voices. Thus, the goal of therapy can be seen as turning problematic experiences into personal resources.

This approach suggests that conditions of worth and other fixities within clients can be understood as traces of previous experience that have become problematic. For example, current experience may be opposed by introjected representations of significant others who imposed external systems of values. The opposing internal parts of the person can be considered as separate internal voices that act and speak. In an accepting relationship, internal discrepancies can be voiced, examined, and resolved through compromise or creative synthesis.

Gloria's ambivalence about telling her daughter about having sex outside of marriage illustrates such conflicting internal multiplicity.

Gloria: I want to approve of me always, but my actions won't let me. I want to approve of me. [pauses.] I—I think—[strains face] . . .

Rogers: I realize . . . you—alright, but let me—I'd like to understand it. You sound as though your actions were kind of outside of you. You want to approve of you, but what you do somehow won't let you approve of yourself.

Gloria: Right. [pauses.] Like I feel that I can't approve of myself regarding, for example, [smiles] my sex life.

Rogers: Mhm, mhm.

Gloria: This is the big thing. If I really fell in love with a man, and I respected him and I adored him, I don't think I would feel so guilty going to bed with him, and I don't think I would have to make up any excuses to the children because they could see my natural caring for him.

Rogers: Mhm, okay.

Gloria: But when I have the physical desires and I'll say, "Oh, well, why not," and I want to anyway, but I feel guilty afterwards. I hate facing the kids, I don't like looking at myself, and I rarely enjoy it.

The therapeutic task here can be understood as providing a context in which the opposing parts of the self—such as Gloria's actions and her approval—can each be heard and can work toward ways of understanding each other and engaging in joint action. By reflecting each internal voice as it spoke, Rogers allowed each to hear the other and build meaning bridges with each other (see the more detailed examination of similar processes in other cases in Mosher et al., 2008; and Stiles & Glick, 2002).

> Rogers: I guess, judging from your tone of voice, you sound as though you hate yourself more when you lie than you do in terms of things you disapprove of in behavior.
>
> Gloria: I do. I do because this has really bothered me. This happened with Pammy [Gloria's daughter] about a month ago and it keeps coming to my mind. I don't know whether to go back and talk to her about it or wait. She may have even forgotten what she asked me, but uh—it just . . .
>
> Rogers: The point is, you haven't forgotten.
>
> Gloria: I haven't. . . . No, I haven't. And I would like, at least, to be able to tell her that I remember lying and I am sorry I lied. . . . [pauses.] I do—Now I feel like—now that's solved—and I didn't even solve a thing, but I feel relieved.

Gloria's sense of relief seemed to reflect a new meaning bridge. As the conflicting positions were expressed and reflected by Rogers, each internal part felt heard and understood. Within this mutual understanding, Gloria's internal voices caused each other less distress, and they could work together on ways to resolve the practical problem of dealing with her sexual feelings while maintaining an honest relationship with her daughter. The practical problem was not immediately solved, but a psychological barrier to finding a solution had been overcome. For Gloria, it appeared to be a CE.

CORRECTIVE EMOTIONAL EXPERIENCE IN PERSON-CENTERED THERAPY AND CONTEMPORARY RELATIONAL DYNAMIC PSYCHOTHERAPY: SORT OF THE SAME, BUT NOT REALLY

Having begun this chapter by contextualizing Rogers's view of CE within the classical psychoanalytic tradition, we conclude by contrasting the person-centered model with a contemporary psychodynamic view on this construct. But first, to review: The classical Freudian view is not only embedded in a drive–conflict model but, from another metatheoretical perspective, also holds that insight is corrective (i.e., that knowledge is power). As one becomes aware of the unconscious determinants of one's behaviors, one is able to assume conscious control over them. In contrast, Alexander's (1946) concept of CE was that experience in therapy could alter behavior directly, without conceptual mediation, although it might subsequently lead to insight or understanding. If, for example, one was deprived of love from one's mother as a child, the love of the therapist could correct that, without the person necessarily understanding how he or she had repressed the knowledge, or how that repression had woven itself through his or her personality. In this respect, Alexander's views were consistent with later object relational perspectives on the nature of healing in psychotherapy.

Contemporary relational dynamic thought has much in common with positions articulated by Rogers (1957) more than 50 years ago, although this is often overlooked. Both emphasize the mutative elements of the client–therapist relationship, suggesting that the therapist's openness, empathy, and acceptance are the keys to clients' ability to make significant changes in their lives. The late Stephen Mitchell, leading architect of the current brand of relational therapy, wrote a book titled Relationality: From Attachment to Intersubjectivity (2000) without referencing Rogers, even though Mitchell was a gifted synthesizer of multiple theoretical traditions within the psycho-analytic canon (Farber, 2007). Mitchell's focus in this book was on extrapolating new ways of understanding and relating to clients from the work of early object relations theorists (e.g., Fairbairn), attachment theorists (e.g., Bowlby), and more contemporary analysts (e.g., Loewald).

More recently, Wachtel's (2008) characterizations of the CE in contemporary relational therapy strongly resemble ideas from the classical person-centered paradigm. Wachtel suggested that

> the approach described here aims to help the patient reappropriate the aspects of his self-experience and affective life that have been cast aside under the pressure of anxiety, guilt, and shame. It regards support not as antithetical to effective self-exploration but as the very ground of such exploration, providing the safety and encouragement necessary for exploration to proceed in a manner that truly expands the self. (p. 220)

Moreover, Wachtel acknowledged that in this newer iteration of psychodynamic therapy, the process

> is less centered on the therapist's role as interpreter and more attuned to her role as a participant in new relational experiences. . . . Such an approach is more focused on the immediate and affective interchange that has variously been called, among other conceptualizations, corrective emotional experience. (p. 221)

What, then, of differences between psychodynamic perspectives—classical or contemporary—and person-centered perspectives on CEs? Although the therapist's genuineness, support, and emotional engagement with his or her clients are far more integral to the work of contemporary psychodynamic therapists than they were to their counterparts of half a century ago, psychodynamically oriented psychotherapists of today still tend to privilege understanding and cognition. This position might be articulated as follows: I can and should connect with my clients; I can and will acknowledge my mistakes and my place in the therapeutic discourse and relationship with my clients; and I can and will be far more genuine, giving, and emotionally resonant than my analytic predecessors. But I am at heart a psychodynamically oriented therapist, and I still believe that the expression of feelings, as powerful as this is, should be accompanied by subsequent attempts to understand what happened and to process the meaning of new experiences.

Theoretically, the psychodynamic focus on understanding, even if it is only a part of the therapeutic equation, still remains distinct from a person-centered suggestion that the experience itself needs no added cognitive explanation. Rogers did not ask Gloria how and whether his articulated sense that she would make a "good daughter" fulfilled her long-standing and apparent need for a good (or good enough) father. He did not question what qualities were present in their interaction that were lacking in her relationships with other men, and he did not pursue—although Gloria provided opportunities to do so—the ways in which her choices regarding career and men were overdetermined by her apparent need to provoke her father. From a person-centered perspective, understanding feelings or maladaptive patterns is at best incidental to the growth process.

Although person-centered therapy aims to symbolize experience—that is, to articulate and share experience through explicit verbal and nonverbal signs—it does not aim to give clients a cognitive or historical understanding of how conditions of worth are paralyzing them or attempt to review childhood memories to show how parents' imposed values contribute to their distress. Instead, it seeks to provide a relationship in which clients realize they are valued no matter what they experience. Thus, successful person-centered therapy typically consists of a series of CEs—episodes in which clients gingerly discuss previously avoided or denied aspects of experience, experience the therapist as not judging them, and come to accept that aspect of themselves. Through such series of CEs, clients come to trust themselves and to learn to listen more closely to themselves. Like Gloria, they become more empowered, feeling more efficacious and able to make decisions. Feeling more accepting and capable, clients no longer fear strong emotions and become able to establish more open, accepting, and reciprocally fulfilling relationships. Conversely, having learned to trust in and listen to all of one's self, they do not let intense emotion blot out multiple voices within (Stiles, Osatuke, Glick, & Mackay, 2004).

REFERENCES

Alexander, F. (1946). The principle of corrective emotional experience. In F. Alexander & T. M., French (Eds.), *Psychoanalytic therapy: Principles and application* (pp. 66–70). New York, NY: Ronald Press.

Bohart, A. C., & Tallman, K. (2010). Clients as active self-healers: Implications for the person-centered approach. In M. Cooper, J. C. Watson, & D. Holldampf (Eds.), *Person-centered and experiential therapies work: A review of the research on counseling, psychotherapy and related practices* (pp. 91–131). Ross-on-Wye, Wales, United Kingdom: PCCS Books.

Brinegar, M. G., Salvi, L. M., Stiles, W. B., & Greenberg, L. S. (2006). Building a meaning bridge: Therapeutic progress from problem formulation to understanding. *Journal of Counseling Psychology, 53,* 165–180. doi:10.1037/0022-0167.53.2.165

Farber, B. A. (2007). On the enduring and substantial influence of Carl Rogers' not-quite essential nor necessary conditions. *Psychotherapy: Theory, Research, & Practice, 44,* 289–294. doi:10.1037/0033-3204.44.3.289

Farber, B. A., Brink, D., & Raskin, P. (1996). *The psychotherapy of Carl Rogers: Cases and commentary.* New York, NY: Guilford Press.

Farber, B. A., & Doolin, E. M. (2011). Positive regard and affirmation. In J. C. Norcross (Ed.), *Psychotherapy relationships that work* (2nd ed., pp. 168–186). New York, NY: Oxford University Press. doi:10.1093/acprof:oso/9780199737208.003.0008

Gendlin, E. T. (1961). Experiencing: A variable in the process of therapeutic change. *American Journal of Psychotherapy, 15,* 233–245.

Gendlin, E. T. (1966). Existentialism and experiential psychotherapy. In C. Moustakas (Ed.), *Existential child therapy* (pp. 206–246). New York, NY: Basic Books.

Gendlin, E. T., & Rogers, C. R. (1967). The conceptual context. In C. R. Rogers, E. T. Gendlin, D. J. Kiesler, & C. B. Truax (Ed.), *The therapeutic relationship and its impact: A study of psychotherapy with schizophrenics* (pp. 3–22). Madison: University of Wisconsin Press.

Hart, J. T., & Tomlinson, T. M. (Eds.). (1970). *New directions in client-centered therapy.* Boston, MA: Houghton-Mifflin.

Mitchell, S. A. (2000). *Relationality: From attachment to intersubjectivity.* Hillsdale, NJ: Analytic Press.

Mosher, J. K., Goldsmith, J. Z., Stiles, W. B., & Greenberg, L. S. (2008). Assimilation of two critic voices in a person-centered therapy for depression. *Person-Centered and Experiential Psychotherapies, 7,* 1–19. doi:10.1080/14779757.2008.9688449

Rice, L. N. (1984). Client tasks in client-centered therapy. In R. F. Levant & J. M. Shlien (Eds.), *Client-centered therapy and the person-centered approach* (pp. 182–202). New York, NY: Praeger.

Rice, L. N., & Saperia, E. P. (1984). Task analysis and the resolution of problematic reactions. In L. N. Rice & L. S. Greenberg (Eds.), *Patterns of change* (pp. 29–66). New York, NY: Guilford Press.

Rogers, C. R. (1957). The necessary and sufficient conditions of therapeutic personality change. *Journal of Consulting Psychology, 21,* 95–103.

Rogers, C. R. (1959). A theory of therapy, personality, and interpersonal relationships as developed in the client-centered framework. In S. Koch (Ed.), *Psychology: A study of Science: Vol. 3. Formulation of the persona and the social context* (pp.184–256). New York, NY: McGraw-Hill.

Rogers, C. R. (1961). *On becoming a person.* Boston, MA: Houghton Mifflin.

Rogers, C. R. (1980). *A way of being.* Boston, MA: Houghton Mifflin.

Rogers, C. R., Gendlin, E. T., Kiesler. D. J., & Truax. C. B. (Eds.). (1967). *The therapeutic relationship and its impact: A study of psychotherapy with schizophrenics.* Madison: University of Wisconsin Press.

Rogers, C. R., & Wood, J. K. (1974). Client-centered theory: Carl R. Rogers. In A. Burton (Ed.), *Operational theories of personality* (pp. 237–254). New York, NY: Brunner/Mazel.

Shostrom, E. L. (Producer). (1965). *Three approaches to psychotherapy* (Part 1) [Film]. Orange, CA: Psychological Films.

Stiles, W. B. (2011). Coming to terms. *Psychotherapy Research, 21,* 367–384. doi:10.1080/10503307.2011.582186

Stiles, W. B., Elliott, R., Llewelyn, S. P., Firth-Cozens, J. A., Margison, F. R., Shapiro, D. A., & Hardy, G. (1990). Assimilation of problematic experiences by clients in psychotherapy. *Psychotherapy: Theory, Research, & Practice, 27,* 411–420. doi:10.1037/0033-3204.27.3.411

Stiles, W. B., & Glick, M. J. (2002). Client-centered therapy with multivoiced clients: Empathy with whom? In J. C. Watson, R. Goldman, & M. S. Warner (Eds.), *Client-centered and experiential therapy in the 21st century: Advances in theory, research, and practice* (pp. 406–414). London, England: PCCS Books.

Stiles, W. B., Osatuke, K., Glick, M. J., & Mackay, H. C. (2004). Encounters between internal voices generate emotion: An elaboration of the assimilation model. In H. H. Hermans & G. Dimaggio (Eds.), *The dialogical self in psychotherapy* (pp. 91–107). New York, NY: Brunner-Routledge. doi:10.4324/9780203314616_chapter_6

Wachtel, P. (2008). *Relational theory and the practice of psychotherapy.* New York, NY: Guilford Press.

Watzlawick, P., Weakland, J., & Fisch, P. (1974). *Change: Principles of problem formation and problem resolution.* New York, NY: Norton.

Winnicott, D. W. (1960). Ego distortion in terms of true and false self. In D. W. Winnicott (1965), *The maturational process and the facilitating environment: Studies in the theory of emotional development* (pp. 140–152). New York, NY: International Universities Press.

Zimring, F. (1996). Rogers and Gloria: The effects of meeting some, but not all, of the "necessary and sufficient" conditions. In B. A. Farber, D. C. Brink, & P. M. Raskin (Eds.), *The psychotherapy of Carl Rogers: Cases and commentary* (pp. 65–73). New York, NY: Guilford Press.

8

AN EXPECTANCY-BASED APPROACH TO FACILITATING CORRECTIVE EXPERIENCES IN PSYCHOTHERAPY

MICHAEL J. CONSTANTINO AND HENNY A. WESTRA

Alexander and French (1946) introduced the therapeutic principle of *corrective emotional experience,* in which a client's ability to repair the conflictual sequelae of prior experiences with his or her early caregivers is made possible through the therapeutic relationship. Although speaking from a psychoanalytic perspective, Alexander and French's operationalization of corrective experience (CE) was actually quite integrative in its incorporation of interpersonal, cognitive, and affective elements. They argued that in behaving differently from the initial conflict situation,

> the therapist has an opportunity to help the patient both to see intellectually and to *feel* the irrationality of his emotional reactions. . . . When one link (the parental response) in this interpersonal relationship is changed through the medium of the therapist, the patient's reaction becomes pointless. (p. 67)

Alexander and French's (1946) construct has now received a wide endorsement across psychotherapy orientations, albeit with varied definitions and foci (some with and some without the *emotional* component of the original definition). Currently, there is no universally agreed-upon notion of what is corrective or what gets corrected, and there is limited formal elaboration of integrative definitions or proposed pantheoretical mechanisms of CEs.

In this chapter, we focus on an integrative psychotherapy approach that underscores clients' expectations as an explanatory construct for CEs. First, we conceptualize client expectancies as powerful treatment factors common to various approaches. Second, we present an integrative definition of CEs (centered on the alteration of expectancies) that encompasses both the clients' experience and the therapists' role across interpersonal, cognitive, and affective domains. Third, we elaborate a four-phase expectancy-based approach to facilitating CEs grounded in social psychological and interpersonal theory. Finally, we discuss the psychological consequences of clients undergoing corrective, expectancy-altering interpersonal, cognitive, and affective experiences in psychotherapy. Across these sections, we highlight both what is corrective and what gets corrected.

CLIENT EXPECTATIONS AS A POWERFUL COMMON TREATMENT FACTOR

Psychologists have long recognized that various expectations play a powerful role in shaping people's perceptions, motivations, and actions in psychotherapy (e.g., Frank, 1961). *Outcome expectations* reflect clients' prognostic beliefs about the personal consequences of engaging in treatment. Such expectations have tended to have a small but significant association with adaptive treatment processes (e.g., alliance quality) and outcomes (see Constantino, Glass, Arnkoff, Ametrano, & Smith, 2011, for a review).

Treatment expectations reflect clients' beliefs about what will transpire during treatment, including expectations about the roles that they and their therapists will adopt and the type of work in which they will engage. Research findings on treatment expectations are more equivocal than those on outcome expectations; however, some studies suggest that confirmation of role expectations is associated with more adaptive processes (e.g., alliance quality) and outcomes (Constantino et al., 2011), as is the shaping of expectations through treatment socialization strategies (see Walitzer, Dermen, & Conners, 1999).

Another set of expectations, although not directly about treatment, is highly relevant to treatment process and outcome. *Interpersonal expectations* reflect self–other beliefs (e.g., expected responses of others) and interactional scripts (e.g., expected exchanges between self and others) that clients carry forward into new relationships, including with the therapist. There has been limited theory and research on interpersonal expectancies as a pantheoretical psychotherapy construct. In one study, though, Ahmed and Westra (2008) found that analogue clients high in outcome expectations had better outcomes but only when hearing a treatment rationale provided by a warm, enthusiastic clinician. The opposite was found for clients with low outcome expectations; they demonstrated good outcomes only when hearing the rationale from a colder, less enthusiastic clinician. These findings speak to the potential importance of therapists matching their clients on levels of enthusiasm and optimism (at least initially), which might reflect a type of interpersonal expectancy confirmation. Other studies, however, have demonstrated that good outcome is associated with disconfirmed interpersonal expectations over time (e.g., Weiss & Sampson, 1986; Westra, Aviram, Barnes, & Angus, 2010).

Reflecting the vast and multidimensional expectancy literature, some have argued that the manipulation, reshaping, and revision of various client expectations are at the foundation of virtually every major psychotherapy model (Beitman, Soth, & Bumby, 2005; R. P. Greenberg, Constantino, & Bruce, 2006). The notion is that clinicians bring to the psychotherapy table an alternative and often unexpected frame of reference to clients' personal constructions and meaning systems. This discrepant frame is required for change in such constructions (Festinger, 1957), and the specific nature of the discrepancies and their delivery is drawn from clinicians' clinical theory.

For example, in psychoanalytic and psychodynamic approaches, clients' repetitious (and expectancy-confirming) attitudes, feelings, and behaviors that are derived from early (and often conflictual) relationships are altered or reshaped through therapists' interpretations (Freud, 1912/1953). Interpersonal therapists purposely engage in exchanges with their clients that disconfirm typical self–other social patterns. By not responding to the client in the same constricted manner as most important others in the client's life, the clinician fosters the client's ability to revise self–other expectations and scripts (Kiesler, 1996). In behavioral therapies, clients are exposed to their feared stimuli to experience directly their erroneous expectation of breakdown (Foa & Kozak, 1986). And in emotion-focused therapies, clients process unresolved emotions, but in a novel, expectancy-disconfirming context of a safe and empathic therapeutic relationship (L. S. Greenberg, Rice, & Elliott, 1993).

CORRECTIVE EXPERIENCES AS A REVISION OF EXPECTATIONS: AN INTEGRATIVE DEFINITION

Reflecting the seeming ubiquity of expectations across different psychotherapies processes and outcomes, we present here an integrative definition of CEs based on the alteration of client expectations (as both CEs in and of themselves and as a precursor to other forms of CEs). We view our operationalization as integrative both because it is based on a factor (i.e., expectations) that cuts across different treatment orientations and because it incorporates multiple levels of functioning (i.e., interpersonal, cognitive, and affective). We view both the client's experience and the therapist's ability to foster various client and dyadic experiences as being central to our CE definition.

Regarding client experience, we view three central forms of expectancy revision as being at the heart of CEs. These speak directly to what we propose gets corrected. In some cases, all three forms of expectancy revision will characterize a CE, although some CEs might involve just one or two. First, at an interpersonal level, a CE might involve an experiential relearning and alteration of rigid relational patterns and expectations through exposure to new interpersonal experiences in the psychotherapy relationship. Second, at a cognitive level, a CE might involve the gradual incorporation of self-relevant information that is inconsistent with one's self and world schemas. Finally, at an affective level, a CE might directly involve the ability to emote freely without the expectation of negative consequence, and/or it might involve the processing and revision of emotion schemes from maladaptive and restrictive to adaptive and guiding (L. S. Greenberg & Paivio, 1997).

The connecting thread across these types of altered expectation is the client's revised working model of self and other (Bowlby, 1988). As one example involving all types in a CE, clients might present to therapy with insecure attachment, a sense of shameful inadequacy, and a fear of openly sharing feelings (based on an expected fear of being ridiculed and/or having their feelings minimized, as has been the case in previous central relationships). However, with a therapist who over time becomes an important attachment figure, and who also fosters emotional disclosure and processing, with corresponding acceptance and valuing, such clients might develop a new self–other model. Within this revised model, these clients can become more securely attached, can begin to emote without the automatic expectation of derision, can begin to replace enduring shame with more adaptive emotion, and can develop new cognitions and emotion-based narratives about how successful and intimate they can be in relationships.

Regarding the therapist's role in promoting a clients's revised self–other model, we emphasize three general skills that are central to the type of CEs advanced here (i.e., revised self–other models across interpersonal, cognitive, and/or emotional levels). These speak directly to what we propose is corrective; that is, what fosters the client's transformation involved in a CE. First, the clinician must provide the favorable conditions under which a client can tolerate previously unexpected interpersonal behavior, self-related feedback or information, and/or emotional experience. To us, these conditions manifest most prominently in the quality and negotiation of the therapeutic alliance. Second, the clinician must eventually respond to the client in a manner that is different and unexpected from how others have responded to the client—

what Kiesler (1996) referred to as "nonconfirmation of the patient's restricted self." Finally, when the client encounters novel and unexpected experiences and perspectives (as the transformative process of revising self–other models unfolds), the therapist must tread lightly while paying constant attention to the client's anxieties, responses, and powerful pulls to revert to what is familiar, as well as to the climate of the therapeutic alliance.

FACILITATING CORRECTIVE EXPERIENCES: AN EXPECTANCY-BASED APPROACH

Expectancy revision appears to have a significant role in most major psychotherapies, as well as in the CE definition formulated at the 2007 Penn State University Conference on the Process of Change: "CEs are ones in which a person comes to understand or experience affectively an event or relationship in a different and unexpected way" (Chapter 1, this volume, p. 5). However, questions remain about how and when to foster, manipulate, confirm, and disconfirm various client expectations. In this section, we present a psychotherapy approach that addresses these questions in the consideration of the CE construct.

Central to our expectancy-based CE approach are two fundamental self-motivations that are associated with different types of expectations. One motivation reflects the need for self-enhancement, or *positivity strivings*. From this perspective, people possess a desire for positive evaluations and interpersonal interactions, as such outcomes foster and maintain favorable self-perceptions (Shrauger, 1975). There is a large literature that supports people's use of strategies to obtain desired positivity (see Baumeister, 1999). However, people also possess *self-verification strivings*; that is, people are motivated to receive self-consistent feedback and behaviors from others because doing so provides them with a sense of psychological control, coherence, prediction, and competence in the crucial domain of knowing oneself (Swann, 1996). Purportedly, the felt security that arises from such self-consistent feedback or behavior protects individuals from the angst that accompanies feeling as though one is unfamiliar with oneself. There is strong evidence that people, including those with negative self-views, use cognitive, behavioral, and interpersonal strategies to satisfy their self-verification needs (see Pinel & Constantino, 2003).

Positivity and verification strivings compete when people have negative self-views. Although most people with negative self-views are quite ambivalent about negative yet verifying feedback, their stronger need might be to feel like they know themselves and are known and understood by others (even if such knowledge maintains a negative self-view). According to Swann (1996), people have not only an *epistemic* motive underlying their desire for self-verification (i.e., to feel the security that accompanies a sense of self-knowing) but also a *pragmatic* motive (i.e., people learn that interpersonal interactions proceed most comfortably and functionally when people view and treat them as they view and treat themselves). It is not surprising then that people use methods to protect the self from incongruent and unexpected feedback and exchange. And to the extent that people are successful in soliciting such verifying feedback and exchange, the self then self-perpetuates and expectancies of self and other become more powerfully entrenched.

This situation, of course, is highly relevant to psychotherapy in that clients often possess negative self-views that are resistant to change and also behave in ways to maintain their self–other expectations despite their (often) maladaptive nature. Thus, the approach advanced below emphasizes the therapist's need to attend to their clients' positivity and verification strivings while developing an interpersonal context conducive to expectancy-altering feedback and exchange that is central to clients' CEs. This approach incorporates the three expectations (outcome, treatment, interpersonal), the three forms of expectancy revision (interpersonal, cognitive, affective), and the three therapist skills (alliance development, disconfirmation of the clients's restricted self, treading lightly in the course of change) discussed above.

Phase 1: Initial Contact

According to this approach, it is important for therapists to foster clients' outcome expectations during the initial contact. As previously described, outcome expectations reflect clients' beliefs about the likely efficacy of engaging in treatment. Not only does the literature suggest that those who have higher prognostic expectations develop better alliances with their therapist and achieve better outcomes, but it also suggests that also fostering outcome expectations inherently attends to clients' positivity strivings (i.e., a self-motivation to evaluate treatment favorably). For example, clinicians might offer general, hope-inspiring statements (e.g., "Your problems are exactly the type for which this therapy can be of assistance") while also expressing some reserved confidence in their own abilities and the treatment (e.g., "Although no course of treatment is foolproof, I do believe that we can work together to help you deal with your problems"). Such mild and non–self-threatening positive feedback might help to engage clients in the early treatment process. At the same time, it is important that clinicians at this stage refrain from disconfirming clients' interpersonal expectations (self–other beliefs and interpersonal scripts), which would likely be too threatening and anxiety provoking this early in treatment. We view this aspect of the initial stage as reflecting the clinician skill of creating a favorable condition that capitalizes on a client's ability to accept positivity (i.e., heightened outcome expectations) in the right context (i.e., the clinician's simultaneous respect for the client's verification strivings). This process is foundational to the subsequent unfolding of the CE.

When using early strategies to foster outcome expectations, it is important to avoid arousing clients' experience of threat and defensiveness or invalidating their concerns regarding change. Using these strategies with a willingness to hear and process client perspectives that deviate from the clinician's own beliefs about the potential for change is important. For example, the clinician can ask the client's permission to provide information about likely or typical treatment outcomes, can express affirming or hope-inspiring statements in an autonomy-preserving manner (e.g., "This is just my opinion of course, and you might disagree, but from my perspective it seems that you have a number of qualities that make you a good candidate for this treatment"), and can elicit the client's reactions to any clinician inputs. Moreover, making room to hear and empathically process client concerns about change may also be important to enhancing early client confidence in the treatment's efficacy. For example, Ahmed, Westra, and Constantino (2010) found that the more clinicians were understanding and affirming as opposed to influencing or controlling during moments of resistance (i.e., client opposition to clinician direction) in the first session, the higher were clients' subsequent outcome expectations. Although validation and autonomy granting are thus foundational to our CE approach, they might also reflect early moments of disconfirmation of the client's self–other models (to the extent that those models are characterized by invalidation and control by significant others). Thus, such moments could reflect some early experiential relearning in interpersonal exchange, which is one type of expectancy revision in our CE paradigm.

At this first treatment step, clinicians can also begin socializing clients to the treatment process, thereby enhancing, or in some cases altering, clients' treatment expectations (i.e., beliefs about what will transpire during treatment). The literature suggests that clients who undergo a pretreatment socialization or role preparation process have been shown to respond better to treatment than those who do not. Furthermore, discussing what to expect in treatment serves important alliance development and engagement functions (which we previously highlighted as one of three important therapist skills according to this approach) because it allows for active collaboration. For example, to the extent that role behaviors or treatment strategies are incompatible with clients' beliefs, clinicians may need to work toward either altering their clients' expectations (while gauging the anxiety that this might pose) or altering the nature of treatment to better meet those expectations. Of course, given the collaborative nature of this process, a hybrid understanding might be achieved. For example, a client might expect psychotherapy to focus exclusively on early childhood, whereas the clinician might tend to work in the here and now. In an effort to frame his or her approach to be consistent with the client's expectations, thereby potentially restoring or even enhancing the client's outlook, the clinician might suggest the following:

> People learn many things early on that have a lasting influence on their present thoughts and feelings. Thus, although we might lean toward discussing the here and now, your childhood will not be off limits, and I suspect that we will learn something quite useful from connecting past to present.

Such collaboration and alliance fostering is consistent with the clinician establishing a favorable condition for change—one of the three therapist skills in our CE approach.

Also at this very early treatment stage, it would benefit clinicians to scrutinize their expectations (perhaps based on their own biases and immediate diagnostic impressions), as well as their reactions to their clients. Taking stock of these reactions is a large part of a constructive case formulation that will later inform expectancy-altering exchanges in the service of CEs. Such clinician reactions have been referred to as *objective countertransference* in interpersonal parlance (Kiesler, 1996) and involve direct feelings being aroused, specific behavioral urges, beliefs about what the client is trying to do to him or her, or how the client wants him or her to behave or react, and images involving concrete interactions with the client. Of course, the initial contact is only the beginning of attending to this process; we envision it continuing at least through the second phase and in some cases throughout the entire treatment.

Phase 2: Early Treatment

As the psychotherapy relationship moves beyond initial contact, clients will begin accessing their self-views, for which they will desire verifying feedback or behavior that will fit their expectations of self and other (even if such expectations are negative). As we have discussed, such verification will promote a sense of control and familiarity in the exchange. Thus, in this stage we argue that clinicians need to provide an optimal dose of verifying, expectancy-consistent feedback and behavior to build a safe and congruent encounter (i.e., one in which the client feels the security of knowing oneself and feeling accurately known by another). Such verification will also foster clients' sense that their therapist is a credible feedback source who confirms their self-concept. Multiple authors have highlighted the importance of stepping into the client's frame of reference at this early stage as a necessary prerequisite (what we present as a favorable CE condition) to the subsequent alteration of self-views and schema-based expectations (e.g., Pinel & Constantino, 2003; Strong & Claiborn, 1982).

Given the importance of client engagement in the psychotherapy process, the meeting of clients' self-verification needs plausibly takes on a central role early in treatment, as failure to do so could leave the still-developing alliance in an unproductive state of tension and/or lead to the dissolution of the relationship altogether. Furthermore, verifying feedback or behavior might provide another type of "favorable condition" (Alexander & French, 1946) under which eventual nonverifying and expectancy-inconsistent behavior can be tolerated.

We argue that there are three nonmutually exclusive ways of providing an adaptive dose of early verification. First, it can be provided (at an affective, interpersonal, cognitive, and/or behavioral level) directly and consciously. Affectively, a psychotherapist can match the client's mood and level of optimism (see Ahmed & Westra, 2008). Interpersonally, the clinician can deliberately provide complementary behaviors to create a functional, integrated, and low anxiety exchange. Theoretically, interpersonal behaviors are complementary if similar in affiliation and opposite in control (Kiesler, 1996).

Thus, a clinician might purposely submit to a dominant client at first, knowing that nonverifying behavior might create too much initial anxiety. As an example, a client might have a defensive tendency to criticize the competence of the therapist and demand that the therapist use a particular theoretical framework. Although the therapist might disagree with this framework and recognize the defensive function of the request, it might build the relationship to submit initially to this client's dominance. The clinician might say, "I can see how invested you are in this approach. Although it is not my typical working style, I would like to hear more about it."

Cognitively, clinicians can provide veridical assessment feedback that matches their client's sense of his or her own problems (Ackerman, Hilsenroth, Baity, & Blagys, 2000). Such direct feedback might also build therapist credibility, as therapeutic shrewdness increases the client's trust that the problems with which they are presenting will be addressed and not invalidated or misunderstood. Such credibility, in turn, may promote greater client faith in any novel, adaptive, and unexpected information that subsequently emerges in the service of change. At a behavioral level, clinicians can first engage in strategies that align with their clients' typical coping styles (even if they believe them to be restrictive), so as to confirm their clients' expected sense of problem resolution (Glass & Arnkoff, 1982).

Second, verification might be achieved more passively. If the therapist is simply careful to not disconfirm clients' self–other expectations, provide highly discrepant self-related feedback, or behave in a starkly noncomplementary manner, clients' security operations might do the rest; in other words, clients might interpret, or distort, more neutral feedback or behavior in a way that conforms to their self–other schemas and expectations (Sullivan, 1953).

Also, therapists will often have no choice but to verify their clients' self–other schemas and expectations. People are experts at achieving felt security by behaving in ways that pull for confirmation of their self–other conceptions (Leary, 1957). The power of such pulls in a psychotherapy context will inevitably hook the therapist into expected patterns of behavior. For example, a charming yet highly dependent client might pull for a therapist to do much more work than is typical. Of course, it will ultimately be important for this clinician to recognize this maladaptive reinforcing behavior to disembed from it as treatment progresses. However, in this early phase, "getting hooked may be necessary for the establishment of the working alliance . . . the client needs to experience some level of acceptance and endorsement of his or her self-presentation by the therapist as a prerequisite for alliance formation (Kiesler, 1996)" (Bernier & Dozier, 2002, p. 35).

Phase 3: Middle Treatment

The priority in this phase is to begin to challenge and to disengage from clients' self–other expectations; that is, to foster experiences that disconfirm or violate clients' expectations (Cashdan, 1988). Cognitively, this disconfirmation could be manifested as a gentle challenge to a client's self-view by presenting unexpected, nonverifying feedback. For example, to a client who has persistently experienced others as treating him as a failure, a therapist might say,

> You strike me as someone who has accomplished a lot in spite of your difficult past. Although it is always a risk to put yourself out there, I have faith that you would be very competitive in applying for these jobs.

This provision of expectancy-inconsistent information is potentially corrective because it comes from a therapist who has built credibility; fostered a favorable therapeutic relationship; and represents a new, antidotal significant other to the client. In this case, a type of cognitive "beneficial uncertainty" (Young & Beier, 1982, p. 264) has been created that might help a client revise his or her own self-beliefs, self-talk, and recapitulations (expected behavior of others based on important others from the past); that is, a CE. Thus, revised recapitulations (based on experience with a novel significant other in the clinician) can be corrective in and of themselves (revisions of self–other scripts) and in addition can provide a necessary mechanism to get to another form of CE (i.e., revision of self-concept as a function of new self–other scripts and exchanges).

Interpersonally and affectively, the clinician thus disengages from being hooked. So as not to overwhelm the client (thereby creating unmanageable anxiety and potential disengagement), the first level of unhooking should involve the provision of an *acomplementary*, or *asocial*, response (i.e., stop doing what is confirming the maladaptive pattern). Some have argued that the primary asocial response in psychotherapy is to metacommunicate (Hill & Knox, 2009; Kiesler, 1996; Young & Beier, 1982), a process in which the clinician speaks openly and directly to the client about their unfolding transactional exchanges and the impact that the therapist is experiencing. Such process commentary is inherently acomplementary in that it is far from the norm for people to speak directly to each other about their relationship dynamics and feelings. This atypical behavior can be another vehicle to creating a type of beneficial uncertainly in the client's expected self–other relationships. Drawing on the earlier example of the dominant, critical client to whom the clinician initially deferred, the clinician in this phase (in response to the client's ongoing challenge to her competence) might disclose, "I often find myself worrying before our meetings. I think it's because I feel there is a good chance that I will feel bullied by you. I wonder what it's like for you to hear me say that?" This process commentary, drawn from an actual case, promoted an important discussion of the client's core theme of wanting intimacy but being afraid of it and thus being hostile.

Furthermore, by not providing the expected complementary response of hostile–submissiveness (to the client's hostile–dominance), the clinician provided a new interpersonal and affective experience to the client (i.e., rather than becoming frustrated and leaving as others have, the therapist was willing to stick with it and talk about it). Acomplementary responses are often corrective in and of themselves. In addition, in some circumstances, they are an intermediate step to CEs, with the correctiveness stemming from the following *anticomplementary* responses.

Anticomplementary responses involve doing the opposite of the initial complementary interaction (Benjamin, 2003; Kiesler, 1996). Drawing again on the previous example of the hostile–dominant client, an anticomplementary response would involve doing the opposite of the typical complement of hostile–submissiveness, that is, friendly autonomy-taking. For example, the therapist might disclose warmly,

> As you were questioning my ability to help, I found myself connecting with how difficult it must be for you when others do not fully appreciate your feelings and needs. With that powerful connection, I felt closer to you than I have at any point in our work . . . like I really want to get to that point of full appreciation and understanding.

In this exchange, the therapist is affiliative (vs. hostile) while also taking more of the lead in the exchange (vs. simply accepting the client's dominance). Furthermore, in both content and process, the therapist is attempting to foster unexpected intimacy and prizing of the client. Again, although threatening, such expectancy-disconfirming behavior and feedback can be interpersonally and emotionally corrective under conditions of beneficial uncertainty (i.e., coming from a therapist who has built credibility, fostered a therapeutic alliance, and represents a new significant other to the client). It is important to note that neither acomplementary nor anticomplementary responses or feedback are single interventions or isolated moments. Rather, these are evolving processes that require psychotherapist attunement, responsiveness, and involvement—what Sullivan (1953) referred to as *participant observation*.

Such participant observation is central in this approach to facilitating CEs in that with any level of threat comes anxiety. Thus, in delivering expectancy-challenging interventions, the clinician needs to tread lightly (Pinel & Constantino, 2003; Sullivan, 1953)—the third therapist skill highlighted in this approach. Furthermore, therapists need to be responsive and flexible in balancing complementary and acomplementary or anticomplementary exchanges. As Bernier and Dozier (2002) noted,

> It appears that harmonious and gentle switches between complementary and noncomplementary exchanges over the course of treatment may maximize therapeutic gains, presumably by providing . . . a safe and confirming environment along with appropriate challenges likely to induce change and growth. (p. 36)

In our approach, the safety comes from complementary exchanges providing a verifying function, whereas the noncomplementary exchanges provide a gradual change function. With balance in these processes across time, clients' anxiety level will be challenged but also manageable as they engage in experiential relearning of interpersonal exchange, incorporate novel and previously unexpected information about self, and revise self- and other-related emotion schemes (the three types of expectancy revision that we described as being at the heart of CEs).

As clients will often have ambivalence around novelty and change, it is important for therapists to be of aware of potential moments of extreme self-dissonance and/or relational tension because of too much self–other expectancy-disconfirmation at the expense of the client feeling verified, validated, and grounded. Thus, any emergent alliance ruptures need to be attended to, with perhaps metacommunication as a promising strategy (Safran & Muran, 2000). Not only does this strategy address ruptures directly but also acomplementarity holds the promise of being neither too reinforcing of old maladaptive patterns nor too challenging with starkly opposite behaviors or feedback. In other words, metacommunication might be a vehicle through which treading lightly is achieved in the psychotherapy process.

In this third phase, disrupted relational, cognitive, and affective patterns are CEs; that is, transformative experiences that help people revise their working models of self and other based on the manageable receipt of unexpected reactions or feedback from a newly important other (the therapist). Interestingly, so too might be the treading lightly via metacommunication and balancing of acceptance–consistency and change–novelty. The very process of understanding, appreciating, and responding to an individual's competing self-strivings can be powerfully corrective, as prior important relationships may have been devoid of these adaptive processes. Elaborating on what is corrected, our approach suggests that it is both recapitulations (i.e., expected reactions and dynamics of others) and self-conceptions (with revised recapitulations as a precondition for self-concept change). Self-concept change meets the spirit of introjection—treating oneself as important others have treated you (Sullivan, 1953). To the extent that the therapist becomes important to the client and engages in the three primary skills (i.e., alliance development and negotiation, disconfirmation of the client's restricted self, treading lightly in the course of change), the client can begin to treat himself or herself in a healthier manner (i.e., letting go of fantasy residues of early attachments and responding more accurately in the present to both self and others; Benjamin, 2003). As we mentioned previously, these psychotherapist skills and conditions are what we view as corrective (or what facilitate CEs) in this approach.

Phase 4: Late Treatment

With revised interpersonal expectations and introjections, the goal of the final phase involves the confirmation, or reinforcement, of new expectations. Using similar social psychological principles, the therapist can verify and complement the more adaptive and positive self-views that the client is trying on to help foster greater self-certainty (i.e., the conviction with which the client believes that these new self-conceptions truly reflect who he or she is). With these revised positive self-conceptions and expected self–other behavior, clients' positivity and self-verification strivings would no longer be at odds (at least not to as salient of a degree). Such harmony between what were likely competing motives at the start of therapy would likely be reflected in less anxiety and change ambivalence in the client, as well as less alliance tension in the therapy relationship and revised interpersonal scripts in relationships outside of therapy. These changes would all be markers for the client's termination readiness.

CONSEQUENCES OF CORRECTIVE EXPERIENCES

According to our treatment approach and perspective, there are multiple, equally important psychological consequences of CEs. First, clients probably adopt a wider array of relationship definitions and behaviors (i.e., a broader script with less rigid self–other expectations). Second, clients improve, we hope, their ability to receive and to initiate a range of relationship bids without experiencing significant threat to self. Third, clients often develop new, more adaptive cognitive and emotion schemes, and emotion-based narratives. Finally, clients might develop a wider array of self-definitions and behaviors (i.e., broader intrapsychic schemas or introjections).

EMPIRICAL SUPPORT

Presently, there is some research to support the general efficacy of the individual phases of the above model. For example, relative to Phase 1, there is preliminary evidence for the efficacy of augmenting cognitive therapy (CT) for depression with first session outcome expectancy-enhancement (EE) strategies (Constantino, Klein, Smith-Hansen, & Greenberg, 2009). In this 16-session pilot study, CT + EE clients reported less early treatment hopelessness and less early treatment depression than CT-only clients. However, this study did not directly test the influence of EE interventions on the actual CE process. According to our approach, fostering positive expectations should be foundational in our CE process in that it promotes client engagement by meeting positivity needs while avoiding threat to self. Thus, future empirical work should focus on engagement measures (e.g., attendance beyond Session 1) as dependent variables both with quantitative methods (e.g., trials testing the aforementioned EE module) or qualitative methods (e.g., interviewing therapists and clients immediately following the first session, perhaps while watching the video, to determine critical moments that facilitated the client's desire to return to the next session). Furthermore, to the extent that open-ended questions can elicit clients' recollections of CEs (see Chapter 10, this volume), it would be interesting to see whether clients recall the therapist's fostering of outcome expectations or provision of validation and autonomy granting as aspects of what was corrective for them.

Relative to Phase 2, Constantino et al. (2005) found that similarity between client-perceived therapist behavior and client self-directed behavior (introject) early in treatment was positively associated with early alliance quality in cognitive behavior therapy for generalized anxiety disorder. Further, some findings point to the importance of providing veridical assessment feedback for alliance development (e.g., Ackerman et al., 2000). Ackerman et al. (2000) argued that the relational benefits of such veridical feedback might be the result of greater responsiveness to clients' self-verification needs. Again, it will be important for future research to examine more directly the influence of therapists' verification of their clients' self-concepts and self-directed behaviors on the CE process that we have outlined in this chapter. As Phase 2 is largely foundational in creating a favorable condition for subsequent challenging of and disengagement from clients' self–other expectations, it would be interesting to see whether clients recalled the importance of this foundational process in qualitative analyses of recalled CEs. Process coding would also allow for correlating the frequency or quality of therapist verifying exchanges, or both, with model-relevant outcomes, such as perceptions of therapist credibility.

Regarding Phase 3, numerous studies support the clinical value of high–low–high complementarity patterns across treatment (e.g., Tracey & Ray, 1984). Furthermore, several studies point to the value of using metacommunication. For example, brief relational therapy, which is centered on using metacommunication to address alliance ruptures, had lower dropout rates than short-term psychodynamic and cognitive behavior therapies (Muran, Safran, Samstag, & Winston, 2005). Drawing on similar principles for addressing emerging alliance ruptures, Castonguay et al. (2004) developed an integrative CT for depression. Promising preliminary support for this treatment's efficacy has been demonstrated in comparison to a waiting-list control (Castonguay et al., 2004) and to standard CT (Constantino et al., 2008). Future research could more directly examine the contribution of the expectancy-disconfirming strategies (e.g., observer coded) that characterize Phase 3 by comparing their ability to differentiate clients who demonstrate significant revisions of their self–other expectations or actual self–other behavior (as per self, other, and/or observer reports of such revisions) from those who do not. A similar research design could examine whether the Phase 3 strategies differentiate clients who report significant changes in their self-concept from those who do not.

Finally, with respect to Phase 4, fine-grained analyses of client–therapist process indicate that a greater proportion of positive complementarity differentiates good from poor outcome cases (e.g., Henry, Schacht, & Strupp, 1986). Of course, it will be important to test whether confirming, or reinforcing, clients' new and adaptive self-conceptions in the later phase of treatment is directly related to, or recalled as an important process in, CEs. And, in addition to further research extending these phase-based findings, it will be important to test the entire approach. Task analysis (see L. S. Greenberg, 2007) might be particularly well suited for further developing, refining, and testing the theoretical model behind the four treatment phases. Such research would prove useful in enhancing understanding of how expectation confirmation and disconfirmation underlie CEs in psychotherapy.

CONCLUSION

The proposed integrative psychotherapy approach privileges various client expectations as an explanatory construct for CEs in psychotherapy. The approach draws heavily on the social psychological and interpersonal principles of positivity, verification, social influence, complementarity, and meta-communication. It suggests that through an evolving sequence of three primary therapist skills that are corrective (i.e., alliance development and negotiation, disconfirmation of the client's restricted self, treading lightly in the course of change), clients will have one or more of three novel and unexpected experiences (i.e., experiential relearning of interpersonal exchange, incorporation of novel and previously unexpected information about self, and revision of self- and other-related emotion schemes). Through the interaction of the therapist's corrective skills and the client's new experiences, the client will develop new and more adaptive recapitulations and introjections (i.e., this is what gets corrected). Although the specific components of our approach are not completely novel conceptions, the approach's focus on expectancy and expectancy change as a unifying thread and proposed pantheoretical mechanism of CEs is novel.

REFERENCES

Ackerman, S. J., Hilsenroth, M. J., Baity, M. R., & Blagys, M. D. (2000). Interaction of therapeutic process and alliance during psychological assessment. *Journal of Personality Assessment, 75,* 82–109. doi:10.1207/S15327752JPA7501_7

Ahmed, M., & Westra, H. A. (2008, September). *Impact of counselor warmth on attitudes toward seeking mental health services.* Paper presented at the meeting of the North American Chapter of the Society for Psychotherapy Research, New Haven, CT.

Ahmed, M., Westra, H. A., & Constantino, M. J. (2010, June). *Interpersonal process during resistance in CBT associated with high vs. low client outcome expectations: A micro-process analysis.* Paper presented at the 41st Society for Psychotherapy Research International Meeting, Asilomar, CA.

Alexander, F., & French, T. M. (1946). *Psychoanalytic therapy: Principles and application.* New York, NY: Ronald Press.

Baumeister, R. F. (1999). The self. In D. T. Gilbert, S. T. Fiske, & G. Lindzey (Eds.), *The handbook of social psychology* (4th ed., Vol. 1, pp. 680–740). New York, NY: Oxford University Press.

Beitman, B. D., Soth, A. M., & Bumby, N. A. (2005). The future as an integrating force through the schools of psychotherapy. In J. C. Norcross & M. R. Goldfried (Eds.), *Handbook of psychotherapy integration* (2nd ed., pp. 65–89). New York, NY: Oxford University Press.

Benjamin, L. S. (2003). *Interpersonal reconstructive therapy: An integrative personality-based treatment for complex cases*. New York, NY: Guilford Press.

Bernier, A., & Dozier, M. (2002). The client–counselor match and the corrective emotional experience: Evidence from interpersonal and attachment research. *Psychotherapy: Theory, Research, & Practice, 39*, 32–43. doi:10.1037/0033-3204.39.1.32

Bowlby, J. (1988). *A secure base: Parent–child attachment and healthy human development*. New York, NY: Basic Books.

Cashdan, S. (1988). *Object relations therapy: Using the relationship*. New York, NY: Norton.

Castonguay, L. G., Schut, A. J., Aikins, D., Constantino, M. J., Laurenceau, J. P., Bologh, L., & Burns, D. D. (2004). Repairing alliance ruptures in cognitive therapy: A preliminary investigation of an integrative therapy for depression. *Journal of Psychotherapy Integration, 14*, 4–20. doi:10.1037/1053-0479.14.1.4

Constantino, M. J., Castonguay, L. G., Angtuaco, L. A., Pincus, A. L., Newman, M. G., & Borkovec, T. D. (2005, June). *The impact of interpersonal–intrapsychic complementarity on the development and course of the therapeutic alliance*. Paper presented at the 36th Annual Meeting of the Society for Psychotherapy Research, Montreal, Quebec, Canada.

Constantino, M. J., Glass, C. R., Arnkoff, D. B., Ametrano, R. M., & Smith, J. Z. (2011). Expectations. In J. C. Norcross (Ed.), *Psychotherapy relationships that work: Therapist contributions and responsiveness to patients* (2nd ed., pp. 354–376). New York, NY: Oxford University Press.

Constantino, M. J., Klein, R., Smith-Hansen, L., & Greenberg, R. (2009, October). *Augmenting cognitive therapy for depression with an expectancy enhancement module: Preliminary efficacy*. Paper presented at the meeting of the Canadian Chapter of the Society for Psychotherapy Research, Montreal, Quebec, Canada.

Constantino, M. J., Marnell, M., Haile, A. J., Kanther-Sista, S. N., Wolman, K., Zappert, L., & Arnow, B. A. (2008). Integrative cognitive therapy for depression: A randomized pilot comparison. *Psychotherapy: Theory, Research, & Practice, 45*, 122–134. doi:10.1037/0033-3204.45.2.122

Festinger, L. (1957). *A theory of cognitive dissonance*. Evanston, IL: Row, Peterson.

Foa, E. B., & Kozak, M. (1986). Emotional processing of fear: Exposure to corrective information. *Psychological Bulletin, 99*, 20–35. doi:10.1037/0033-2909.99.1.20

Frank, J. D. (1961). *Persuasion and healing: A comparative study of psychotherapy*. Baltimore, MD: Johns Hopkins Press.

Freud, S. (1953). The dynamics of transference. *Standard Edition, 12*, 97–108. London, England: Hogarth Press. (Original work published 1953)

Glass, C. R., & Arnkoff, D. B. (1982). Think cognitively: Selected issues in cognitive assessment and therapy. In P. C. Kendall (Ed.), *Advances in cognitive–behavioral research and therapy* (Vol. 1, pp. 35–71). New York, NY: Academic Press.

Greenberg, L. S. (2007). A guide to conducting a task analysis of psychotherapeutic change. *Psychotherapy Research, 17*, 15–30. doi:10.1080/10503300600720390

Greenberg, L. S., & Paivio, S. (1997). *Working with emotions in psychotherapy.* New York, NY: Guilford Press.

Greenberg, L. S., Rice, L. N., & Elliott, R. (1993). *Facilitating emotional change: The moment-by-moment process.* New York, NY: Guilford Press.

Greenberg, R. P., Constantino, M. J., & Bruce, N. (2006). Are expectations still relevant for psychotherapy process and outcome? *Clinical Psychology Review, 26,* 657–678. doi:10.1016/j.cpr.2005.03.002

Henry, W. P., Schacht, T. E., & Strupp, H. H. (1986). Structural analysis of social behavior: Application to a study of interpersonal process in differential psychotherapeutic outcome. *Journal of Consulting and Clinical Psychology, 54,* 27–31. doi:10.1037/0022-006X.54.1.27

Hill, C. E., & Knox, S. (2009). Processing the therapeutic relationship. *Psychotherapy Research, 19,* 13–29. doi:10.1080/10503300802621206

Kiesler, D. J. (1996). *Contemporary interpersonal theory and research: Personality, psychopathology, and psychotherapy.* New York, NY: Wiley.

Leary, T. (1957). *Interpersonal diagnosis of personality: A functional theory and methodology for personality evaluation.* New York, NY: Ronald Press.

Muran, J. C., Safran, J. D., Samstag, L. W., & Winston, A. (2005). Evaluating an alliance-focused treatment for personality disorders. *Psychotherapy, 42,* 532–545. doi:10.1037/0033-3204.42.4.532

Pinel, E. C., & Constantino, M. J. (2003). Putting self psychology to good use: When social psychologists and clinical psychologists unite. *Journal of Psychotherapy Integration, 13,* 9–32. doi:10.1037/1053-0479.13.1.9

Safran, J. D., & Muran, J. C. (2000). *Negotiating the therapeutic alliance: A relational treatment guide.* New York, NY: Guilford Press.

Shrauger, J. S. (1975). Responses to evaluation as a function of initial self-perceptions. *Psychological Bulletin, 82,* 581–596. doi:10.1037/h0076791

Strong, S. R., & Claiborn, C. D. (1982). *Change through interaction: Social psychological processes of counseling and psychotherapy.* New York, NY: Wiley.

Sullivan, H. S. (1953). *The interpersonal theory of psychiatry.* New York, NY: Norton.

Swann, W. B., Jr. (1996). *Self-traps: The elusive quest for higher self-esteem.* New York, NY: Freeman.

Tracey, T. J., & Ray, P. B. (1984). Stages of successful time-limited counseling: An interactional examination. *Journal of Counseling Psychology, 31,* 13–27. doi:10.1037/0022-0167.31.1.13

Walitzer, K. S., Dermen, K. H., & Conners, G. J. (1999). Strategies for preparing clients for treatment: A review. *Behavior Modification, 23,* 129–151. doi:10.1177/0145445599231006

Weiss, J., & Sampson, H. (1986). *The psychoanalytic process: Theory, clinical observations, and empirical research*. New York, NY: Guilford Press.

Westra, H. A., Aviram, A., Barnes, M., & Angus, L. (2010). Therapy was not what I expected: A preliminary analysis of concordance between client expectations and experience of cognitive-behavioural therapy. *Psychotherapy Research, 20,* 436–446. doi:10.1080/10503301003657395

Young, D. M., & Beier, E. G. (1982). Being asocial in social places: Giving the client a new experience. In J. C. Anchin & D. J. Kiesler (Eds.), *Handbook of interpersonal psychotherapy* (pp. 262–273). Elmsford, NY: Pergamon.

9

CORRECTIVE EXPERIENCES: WHAT CAN WE LEARN FROM DIFFERENT MODELS AND RESEARCH IN BASIC PSYCHOLOGY?

FRANZ CASPAR AND THOMAS BERGER

In this book, corrective experiences (CEs) are discussed from the perspective of several approaches to psychotherapy. This chapter does not rely on a specific psychotherapeutic approach but rather endeavors to use general psychological models to shed light on processes underlying CEs. Arguably, professional psychotherapy not only should demonstrate its effectiveness but also should be based on scientifically sound concepts. When phenomena such as CEs are discussed, considerable benefit might be gained from looking into basic domains of psychology and neighboring fields for useful concepts and empirical findings.

BEYOND TRADITIONAL MODELS OF COGNITIVE–EMOTIONAL FUNCTIONING

Several well-known constructs (e.g., schemata, scripts, plans) have emerged from traditional—information processing—cognitive models. As illustrated in this book (see, e.g., Chapter 2), some of these constructs have been integrated in the conceptual framework of major psychotherapy approaches. These constructs are relatively easy to grasp (e.g., Caspar, 2007). However, they also have limits when it comes to understanding complex phenomena. In this chapter, we discuss concepts associated with newer models of cognitive science (i.e., connectionist and self-regulation models; interested readers can find some of these models described in greater detail in Caspar & Berger's, 2007, work on insight).

Connectionist Models

Although neural network, or connectionist, models experienced a revival about 20 years ago, our experience is that only a few therapists are familiar with them. We therefore give a very brief introduction to these models, referring those who wish to read more about them to Caspar (1998); Caspar and Berger (2007); and Caspar, Rothenfluh, and Segal (1992). By referring to connectionist models as a family, we emphasize that there are several models sharing some, but not all, elements and properties. Although the terms *neural network models* and *connectionist models* are somewhat interchangeable, we prefer the latter term, as it refers to an important property of these models (the connectivity between nodes, see below) while not presupposing that the models correspond to the functioning of human neuronal systems. Such a correspondence seems plausible, yet it is, strictly speaking, something that remains to be demonstrated systematically. The connectionist models can be formulated precisely by mathematical formula, but in this chapter, we ask readers to understand them more as metaphors for what happens in the brain (Caspar et al., 1992; Smolensky, 1986).

Most connectionist networks share three main properties: First, they are *subsymbolic*, in that their basic units (nodes) do not represent things or facts as they are labelled in everyday language. Subsymbolic means that no single unit in a processing network is a symbol for a thing or a concept. Rather, knowledge is distributed among interconnections of nodes. For example, a dog, or the pain feared from its bite, is not represented by one node but by a more complex network of nodes. When a person's dog phobia decreases, it is not that single nodes (for dog, pain, avoidance behavior, a conflicting macho view of oneself, etc.) change but rather that the whole network of small nodes changes. Traditionally, it is easier to think of something that needs to be changed by some changing agency (critics also speak of a homunculus). However, the second property of typical connectionist networks is that the structures themselves change, and thus there is no distinction between the changing agent and changed content. Rather, structures develop and change by modifying the connections between the nodes of which they consist. Connectionist scholars refer to information processing as a process of spreading activation that can take place simultaneously across partial structures and in parallel, that is, simultaneously in the whole network.

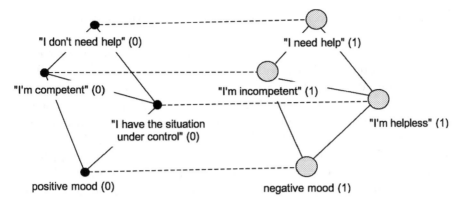

Figure 9.1. Competing patterns of competence versus incompetence with patients with borderline personality disorder.

The third guiding principle of connectionist models is that they are driven by the principle of minimizing tension. Tension is built up when connections between simultaneously activated nodes are negative (e.g., in Figure 9.1 between "I have the situation under control" and "I'm helpless"). Tension is low when, in the case of positive connections, all the activated elements are consistent or, in the case of negative connections, one element is activated and the other (inconsistent or opposite) is deactivated.

There is a tendency for patterns of positively connected nodes to be simultaneously activated (e.g., memories of situations in which one has performed well are triggered when positive self-esteem is activated) and for negatively connected nodes and patterns to be deactivated (e.g., memories of when one has failed are suppressed when positive self-esteem is activated). The entire network representing an individual's functioning includes connections of various degrees of tension. The sum of all individual tensions between single nodes results in a total tension of the entire network. Over time, a network will change (e.g., self-esteem can vary, and so do the patterns of connections associated with a feeling of self-esteem). The probability that a network will get and remain in a specific state, however, is higher for states that are relatively low in tension (in comparison with states that are higher in tension). This tendency to settle in states with relatively low tension can be brought about in several ways, the most relevant in our context being that large patterns of consistent elements dominate a network for some time while suppressing (deactivating) competing patterns (e.g., when self-esteem is high, memories of failures are suppressed). The simultaneous activation of competing patterns (holding elements with negative connections between each other) would increase the overall tension and is thus avoided. This kind of information processing and regulation is designated as *self-organized*, which means that no conscious control or representation is needed.

Needless to say, the properties described here can appear rather abstract, in part because connectionist networks operate at a subsymbolic level. Figure 9.1 is an attempt to illustrate how connectionist networks can symbolically reflect the activation of meaningful contents. Depicted in Figure 9.1 are two networks of nodes, each involving a pattern of cognitive and emotional elements that fit together well within, but not between, the patterns. On the left is the currently deactivated *competent* pattern; on the right is the currently activated *incompetent* pattern. These two patterns are not likely to be activated at the same time, as this would lead to a high level of tension between the negatively connected elements (which is indicated in the figure by the dashed lines). However, these incompatible patterns can be activated alternatively, with a person oscillating between a pattern of competence and a pattern of incompetence. Such a process of oscillation is frequently encountered in therapy, when clients are sometimes dominated by maladaptive experiences and at other times by positive (including corrective) experiences.

Connectionist models can also provide a metaphor (called *tension landscape*, see Figure 9.2) representing how clients are likely to stay in, move out, or return to different states. When there is minimum tension, the system (client) is described as being at the point of *global minimum* (the absolutely deepest point in Figure 9.2). This ideal state is hardly ever reached, as most systems experience some states of incompatibility between patterns of expe-

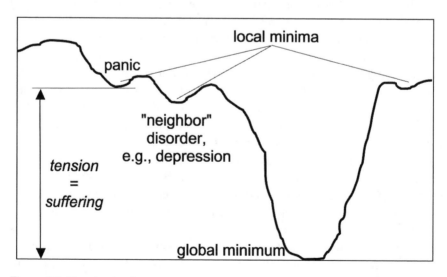

Figure 9.2. Tension landscape.

rience. The most typical relatively stable states are called *local minima*, or states in which the tension of one state (altitude in Figure 9.2) is relatively low in comparison with those of neighboring states. As a consequence, the local minimum cannot be escaped from without an increase in tension (i.e., "climbing over a height").

Local minima represent states in which many elements, such as cognitions, emotions, behavior, biological states, and the environment, fit together well. For example, depression is a state in which many maladaptive elements fit together. For example, if a therapist tries to introduce positive cognitions by saying, "You seem to have a lot of things going for you: You are smart, well-educated, and have a lot of professional experience," the patient who is depressed may respond through the lens of his or her depression, with something along the lines of, "Yes, but I have not accomplished much of any value with all I have!" The attempt to introduce a seemingly positive element resulted in an increase of tension that was immediately "repaired" (compensated for) by the patient. Within the context of the landscape metaphor, the therapist has attempted to help the patient to climb a hill, but the patient experienced a tension increase and then rolled back to the initial position. In this example, as with many other instances in clinical work, the therapist interventions hold the potential for being corrective but are either not strong enough or are counteracted, so that (at best) only some momentary, but no lasting, change results.

As suggested in the previous example, change is most typically triggered by new input. Inconsistencies in the system, caused partly by internal tension but largely by new input, are the driving force for change. As can easily be understood by the landscape metaphor and modeled more precisely using mathematical formula, it is easier to bring about change in a flat landscape than in one with steep hills and valleys. In connectionist or neural network simulations, the steepness of the landscape is influenced by neuromodulators (e.g., dopamine, noradrenaline), motivational or emotional variables (e.g., goals, wishes, needs), and emotional arousal. Thus, the more dopamine or noradrenaline, the steeper the valleys and the harder to bring about change. On the other hand, it would be maladaptive for a system to oscillate between states all the time, as illustrated on a clinical level by patients with borderline personality disorder, who often alternate between seeking and repelling close relationships. So it is easy to see that the interplay between openness to change (flattening) and return to stability (steepening) is crucial. Remaining at the metaphorical level, drawings such as Figure 9.2 can be used in therapy to communicate with clients. In our experience, most of them understand easily and intuitively why it is that they experience an increase in tension when therapists attempt to change painful, but established, behavioral patterns in therapy. One can discuss with them what it would mean to facilitate change by filling up valleys (e.g., by removing reinforcement associated with their disorder, such as lenience and attention), by leveling off peaks (e.g., by disputing how difficult a much-dreaded change will actually be), or (reflecting the real Swiss landscape) by digging tunnels (e.g., by creatively circumventing difficulties).

On the basis of the brief description of the basic foundations of the a connectionist model, the following implications can be derived with regard to the process of change in general and CEs in particular:

- The representation in whole patterns of subsymbolic nodes, instead of single, meaningful nodes, means that old patterns can easily be restored, even if some elements in the network have been changed. This accounts for the longevity and the resistance of strong, established patterns.
- Related to the previous point, existing patterns strongly influence whether an input becomes an experience that changes the existing structure and whether such a change lasts.
- Therapeutic strategies that foster continuous input over extended time or deal with a strong one-time input over extended time have a higher chance of bringing about CEs with lasting effects than one or a few therapeutic interventions that stick out in bringing about change. For example, the long-term, stable, reliable therapeutic relationship, which can by definition not unfold its impact within a very time-limited situation, is at least as important as specific techniques (assuming that the impact of techniques and relationship can be separated at all).
- Even if at times one factor seems to strongly determine how a system functions, it is typical that many factors are actually involved. Interaction of therapeutic variables is more typical than main effects. As a consequence, a patient cannot normally tell how a change came about, or at least is only partially accurate.
- The interconnectedness with the environment can lead to new input that stimulates change but also to stability and rigidity that could hardly be found with an isolated person.
- The effectiveness of therapeutic interventions may depend on their impact at one or several points in the existing networks. Side effects of interventions (e.g., side effects of therapeutic techniques on the therapy relationship) may be crucial in increasing or decreasing the chances of experiences to occur and have a lasting corrective effect.

- The current state also strongly influences whether and how an experience occurs and whether it can have a lasting effect. It may be advantageous, or even necessary, to first concentrate on bringing the patient into a favorable learning state, such as working on his or her motivational or emotional state before engaging with the content of a desired CE. Strong experiences may be needed or useful to not only feed in new information but also to "heat up the system" sufficiently.
- The therapist and patient have limited influence on how change occurs. They can change probabilities, but there is still a largely autonomous system.
- The metaphor of local minima may help to understand why it may be difficult for change to occur in a more steady, continuous way and why a strong and/or coordinated impact may be needed to bring about discontinuous change.

Combined Regulation Models

Typical traditional concepts, such as schemata and plans, can to some extent be simulated within connectionist models. One might therefore argue that connectionist models are more advanced and comprehensive approaches, although they are somewhat more difficult to understand for theoretical and practical reasons (e.g., how to represent subsymbolic nodes). One might also argue that one should use the most simple available models for explaining clinical phenomena. Similarly, in physics, Newtonian models are incorrect from a quantum physics perspective, but they are still sufficient and more practical for modeling the flight of a baseball. It is the very coordination of more traditionally functioning and self-organized (connectionist) functioning parts of the entire regulation system, however, that holds the key for understanding some phenomena relevant to CE. Combined regulation models provide theoretical avenues for such a needed coordination.

For illustration purposes, we briefly discuss the case of a patient who has marital problems based on his jealousy of his 1-year-old son. He knows that a new child is a challenge for a couple, but he also knows (intellectually) that there is space for two in his wife's heart. His childhood was characterized by a stiff competition with his younger brother for his parents' attention. His childhood experience was that there was only space for one. As their marital counselor conveyed to the couple, the client's perceived competition with his child provided him with the opportunity for a CE. Even though the client recognized that he longed for such an experience, he behaved in a highly maladaptive way (e.g., withdrawing and not talking to his wife for days) whenever he thought he was not getting enough attention. Although he was able to see that his behavior was maladaptive, he felt blocked and was unable to fix the problem. From an outside perspective, he functioned well in his rational, traditional regulation when he was calm. The problem was that his jealousy seemed to be regulated in a self-organized, maladaptive way that was out of his conscious control.

This kind of situation, experience, and behavior is well explained by the regulation model developed by Carver and Scheier (2002), specifically because it combines both traditional goal-directed and self-organized (typical connectionist) functioning (see Figure 9.3). The traditional part of the self-regulation (not to be confounded with self-organization, as described below) or feedback control model holds that human behavior is determined by goals. At the core of this view is a discrepancy-reducing feedback loop in which an input value (a perception) and a reference value (or goal) are compared in a comparison function. The output function (or behavior) is then adjusted so that the individual moves (at least in his or her perception) closer to his or her reference value or goal. From the perspective of this model, the client in the above example was driven by a goal of getting attention from his wife. The rational side says that there is enough attention, and even if not, he will (output function) do something reasonable to get more attention from his wife (e.g., finding a babysitter and going out with his wife for an undisturbed evening), which would have a good impact on his environment (wife), and which in turn would lead to a positive input (wife behaving nicely and attentively toward him), which should, in theory, lead him to conclude that everything is okay. In reality, however, a second, self-organized part (in

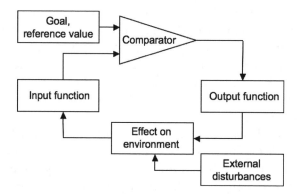

Figure 9.3. Feedback loop. Goals correspond to desired states, which are compared by the comparator as reference values against the (perceived) actual state. The output function means behavior serving the purpose of bringing the environment (or internal states, or both) into better correspondence to one's goals if the comparator finds a discrepancy. The process is made more difficult by disturbances in the external world.

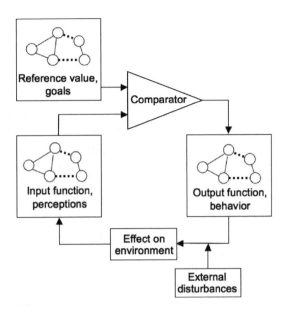

Figure 9.4. Self-organization within a feedback loop. Traditional, consciously functioning elements in the output function, input function, and goals are replaced by self-organized processes.

our case the client's jealous state) also plays a role. According to Carver and Scheier, every element in the regulation model in Figure 9.3 can be filled or replaced by self-organized processes, as illustrated in Figure 9.4.

In most life situations, the replacement of a goal-directed regulation by a self-organized one is adaptive. Based on previous training of people's information processing networks throughout life, a self-organized regulation helps them pursue and observe more goals, produce more behavior, and process more input than they could through using deliberate, conscious functioning. However, although often adaptive, such self-organized processes can also sometimes be maladaptive. A harmless example is when one of the authors poured salt into coffee while engaging in conversation. His attention (traditional control) was on trying to convince another person about a firmly believed-in viewpoint. This conscious attempt absorbed most of his resources, so that pouring sugar into the coffee was delegated to self-organization. Unfortunately, there was salt on the table in little paper bags, similar to those that are frequently used for sugar in different parts of the world. As typical for connectionist self-organized information processing, a partial input (package) was sufficient to activate the whole pattern "sugar for coffee." Such little errors are easily compensated for by the advantage of delegating tasks to self-organized regulation, that is, saving attention and information processing resources, and thus enabling the individual to do many things in parallel.

Needless to say, it is another story when dominating patterns push to rule over the regulation processes in a maladaptive way. In the example of the jealous client, the goal of getting exclusive attention can become overvalued at the expense of other goals, such as maintaining a good, stable relationship with one's wife or being a good father. The comparator function of self-regulation would then almost unavoidably detect a difference between the actual situation and the client's strongest desire. This comparison could then lead to behaviors, which once started, are out of one's control, even if in his conscious, traditional functioning, he may be well aware that he is behaving maladaptively and would like to stop acting that way. Such maladaptive behavior, of course, would make it difficult for his wife to show positive affection. Even if she were to neglect him only in minor ways (while mostly behaving attentively), it is likely that his self-organized perceptions would interpret such minor signs of inattention as confirming that he is neglected.

How can this client gain the CE that there is enough space for two? Not an easy task, even for a cooperative patient and therapist! The more difficult the task, the more important a good understanding of how the system works. For this, appropriate general models have been proposed here, complementing the requirement of a good individual case conceptualization. Referring to Baumeister, Gailliot, De Wall, and Oaten (2006; see below), a resource-oriented mobilization of his strengths, along with increasing awareness and conscious control (e.g., Meichenbaum, 1977; see below), would be important parts of the fight against the self-organized aberrations from what he consciously wants.

The view that this might only be an issue of replacing "exclusive attention" with "enough attention" (as a rational emotive therapist might argue) is likely to fall short of doing justice to the completely different processes underlying the enough attention (corresponding to a traditional functioning) versus the excessive exclusive attention (brought about by self-organized processes against the conscious will of the man). A clinically useful perspective, in our opinion, can be found in Grawe's (2004) concept of conflict schema (see also Chapter 15, this volume). Such a schema (not to be confused with a simple conflict between two or more schemata) combines opposite approach and avoidance components. The approach component cannot be set into action without automatically and unavoidably activating strong negative emotions and compelling avoidance behavior. As is illustrated later in an example derived from control mastery theory, the individual is thus not likely (at least not without the help of external events, such as therapy) to have the CEs that would ultimately occur by following through with the approach behavior. Within the lens of the Carver and Scheier (2002) model, the approach behavior is most likely operating within the paths of traditional regulation, but it is also an activating, self-organized, unconscious control process, automatically leading a counteracting dynamic to ensue. From this perspective, a solution is impossible without gaining control over these self-organized processes, unless one gives up the more adaptive approach behaviors for good, as it is sometimes observed clinically.

To prevent misunderstandings, it is important to mention that Carver and Scheier's (2002) model does not imply that it is always optimal or necessary to move from the self-organized to the more consciously, deliberately controlled processes. Ultimately, the goal is to leave the regulation of goals, behaviors, and perceptions to (a more adaptive) self-organized control. Smooth, effective control within the context of a good harmony across an individual's goals requires the effortless working of self-organized processes. The task of psychotherapy is not only to deautomatize (as Greenberg and Elliott, Chapter 6, this volume (p. 91), put it, "The client thus is encouraged to exert mental effort to . . . interrupt the old maladaptive response") but also to reautomatize (as argued by Goldfried, Chapter 2, this volume, one of the goals of all therapy is to help the client moving from a state of *conscious competence* to one of *unconscious competence*). One way to understand this dual task of therapy is to imagine the difference between a person at a party or in an intimate situation whose behavior is exclusively under deliberate, conscious control, as opposed to another individual who is at least partly smooth and spontaneous as a result of automatization and self-organization.

Although self-regulation models can provide new perspectives about how change of complex clinical situations can be fostered, they can also be helpful in understanding (as described in detail above) how organisms keep particular variables constant. An interesting issue, in fact, is whether the striving of a system for stability also implies a drive toward fighting or warding off CEs. The crucial question when trying to assess whether the striving for stability will work against a CE is, Does the occurrence of a CE mean a short- to medium-term destabilization (tension increase), or rather a reduction of threats to what an individual's feedback-control system tries to achieve (tension reduction)? In other words, Is destabilization by CEs possibly positive, because stable, but maladaptive, structures may not be in line with higher order desired values, thus creating tension that can be reduced?

To address these questions, we use an example (described in the control mastery theory of Weiss, Sampson, & The Mount Zion Research Group, 1986) in which the regulation in the interest of an anxiety-reducing maladaptive pattern is incompatible with a regulation in the interest of growth-related patterns and values. In this example, the professional success of a man is being regulated by his need to keep his guilt feelings below a threshold because he expects that it would be unbearable if he were to outperform his loser father. Success thus means an increase in guilt feelings, which are (automatically and unavoidably, from the perspective of Grawe's, 2004, concept of conflict schema) torpedoed before becoming too threatening. Limiting guilt is one desired value in the patient's functioning. To make things more complicated, there are other values, such as achieving and maintaining good self-esteem or earning sufficient money to provide for his three children. The comparator will thus not be satisfied when only guilt feelings are minimized.

To come back to the two questions above, CEs in this case are likely to lead to both the destabilization of old patterns and to a better satisfaction of other, more recently activated values. Specifically, having the client experience the lack of decompensation of his father from his success (or experiencing that he is able to deal with his father showing distress) will not only destabilize his regulation processes based on guilt but will also likely open new possibilities for the above-mentioned newer values (growth) or help stabilize the patterns serving them.

WHAT FACILITATES CORRECTIVE EXPERIENCES IN THERAPY?

Experiences can be corrective only if the organism learns. In the following section, we try to derive ideas of how this can be brought about, based on the models described so far. We present these views as *perspective models*, the function of which is to provide potentially useful ideas. Foppa (1984) and Bunge (1967) have emphasized the value of such models, arguing that they can be used or built upon even in the absence of the precise and comprehensive support that researchers typically demand from explanatory models.

The most important contribution of regulation models is not the techniques or strategies (or input) that can be used to foster CE as far as their content is concerned, but it is rather about the conditions that increase the probability of states favorable for CEs to take place (one might say, the instrumental conditions for CEs to take place). Generally, we know that a medium level of arousal is favorable for learning. In terms of a connectionist metaphor, high arousal means steeper slopes in the tension landscape and increased difficulty of moving into different states. Some patients are underaroused, either generally or in relation to specific problems, and need problem activation. But most patients are overaroused and need to have help in reducing the arousal.

The most important means for either increasing or reducing arousal is a good therapeutic relationship. Such a relationship is likely to have an impact at cognitive levels (providing confidence), emotional levels (fostering feeling of being sheltered, liked, and accepted), and biological levels (calming down neuromodulators, such as noradrenaline, and hormones, such as oxytocin). One could also argue that resource-activating interventions emphasizing a patient's positive capabilities and potentials (Grawe, 2004) are likely to have a calming effect because they convey that the therapist sees and acknowledges the patient's strengths and positive motives, as opposed to seeing him or her as a bundle of problems. These interventions can also have a calming effect by strengthening the view that there are some problems, but it should be possible for therapists and clients to work together to solve them, given all the available resources.

A second related issue involves presenting the client with a rationale for his or her problem that will help him or her agree with the tasks and goals of therapy. As we mentioned earlier, the tension landscape metaphor can be used with the patient, or for the therapist alone, to develop ideas about how the landscape would have to change to make reaching a different state feasible (e.g., filling up valleys by spoiling advantages of a maladaptive pattern, lowering summits by discussing whether they are actually as high as suspected, and finding ways around or through obstacles, as described above).

A third issue is the strengthening of the approach tendencies, which brings the system into a state in which it is more open, ready to take risks, and prone to change, as opposed to the depressive "trying is the first step to failure" (Homer Simpson). As Schwarz (2001) demonstrated, positive states facilitate productive self-organization in the sense of creative, intuitive processing. This change is related to an increased activity of the prefrontal cortex (Grawe, 2004), which is needed for an individual to become aware of his or her needs, and which in turn facilitates CEs that are in line with actual needs. As pointed out by Greenberg and Elliott in Chapter 6 of this volume, CEs can also involve the experience of new, alternative emotions. From a connectionist point of view, experiencing new emotions strengthens new patterns, which would be incomplete and more at risk of being abolished if the emotional component were lacking. When discussing the strengthening of approach tendencies, Grawe (2004) recommended helping the patient have mastery experiences to bring the brain into an approach mode (for a description of neurobiological determinants of the approach vs. the inhibition system, see Grawe, 2006; Strauman & Wilson, 2010).

A fourth issue related to the conditions necessary for CEs to take place is the control over maladaptive self-organizing processes that interfere with the patient's conscious wants. Among the therapeutic interventions that can facilitate this goal are analysis (the therapist and patient have to understand how processes concretely evolve), metacommunication, and planning of alternative action. Self-observation by the patient, even outside of therapy, may also be necessary to get the relevant information and to allow the patient to experience with more awareness how he or she is pulled into old patterns. If the automatisms are not deeply grounded, they can be interrupted relatively easily. Some people typically turn on the water for no apparent reason and counter to their environmental consciousness while brushing their teeth, but they find it easy to fight this habit and turn off the water as soon as they become aware of it. Self-instruction in the sense of Meichenbaum (1977) seems very suitable to take control, not only over overt behavior but also over internal regulation. In addition, the availability of mindfulness techniques opens a new pathway to accept the existence of automatisms without being controlled by them. Exhaustion may be a possible cause of failure of successful regulation (Baumeister, Gailliot, De Wall, & Oaten, 2006; Vohs & Heatherton, 2000). In such a situation, it may be of primary importance to help the patient do something against excessive fatigue. When the automatisms are more deeply engrained, as in Grawe's (2004) conflict schemata, more stabilization and building up of trust and motivation may be needed to get the patient to the point at which he or she is able to let himself or herself have a CE. In turn, a CE may be an important part of a relearning process.

A fifth issue is that patients often do not notice that a current experience differs objectively from earlier experiences and therefore do not gain corrective information from it. Although connectionist models suggest that much learning takes place without awareness, it is very plausible that learning is more efficient when attention is directed toward the new input. Strategies for greater awareness are available in problem solving or self-instruction approaches (e.g., the explicit interpersonal discrimination exercise in McCullough's [2000] cognitive behavioral analysis system of psychotherapy).

An additional consideration is related to the question of how the system brings about CEs in a dynamic interplay among values, goals, and motives as different as earning money, protecting old sore spots, gaining the affection of one's child, seeking satisfaction of sexual desires, and taking care of one's parents. What enables people to know what is really important in a world of such incommensurable variables? Baumeister, Vohs, DeWall, and Zhang (in press) proposed the signal function of emotion as providing a common currency for comparing within a wide range of things that may occur to or that may be achieved. This perspective underlines the importance of emotions in the process of developing and experiencing CEs.

HOW TO INCREASE THE PROBABILITY THAT CORRECTIVE EXPERIENCES HAVE A LASTING IMPACT

An experience cannot be considered corrective unless the change lasts for some time. Thus, the brain needs to be retrained, which requires a repeated activation of the relevant structures. A wide variety of psychotherapeutic techniques related to this have already been developed, from writing statements describing the new experiences on cards and reading them daily, to behavioral exercises. The latter have a high potential of not only activating whole patterns as opposed to isolated modalities (only behavior, cognition, emotion, etc.) but also evoking and establishing reactions in the environment. Larger change patterns have a higher a priori chance of lasting and of remodeling the brain over extended time than do changes in isolated modalities or elements.

Another issue to consider is that motivations may remain within the patient or his or her environment that are incompatible with the CEs and thus work toward setting the system back to the old state. A traditional view would be to look for instrumental functions of the old state. For example, if a person does not dare believe she is able to achieve something, she would not even try. In therapy, she may be encouraged to consider the possibility that she can achieve more than she thought. The therapeutic relationship may give her enough confidence to try new behaviors, and these positive experiences, along with praise in individual or group therapy, may feel good and help to establish new patterns. After the termination of successful therapy, the client may consider striving toward more difficult achievements, which have a higher risk of failure. This failure may reactivate the low self-esteem and low self-efficacy that lead to devastating failure: Better to not even try than to be confronted with concrete proofs of insufficiency!

FINAL COMMENTS

The goal of this chapter was to demonstrate that basic concepts and findings in cognitive psychology may improve understanding of CEs. Because the implications derived from these models were derived from basic science, they are likely to be relevant to therapists of different orientations. Many crucial questions have not been addressed in this chapter (e.g., Are there successful therapies that have no CEs? Is conscious understanding a necessary ingredient for CEs?). However, we hope to have contributed to the development of concepts and interpretation of clinical phenomena by facilitating access to some contributions from basic science that seem to have some applicability to CEs.

REFERENCES

Baumeister, R. F., Gailliot, M., De Wall, C. N., & Oaten, M. (2006). Self-regulation and personality: How interventions increase regulatory success, and how depletion moderates the effects of traits on behavior. *Journal of Personality, 74,* 1773–1801. doi:10.1111/j.1467-6494.2006.00428.x

Baumeister, R. F., Vohs, K. D., DeWall, C. N., & Zhang, L. (in press). How emotion shapes behavior: Feedback, anticipation, and reflection, rather than direct causation. *Personality and Social Psychology Review*.

Bunge, M. (1967). *Scientific research: Vol. 2. The search for truth*. New York, NY: Springer.

Carver, C. S., & Scheier, M. F. (2002). Control processes and self-organization as complementary principles underlying behavior. *Personality and Social Psychology Review, 6*, 304–315. doi:10.1207/S15327957PSPR0604_05

Caspar, F. (1998). A connectionist view of psychotherapy. In D. J. Stein & J. Ludik (Eds.), *Neural networks and psychopathology* (pp. 88–131). Cambridge, England: Cambridge University Press. doi:10.1017/CBO9780511547195.006

Caspar, F. (2007). Plan analysis. In T. Eells (Ed.), *Handbook of psychotherapeutic case formulations* (2nd ed., pp. 251–289). New York, NY: Guilford Press.

Caspar, F., & Berger, T. (2007). Insight and cognitive psychology. In L. Castonguay & C. Hill (Eds.), *Insight in psychotherapy* (pp. 375–399). Washington, DC: American Psychological Association. doi:10.1037/11532-018

Caspar, F., Rothenfluh, T., & Segal, Z. V. (1992). The appeal of connectionism for clinical psychology. *Clinical Psychology Review, 12*, 719–762. doi:10.1016/0272-7358(92)90022-Z

Foppa, K. (1984). Operationalisierung und der empirische Gehalt psychologischer Theorien [Operationalization and the content of psychological theories]. *Psychologische Beiträge, 26*, 539–551.

Grawe, K. (2004). *Psychological therapy*. Toronto, Ontario, Canada: Hogrefe & Huber.

Grawe, K. (2006). *Neuropsychotherapy. How the neurosciences can inform effective psychotherapy*. Mahwah, NJ: Erlbaum.

McCullough, J. P. (2000). *Treatment for chronic depression: Cognitive behavioral analysis system of psychotherapy*. New York, NY: Guilford Press.

Meichenbaum, D. (1977). *Cognitive behavior modification: An integrative approach*. New York, NY: Plenum Press.

Schwarz, N. (2001). Feelings as information: Implications for affective influences on information processing. In L. L. Martin & G. L. Clore (Eds.), *Theories of mood and cognition* (pp. 159–176). Mahwah, NJ: Erlbaum.

Smolensky, P. (1986). Information processing in dynamical systems: Foundations of harmony theory. In D. E. Rumelhart, J. L. McClelland, & The PDP Research Group (Eds.), *Parallel distributed processing: Explorations in the microstructure of cognition* (pp. 194–281). Cambridge, MA: MIT Press.

Strauman, T. J., & Wilson, W. A. (2010). Individual differences in approach and avoidance behavioral activation/inhibition and regulatory focus as distinct levels of analysis. In R. H. Hoyle (Ed.), *Handbook of personality and self-regulation* (pp. 447–473). Malden, MA: Blackwell. doi:10.1002/9781444318111.ch20

Vohs, K. D., & Heatherton, T. D. (2000). Self-regulatory failure: A resource-depletion approach. *Psychological Science, 11*, 249–254. doi:10.1111/1467-9280.00250

Weiss, J., Sampson, H., & The Mount Zion Psychotherapy Research Group. (1986). *The psychoanalytic process: Theory, clinical observation, and empirical research.* New York, NY: Guilford Press.

II

EMPIRICAL INVESTIGATIONS OF CORRECTIVE EXPERIENCES

10

CLIENTS' PERSPECTIVES ON CORRECTIVE EXPERIENCES IN PSYCHOTHERAPY

LAURIE HEATHERINGTON, MICHAEL J. CONSTANTINO,
MYRNA L. FRIEDLANDER, LYNNE E. ANGUS,
AND STANLEY B. MESSER

Although there has been considerable theorizing regarding the nature of corrective experiences (CEs) in psychotherapy (Alexander & French, 1946; Wallerstein, 1990), little is known about what psychotherapy clients perceive to be corrective and whether these perceptions square with theoretical accounts. This lack is notable considering that CEs ultimately belong to the client and that a client's subjective sense of what is corrective represents a unique and essential vantage point on therapy process and outcome (Hadley & Strupp, 1977; Strupp & Hadley, 1977). There is, however, substantial research on clients' perspectives on their treatment in general and on helpful events more specifically. Prominent in such change process research is the qualitative *helpful factors* method (Elliott, 2010), which is used to ask clients directly what they found helpful or unhelpful in their treatment. Such inquiry has generally taken two forms (Elliott, 2010): (a) a qualitative post- or during-treatment interview (e.g., the Change Interview; Elliott, Slatick, & Urman,

We gratefully acknowledge the contributions of Rebecca Ametrano, Shaina Bernardi, Laura Christianson, Joan DeGeorge, Lisa Grinfeld, Hsin-Hua Lee, Fern Kagan, Laura Kortz, Hanna Seifert, and Joshua Wilson to the work presented in this chapter. We also thank the Dean's Fund at one training clinic and the training clinic itself at another setting for their financial support of this project.

2001) or (b) a postsession questionnaire, which tends to be open ended, although occasionally accompanied by objective rating scales (e.g., the Helpful Aspects of Therapy Form; Llewelyn, 1988).

Several landmark studies on helpful factors reflect this methodological pluralism. Analyzing responses to a quantitative survey (i.e., the Therapy Session Report) following each session, Orlinsky and Howard (1975) found that clients reported the following kinds of helpful experiences: engaging in mutual collaboration with the therapist, viewing the therapist as emotionally present, feeling autonomous and openly introspective, and exploring significant relationships in a problem-oriented manner. Analyzing content from video-assisted recall interviews with one client who received dynamic experiential therapy and another who received cognitive therapy, Elliott, James, Reimschuessel, Cislo, and Sack (1985) found that both clients viewed insight into self and self–other relationships as particularly helpful. Moreover, consistent with the theory-specified treatment approaches, the client who was seen in dynamic experiential therapy also found awareness and involvement with the therapist to be helpful, whereas the client in cognitive therapy also found the therapist's reassurance to be helpful. Across multiple studies using various methodologies and heterogeneous assessment occasions, the most common client-indicated helpful impacts were self-understanding and insight, self-awareness, therapist guidance, responsibility taking, catharsis, reassurance, relief, and feeling understood (see Elliott & James, 1989, for a review).

Several systematic meta-analyses have also been conducted on the qualitative helpful impacts literature. For example, synthesizing data from 14 studies of person-centered experiential therapies, Greenberg, Elliott, and Lietaer (1994) found 14 helpful aspects of therapy that were organized into four overarching factors: positive relational environment (e.g., empathy), clients' therapeutic work (e.g., self-disclosure), therapists' facilitations of clients' work (e.g., giving feedback), and client changes (e.g., positive feelings). Timulak (2007), in a qualitative meta-analysis of seven studies (reflecting various treatments) on significant events, found nine categories of client-indicated helpful impacts: awareness–insight–self-understanding, reassurance–support–safety, behavioral change–problem solution, empowerment, relief, exploring feelings–emotional experiencing, feeling understood, client involvement, and personal contact.

Research has also addressed clients' perspectives on critical incidents in the formation of a therapeutic alliance with their therapist (e.g., Bedi, Davis, & Arvay, 2005; Bedi, Davis, & Williams, 2005; Fitzpatrick, Janzen, Chamodraka, & Park, 2006; Mohr & Woodhouse, 2001). Given the centrality of the client–therapist relationship in many theoretical perspectives (Constantino, Castonguay, & Schut, 2002), this literature also has an indirect bearing on understanding of CEs from the client's vantage point. Across these studies, clients emphasized therapist friendliness, therapist provision of positive commentary, and humor as important in alliance development. In a more recent study of depressed clients working with experienced therapists, Fitzpatrick, Janzen, Chamodraka, Gamberg, and Blake (2009) found that clients endorsed the following therapist behaviors as fostering alliance development: demonstrating interest, providing support, communicating understanding, and remaining nonjudgmental. Clients also endorsed their own ability to disclose and open up to their therapist as important alliance-fostering factors.

Although research on critical events and helpful impacts provides some evidence of what clients view as helpful in psychotherapy in general and in developing a favorable therapeutic alliance specifically, these findings do not necessarily speak to the nature of the psychological change or address specifically what clients perceive to be corrective about their experiences in psychotherapy. In a variety of theoretical accounts of the psychotherapy process, CEs are often identified as novel, experiential, and unexpected. In many cases, CEs are posited to entail a significant positive shift, transformation, or change in psychological functioning that is personally meaningful to the client (e.g., Alexander & French, 1946; Angus & McLeod, 2004; Foa & Kozak, 1986; Greenberg, Rice, & Elliott, 1993; Kiesler, 1996; Safran & Muran, 2000; Strachey, 1934; Strupp & Binder, 1984). Helpful events, although positively perceived by clients, do not necessarily reflect such transformative changes. For example, clients might find it helpful to self-disclose, but self-disclosures are not necessarily corrective in the sense of experiencing emotional, relational, cognitive, or behavioral transformation or reorganization. Consequently, it seems important to differentiate what clients view as helpful from what they view as *corrective*. Furthermore, the client's perspective on CEs can help clarify the definition of this important, yet conceptually elusive, construct, which to date has primarily referenced psychotherapists', but not clients', understandings of change processes. Because it is possible that a client's perspective on what is corrective may be different from that of a mental health professional or theorist (Hadley & Strupp, 1977), we reasoned that it is important not only to explore what clients feel has changed but also to ascertain their perceptions on how such change experiences come about (e.g., Bridges, 2006).

To this end, the purpose of the current discovery-oriented, multisite qualitative study was to provide an in-depth analysis of clients' subjective, during-treatment perceptions of CEs in psychotherapy. The primary investigators (i.e., the five coauthors of this chapter) represent multiple theoretical orientations (psychodynamic, emotion-focused, family systems, cognitive behavior, and interpersonal) and had access to a variety of community-based clinical samples representing varied individual psychotherapy approaches. Adopting a two-step methodological strategy, we developed an open-ended questionnaire and a transtheoretical coding system informed by the following definition of CE formulated by participants of the 2007 Penn State University (PSU) Conference on the Process of Change: "CEs are ones in which a person comes to understand or experience affectively an event or relationship in a different and unexpected way" (Chapter 1, this volume, p. 5).

Specifically, we addressed the following research questions: (a) What are the core categories and properties that emerge from clients' accounts of corrective, or significant and meaningful, experiences of change in psychotherapy sessions? (b) How do clients understand these experiences to have come about, that is, what are their commonsense explanations of the mechanisms of meaningful change experiences? and (c) To what extent are clients' accounts of corrective, or significant and meaningful change experiences, similar or dissimilar across different clinical settings and therapy orientations? For our initial inquiry into clients' descriptions of meaningful experiences of change, we intentionally avoided the use of theory-specific and potentially leading terms such as *corrective experiences*, to more fully access what clients experience as corrective in therapy sessions, from their own frame of reference.

METHOD

Settings and Treatment Orientation

The study was conducted simultaneously in five sites, four in the United States and one in Canada, where the authors were affiliated either as faculty or in a research–practice collaborative. Because the sites were heterogeneous, the study included a wide range of clients and treatments.

University Training Clinic 1

This first university training clinic (UTC1) for doctoral students (as well as some postdoctoral trainees) serves both community and student clients. It is located at a large state university in a small U.S. city. Adult clients present with a range of Axis I and II conditions, excluding acute suicidality or homicidality, florid psychosis, and/or current and primary substance dependence. The clinicians at this site conduct various forms of psychotherapy. The therapists in the current study reported being influenced most strongly by cognitive behavioral, psychodynamic, and integrative or eclectic approaches. All clients were seen on a fee-for-service, sliding scale basis.

University Training Clinic 2

The second university training clinic (UTC2) is located at a large state university in a midsized U.S. city and serves both community clients and students. Adult clients present with a range of Axis I and II conditions, excluding acute suicidality or homicidality and florid psychosis. The self-reported therapeutic orientations for therapists in the current study were cognitive behavioral and psychodynamic. All clients were seen on a fee-for-service, sliding scale basis.

University Training Clinic 3

This Canadian, third university training clinic (UTC3) is located at a large university in a large urban area. Adult clients present with a range of Axis I and II conditions, excluding acute suicidality or homicidality, florid psychosis, sexual abuse, eating disorders, and/or current and primary substance dependence. The therapeutic orientation at this site is client-centered, experiential psychotherapy with specialized training in marker-guided emotion-focused therapy interventions. Although most clients in the present study were referred for treatment by the university's student counseling service (with payment provided by university-based student fees), several clients were referred by the university's psychology department clinic on a fee-for-service, sliding scale basis.

Community Mental Health Center

This community mental health clinic (CMHC) is located in a small U.S. city surrounded by a rural area. Adult clients in the sample presented with various anxiety disorders and a range of comorbid conditions, such as depression and substance use. They were treated by therapists who are trained members of a cognitive behavioral treatment team. Most clients had third-party payers, about half through public assistance and half through private health insurance.

Hospital-Based Practice

This outpatient practice is administered by the psychiatry faculty of a teaching medical college in a moderate-sized U.S. city. The clients in this sample, who had a range of Axis I disorders, primarily anxiety and depression, were treated by one highly experienced clinician using short-term dynamic psychotherapy. Most clients had third-party payers, either through public assistance or private health insurance.

Participants

Clients

In total, there were 76 clients, 50 women (65.8%) and 26 men (34.2%), with an average age of 30.8 years ($SD = 11.9$ years). Of the 72.4% of clients who reported their race/ethnicity, the majority in each site identified as White/non-Latino(a). Clients seen in the three UTCs tended to be more highly educated than those in the two other settings. The majority of clients in the entire sample ($N = 51$; 67.1%) had some previous psychological treatment, ranging from fewer than 3 months to 3 years or more.

Therapists

There were 39 participating therapists (33 women and six men). Additional demographic information on therapists is limited because two sites did not provide demographic data about participants. However, of the three sites reporting therapist characteristics (UTC1, the CMHC, and the hospital-based practice), the average age was 32.4 years ($SD = 10.9$ years). With respect to race/ethnicity, three of these therapists were Asian American and 10 were White/non-Latino(a). Therapists' experience levels ranged from doctoral trainees in supervised practicum training to highly experienced, full-time clinicians.

Questionnaire

Clients completed a two-item, open-ended questionnaire after every fourth session. The first question (Q1) assessed the nature of the CE (i.e., What changed?) and was worded,

> Have there been any times since you started the present therapy that you have become aware of an important or meaningful change (or changes) in your thinking, feeling, behavior, or relationships? This change may have occurred in the past four weeks or any time during the present therapy. Please describe such change (or changes) as fully and vividly as possible.

In developing this question, we were simultaneously informed by the PSU conference's definition of CE, and we purposely avoided the word *corrective*. As commonly used (vs. its particular usage in the psychotherapy literature), *corrective* could be interpreted to mean that the experience needed to be remedial, that is, that something was "incorrect" previously but was "corrected" in therapy; we worried that this terminology could be both off-putting for clients and potentially misleading. Further, we wished to phrase the question in such a way to allow for responses that might reflect not only the reduction of symptoms or personal problems but also growth or development or, contrariwise, that no change had occurred. Thus, the question was deliberately phrased to focus on the experience of moving from one place to another, psychologically—within session, over the course of several sessions, or sometimes between sessions, but always linked to what had happened during sessions. The second question (Q2) assessed the mechanism of change (i.e., How did the change happen?) and was worded, "If yes, what do you believe took place during or between your therapy sessions that led to such change (or changes)?"

Procedure

The procedures were designed to make the research task as easy and nonthreatening as possible for clients and therapists. In each setting, clients were asked to participate in a study of "clients' perceptions of psychotherapy" and signed a written consent. Although the mechanics of data collection varied somewhat as required by the rules and routines of each site, as described below, at all sites the procedures ensured that someone other than the therapist requested consent, all clients got the same information about the study and the same questionnaires, and the therapists did not see the protocols.

At UTC1, 22 clients (i.e., consecutive adult outpatient referrals during the study period) were asked during initial phone screening whether they would be interested in hearing about research opportunities during their intake interview. Thirteen (59%) clients agreed to hear about the research opportunities, whereas nine (41%) declined. Of the 13 who initially agreed, 10 (77%) consented to participate in the study after meeting with a research assistant before their intake interview, whereas three (23%) declined. Participants completed the study questionnaire following every fourth session. For all but one client, data collection began at Session 4 (for one client, the Session 4 occasion was missed and thus Session 8 was the initial data point). Guided by research assistants, clients completed the questionnaire on a desktop computer following their appointment. Clients received $10 for each questionnaire completed. There were 30 protocols completed by the 10 participants at UTC1. The number of protocols completed per client ranged from one to eight, with an average of three.

At UTC2, the clinic coordinators asked potential clients during the phone screening whether they were willing to participate in the study. Of approximately 75 clients who were asked to participate, 36 agreed, and of these, 19 filled out at least one questionnaire. Guided by a research coordinator, clients completed the questionnaire in the waiting room and returned it to a locked box in a sealed envelope. For the first 10 clients (six women and four men) whose questionnaires (range = 1–9) were coded, there were 53 protocols in all, averaging 5.3 per client. Clients received $10 compensation for completing two or fewer or upon withdrawing from the study, and $25 for filling out at least three questionnaires. Efforts were made to collect data after every fourth session, although this varied at times because of clients' schedules and holidays.

At UTC3, 20 clients were asked at the time of their initial assessment sessions to review and sign, if willing to participate, an informed consent that described the purposes of postsession measures, including the CE questionnaire used in this study. All clients who were asked consented. The CE questionnaire was included in a plain envelope that was handed to the client, who then deposited it in a ballot-type mailbox on completion. Clients were not compensated for participating in this study. The number of protocols completed at UTC3 was 43. The number of protocols completed by each client ranged from one to three, with an average of two.

At the CMHC, when clients checked in for their fourth appointment, the receptionist informed them about the ongoing study and gave them a written description with the consent. All clients who were asked consented to participate. After the fourth session, when clients returned to the waiting area, the receptionist gave them the questionnaire and an envelope; participants completed the questionnaire in the reception lobby, sealed it in the envelope, and dropped it in a ballot-type box at the receptionist's desk, which was used exclusively for this purpose. Clients were not compensated for their participation. There were 22 participants, and a total of 24 protocols were completed (two clients also completed the questionnaire after Session 8).

In the hospital-based practice, the therapist informed clients with whom he was working about the study and asked whether they were interested in learning more about it. The names and phone numbers of interested clients were forwarded to a graduate research assistant, who contacted the client to explain the purpose and nature of the study, including all ethical considerations. Those who agreed to participate were given a written consent at their next appointment, which they signed and returned to the receptionist. After relevant sessions, the therapist handed the client the questionnaire, precoded with a random number and the session number, along with an envelope. Clients completed the questionnaires in the waiting room and returned the sealed envelopes to the receptionist, who placed them in a ballot-type box at her desk. Clients were not compensated for their participation. Of the 18 clients recruited for participation, 14 (78%) consented. Eleven of the 14 clients had been in therapy for more than four sessions when data collection began, and the other two clients began their participation after their fourth session.

Thus, across the five sites, the overall response rate was 82%. We collected a total of 218 protocols from the 76 clients, and the number of protocols completed by each client ranged from one to 11.

Coding Clients' Perceptions of Corrective Experiences

Development of the Coding System

To analyze the CE protocols emerging from each of the research sites, we developed a transtheoretical coding system that involved collaboration among the five authors of this chapter, each working in his or her own lab on the coding as described below. To develop a clinically grounded representation of client CEs, we adopted a constant comparison method for examining the meaning units and generating categories (Strauss & Corbin, 1990). Constant comparison involves the creation of new categories when meaning units from the raw data cannot yet be classified into an existing category. In this sense, we were constantly moving between the raw data and the emerging categories that organize those data in an effort to establish a final, encompassing set of categories.

We first collectively reviewed the initial data gathered from a sample of CE questionnaire protocols in two sites (the hospital-based practice and UTC2), segmented the clients' responses into individual meaning units (i.e., single complete thoughts), and created a preliminary list of CE categories based on these meaning units (i.e., the unit of analysis). As data emerged from the other three sites, this initial list of CE categories was expanded by the addition of more exemplars from these sites. This collaborative process resulted in the first draft of a protocol-based coding system and manual.

Next, each investigator created a team (with one or two research assistants) to code CE protocols collected at his or her respective site, using the draft coding manual. All research teams were notified when new meaning units emerged that could not be adequately characterized by the preliminary codes (i.e., constant comparison) and seemed to require the addition of new codes. At that time, all previous protocols were reexamined carefully for the presence or absence of the emergent new code. Elaboration and refinement of the coding system by the group thus continued until no new categories emerged across sites and saturation for the identification of CE codes had been achieved. New CE protocols were coded continuously until each site had achieved a sample of at least 20 client protocols. Within each team, the judges coded the meaning units, negotiating discrepancies to consensus.

Finally, collaborative discussion among all investigators resulted in a hierarchical, thematic grouping of individual codes. For example, the major category *new experiential awareness* includes subcategories such as *new experiential awareness of emotions* and *new experiential awareness of patterns in interpersonal relationships*. A final coding manual was produced that included paradigmatic examples for all categories.

Two additional coding procedures were identified early in the evolution of the coding system and were adhered to by coding teams at each site. First, it became clear that clients' responses sometimes contained more than one meaning unit. For example, in response to Q2, one client expressed two different complete thoughts: "Talking about my feelings in therapy with regards to my childhood, specifically my parents and how they made me feel" and "forcing myself to think about the sessions between therapy appointments." In cases like these, the response was divided, and the coders were instructed to apply the best-fitting code to each meaning unit separately. Across the 218 protocols, there was a total of 423 meaning units for Q1 and 353 meaning units for Q2.

Second, we noticed that occasionally a client gave an answer in response to Q1 (What was the change?) that was actually an answer to Q2 (How did it happen?). For example, one client wrote in response to Q1, "I am able to feel emotions I normally do not allow myself to feel on a normal basis/I freely cry during the sessions, which afterwards feels like a big weight is lifted off of my shoulders" (slash added for segmenting meaning units). The first meaning unit is a direct answer to Q1, citing a new emotional awareness. The second meaning unit, however, is an explanation of how that change occurred and thus is an answer to Q2, citing getting relief by being encouraged to own and express feelings. In cases like these, the latter meaning unit was coded as a response to Q2, using the categories that comprised explanations of how changes occurred.

Final Coding System and Manual

For Q1, seven major categories emerged that captured clients' phenomenology of CEs.[1] Most of the major categories also contained thematically linked subcategories that further differentiated clinically significant properties identified in the CE protocols. For a full listing of Q1 major categories and subcategories, see Table 10.1.

Category 1 encompassed responses that indicate the experience of *change in the sense of self, a stronger, positive sense of self*, reflected by examples such as, "Somehow, therapy helps me feel better about myself. I don't really know how to better explain it than that" and "I feel like I have mentally been getting stronger."

Category 2 encompassed *new experiential awareness* in some area other than the sense of self. Because this category proved to be a rich and deep one, we refined it to include six subcategories, such as (*new experiential awareness...*) ... *that a problem exists* (e.g., "I feel resentment and anger that I was not aware of before"), ... *of patterns in interpersonal relationships* (e.g., "I never really knew how much being angry scares me and reminds me of people who have hurt me in the past. That is probably why I just clam up when I'm angry. I'd rather make excuses for other people's bad behavior than let myself get angry"), ... and *of emotions* (e.g., "I am more aware of my detachment in everyday living").

Category 3, by contrast, captured responses that cited *new perspectives* (*more cognitive than experiential*). Rather than focus on feelings or emotions,

---

[1]A list of the coding categories is available upon request from the first author at lheather@williams.edu.

TABLE 10.1
Percentages of Coded Meaning Units Across Categories for Clients' Accounts of What Was Corrective

			Treatment setting: Orientation (No. of clients/no. of protocols)				
What changed?	UTCs: Psychodynamic or interpersonal (5/29)	UTCs: Cognitive behavioral (7/31)	UTC: Integrative (8/23)	UTC: experiential (20/43)	CMHC: Cognitive behavioral (22/24)	Hospital-based practice: psychodynamic (14/68)	Total across sites (76/218)
1. Change in the sense of self, stronger, positive sense of self	0.00	5.36	4.55	3.33	5.26	3.70	3.55
2. New experiential awareness	1.67	0.00	2.27	2.22	0.00	0.00	0.95
(Major category % including subcodes a–f)	(38.33)	(28.57)	(13.64)	(44.44)	(10.53)	(35.56)	(32.39)
a. . . . that a problem exists	6.67	3.57	0.00	13.33	2.63	5.19	6.15
b. . . . of personal strengths	0.00	0.00	0.00	0.00	2.63	0.00	0.24
c. . . . of personal needs	0.00	3.57	0.00	1.11	0.00	4.44	2.13
d. . . . of emotions	25.00	10.71	6.82	16.67	2.63	17.78	15.13
e. . . . of patterns in interpersonal relationships	5.00	1.79	2.27	2.22	0.00	7.41	4.02
f. . . . of the need to change behavior	0.00	8.93	2.27	8.89	2.63	0.74	3.78

(continues)

TABLE 10.1
Percentages of Coded Meaning Units Across Categories for Clients' Accounts of What Was Corrective (*Continued*)

What changed?	Treatment setting: Orientation (No. of clients/no. of protocols)						
	UTCs: Psychodynamic or interpersonal (5/29)	UTCs: Cognitive behavioral (7/31)	UTC: Integrative (8/23)	UTC: experiential (20/43)	CMHC: Cognitive behavioral (22/24)	Hospital-based practice: psychodynamic (14/68)	Total across sites (76/218)
3. *New perspectives (more cognitive than experiential)*	1.67	1.79	2.27	11.11	2.63	3.70	4.49
(Major category % including subcodes a–f)	(38.33)	(17.86)	(22.73)	(28.89)	(10.53)	(28.89)	(26.48)
a. *...on relationships with family members or romantic others*	13.33	5.36	4.55	4.44	2.63	8.15	6.86
b. *...on relationships with friends or coworkers*	0.00	1.79	0.00	0.00	0.00	2.96	1.18
c. *..on relation between past & present*	11.67	0.00	0.00	1.11	0.00	7.41	4.26
d. *...on self*	8.33	3.57	13.64	6.67	2.63	5.19	6.38
e. *...on life*	0.00	3.57	0.00	5.56	2.63	0.00	1.89
f. *....on therapeutic process*	3.33	1.79	2.27	0.00	0.00	1.48	1.42
4. *Recognition of hope, or reason to hope*	0.00	3.57	0.00	1.11	10.53	0.74	1.89

5. Acquisition or use of specific new skills (e.g., meditation, exercise, mindfulness, challenging automatic thoughts, deep breathing)	0.00	1.79	6.82	0.00	21.05	0.00	2.84
6. Changes in behavior (Major category % including subcodes a–e)	0.00 (16.67)	3.57 (28.57)	4.55 (47.73)	0.00 (13.33)	5.26 (42.11)	0.00 (27.41)	1.42 (26.48)
a. behaving in new ways with others	13.33	7.14	18.18	2.22	13.16	17.78	12.06
b. taking on new challenges	0.00	0.00	2.27	1.11	2.63	1.48	1.18
c. reacting differently to stress	0.00	3.57	9.09	4.44	0.00	2.22	3.07
d. reduction in psychological symptoms	1.67	8.93	9.09	2.22	21.05	4.44	6.15
e. change in internal dialogue	1.67	5.36	4.55	3.33	0.00	1.48	2.60
7. No or minimal change	6.67	10.71	0.00	8.89	0.00	1.48	4.73
8. Recognition of, or feeling that, things are getting worse	0.00	3.57	0.00	0.00	0.00	0.74	0.71
9. Change in relationship with my therapist (Major category % including subcodes a–c)	0.00 (0.00)	0.00 (0.00)	0.00 (0.00)	0.00 (0.00)	0.00 (0.00)	0.74 (1.48)	0.24 (0.47)
a. closer/better relationship	0.00	0.00	0.00	0.00	0.00	0.74	0.24
b. more distant/worse relationship	0.00	0.00	0.00	0.00	0.00	0.00	0.00
c. other change or shift in relationship	0.00	0.00	0.00	0.00	0.00	0.00	0.00
10. Uncodable	0.00	0.00	4.55	0.00	0.00	0.00	0.47

Note. UTC = university training clinic; CMHC = community mental health clinic.

these responses were more intellectual (cognitive), reflected in the verbs that clients used to describe their CEs (e.g., *think, see, know*). This category included six subcategories, such as *new perspectives (more cognitive than experiential) ... on relationships with friends or coworkers* (e.g., "I've really become aware of the issues with my boss and know that relates to my feeling like a screwup. I see more clearly how those interactions have colored my self-opinion"), ... *on the relation between past and present* (e.g., "I think I have become more aware of how much events in the past have and continue to affect my life in the present"), and ... *on oneself* (e.g., "In general I have become much more aware of why I have made the decisions even bad ones and what my thinking was behind those decisions, this is the most important part").

Category 4 reflected the experience of *recognition of hope, or reason to hope*. For example, one client noted, "After my first session I had a feeling of relief, of hopefulness. I felt like I finally had taken the first step to feeling better/more in control."

Category 5 captured *acquisition or use of specific new skills*. Here, clients cited skill acquisition, such as meditation, exercise, mindfulness, challenging automatic thoughts, or deep breathing, as CEs in their therapy, such as, "I catch my negative thoughts and turn them to positive. I've developed a self-care process daily for myself" and "I've learned many skills that help me get through times I feel like giving up and when it all feels hopeless. Meditation, breathing exercises, facing my fears."

Category 6 encompassed *changes in behavior*. Several clear subcategories included *behaving in new ways with others* (e.g., "I am participating in my relationships with my parents more like an adult" and "changes in ways I have dealt with friendships, especially with guys"), *taking on new challenges* (e.g., "I have started a business and deal with challenges rather than giving up as I did in the past"), *reacting differently to stress* (e.g., "I have found myself calming down. Reacting differently to stressful situations"), and *reduction in psychological symptoms* (e.g., "I've been better at controlling my overeating").

Category 7, *no or minimal change*, allowed for coding responses that indicated that clients were not aware of any important or meaningful changes in their thinking, feelings, behavior, or relationships. Category 8, *recognition of, or a feeling that, things are getting worse*, allowed for responses that indicated negative change. Category 9, *change in relationship with my therapist*, was used for responses that cited shifts in the therapeutic relationship itself as corrective. Category 10, *uncodable*, was used in a only a few instances.

For Q2, the most salient dimension on which clients' answers differed was the *locus of the change*, that is, the agent or agents who were explicitly named or implicit in clients' accounts of the CE mechanisms. For example, a client who felt that what changed was her awareness of how often she felt afraid in situations wrote, "I reflected a lot on our discussions in therapy and it was easier to spot those instances when I was acting based on fear, then I took an active approach to try and change that." In this case, the client is the agent; from her perspective, it was her own reflections on the therapy material and her active approach to try and change something that were salient. Another client, explaining her realization that she tended to flee or make hasty decisions in the face of a mess and that her controlling nature prevented her from wading through conflicts to reach better results wrote, "My therapist actually pointed this out (i.e., led me to it)." Here, the causal explanation for the client's realization was exclusively the therapist's intervention.

Another client wrote, "My therapist asked me to consider my level of dedication to our therapy sessions and the skills emphasized during them. This led me to question my dedication to anything and (almost) everything substantial in my life." This questioning, she believed, brought about a helpful awareness of her pattern of being overcommitted and feeling overwhelmed. Thus, she saw that she and the therapist worked together to bring about the CE. Rarely, clients attributed change to events that happened outside of therapy or to the therapeutic work on the meaning of those external events. One client, who had come to a realization about the effects of social class on life outcomes, noted,

> There was nothing directly related to therapy sessions that prompted me to undergo these changes.... I simply [went to a conference at an elite university] over this past weekend, and my awareness of how I lack significant amounts of different forms of capital was pushed to the forefront of my mind.

Another client cited "winter break, and start of medication" as accounting for her decreased depression.

Thus, answers to Q2 were first coded according to the locus of change: *something the therapist did; something the client did; something the client and therapist did together;* or *something external.* Within these major categories, subcategories concerning the *nature of the change* were created using the same procedures described above. For a full listing of Q2 major categories and subcategories, see Table 10.2. For the category *something the therapist did,* the substantive interventions included subcategories such as *provided new understandings of the basis of the client's problems, helped the client uncover or revisit past problematic feelings or events, encouraged clients to own and express feelings, provided acceptance* (variously referred to as *unconditional positive regard, nonjudgmental attitude, warmth, empathy*), *taught specific techniques* (e.g., breathing exercises, mindfulness), and *gave advice or suggestions that the client uses.*

Explanations that implied *something the client did* yielded subcategories reflecting the implementation of *implemented specific techniques outside therapy* (deep breathing, yoga), *self-reflection or greater awareness, disclosure in therapy*

TABLE 10.2
Percentages of Coded Meaning Units Across Categories for Clients' Accounts
of How Corrective Experiences (CEs) Occurred

| | Treatment setting: Orientation (No. of clients/no. of protocols) | | | | | | |
How changes occurred?	UTC: Psycho-dynamic–interpersonal (5/29)	UTC: Cognitive behavioral (7/31)	UTC: Integrative (8/23)	UTC: Experiential (20/43)	CMHC: Cognitive behavioral (22/24)	Hospital-based practice: psychodynamic (14/68)	Total across sites (76/218)
1. *Something the therapist did* (Major category % including subcodes a–h)	1.85 (37.04)	0.00 (19.61)	6.67 (22.22)	0.00 (24.56)	3.23 (41.94)	0.00 (31.30)	1.42 (29.18)
a. *Provided new understanding of the basis of the client's problems*	5.56	0.00	0.00	3.51	12.90	4.35	3.97
b. *Helped client uncover or revisit past problematic feelings or events*	3.70	0.00	0.00	10.53	0.00	6.09	4.25
c. *Directed to pay attention*	7.41	5.88	2.22	5.26	0.00	1.74	3.68
d. *Observed client's patterns of thoughts, feelings, behavior*	3.70	7.84	4.44	0.00	0.00	3.48	3.40
e. *Encouraged client to own & express feelings*	7.41	0.00	0.00	0.00	0.00	6.96	3.40
f. *Provided acceptance, unconditional positive regard, nonjudgmental attitude, warmth, empathy*	5.56	1.96	6.67	5.26	9.68	6.96	5.95

g. Taught specific techniques (e.g., breathing exercises, mindfulness)	0.00	1.96	2.22	0.00	6.45	0.87	1.42
h. Gave advice or suggestions that client uses	1.85	1.96	0.00	0.00	9.68	0.87	1.70
2. Something the client did (Major category % including subcodes a–o)	0.00 (29.63)	0.00 (35.29)	2.22 (37.78)	0.00 (57.89)	0.00 (25.81)	0.00 (50.43)	0.28 (42.49)
a. Implemented specific techniques outside therapy	0.00	5.88	0.00	1.75	6.45	1.74	2.27
b. Implemented something learned in therapy to daily life	3.70	5.88	13.33	1.75	0.00	4.35	4.82
c. Learned to recognize patterns	3.70	1.96	2.22	0.00	0.00	3.48	2.27
d. Self-reflection or greater awareness	5.56	11.76	2.22	3.51	0.00	10.43	6.80
e. Self-realization or insight	3.70	1.96	4.44	8.77	6.45	8.70	6.23
f. Reviewing therapy experiences between sessions	0.00	0.00	2.22	7.02	3.23	5.22	3.40
g. Disclosure in therapy about disturbing experiences & situations (overcoming avoidance)	3.70	0.00	2.22	17.54	0.00	5.22	5.38
h. Taking responsibility for own problematic behavior or role in contributions to problems	0.00	3.92	0.00	1.75	3.23	0.87	1.42
i. Tried to be trusting, honest, and/or cooperative with therapist	1.85	0.00	0.00	3.51	3.23	1.74	1.70
j. Paying attention to/mimicking others who are successful	0.00	0.00	0.00	1.75	0.00	0.00	0.28

(continues)

TABLE 10.2

Percentages of Coded Meaning Units Across Categories for Clients' Accounts
of How Corrective Experiences (CEs) Occurred   *(Continued)*

		Treatment setting: Orientation (No. of clients/no. of protocols)					
How changes occurred?	UTC: Psycho-dynamic–interpersonal (5/29)	UTC: Cognitive behavioral (7/31)	UTC: Integrative (8/23)	UTC: Experiential (20/43)	CMHC: Cognitive behavioral (22/24)	Hospital-based practice: psychodynamic (14/68)	Total across sites (76/218)
k. *Not thinking as much*	0.00	0.00	0.00	1.75	0.00	0.00	0.28
l. *Remembered or recalled something*	0.00	0.00	0.00	0.00	0.00	0.87	0.28
m. *Allowing self to feel (differently or more deeply)*	1.85	0.00	0.00	3.51	0.00	7.83	3.40
n. *Tried to change beliefs*	5.56	0.00	6.67	0.00	0.00	0.00	1.70
o. *Exploring feelings at a deeper level*	0.00	3.92	2.22	5.26	3.23	0.00	1.98
3. *Something client & therapist did together*	0.00	0.00	4.44	0.00	3.23	0.00	0.85
(Major category % including subcodes a–f)	(20.37)	(17.65)	(31.11)	(10.53)	(9.68)	(15.65)	(17.28)
a. *Role playing*	0.00	5.88	0.00	5.26	0.00	1.74	2.27
b. *Overcoming faulty logic in thinking*	1.85	1.96	6.67	0.00	0.00	0.87	1.70
c. *Focusing on the past*	0.00	1.96	2.22	0.00	0.00	5.22	2.27

d. Discussing something specific	9.26	1.96	8.89	0.00	0.00	6.09	4.82
e. Developed therapeutic relationship	1.85	0.00	0.00	0.00	3.23	0.00	0.57
f. Collaborating or coconstructing to make sense of things	7.41	5.88	8.89	5.26	3.23	1.74	4.82
4. Something external (Major category % including subcodes a–d)	0.00 (3.70)	1.96 (11.76)	0.00 (0.00)	0.00 (3.51)	0.00 (22.58)	1.74 (1.74)	0.85 (5.38)
a. Changes in external demands in work and/or social domains	0.00	3.92	0.00	0.00	6.45	0.00	1.13
b. Changes in daily routine	0.00	1.96	0.00	0.00	3.23	0.00	0.57
c. Specific event that prompted reflection or other CEs	3.70	1.96	0.00	3.51	0.00	0.00	1.42
d. Medication	0.00	1.96	0.00	0.00	12.90	0.00	1.42
5. Doesn't know, not sure, uncodable	9.26	15.69	8.89	3.51	0.00	0.87	5.67

Note. UTC = university training clinic; CMHC = community mental health clinic.

about disturbing experiences and situations (*overcoming avoidance*), and *allowing self to feel* (*differently or more deeply*). Subcategories under *something the client and therapist did together* included *role playing*, *overcoming faulty logic in thinking*, *discussing something specific*, and *collaborating or coconstructing to make sense of things*. The content of the *something external* explanations included changes or events that the client did not initiate, for example, *changes in external demands in work and/or social domains*, *changes in daily routine*, *specific events that prompted reflection or other CEs*, and *medication* as the explanations for the changes they described.

RESULTS

At a purely descriptive level, the variability in the range and depth of responses to Q1 was immediately evident. Clients cited meaningful movement in the domains of affect, for instance, "My relationship with myself has changed a lot.... I am now very attuned to my feelings and try not to push them down"; cognition, for instance, "What changed firstly is that I became able to recognize patterns or issues that kept coming up. Secondly, I have changed the way I approach things by changing [or trying to change] my internal dialogue"; behavior, for instance,

I have started a business and deal with challenges rather than giving up as I have done in the past. I have seen my father for the first time in 10 years, and I am seeing him again soon and it feels like my choice;

and relationships, for instance,

Therapy has really changed the way I view my relationship with my parents. I have a better understanding of my rights as a person in my relationship with them, and I feel like I can participate in my relationship with them as an adult.

Additionally, it was clear that some clients provided deeply personal and elaborated responses that identified having achieved a new realization in therapy along with a significant and meaningful shift in thinking, feeling, and behaving; for example,

I realized that I am not worthless. Which to most people is an obvious thing, but it's taken me a long time to reach that conclusion. One day I was thinking about something, I don't remember what, and I thought "Duh, it's not like I'm worthless or something." And I quickly realized what a huge change in thinking that was. For most of my teen/adult life, I had taken refuge in the belief that I was not just worthless, but pretty much every negative thing one can be. And every time I did even the tiniest thing wrong, I would beat myself up for it and reinforce those feelings. But now I'm like "I'm not perfect, no one is. I make mistakes, but that doesn't make me worthless." Even in those moments where I do something wrong and I feel horrible, I still have worth. And it's not just that I can say these words; I feel them too. It is a genuine change in my thinking.

In contrast, other clients provided far less elaborated accounts that entailed the identification of a new awareness of a shift in thinking or feeling that may or may not have resulted in new ways of being in the world (e.g., "Realizing that my relationship with my husband is not as open as I have thought. I feel put under a microscope over the years and I feel resentment and anger that I was not aware of before" and "I have started a business and deal with challenges rather than giving up as I did in the past"). Some responses explicitly cited awareness that the change was novel or unexpected, that is, events that explicitly met the PSU conference definition of CEs, for instance,

> Before, when people told me I was too hard on myself, I disagreed. I would concede that I was hard on myself, usually very hard on myself, but never TOO hard. A few weeks ago, I realized that I AM too hard on myself,

whereas other clients did not report anything explicitly new or unexpected, for instance, "I've learned many skills that help me get through times I feel like giving up and when it all feels hopeless. Meditation, breathing exercises, facing my fears."

The coding system provided the frame for categorizing the different types of responses and for representing the proportions of all meaning units encompassed by each code. These proportions are displayed in Tables 10.1 (for Q1) and 10.2 (for Q2) for the total sample, as well as separately across the different subsamples. Note that although there were five sites, the tables include columns for six subsamples. For the three UTCs, we separated the data on the basis of whether the therapists in training were treating their clients from psychodynamic, cognitive behavioral, integrative, or experiential approaches. All of the integrative cases were treated at UTC1, and all of the experiential cases were treated at UTC3. The psychodynamic and cognitive behavioral samples combined data from UTC1 and UTC2 (by orientation type). The hospital-based practice sample was solely psychodynamic, and the CMHC sample was solely cognitive behavioral.

Clients' Accounts of What Was Corrective

The most frequently cited CE was *new experiential awareness*, which accounted for roughly 30% to 40% of all meaning units in four of the six samples. This finding suggests that clients experienced as corrective the shift from a state of not knowing to knowing something that was personally important and relevant to their presenting problems or for concerns that arose during treatment. This shift, by definition, involved an uncovering of experience or feelings that clients typically described as having occurred gradually ("I have become more aware of how often I blame myself for things and let people walk all over me") rather than a more sudden "aha" experience, such as "Just today I realized I have not been in touch with or have been denying my feelings." Theorists and therapists apply various terms, such as *insight, awareness,* and *self-understanding,* that cast different shades of meaning on this experience. In these data, the most salient distinctions among the responses related to differences in the domains in which the awareness occurred, which ranged from the most simple awareness that a problem or issue exists ("Never, ever [until yesterday] have I even been able to see that I have an eating disorder living inside me"), to more complex understandings about emotions, about the connections between two or more feelings, or between feelings and interpersonal situations.

The proportion of these kinds of answers was followed closely by the proportion of answers that articulated a New perspectives (*more cognitive than experiential*) flavor, for example, "I felt a shift in … having alternative perspectives about different situations in my life" and "I think I have become more aware of how much events in the past have and continue to effect [sic] my life in the present." Across the five samples, these responses accounted for 11% to 38% of all meaning units and were particularly salient in the samples with high proportions of *new experiential awareness*. Together, these two categories comprised more than 73% of all responses in two of the samples, 64% in a third sample, and almost 59% in the fourth sample. At least for these clients, psychotherapy involved bringing to awareness previously unacknowledged material and/or the experience of understanding—about relationships, about the relationship between past and present, or about the self.

In the four samples discussed above, a modest to large proportion (48% and 41% in the UTC1: integrative and CMHC: cognitive behavior therapy [CBT] samples, respectively) of meaning units articulated some kind of *changes in behavior* as the CE, for example, "I stopped self-medicating with substances, and asked people in my life to stay away so I could rehab and get better" and "I am reducing my extracurricular involvement and my work load for this academic year." Fewer clients cited the acquisition or use of specific new skills and/or information.

Finally, few clients reported having experienced no change or a change for the worse. Whereas a few clients specifically identified a *change in the relationship with the therapist* as the CE, the person of the therapist and his or her contributions to the therapy relationship were often identified by clients in their answers to Q2 as key to how they understood significant change to have happened in therapy sessions.

Clients' Accounts of How Corrective Experiences Occurred

Clients' responses to Q2 were also wide ranging. The data indicated that, in general, change was attributed primarily to *something the client did* (ranging from 26% to 58%, with an average of 42% across samples) or *something the therapist did* (ranging from 20% to 42%, with an average of 29% across samples). However, there was considerable variability across samples. Responses in which the therapists' and clients' efforts in tandem were cited as accounting for CE were less frequent but not absent, ranging from 10% to 31%, with an average across samples of 17%; this percentage also varied considerably. In general, external factors were the least salient in clients' accounts of change processes, and among these, the most frequent subcategory was the one related to psychotropic medication.

Beyond the categories reflecting the change agent, the *content* of the explanations proved varied and interesting. With regard to what the therapist did, answers that articulated some version of providing acceptance or empathy, directing the client to pay attention to certain things, and teaching specific techniques were the most frequent. With regard to clients' own behavior, the most frequent responses were those articulating some version of being self-reflective or attentive to one's own behavior, thoughts, or feelings and coming to a particular insight.

The data revealed that clients think broadly about corrective experiences. That is, they think both about what they do within sessions (learning to recognize patterns of various kinds, disclosure in therapy) and about what they do between sessions (implementing specific techniques, reviewing therapy sessions) in accounting for CEs in treatment.

Corrective Experiences Across Samples

Within the generally high rates of meaning units relating to experiencing or thinking about things differently, there was considerable variability across samples. In this section, we draw readers' attention to this variability, not to make statistical comparisons or to draw conclusions about the causes of the variability (comparisons are purely descriptive of this sample, not inferential) but rather to raise questions about it for practice and future research.

References to *new experiential awareness* were less common in clients whose therapists identified with CBT orientations, whether at the UTCs or at the CMHC, as were references to new perspectives of a more cognitive type. Moreover, the clients in the CMHC CBT sample were more likely to cite as corrective the acquisition or use of new skills and information and changes in their own behavior. Clients from this sample provided shorter and more concrete responses than those in psychodynamic treatment, especially those seen in the hospital-based practice.

Regarding clients' perspectives on how their CEs came about, there was also variability across site/orientation. First, nearly 60% of all client explanations in treatment with therapists who were self-identified as client-centered or experiential were coded as *something the client did*. For example, one client wrote, "The realizations happened in the last couple of weeks because I started reflecting on what we've talked about between our sessions—I didn't do that before." These kinds of responses were also particularly common in the hospital-based practice–psychodynamic sample (roughly 50% of the meaning units), but the proportion for clients in the UTC psychodynamic therapy sample was lower, just under 30% and comparable to the proportions in the other two UTC samples (recall that the UTC psychodynamic and UTC cognitive behavioral cases reflect a blend of clients from UTC1 and UTC2). *Something the therapist did* also loomed relatively large as an explanation for CEs from the perspective of clients in the hospital-based practice's psychodynamic treatment, as well as for clients in the UTC psychodynamic treatment, and the CMHC cognitive behavioral treatment. Within this category, however, the specific subcategory values were not distributed evenly across samples. Table 10.2 shows, for example, that *helped the client uncover or revisit past problematic feelings or events* and *encouraged clients to own and express feelings* were found in the protocols of clients in both psychodynamic samples but not in the two CBT samples.

As noted earlier, responses citing the therapist and client together as agents were less frequent overall. An exception to this is the relatively high frequency of collaboration in the UTC integrative therapy sample. One paradigmatic example was, "We worked on trying to develop a positive sense of self and ignore the negative messages that people send to me." Finally, *something external* in general accounted for an even smaller, almost negligible, proportion of answers to Q2. The clients who did mention external factors tended to come from the UTC: CBT or the CMHC: CBT samples (e.g., "I got on the right meds and stayed on them" and "I decided to eat less and exercise more").

DISCUSSION

First, it was clear that clients do have, and are able to verbalize, their own opinions about CEs in therapy, as well as a sense of what (and who) brought about the changes they experienced. Overall, few clients perceived little or no change, despite the fact that the questionnaire allowed for these kinds of responses (however, it is important to note that by design, only clients who had reached the fourth session were included in the sample; thus, there might have been clients who felt that they were not benefitting from treatment who had already discontinued treatment before Session 4). Moreover, the responses offered by these clients echoed changes that scholars write about, such as significant and meaningful changes in thoughts, feelings, behaviors, relationships, and overall sense of self. Nonetheless, clients' accounts of what is corrective in therapy, and how that came about, were largely based on their own phenomenological experience and constructions of that experience. Simply stated, it is essential to understand what constitutes a client's experience of a meaningful corrective shift in therapy, in addition to the more theoretical accounts or maps provided by therapists, to fully understand the territory of psychotherapeutic change (Hadley & Strupp, 1977).

In designing the study, we deliberately provided an unstructured opportunity for clients to share their accounts of CEs with us, and as noted earlier, we were struck by the range and depth of those accounts. In trying to understand the corpus of these accounts, we started from the ground up with a careful reading of their narratives and an analytic strategy that produced a transtheoretical measure of clients' perspectives on CEs. The coding system resulted from the collaborative analysis of five researchers representing distinct therapy traditions, using client protocols emerging from differing clinical settings and treatments. Thus, by design, the results were not constrained by predetermined categories and assumptions. The give and take among the researchers was an important aspect of the process of our work and resulted in a coding system and manual that, to our knowledge, is unique in its transtheoretical nature.

Although Alexander and French's (1946) term *corrective emotional experience* refers to a therapeutic relationship that differs from other relationships, our respondents rarely identified this specific awareness as a meaningful change in their postsession protocols. On the rare occasions that clients did provide an account of a CE that included mentions of the therapeutic relationship, these occurred in the longer term psychodynamic treatment with a highly experienced therapist. Perhaps it takes posttherapy reflection to achieve this awareness, if clients develop it at all. It may be an important feature of change but one that is not easily verbalized.

On the other hand, it should be noted that numerous client accounts of how CEs happened in therapy sessions did refer to therapist factors such as empathy, positive regard, asking questions, and so on. Thus, it appears that clients tend to be much more aware of how specific therapist in-session responses facilitate intrapersonal experiences of significant change and are far less attuned to shifts or changes in the interpersonal nature or dynamics of the therapeutic relationship itself. It is interesting that in the current sample, only 10% of the meaning units from clients undergoing experiential therapy were something that the therapist and client did together. This contrasts with the findings that (a) clients' ratings of the alliance between therapist and client are at least modest predictors of therapeutic outcome in many therapeutic approaches, including experiential therapies of depression (Castonguay & Beutler 2006); and (b) in an intensive narrative process coding system relational theme analysis (Brunshaw, 2005) of three good- and three poor-outcome experiential therapies of depression, a focus on the therapist–therapy relationship was identified as one of the five most frequently occurring relational foci in consecutive therapy session transcripts.

Beyond the relationship, CEs in most forms of treatment are also related to specific techniques. It was interesting that "providing a new understanding of the basis of the clients' problem" was cited across samples, although we can imagine that the nature of that understanding might be different in CBT versus psychodynamic therapies, for example. Responses that referred to the therapist giving advice or suggestions that the client used or to teaching specific practices (mindfulness) or habits of thinking (monitoring automatic thoughts) accounted for 16% of meaning units in the CMHC cognitive behavioral sample (vs. 2%–4% in the other samples), perhaps reflecting the didactic feature of CBT and the nature of this sample. Any explanations must be considered tentative, however, as not only the nature of the client samples but also the experience levels of the therapists differed across sites. For example, the relatively higher proportion of responses citing "something the therapist and client did together" as reflecting how the CE came about in the UTC1:integrative sample might be due to the relative inexperience of therapists in this sample. That is, we suspect that the trainees who described themselves as integrative were likely to be trying to develop their identity as therapists. Thus, their integrative identity might reflect a process of trying on different theoretical approaches, or even working primarily using basic helping skills, which may have been experienced by their clients as collaboration and equity in the process, that is, a fairly even sharing of agency.

In this vein, we note several limitations of the study, which are related to its descriptive, exploratory nature. Our results do not permit firm conclusions about whether certain types of client perceptions are related to their being treated by therapists with particular therapeutic orientations. There was overlap between the setting (UTC, hospital-based practice, CMHC) and the theoretical orientations represented in those settings. For example, emotion-focused therapy was represented at only one UTC. Although this confounding was only partial (CBT was represented at a UTC and a CMHC; psychodynamic therapy was represented at a UTC and a hospital-based outpatient practice), it would have been preferable if site and orientation were completely crossed. Other limitations include the lack of formal assessment of interjudge reliability, which should be undertaken in the future as the coding system is further developed, and the possible effects of the language of our questions on the responses given. In striving to write nonleading questions (and specifically to avoid the term *corrective*), we probably pulled a wider range of client responses than those covered by a strict adherence to the experience of *novel or unexpected changes* of the PSU conference definition.

Finally, in any study—but especially in qualitative studies of this type— there is the possibility that researchers' biases affected the identification of themes and categories in clients' responses. In the present coding system, the subcategory *new awareness of emotion*, for example, is quite refined relative to other subcategories, with subsubcategories including *opening up or feeling new or changed emotions*, *awareness of a relationship between two or more different feelings*, and *awareness of a relationship between a situation or interpersonal interaction and emotion*. Furthermore, we made a major distinction between a new experiential awareness and a new cognitive perspective, which may have reflected a particular way of parsing the realm of CEs. On the other hand, having a research team composed of individuals with expertise in different theoretical perspectives was a strength of the study insofar as the team members provided checks on potential biases in understanding the data that were specific to one particular orientation.

The results answer some questions and raise others. First, what is the scope of the CEs that clients shared with us? Just as psychotherapy research has described "small o" outcomes as the course of therapy proceeds (e.g., increased ability to identify automatic thoughts in cognitive therapy, "softening" events in emotion-focused couples therapy) versus "big O" outcomes at the termination of therapy (e.g., clinically significant decreases in depression, significantly improved marital satisfaction), might there be "small" and "big" CEs? One of our clients, for example, stated that her therapist's questioning brought about a helpful awareness of her pattern of being overcommitted (small o) and feeling overwhelmed in therapy that had also generalized to other aspects of her life (big O). A fruitful topic for future research is whether these kinds of small corrective yet personally meaningful steps might build over time and lead to major CEs of the kind that Alexander and French (1946) reported. Another unanswered question is whether these kinds of subjective experiences are eventually linked to feeling and functioning better.

Second, it would be interesting to discover whether these kinds of links (e.g., a new awareness in therapy being connected with improved interpersonal relationships) are consciously made by clients as they reflect on their treatment after termination. We are currently examining the posttherapy accounts of CEs with a subset of clients, many from this data set. We also observed that clients' accounts varied in their scope, with the more specific accounts coming from clients in CBT and the broader ones from clients in psychodynamic treatment, regardless of the setting in which the therapy was conducted. Further research is needed to ascertain whether this observation is robust and to what extent it reflects the kinds of narratives about CEs that therapists of different theoretical persuasions implicitly or explicitly communicate to clients.

Another question that often arises in this kind of research concerns the truth value of people's accounts of elements of psychotherapy and psychotherapeutic change. It has been well documented that there are differences between clients', therapists' and outside observers' perspectives on therapy (Hadley & Strupp, 1977). For example, therapists', clients', and observers' perspectives on the strength of the alliance within a given therapy relationship often differ, with clients' perspectives generally found to be more predictive of outcomes than that of therapists (Horvath & Symonds, 1991). How can one make sense of these differences, and how should one treat the validity of the varying accounts and perspectives?

In discussing designs for change process research, Elliott (2010) addressed the differing perspectives issue head on when assessing the limitations of the "qualitative helpful factors design." Elliott noted that clients' accounts, even highly compelling ones, may be riddled with attributional errors, namely, that clients may not be able to access and articulate what really happened in therapy. Elliott further acknowledged that proponents of quantitative methods are likely to dismiss such data as "testimonial" (p. 127).

Although our data may indeed be testimonial, they are nonetheless clinically important, because they represent clients' conscious theories or understandings of how change processes come about in psychotherapy. It is this understanding, regardless of its objective or truth value from an outsider's perspective, that will shape and inform clients' working theory of therapy and whom they deem responsible for significant changes (themselves and/or the therapist). Truthful or not, clients' perspectives have consequences. The client who believes that an improvement in his or her anxiety symptoms is due to having mastered mindfulness is likely to have a greater sense of agency than a client who attributes symptom reduction to having taken a new medication, for example. This consideration brings us back full circle, to our initial assertion that the experience of change, corrective or not, is the client's experience, worth asking about and worth studying in its own right, alongside the accounts of therapists and theorists. Thus, we hope that this initial investigation succeeds in contributing our clients' voices to the other voices represented by the chapters in this volume.

REFERENCES

Alexander, F. (1950). Analysis of the therapeutic facto[r] *The Psychoanalytic Quarterly, 19,* 482–500.

Alexander, F., & French, T. M. (1946). *Psychoanalytic t[h]* New York, NY: Ronald Press.

Angus, L., & McLeod, J. (Eds.). (2004). *Handbook o[f] .... ana psychotherapy: Theory, research, and practice.* Thousand Oaks, CA: Sage.

Bedi, R. P., Davis, M. D., & Arvay, M. A. (2005). The client's perspective on forming a counseling alliance and implications for research on counsellor training. *Canadian Journal of Counselling, 39,* 71–85.

Bedi, R. P., Davis, M. D., & Williams, M. (2005). Critical incidents in the formation of the therapeutic alliance from the client's perspective. *Psychotherapy: Theory, Research, & Practice, 42,* 311–323. doi:10.1037/0033-3204.42.3.311

Bridges, M. R. (2006). Activating the corrective emotional experience. *Journal of Clinical Psychology, 62,* 551–568.

Brunshaw, J. (2005). *Process of change in emotion-focused therapy: Narrative theme analysis and the development and application of a change process model.* Unpublished doctoral dissertation, Department of Psychology, York University, Toronto, Ontario, Canada.

Castonguay, L. G., & Beutler, L. E. (Eds.). (2006). *Principles of therapeutic change that work.* New York, NY: Oxford University Press.

Constantino, M. J., Castonguay, L. G., & Schut, A. J. (2002). The working alliance: A flagship for the "scientist-practitioner" model in psychotherapy. In G. S. Tryon (Ed.), *Counseling based on process research: Applying what we know* (pp. 81–131). Boston, MA: Allyn & Bacon.

Elliott, R. (2010). Psychotherapy change process research: Realizing the promise. *Psychotherapy Research, 20,* 123–135. doi:10.1080/10503300903470743

Elliott, R., & James, E. (1989). Varieties of client experience in psychotherapy: An analysis of the literature. *Clinical Psychology Review, 9,* 443–467. doi:10.1016/0272-7358(89)90003-2

Elliott, R., James, E., Reimschuessel, C., Cislo, D., & Sack, N. (1985). Significant events and the analysis of immediate therapeutic impacts. *Psychotherapy: Theory, Research, & Practice, 22,* 620–630. doi:10.1037/h0085548

Elliott, R., Slatick, E., & Urman, M. (2001). Qualitative change process research on psychotherapy: Alternative strategies. In J. Frommer & D. L. Rennie (Eds.), *Qualitative psychotherapy research: Methods and methodology* (pp. 69–111). Lengerich, Germany: Pabst Science.

Fitzpatrick, M., Janzen, J., Chamodraka, M., Gamberg, S., & Blake, E. (2009). Client relationship incidents in early therapy: Doorways to collaborative engagement. *Psychotherapy Research, 19,* 654–665. doi:10.1080/10503300902878235

[handwritten margin note: CE's mostly focused on benefits of Transference]

Fitzpatrick, M. R., Janzen, J., Chamodraka, M., & Park, J. (2006). Critical incidents in the process of alliance development: A positive emotion exploration spiral. *Psychotherapy Research, 16*, 486–498. doi:10.1080/10503300500485391

Foa, E. B., & Kozak, M. (1986). Emotional processing of fear: Exposure to corrective information. *Psychological Bulletin, 99*, 20–35. doi:10.1037/0033-2909.99.1.20

Greenberg, L., Elliott, R., & Lietaer, G. (1994). Research on experiential psychotherapies. In A. E. Bergin & S. L. Garfield (Eds.), *Handbook of psychotherapy and behavior change* (4th ed., pp. 509–539). Oxford, England: Wiley.

Greenberg, L. S., Rice, L. N., & Elliott, R. (1993). *Facilitating emotional change: The moment-by-moment process.* New York, NY: Guilford Press.

Hadley, S. W., & Strupp, H. H. (1977). Evaluations of treatment in psychotherapy: Naiveté or necessity? *Professional Psychology, 8*, 478–490. doi:10.1037/0735-7028.8.4.478

Horvath, A. O., & Symonds, B. D. (1991). Relation between the working alliance and outcome in psychotherapy. *Journal of Counseling Psychology, 38*, 139–149. doi:10.1037/0022-0167.38.2.139

Kiesler, D. J. (1996). *Contemporary interpersonal theory and research: Personality, psychopathology, and psychotherapy.* New York, NY: Wiley.

Llewelyn, S. P. (1988). Psychological therapy as viewed by clients and therapists. *British Journal of Clinical Psychology, 27*, 223–237. doi:10.1111/j.2044-8260.1988.tb00779.x

Mohr, J. J., & Woodhouse, S. S. (2001). Looking inside the therapeutic alliance: Assessing clients' visions of helpful and harmful psychotherapy. *Psychotherapy Bulletin, 36*, 15–16.

Orlinsky, D. E., & Howard, K. I. (1975). *Varieties of psychotherapeutic experience: Multivariate analyses of patients' and therapists' reports.* New York, NY: Teachers College Press.

Safran, J. D., & Muran, J. C. (2000). *Negotiating the therapeutic alliance: A relational treatment guide.* New York, NY: Guilford Press.

Strachey, J. (1934). The nature of the therapeutic action of psychoanalysis. *The International Journal of Psychoanalysis, 15*, 127–159.

Strauss, A., & Corbin, J. (1990). *Basics of qualitative research.* Newbury Park, CA: Sage.

Strupp, H. H., & Binder, J. (1984). *Psychotherapy in a new key: A guide to time-limited psychodynamic therapy.* New York, NY: Basic Books.

Strupp, H. H., & Hadley, S. W. (1977). A tripartite model of mental health and therapeutic outcomes: With special reference to negative effects in psychotherapy. *American Psychologist, 32*, 187–196. doi:10.1037/0003-066X.32.3.187

Timulak, L. (2007). Identifying core categories of client-identified impact of helpful events in psychotherapy: A qualitative meta-analysis. *Psychotherapy Research, 17*, 305–314. doi:10.1080/10503300600608116

Wallerstein, R. S. (1990). The corrective emotional experience: Is reconsideration due? *Psychoanalytic Inquiry, 10*, 288–324. doi:10.1080/07351690.1990.10399609

11

CORRECTIVE RELATIONAL EXPERIENCES: CLIENT PERSPECTIVES

SARAH KNOX, SHIRLEY A. HESS, CLARA E. HILL,
ALAN W. BURKARD, AND RACHEL E. CROOK-LYON

We focus in this chapter on *corrective relational experiences* (CREs), which we define as specific times in therapy when the client feels a distinct shift, such that she or he comes to understand or experience affectively the relationship with the therapist in a different and unexpected way, and is thereby transformed in some manner. Our research follows in the tradition established by Alexander and French (1946) of corrective emotional experiences and Goldfried (1980) of corrective experiences. We focus here, however, only on those experiences that occur within the context of, and because of, the therapeutic relationship. Given the empirically demonstrated importance of the therapeutic relationship to therapy process and outcome (see Norcross, 2002), it makes sense to study corrective experiences within the context of the therapeutic relationship. Thus, our definition is consistent with that adopted at the Pennsylvania State University conference

The order of the second and third authors is alphabetical; both contributed equally to this project. We thank Jen Dahne, Laura Hartmann, Jennifer Jeffery, Trisha Makovsky, and Beth Sleeper for transcribing the interviews. We also thank Arpana Inman and Nick Ladany for reading a draft of this chapter.

on corrective experiences, except that we focus on the relational aspect of such experiences.

Globally, CREs provide clients with "a real-life experience of change in the here-and-now relationship with the therapist" (Teyber, 2006, p. 20) and thus potentially give clients healing responses to their long-standing relationship patterns. CREs rely on therapists responding differently (e.g., more supportively) to clients than have others in clients' pasts. As stated by Levenson (2003), therapists facilitate such experiences by responding to clients helpfully, maturely, and respectfully, thereby undermining clients' dysfunctional styles. Because of the therapist's response, it is speculated that clients' relational schemas become both more flexible and more broad, for clients realize that they need not respond in their customary (and usually problematic) ways. Thus, when therapists respond differently than clients have previously experienced, clients discover that they, too, can interact differently, and then they can begin to alter their troubling relationship patterns with others in their lives. Clients thus resolve, instead of repeat, their earlier maladaptive behavior patterns (Teyber, 2006).

More specifically, CREs are based on the assumption that the therapy relationship itself serves as the source of the corrective experience. Clients may encounter healing responses in their lives outside of therapy and may even be able to gradually adopt more adaptive relational patterns by vicariously watching others' interactions, but our belief is that the therapy relationship is a potent, and as yet relatively empirically unexamined, source of such transformational experiences. In the intense crucible of therapy, the therapy relationship is pivotal to clients' transformation and improved functioning, for it is "restitutive in its own right" (Cohen, 2008, p. 230). In addition, although the entire relationship might well be healing, we were most interested in examining here specific events in therapy that clients considered to be corrective. Our thought was that by studying specific events, we might be able to learn more about the mechanism of change involved in CREs.

For this study, we chose to investigate CREs of clients who were also therapists-in-training. Our thinking was that because of their natural inclinations and training, therapists-in-training would be more able to reflect and articulate their experiences than would clients who are not also therapists. In addition, we used consensual qualitative research (CQR; Hill et al., 2005; Hill, Thompson, & Williams, 1997), a method that fosters in-depth examination of phenomena and uses a team of researchers to achieve a common understanding of the data. CQR's inductive nature also allows unanticipated findings to emerge (i.e., researchers explore participants' experiences without any predetermined responses in mind). Finally, CQR lets researchers use participants' own language as the foundation of data analysis.

METHOD

Participants

Clients

The 12 participants (10 women, two men; all White) ranged in age from 27 to 54 years old ($M = 38.25$, $SD = 10.33$); all were therapists-in-training at the time of the CRE. With regard to their theoretical orientation, they rated (using a 5-point scale, where $1 = low$, $5 = high$) humanistic–existential approaches 4.00 ($SD = 0.74$), psychoanalytic or psychodynamic 3.33 ($SD = 1.23$), and behavioral or cognitive behavioral 2.27 ($SD = 1.01$). They had been in therapy between one and six times ($M = 3.17$, $SD = 1.70$) and had seen between one and five therapists ($M = 2.75$, $SD = 1.42$) for between 18 and 500+ sessions ($M = 167.58$, $SD = 147.67$). With regard to the therapy in which the CRE occurred, participants reported having had between 12 sessions and 12 years of primarily weekly, individual therapy.

Therapists

As reported by the clients, the 12 (seven men, five women; 11 White, one South Asian) therapists ranged in age from early 30s to early 70s. With regard to theoretical orientation, five were described as Jungian; four as eclectic; and three as other (e.g., humanistic, psychodynamic, cognitive behavioral, feminist). They were reported to have had between 10 and 25+ years of experience as therapists. Of the nine participants who reported the place of treatment, eight saw their therapist in her or his private practice, and one at an agency.

Interviewers and Judges

The first three authors (all European American women) were the interviewers and judges on the primary team. The remaining two authors (both European American; one woman, one man) were auditors on the study. All were faculty members in graduate programs in counseling (either counseling psychology or counselor education). Ages ranged from 36 to 58 years. The authors' biases and expectations appear in Appendix 11.1; the potential influence of these biases and expectations was monitored throughout the research process.

Measures

Demographic Form

Participants provided basic information on the demographic form: age, sex, race/ethnicity, their own theoretical orientation as therapists, number of times they had been in therapy, number of therapists seen, estimated total number of therapy sessions, estimated total weeks in therapy, and primary reason or reasons for seeking therapy. Participants also provided their name and contact information so the first interview could be arranged.

Interview Protocol

To develop the interview protocol, the primary team members individually wrote questions based on their experiences as clients and therapists, and then combined these questions in a logical structure and solicited feedback from the auditors. The preliminary protocol was then piloted with one of the primary team members describing to the other two a CRE she had as a client. Based on her feedback, we revised the protocol (simplified wording, reorganized questions, deleted redundant questions). The resulting semistructured protocol (i.e., researchers followed a set of standard questions, and probed as deemed appropriate to acquire more detailed information; see Appendix 11.2) opened with the definition of CREs (see beginning of chapter) and a reminder about confidentiality. The first question asked participants to set the stage for the CRE by describing the therapy experience in which it occurred (therapy relationship, concerns addressed in therapy) and also asked about how the entire therapy may have been a healing experience. Next, the protocol focused on the specific CRE (what was happening in therapy before the CRE, what made the CRE corrective, how the CRE was transformative in therapy and also in other relationships, and how the CRE affected participants' own clinical work). The follow-up interview involved questions about a second CRE within the same therapy and also included questions about clarifications or additions to content from the first interview. (Because not all participants had two CRE examples, we analyzed only the data arising from each participant's first example.) The interview closed with a question about why participants chose to take part in the study and how the interview had affected them.

Procedures for Collecting Data

Recruiting Participants

Students in, or graduates of, the primary researchers' academic programs, as well as the researchers' colleagues, were asked to participate and also to share study information with their peers. Interviewers did not interview anyone from their own current institution. Because of the snowball method of recruiting, we do not know how many people were ultimately contacted, but the proportion who participated seemed small; several people noted that they had not been in therapy or could not identify a salient CRE.

Interviewing

Each member of the primary team completed both the initial and follow-up audiotaped telephone interviews with four or five participants. At the end of the approximately 60-minute first interview, the interviewer arranged for the follow-up interview. The approximately 20- to 60-minute follow-up interview (the length of the follow-up interview depended on whether the participant had a second CRE) occurred about 2 weeks later and before data analysis had begun on the case.

Transcripts

Interviews were transcribed verbatim (except for minimal encouragers, silences, and stutters). Any identifying information was deleted from transcripts, and each participant was assigned a code number to ensure confidentiality.

Procedures for Analyzing Data

Data were analyzed by following the steps of CQR (Hill et al., 1997, 2005). This qualitative method relies on research team members achieving consensus regarding data classification and meaning as they complete the three steps of data analysis (domain coding, which involves organizing the data into topic areas; core ideas, which involves summarizing or abstracting the data for each case within each domain; and cross-analysis, which involves developing categories that capture themes within domains across cases); two auditors reviewed each step. In addition, we continuously went back to the raw data to check all of the judgments, and we revised the cross-analyses numerous times until everyone was satisfied that the results reflected the raw data as closely as possible.

All participants were sent a draft of the final results of the study and asked to comment and to confirm that their confidentiality had been protected. Seven participants responded with minor changes, which have been incorporated.

RESULTS

Here, we present the findings that emerged when participants described their CREs as therapy clients (see Table 11.1). We provide not only the categories that emerged in the cross-analysis but also interview excerpts or core ideas to more vividly depict the findings. For all findings, we followed CQR guidelines with regard to labeling category frequencies, such that categories that emerged for all or all but one case (11 or 12) were considered

TABLE 11.1
Results Domains and Categories

Domain and *category*	Frequency
General background for this therapy	
Positive outcomes of therapy	General
Relationship with therapist	
Positive elements	General
Ruptures, problems, or frustrations	Variant
Concerns addressed in therapy	
Graduate school or professional development	Typical
Interpersonal	Typical
Intrapersonal	Typical
CRE antecedent	
Participant deeply involved in therapy process	Typical
Rupture between therapist and participant	Variant
CRE event	
Type of event	
Resolution of rupture	Variant
Rescue of client	Variant
Reassurance or normalization	Variant
Participants' actions during CRE	
Explored thoughts and feelings	Typical
Asserted self or feelings	Typical
Dissociated, avoided, or felt vulnerable	Variant
Therapists' actions during CRE	
Empathized, reflected, or accepted	Typical
Became active and directive	Variant
Used immediacy	Variant
Invited exploration	Variant
Responded to rupture	Variant
Reassured or normalized	Variant
CRE consequences (as a result of event)	
Positive intrapersonal changes in participant	General
Improvement in therapy relationship	
Deeper relationship	Typical
Saw therapist in new way	Variant
Positive changes in participant's relationships with others	Typical
Positive changes in participant's work as therapist or therapist-in-training	
Able to do better work with clients	Typical
Used CRE as model for work with clients	Variant
Attended more to therapy relationship with clients	Variant
Effect of interview	
Positive emotions	
Opportunity for reflection about CRE	General
Good experience	Typical
Motivated participant to talk with others	Variant
Realized positive things about therapy	Variant
Negative emotions	Typical

Note. CRE = corrective relational experience. General = 11 or 12 cases; typical = seven–10 cases; variant = two–six cases.

general, those that emerged for more than half and up to the cut-off for general (seven to 10) were considered typical, and those that emerged for between two and half of the cases (two to six) were considered variant. Findings that arose solely in a single case were placed into an "other" category and are not reported in this chapter.

GENERAL BACKGROUND FOR THE THERAPY IN WHICH THE CORRECTIVE RELATIONAL EXPERIENCE OCCURRED

Positive Outcomes of Therapy

Participants generally reported that the therapy in which the CRE occurred had positive outcomes. For instance, participants noted that they learned a lot about themselves and others through the therapy, that therapy gave them the confidence to speak to others about difficult topics, and that they now knew what to do when they began, as one participant stated, to "wallow in their own junk."

Relationship With Therapist

Positive Elements

Participants generally had positive relationships with their therapists. Several noted, for example, that the whole relationship was healing and that they felt safe with their therapists. As an illustration, one participant stated that she respected and admired her therapist and felt that she could talk with him about anything; another described the therapeutic relationship as "good and strong."

Ruptures, Problems, or Frustrations

Variantly, however, some participants acknowledged difficulties in the relationship. In one case, the participant was frustrated because there were things bothering her that, had her therapist done an intake, the therapist would have known, and the participant would not have had to disclose this potentially shameful information after therapist and participant already knew each other. Another participant felt a rupture when his therapist switched from an interpersonal style to a more directive and systematic desensitization approach during the second half of therapy: The participant stated that he longed for the honesty and empathy that had been present during the earlier phase of therapy.

Concerns Addressed in Therapy

Graduate School or Professional Development

Typical therapy concerns focused on graduate school or professional development. For example, one participant noted that she talked about her professional identity and development, as well as the process of completing her doctoral degree and its impact on her relationships. Another indicated that he sought therapy early in graduate school to "improve [himself] and work out things."

Interpersonal

Interpersonal concerns were also a typical focus of therapy. One participant reported, for instance, that her therapy attended to her concerns about her marriage and her eventual divorce; another noted that he worked in therapy on how he presented himself to others, and also on the relationship between his family dynamics and his current struggles.

Intrapersonal

Also typically addressed were intrapersonal topics. One participant admitted that she was very depressed, cried frequently, struggled with school, and felt powerless to make changes in her life; another indicated that her therapy focused on her loneliness and sexuality; a third stated that she was seeking to "do some individuating" and work on her "adult womanness."

CORRECTIVE RELATIONAL EXPERIENCE ANTECEDENT

Participant Deeply Involved in Therapy Process

Participants typically described that they were actively and deeply involved in the therapy process before the CRE. In one case, the participant reported that she was crying about something intensely and was retreating and hiding in her sadness and tears. In another case, the participant stated that he was talking about feeling judged by professors and feeling a need to say all the "right things" so that they would not think that they had erred in letting him into the doctoral program; he noted, as well, that he also tried to do all the right things in therapy and be the "perfect client" so that the therapist would like him.

Rupture Between Therapist and Participant

Variantly, a misunderstanding or rupture between therapist and participant was identified as the CRE antecedent (such antecedents occurred only in the "resolution of rupture" type of event; see below). As an example, one participant was not feeling heard by her therapist, which frustrated her. She then decided to communicate her frustration to her therapist (rather than drop out of therapy, as she had in the past), so she wrote in her journal about these feelings and later showed the journal to her therapist. In a second example, the participant stated that her therapist believed that he was a "blank slate" and that anything that occurred between them reflected the participant's issues, leaving the participant with a sense of powerlessness at not being able to have a say in the therapy.

CORRECTIVE RELATIONAL EXPERIENCE EVENT

Type of Event

On the basis of our overall understanding, we categorized the events into three overall types, all of which were variant. First, some events involved the resolution of a rupture between therapist and client. For instance, one client described her usually strong relationship with her therapist as temporarily ruptured when, after canceling her session on September 11, 2001, because she thought her non-European American therapist would be distracted by the her "little problems," the client received a bill for the cancelled session. The client believed that the bill indicated that her therapist was angry at her, and she felt that "his hand came out of the piece of paper and slapped me on the face." It took the therapist and client 2 years to work through this incident, during which time the therapist did eventually admit that he was mad at the client and revealed that he thought the client's cancellation meant that she considered him a terrorist. His acknowledging his error was healing because it enabled the participant to admit and accept that nobody is perfect.

In the second type of event, therapists rescued clients who were feeling extremely distressed. As an illustration, one client struggled to remain psychologically present in session when she cried and became intensely upset. During one such occasion, the therapist "barked" the client's name and said "come back," penetrating the client's bubble and calling her back to the surface. The client realized that she often used her emotions to retreat and avoid, and she described the experience of being called back to the present as "potently in the here-and-now... all of a sudden these clouds just kind of part and you're like, 'I just saw myself.'"

The third type of event involved therapists reassuring or normalizing clients' concerns. As an example, a male client was struggling with sexual concerns (e.g., perceived high sex drive, history of childhood sexual activity). His female therapist asked him if he felt "broken," to which the client agreed.

He felt that the way his therapist asked this question suggested that he was not broken, which helped him challenge his assumptions. The client later asked his therapist if he was "crazy." His therapist reframed that he was "just a curious kid," which also reassured and normalized the client's feelings and allowed him to begin to accept himself.

Participants' Actions During the Corrective Relational Experience

Explored Thoughts and Feelings

Participants typically stated that they explored their thoughts and feelings as part of the CRE. As an example, one participant said that the most corrective aspect of the CRE was allowing herself to acknowledge how much pain she felt, pain that she historically minimized or neglected so that she could take care of others. In a second example, a participant reported that the CRE was one of the first times in his life, inside or outside of therapy, that he allowed himself to be vulnerable.

Asserted Self or Feelings

In this category, participants typically seemed to go beyond just expressing or exploring feelings to strongly taking a stand and asserting themselves. In one case, the participant did not feel that she was "getting [her] stuff across" and was frustrated that her therapist seemed not to be hearing her. Seeking to express herself more clearly and to reach out to her therapist in a different way, the participant gave her journal to her therapist, in which she had written down "what was really troubling" her, as a way of saying "I need you to hear what you're not hearing." Another expressed his anger at the therapy's time constraints, and a third stated that she wanted her therapist to take care of her.

Dissociated, Avoided, or Felt Vulnerable

Participants variantly noted that they dissociated, avoided, or felt vulnerable during the CRE. As an example, one participant was crying deeply, retreating, and hiding in her sadness and tears. In another case, the participant's seemingly confident and competent presentation, one she also maintained in therapy, hid deep insecurities, which she assumed frustrated her therapist's attempts to help her open up.

Therapists' Actions During the Corrective Relational Experience

Empathized, Reflected, or Accepted

According to these participants, therapists typically used empathy, reflection, and acceptance. As an illustration, one therapist said to her client,

"It's really difficult for me to see you in so much pain." In another example, the therapist accepted the participant exactly as he was, a new experience for the participant. In a third example, the participant experienced the CRE as a striking example of the therapist "getting" her.

Became Active or Directive

Therapists also variantly became active and directive. In one case, the therapist verbally "grabbed" the participant and pulled her to the surface (out of her "life sucks" thoughts). As another example, the therapist challenged the participant regarding the latter's keeping up her shield in therapy and not letting the therapist really help.

Used Immediacy

Therapists variantly used immediacy (i.e., directly talking about the relationship). For example, one participant and her therapist used immediacy to discuss what had been going on between them, which illuminated the participant's feeling that she was not effectively communicating her concerns. In a second case, the therapist asked what the participant wanted from the therapist, invited the participant to stay with her emotions, and assured the participant that the therapist would "hold that."

Invited Exploration

Therapists' variantly invited exploration. For instance, one therapist asked the participant, "Where are the tears coming from?" in an effort to help the participant find and connect to her bodily felt emotions. In another case, when the participant had to terminate because of insurance limitations, the therapist stated the reality of the termination and asked the participant what they should do about that reality.

Responded to Rupture

Variantly, therapists were responsive to a therapeutic rupture. For example, a participant reported that her therapist eventually realized how much his own difficulties had interfered with what the participant needed from him and from therapy; in a second case, a therapist's ability to acknowledge his error enabled the therapist and client to work through their tension.

Reassured or Normalized

Finally, therapists variantly reassured and normalized. In one case, the therapist normalized the client's sexual behaviors; in another case, the therapist assured the participant that they would not terminate until the client was in a "safe place" and could function.

CORRECTIVE RELATIONAL EXPERIENCE CONSEQUENCES

Positive Intrapersonal Changes in Participant

After the CRE, participants generally reported a range of positive intrapersonal changes. They felt more self-assured (one therapist even commented to a participant, "You look taller to me today"), took better care of themselves, were better able to resolve some of their own struggles, were more able to trust their own emotions, achieved insight (one participant came to understand that nobody, including her therapist, was perfect, and that imperfection may provide useful material for the therapy; another realized that his anxiety need not destroy his relationship with his therapist), and accepted themselves more.

Improvement in Therapy Relationship

Deeper Relationship

After the CRE, participants typically noted a deeper and more meaningful relationship with their therapists. One participant noted, for instance, that his therapy became more valuable and meaningful because he was able to open up more; another started to connect better with her therapist; a third trusted her therapist more deeply.

Saw Therapist in a New Way

Participants variantly saw their therapists in a new way after the CRE. In one case, the participant saw her therapist as a human being with his own flaws and biases, his own "shadows and demons" to fight; in another case, the participant gained a greater appreciation for what his therapist brought to the therapy and was humbled at how much his therapist tolerated from the participant.

Positive Changes in Participant's Relationships With Others

Participants also typically reported positive changes in their relationships with others. One participant indicated that she was able to make better connections with faculty in her program and was gentler with her husband; another participant felt more assertive and present with others, took more healthy risks, and thought rather than just going along with others.

Positive Changes in Participant's Work as Therapist

Able to Do Better Work With Clients

The CREs also affected participants' clinical work, in that participants typically were able to do better work with their own clients. For instance, one noted that the CRE allowed her to be more present with "scarier" client material and to be less judgmental or blaming of clients. A second participant reported that the CRE permitted her to let go of her need to be perfect and in control in sessions, enabling her to be more flexible, more able to explore client affect, and more able to abandon her need to have an agenda for sessions.

Used Corrective Relational Experience as a Model for Work With Clients

Participants variantly reported that they used the CRE as a model for working with clients. One participant noted that her initial reaction to her therapist's CRE intervention (acknowledging how hard it was to see the participant in such pain) was, "That's a really great intervention. I'm going to stick it in my pocket and use it someday." A second participant reported that the empty chair work in her CRE was helpful and gave her strategies to use with her own clients.

Attended More to Therapy Relationship With Clients

Participants variantly stated that the CRE enabled them to be more attentive to the therapy relationship with their clients. In one instance, the participant asserted that after the CRE, he tried to shed the "therapist" role and just be himself in the room with the client. Another participant stated that the CRE taught him the importance of warmth and rapport with clients, and a third acknowledged that he was able to be more available as a therapist when with clients and that he sensed that his clients felt more understood.

EFFECT OF INTERVIEW

Positive Emotions

Opportunity for Reflection About Corrective Relational Experience

Participants generally felt that the interview provided an opportunity for them to reflect about their CREs. One stated that the interview brought together some of her therapy experiences and helped her perceive more clearly the shifts and changes in herself and in her therapy; another indicated that the interview made him realize that CREs are moments of deep connection between people.

Good Experience

Typically, participants also described the interview as an engaging and good experience, one in which they felt supported by the interviewer. For instance, one person indicated that the interview itself was a CRE, for the interviewer reacted positively and normalized his feelings; another noted that the interview was fun and engaging; a third stated that the interviewer validated the participant and helped her differentiate between some of her clinical issues and reality.

Motivated Participant to Talk With Others

Variantly, the interviewer spurred participants to talk with others in their life about their therapy experiences. As an example, one participant spoke with her supervisor about the study and the effects of CREs; another made plans for a phone session with her therapist; a third shared her interview experience with her sister, something she previously would not have done.

Realized Positive Things About Therapy

The interview also variantly helped participants realize positive things about their therapy. One participant noted that the interview allowed him to remember the progress he made in therapy and the power of the sessions, rather than focusing on "the places that therapy didn't go"; another participant acknowledged that the interview made her think about her therapy experience more positively, consider it from a different angle, and remember the good she got from therapy.

Negative Emotions

Also typical, however, were negative emotions evoked by the interview. One participant felt pretty down after the interview and was thrown back into her affective experiences more than she anticipated; another participant acknowledged that she felt vulnerable because she shared more of herself than she intended, but she also wanted to make a point.

DISCUSSION

Through our interviews of therapy clients, we sought to develop a deep understanding of clients' perspectives on CREs that occurred within the context of, and because of, the therapeutic relationship. As a whole, then, these participants described their CREs as powerful and transformative events in therapy, events whose effects, both intra- and interpersonal, remained long after treatment had ended. Broadly speaking, the CREs arose from therapies characterized by successful outcomes and strong therapy relationships, and occurred when participants (as clients) were deeply engaged in addressing the very concerns that brought them to seek help. It is intriguing that there was no predominant type of CRE event. Each event, however, involved a range of actions by both participant and therapist, and led to marked changes in participants themselves, their own therapy, their work with their clients, and their relationships with others. We discuss these findings in more detail next.

We note first that these CREs emerged during the course of therapies that participants described in quite positive terms with regard to both outcome and therapeutic relationship. Although this is by no means a surprising finding, it adds further affirmation to the importance of the relationship for therapy process and outcome (Norcross, 2002), given that a good therapy relationship may provide a vital foundation for CREs to occur. Not all was perfect, however, for ruptures and frustrations before the CREs were also in evidence. Nevertheless, such difficulties seemed not to undermine participants' sense of the overall benefit of the therapy, probably because these occasional moments of tension seem to have been resolved. Furthermore, and as we discuss below, the difficulties may have rendered the CRE even more potent and transformative in the apparent healing of what may have been, even if only temporarily, a contentious bond.

The topics addressed in the therapy demonstrated no particular pattern, but certainly reflected the range of concerns likely salient for any client, including professional struggles, as well as both intra- and interpersonal difficulties. Despite their status as therapists-in-training, then, these participants appeared to face challenges similar to those of non-therapist clients.

As antecedent to the CREs, participants were most often intensely engaged in the therapy process. Thus, they were doing the hard work of therapy, were grappling with their areas of difficulty, and were immersed in the therapy endeavor. Occasionally, the precursor to the CRE consisted of a disruption of the therapy relationship or process, a rupture. Participants and therapists in some way missed each other, leading to a period of tension in their relationship. Clearly, however, corrective or transformational experiences need not arise solely out of such conflictual circumstances; they may, in fact, arise from the expected and ongoing therapy processes.

Given the extant literature asserting the power of rupture repair in therapy (e.g., Safran, Muran, Samstag, & Stevens, 2002), we were surprised that such breaches emerged as only a variant category here, one of no greater frequency than the other two types of CRE events (i.e., rescue of client, reassurance or normalization). Although ruptures may indeed provide fertile fodder for CREs, other conditions appear equally favorable for such transformational events in therapy. In some cases, participants benefitted from an immediate, rescue-type of intervention, one in which the therapist quite powerfully pulled the participant back from the figurative abyss and directed her or him to reengage with the supportive presence of the therapist. In other cases, therapists' reassurances that participants' struggles were quite normal provided palpable relief and comfort, affirming Cohen's (2008) description of the therapy relationship as itself restitutive.

For CREs to occur, both participant and therapist had to be actively involved throughout the event. Participants, for instance, had to be willing to examine their thoughts and feelings, and also to assert themselves or their emotions. In essence, they had to be willing to stay fully engaged in the work of therapy, even when doing so was difficult or uncomfortable. These participants' willingness to remain engaged may also speak to the strength of the therapeutic relationship: Had they not felt a sense of safety, had they not experienced their therapists as providers of a nurturing space, they may well not have been able to allow themselves to experience the vulnerability that is often necessary for healing and growth. Participants' active involvement was thus central to the CRE. Only occasionally did their actions depict disengagement, such as withdrawal or retreat.

Therapists were similarly perceived as being engaged in the CRE, and they most prominently provided participants with empathy and acceptance. Thus, they remained fully present as participants grappled with their therapy concerns, providing a safe and compassionate space in which the work of therapy could occur. Participants experienced their therapists as neither critical nor judgmental, which likely fostered conditions in which corrective and transformative experiences might indeed arise. In addition, therapists also were perceived as engaging with participants in a variety of other supportive ways, such as using immediacy, fostering exploration, or responding to a potential rupture. In so doing, they may well have responded in ways quite different from significant others in participants' pasts and thus began to challenge participants' assumptions about the futility (at best) or the pain (at worst) of entering into relationships with others (Levenson, 2003).

For participants, the fruits of these labors were remarkable. All noted welcomed transformations within themselves, and most also experienced improvement in their therapy relationship, in their relationships with others, and in their work with their own clients. As is hoped, then, the effects of these CREs extended well beyond the therapy itself, enabling participants to enjoy improved intra- and interpersonal functioning. Echoing Teyber (2006), their lives were changed in the here and now of the therapy relationship, and they began to productively alter their long-standing relational patterns. Their now broader and more flexible relational schemas likely also contributed to participants' ability to engage with others more healthily, allowing them to resolve rather than repeat earlier problematic behavior patterns.

Given the power of these CREs, it is not surprising that most participants found the research interview to be a positive experience, for it often stimulated further reflection about the CRE itself. It is also not surprising that negative emotions were reported by a few participants: Describing therapy experiences, even if ultimately deemed positive, may well reevoke some of the difficult material that led to therapy and thus may render participants vulnerable when asked to share such struggles with an interviewer.

Limitations

Given that our findings are based on qualitative data, we cannot know that the therapist interventions mentioned causally led to the occurrence or resolution of the CREs. The findings do, however, reflect our participants' (i.e., clients') descriptions of and attributions regarding the process and outcome of the CREs.

Furthermore, this study relies on only the participants' (i.e., clients') perspective of CREs. As such, we do not know how therapists experienced these events. In addition, most of the participants were women, and all were European American, so we are uncertain as to the effect of gender or race/ethnicity on CREs. Participants were also therapists-in-training and had a fair amount of experience as clients, and thus were well informed about therapy process and relationships. How those without such experiences, as well as those not in the mental health profession, might describe CREs is yet to be determined. Generalizing from this sample should thus be done with caution. Furthermore, participants characterized the therapies in which the CREs occurred as positive; it is possible that CREs arising in less favorable therapy conditions would be experienced differently. Several participants' therapists were also identified as Jungian, and we do not know to what extent, if any, this orientation may have affected the CREs. Finally, participants received a copy of the interview protocol before participating in the study. Doing so allowed them to make fully informed consent regarding what they would be asked to discuss and also enabled them to think about their therapy experiences before the interview itself; it may, however, also have affected their descriptions of their CREs such that they gave more socially desirable responses than they would have if they had not had the opportunity to reflect on their experiences.

An interesting methodological limitation involves the focus on specific events for this study. Although we initially intended that participants would talk about discrete experiences within individual sessions (as events are studied when examining transcripts of sessions), it quickly became apparent that participants could not easily identify discrete moments (e.g., one event was described as lasting more than 2 years). Because we were looking for transformative events rather than discrete interventions (e.g., therapist self-disclosure), it makes sense that some of these events would take place over longer periods of time. Methodologically, however, we wonder whether brief events have the same impact as events that transpire over a longer period of time. We note, as well, that the diversity of events obtained makes it difficult to define or operationalize CREs clearly.

Future Directions in Research, Training, and Practice

We remain curious about the three distinct types of CRE events that arose here, with none emerging more predominantly than the others. In addition, closer analysis of the findings revealed no definitive pattern for the categories for the different types of CRE events (e.g., resolution of rupture events did not follow a pattern distinct from that of rescue, or reassurance or normalization, events). As noted previously, the extant literature (Safran et al., 2002) suggests that CREs likely arise from therapy ruptures, but such was not solely the case here. Further investigation into the presence, or absence, of any such patterns in CREs may be warranted. In addition, how do CREs relate to other types of good moments in therapy, in which clients experience marked change, improvement, movement, or progress (Mahrer, White, Howard, & Gagnon, 1992), and what therapist "operations and methods" (Mahrer et al., 1992, p. 253) may contribute to such moments?

We also wonder about the implications of these results for training therapists. How might new therapists be trained, for instance, to become attuned to when their clients are, or are not, having corrective experiences? Empathy, reflection, and acceptance emerged as possible facilitators of CREs, so such skills need to be nurtured among those just entering the mental health professions. And if CREs are not occurring, what might their absence indicate about the therapy, the therapist, or the client?

Finally, we were also intrigued that a number of students and therapists whom we approached to participate indicated that they had not had CREs in their therapy experiences; in addition, they often seemed upset by the lack of such experiences. We wonder what impact the lack of CREs may have had on them as clients, as well as on their growth as therapists. Clearly, additional and equally fertile CRE soil remains to be tilled.

APPENDIX 11.1: AUTHOR BIASES

In examining our biases and expectations, each of the authors responded to the following questions: (a) What role do CREs have in therapy for clients, both in and out of therapy; (b) What might clients and/or therapists do to facilitate corrective relational experiences (CREs); (c) What might clients and/or therapists do to inhibit CREs; and (d) How might being a therapist or therapist-in-training affect the experience of a CRE? We shared the responses that appear below with each other and sought to protect against their unduly affecting our interpretation of the findings.

All of us believed that CREs are powerful, transformative, and positive events in therapy, events that allow clients to see that not only the therapy relationship but also other relationships in their lives can be safe and healing. Two researchers also mentioned that CREs enable clients to alter their cognitive schemas about interpersonal relationships, and two mentioned that CREs also involve clients achieving insight.

With regard to CRE facilitators, all researchers noted that therapists need to provide a safe place in which clients can express their needs and wants, and in which therapists are empathic, compassionate, and sensitive to the therapy relationship. Two researchers also noted that therapists must have the skills to address the relationship openly, including asking questions about relationship patterns, probing for clarity, and exploring clients' thoughts and feelings. Two researchers asserted that clients must trust that the therapist will not "go away" if the relationship becomes difficult and that clients must also be curious and willing to take appropriate risks in the relationship; one noted that client insight would facilitate CREs. One researcher noted that CREs often arise from "stuck moments" in therapy.

All believed that CRE inhibitors included such difficulties as therapists or clients withdrawing or shutting down. Two felt that therapist inattention to the relationship or an inability to address relationship problems would inhibit CREs. In addition, one researcher posited that therapists being inattentive to changes in clients would stifle CREs, as would therapists being "insight dense," interpersonally insensitive, or focusing on other things.

Finally, three researchers felt that clients who were also therapists or therapists-in-training would have a dual awareness during their own CREs as clients: They would be aware of what their therapist was doing as an intervention but would also be engaged affectively in the power of the experience itself. One researcher felt that therapists-in-training would be hesitant to raise relationship problems with their own clients for fear of wounding them or because of cultural prohibitions against such conversations.

A fourth researcher felt that therapists-in-training would feel greater pressure (than non–therapist-in-training clients) to be able to process CRE experiences with their own therapists and when doing so may take a more intellectual than an affective approach to the conversation. This researcher also felt that those more advanced in their training would be better able to discuss such events than those earlier in their training.

APPENDIX 11.2: INTERVIEW PROTOCOL

Thank you very much for your participation in this research on corrective relational experiences (CREs) in psychotherapy. We are most grateful for your willingness to discuss your experiences as a client in psychotherapy.

We define CREs as specific times in therapy when the client feels a distinct shift, such that she or he comes to understand or experience affectively the relationship with the therapist in a different and unexpected way and is thereby transformed in some manner. Note that although the entire relationship might be a healing experience, we are most interested in examining here specific events in therapy that you consider to be corrective. All information will be kept completely confidential by assigning each participant a code number and deleting any identifiers.

First Interview

1. Please set the stage for me by telling me about this therapy experience.
   - Possible probes (therapy relationship, concerns addressed in therapy)
2. In what ways was this entire or whole therapy relationship a healing experience for you?
3. Please tell me about the specific event that was a CRE within this therapy relationship.
   - Possible probes (what going on in therapy before event, what occurred to make it corrective, how event was transformative in therapy and in other relationships in client's life)
   - How did being a therapist or therapist-in-training affect your experience of the event?
   - How did the event affect your work as a therapist or therapist-in-training?
4. What additional thoughts do you have about CREs?

Follow-Up Interview

We'd like to ask you now about a second example of a CRE with this same therapist. If you can recall only one such event, we would still very much welcome your participation in this research . . . you need not describe two events in order to participate.

5. Please tell me about a second specific event that was a CRE within this therapy relationship.
   - Possible probes (what going on in therapy before event, what occurred to make it corrective, how event was transformative in therapy and in other relationships in client's life)
   - How did being a therapist or therapist-in-training affect your experience of the event?
   - How did the event affect your work as a therapist or therapist-in-training?
6. Please tell me about the therapist and the therapy involved in these event or events (Therapist: age, gender, race/ethnicity, theoretical orientation, years of therapy experience; Therapy: length, frequency, modality, setting).
7. Why did you participate in this interview?
8. How did this interview affect you?

REFERENCES

Alexander, F., & French, T. M. (1946). *Psychoanalytic therapy: Principles and applications.* New York, NY: Ronald Press.

Cohen, J. N. (2008). Using feminist, emotion-focused, and developmental approaches to enhance cognitive–behavioral therapists for posttraumatic stress disorder related to childhood sexual assault. *Psychotherapy, 45,* 227–246. doi:10.1037/0033-3204.45.2.227

Goldfried, M. R. (1980). Toward the delineation of therapeutic change principles. *American Psychologist, 35,* 991–999. doi:10.1037/0003-066X.35.11.991

Hill, C. E., Knox, S., Thompson, B. J., Williams, E. N., Hess, S. A., & Ladany, N. (2005). Consensual qualitative research: An update. *Journal of Counseling Psychology, 52,* 196–205. doi:10.1037/0022-0167.52.2.196

Hill, C. E., Thompson, B. J., & Williams, E. N. (1997). A guide to conducting consensual qualitative research. *The Counseling Psychologist, 25,* 517–572. doi:10.1177/0011000097254001

Levenson, H. (2003). Time-limited dynamic psychotherapy: An integrationist perspective. *Journal of Psychotherapy Integration, 13,* 300–333. doi:10.1037/1053-0479.13.3-4.300

Mahrer, A. R., White, M. V., Howard, M. T., & Gagnon, R. (1992). How to bring about some very good moments in psychotherapy sessions. *Psychotherapy Research, 2,* 252–265. doi:10.1080/10503309212331333014

Norcross, J. C. (Ed.). (2002). *Psychotherapy relationships that work: Therapist contributions and responsiveness to patients.* New York, NY: Oxford University Press.

Safran, J. D., Muran, J. C., Samstag, L. W., & Stevens, C. (2002). Repairing alliance ruptures. In J. Norcross (Ed.), *Psychotherapy relationships that work: Therapist contributions and responsiveness to patients* (pp. 235–254). New York, NY: Oxford University Press.

Teyber, E. (2006). *Interpersonal process in therapy: An integrative method* (5th ed.). Belmont, CA: Brooks/Cole.

12

RELATIONAL EVENTS IN ACCEPTANCE AND COMMITMENT THERAPY FOR THREE CLIENTS WITH ANOREXIA NERVOSA: WHAT IS CORRECTIVE?

MARGIT I. BERMAN, CLARA E. HILL, JINGQING LIU, JOHN JACKSON, WONJIN SIM, AND PATRICIA SPANGLER

Relational work or immediacy (i.e., talking in the here and now about the therapeutic relationship) is theorized to be helpful, especially in psychodynamic and humanistic psychotherapies (Hill & Knox, 2009). Benefits are thought to accrue because clients are provided with interpersonal feedback and because problems or ruptures in the therapeutic relationship can be resolved in a healthy way, which helps clients make changes in their relationship patterns outside of therapy. Thus, the overall purpose of this study was to examine relational events (REs) within psychotherapy given that they may lead to corrective relational experiences.

Indeed, recent research has provided preliminary evidence for these claims (see Hill & Knox, 2009). For example, two recent case studies of brief therapy explored the impact of REs (i.e., discussions of the therapeutic relationship; Hill et al., 2008; Kasper, Hill, & Kivlighan, 2008). In both case studies, discussion of the therapeutic relationship had generally positive effects (e.g., clients were better able to express their immediate feelings), but some negative outcomes also emerged in one of the cases (i.e., the client felt awkward, pressured, and uneasy with some of the therapist's immediacy). Hill et al. (2008) concluded that REs may be most powerful when therapists use them to invite clients to express their emotions, to repair therapeutic ruptures, and to help clients consolidate their sense of the therapist as a good object or secure base of attachment. Hill et al. (2008) also suggested that additional qualitative case studies on the therapeutic relationship are needed to better understand in what therapeutic contexts REs are useful and when they may be contraindicated.

We hoped to extend this work in the present study by investigating REs in three cases of anorexia nervosa (AN). We focused on AN because previous studies found that emotional dysregulation, avoidant and anxious attachment, and difficulties in relationships predicted poorer outcome for eating disorders in both clinical trials and naturalistic therapy settings (Bell, 2002; Thompson-Brenner & Westen, 2005). Some research has also suggested that emotional dysregulation, attachment, and difficulties in relationships are associated not only with eating disorder treatment outcome but also with the interventions that therapists choose. For example, therapists using cognitive behavior therapy (CBT) were more likely to treat clients with emotionally dysregulated or constricted eating disorders with a psychodynamic approach, whereas psychodynamic therapists became more directive and used more CBT interventions with clients who were constricted (Thompson-Brenner & Westen, 2005). These findings suggest that attention to the therapeutic relationship may yield a better understanding of the elements of effective eating disorder treatment.

The treatment chosen for investigation in this research was acceptance and commitment therapy (ACT; Hayes, Strosahl, & Wilson, 1999; Heffner & Eifert, 2004). ACT is a third-wave CBT in which relational work is not the main focus of treatment, although self-disclosure by the therapist is encouraged as a tool to emphasize the common humanity and common struggle of the therapist and client. Focusing on a CBT such as ACT seemed particularly interesting given that CBTs are commonly used to treat AN and given the suggestion that CBT therapists treating eating disorders may attend to the therapeutic relationship more with difficult clients. In fact, using the therapeutic relationship to provide a corrective emotional experience was among the primary interventions that CBT-oriented therapists used with clients with emotionally constricted or dysregulated eating disorders in one study (Thompson-Brenner & Westen, 2005). Although this study found poorer outcomes for the dysregulated and constricted groups, a more direct investigation of REs and immediacy interventions in CBT may shed light on when these atypical CBT interventions represent helpful adaptation by therapists to client need and when they represent an inappropriate response from a therapist attempting to manage difficult client behavior.

Although it is possible that ACT therapists may, like other CBT therapists, try to create corrective emotional experiences in therapy with difficult clients with eating disorders, it is important to note that ACT differs from psychodynamic approaches in the conceptualization of corrective experiences. Most forms of psychodynamic therapy seek to help clients understand and break chronic maladaptive interpersonal patterns, often through new relational experiences with the therapist. ACT therapists also use experiential learning in therapy, but the focus is not on relationship patterns but on maladaptive responses to negative internal experiences, such as emotional pain. Negative experiences within the therapeutic relationship thus are handled by ACT therapists in the same way as other forms of pain: with nonjudgmental, mindful observation of the unpleasant experience, followed by a recommitment to moving forward, toward and through pain, in service to pursuing a values-driven life.

As in other forms of therapy, ruptures and relational conflicts are likely common in ACT, particularly because clients generally begin ACT in a (tacit) state of disagreement with the therapist on the basic tasks and goals of therapy. Clients come to therapy to eliminate their emotional pain, whereas ACT therapists seek to undermine such efforts, usually by exposing clients experientially to the failure of their efforts to control their own emotional experiences. Thus, as clients begin ACT, feelings of confusion, anger, distress, and hopelessness can emerge. Therapist anxiety can also arise. Later phases of ACT also offer opportunities for client anger at the therapist, as the therapist tries to facilitate client exposure to, and acceptance of, previously avoided experiences.

To evaluate both the process and outcome of relational experiences in manualized ACT for AN, we used a pretest–posttest mixed quantitative and qualitative case series design with a 1-year follow-up assessment. The quantitative process and outcome data provided a context for the three cases and allowed us to compare the results with normative data. The heart of the study, however, is the clinical qualitative description of the cases. We used the consensual qualitative research method (Hill et al., 2005; Hill, Thompson, & Williams, 1997) as applied to cases (CQR-C; Jackson, Chui, & Hill, 2011), as was used in the two previous case studies of immediacy in interpersonally oriented psychotherapy (Hill et al., 2008; Kasper et al., 2008) to identify and analyze REs in a series of three cases of short-term manualized ACT treatment of AN. Both previous case studies focused on immediacy in therapeutic relationships in which the therapist was an expert in the use of interpersonal therapy and immediacy interventions. Therefore, we sought to investigate REs in a noninterpersonally focused manualized CBT therapy, to determine how often REs occur and what role they play in such therapy.

Our primary interest was determining the helpful (corrective) components of REs. We addressed this in two ways: (a) a qualitative analysis of the therapist interventions used when the clients were exploring versus not exploring the therapeutic relationship and (b) a more global qualitative analysis of the helpful therapist and client variables involved in the REs. We note that although our initial intent was to study corrective relational events (CREs), we could not assume that any of these events were corrective, because we did not have access to clients' inner experiences; rather, we used our clinical judgment from both psychodynamic and ACT perspectives to determine whether events seemed to us to be helpful or corrective.

METHOD

Participants

Clients

"Samia" was a 24-year-old Caucasian female dance teacher with a body mass index (BMI) of 19.1 at pretest.[1] She had a 12-year history of AN symptoms and eating disorder treatment and had been hospitalized four times (twice in the year before her study participation) for inpatient AN treatment as a result of medical instability due to her low weight. She had also been diagnosed with and treated for comorbid posttraumatic stress disorder from chronic childhood sexual abuse by a nonfamilial perpetrator. Samia was taking oral birth control medication as well as 50 mg fluvoxamine daily for depression (the minimum recommended efficacious dose for fluvoxamine in treating depression is 100 mg daily), and lorazepam as needed for anxiety.[2]

"Kate" was a 56-year-old Caucasian female language education specialist; she had a BMI of 18.6 at pretest. She had experienced AN symptoms since an onset in her mid 30s following a divorce (BMI at onset was 14.6). She had received inpatient and outpatient treatment for AN, depression, and interpersonal concerns, which she felt had been effective, although she reported ongoing AN symptoms. Kate reported that she had been diagnosed with dysthymia, although her mood at pretest was normal. She also had a history of chronic childhood sexual abuse by her adoptive older brother. Kate was taking 10 mg fluoxetine daily for depression (the minimum recommended efficacious dose for fluoxetine is 20 mg daily).

---

[1]Standard Centers for Disease Control cutoffs for BMI are < 18.5 = underweight, normal weight = 18.5–24.9, overweight = 25.0–29.9, obese = >30. International Classification of Diseases requires a BMI < 17.5 for a diagnosis of AN; the more commonly used *Diagnostic and Statistical Manual of Mental Disorders* (4th ed., American Psychiatric Association, 1994) leaves the weight criterion largely to the clinician's discretion, stating that it should be below 85% of an individual's ideal body weight, and explicitly stating that "ideal" should be adjusted based on individual characteristics (e.g., presence of medical complications due to low weight). We accepted participants for this study up to a BMI of 20, if they met all other criteria for AN except amenorrhea.
[2]Participants in the study were permitted to take medication while enrolled, provided no medication changes had occurred in the 6 months before study enrollment or during the study.

"Jessie" was a 24-year-old Caucasian female dental hygienist; she had a BMI of 18.7 at pretest. She had been in outpatient multidisciplinary treatment for AN for 1 year before enrollment in the study and had engaged in some brief outpatient medical and psychological treatment for depression in the year before that. She had primary amenorrhea with the exception of a single day of menstrual flow beginning the week before her intake for the current study, her first menstrual period. Jessie also had been diagnosed with osteopenia (abnormally low bone density, precursor to osteoporosis) secondary to AN. She had a history of physical abuse from her father. Jessie was taking 30 mg mirtazapine daily for depression (within the recommended efficacious range for this medication).

Therapist

The therapist (also the first author) was a 34-year-old Caucasian female assistant professor of counseling psychology at a large Midwestern public university at the time of the therapy. Her theoretical orientation was feminist and cognitive behavior. She had completed a 1-year specialty training experience in the treatment of eating disorders at the clinic where the research was conducted and had also completed a 1-year training experience in ACT and other third-wave behavioral therapies during her predoctoral internship. The therapist was supervised by a psychologist who was experienced in the treatment of eating disorders but not in ACT.

Researchers

In addition to the therapist, the research team was composed of a 59-year-old Caucasian female professor and four doctoral students (three female, one male; two White, two Asian international students) in counseling psychology, ranging in age from 24 to 46 years. In terms of biases, all six researchers believed that AN is difficult to treat. Two members of the research team, including the first author, saw ACT as a potentially effective treatment for AN, but the remaining four team members felt skeptical about ACT. Several team members had treated clients with eating disorders; only the first author had used ACT with any client. All team members strongly valued the therapeutic relationship and believed that using immediacy in therapy is a potentially powerful intervention, although all also believed that immediacy is more appropriate and vital for some clients than others. Team members varied in their preference for how much immediacy should be used in therapy.

Outcome Measures

The Symptom Checklist–90—Revised (SCl-90–R; Derogatis, 1994) is a widely used, 90-item self-report measure of general psychopathology. Internal consistency reliability and test-retest reliability have consistently been high in past studies (e.g., Derogatis & Cleary, 1977). Criterion and construct validity evidence is also strong for the instrument. For this study, we used the Global Severity Index (GSI), a general measure of symptomatology.

The Relationship Structures Questionnaire (RS; Fraley, Niedenthal, Marks, Brumbaugh, & Vicary, 2006) is a variant of the Experiences in Close Relationships—Revised Questionnaire that is designed to account for variability in adult attachment across various close relationships; it yields scores for both anxious and avoidant attachment, as well as a global quadrant measure of attachment. Although there is relatively little research specifically on this measure, early data on reliability and validity are promising (Welch & Houser, 2010).

Postsession Measures

Therapist Postsession Evaluation

The therapist evaluated each session using three 7-point Likert-scales (1 = *not at all*, 7 = *extremely*): "How important was today's session to participant's overall recovery?" "How productive was today's session in helping participant recover?" and "How close did you feel to participant during today's session?" Internal consistency alpha for the three items was high for the therapist with all three clients (Samia = .80, Jessie = .92, Kate = .86), so the sum for the therapist with each client was used in subsequent analyses.

Client Postsession Evaluation

Clients evaluated each session using these same three items, with the word *participant* changed to *your* and *you* in the first two items, and to *your therapist* in the third. Alpha for the three items was high for all three clients (Samia = .85, Jessie = .98, Kate = .92), so the sum for each client was used in subsequent analyses.

Procedures: Therapy Phase

Recruitment and Pretreatment Assessment

Prospective clients were adults, on stable medication regimens (i.e., no changes to medication during the study or in the 6 months before participation) who met all criteria for AN, except weight (i.e., participants could have BMI of up to 20) and menstruation (i.e., participants could be menstruating). Prospective participants were recruited by means of referral from therapists and advertisements in a large Midwestern city. Seven prospective participants were initially screened for study inclusion; three met inclusion criteria and enrolled in and completed the study protocol. The therapist met with all three participants for a pretherapy assessment, which included a clinical interview, completion of the SCL-90–R and RS, and informed consent. Height and weight measurements (as well as additional measures not reported here) were also obtained.

Treatment

Clients were seen twice weekly for 17 sessions of individual psychotherapy and two optional family sessions, using a treatment manual adapted by the first author from Heffner and Eifert's (2004) ACT-based self-help workbook for treating AN.[3] Participants were weighed before each session. Sessions were videotaped, and clients and the therapist completed evaluations after each session. Following completion of the therapy, and again 1 year after termination, all participants again completed a clinical interview, the SCL-90–R, and the physical indices (and additional measures not reported here).

Procedure: Analysis Phase

We defined an RE in therapy as a period of time in therapy when the therapeutic relationship was overtly discussed by the therapist and/or the client; the event ended when the topic shifted or the session ended. Nonverbal relational experiences (e.g., a hug at the termination of therapy) were not included unless they were also discussed verbally. Using this definition, between one and six researchers watched each videotaped therapy session for each client and identified all possible REs, which were transcribed verbatim.

Once the initial REs were identified and transcribed, the therapist went back through the videotapes and wrote her experience of the antecedents, process, and consequences of each event. Then, a team of at least three judges (teams rotated for each case but did not include the first author [therapist]) viewed the videotaped events for each case while reading the transcripts and consensually determined whether each RE identified for the case was actually an RE. Some events were discarded at this point if they no longer fit our evolving definition of REs (e.g., in some instances, the therapist inquired if the participant had feedback about the therapy in general and the client indicated that she did not or responded with non–relationship-relevant feedback; in other instances the relationship was very briefly alluded to but was not explicitly discussed).

---

[3]Two of the three clients participated in the optional family sessions; no REs occurred in any of the family sessions, and they were thus not included in any of the analyses described here.

A team of three judges next went sequentially through each of the events again (watching the videotape and reading the transcript) and specified by consensus the antecedents, components of the process of the event (i.e., what the therapist and client did), and consequences of each event. After they completed this task, they coded by consensus the valence of the event (*very positive, mildly positive, neutral, mildly negative,* or *very negative*).

The videotaped event was then watched separately by two other team members (not the first author [therapist]), who made suggestions about changes to the consensus version; these suggestions were considered by the primary team, and changes were made as deemed necessary. The therapist next viewed all of the identified events and noted her feedback about the coding. These comments were reviewed by the primary team, and once again changes were made for a thorough understanding of the event.

In the next step, the team (except for the first author [therapist]) completed a cross-analysis of REs across all three cases, determining themes within and across cases and developing categories of therapist and client actions within the events. The therapist then reviewed the cross analysis and suggested changes.

Because several of the categories were used infrequently and overlapped, judges went back through all the events and collapsed some categories. The final categories for client and therapist actions can be seen in Table 12.1.

Next, four people on the primary team identified when during each of the events the client was exploring (e.g., expressing her feelings) or not exploring the therapy relationship. Two others (including the first author [therapist]) reviewed all of the events and audited everything an additional time. Finally, the four members of the team went back through the audits, going back to the original data when necessary, and made final adjustments to the data.

Four members of the primary team then independently formulated conceptualizations of the relational work with each client, answering several questions: "What was the context in which the REs occurred?" "What were the effects of the relational work?" "What client, therapist, and relational factors contributed to the effects?" Following the Ward method (Schielke, Fishman, Osatuke, & Stiles, 2009), each member independently wrote their answers to these questions and presented their conceptualization to the group. The group then questioned the conceptualizations to try to understand them. Each member then went back and rewrote their conceptualizations. The process continued iteratively until the team arrived at some consensus. At this point, the team divided the responsibility for writing the final document, although all four judges aided in the revisions until all felt that it reflected their views. The other two authors then served as auditors and provided feedback, which the primary team incorporated as appropriate. In

TABLE 12.1
Frequency of Occurrence of Client Exploration Versus No Exploration After Different Therapist Interventions

Intervention	Samia		Kate		Jessie		Total	
	Exp	No	Exp	No	Exp	No	Exp	No
Reflects, validates feelings, supports	6	0	17	6	17	6	40	12
Asks client to explore	7	0	14	4	22	8	43	12
Psychoeducation	1	0	4	13	3	8	8	21
Direct guidance	0	0	1	8	2	7	3	16
Interpretation	1	0	1	0	2	1	4	1
Challenge	0	0	1	6	5	6	6	12
Interrupts, changes topic, denies negative feeling, disagrees with client	0	0	2	7	2	2	4	9
Minimal response, does not acknowledge client's feelings	0	0	0	3	0	0	0	3
Approves, reassures, praises, gives gift or hug	4	0	0	5	4	3	8	8
Seeks client commitment or participation	0	0	1	0	1	5	2	5

Note. Exp = client was productively exploring; no = client was not productively exploring.

addition, the therapist wrote an alternate perspective of her conceptualization of the effects and contributing factors for all three cases. Finally, four judges went through each event and identified by consensus whether the therapist or the client initiated the event.

RESULTS

Outcome Data

Table 12.2 shows scores for the SCL-90–R GSI and weight as indexed by the BMI for the three clients for pretherapy, posttherapy, and at 1-year follow-up. Samia and Kate improved to a clinically significant degree on the SCL-90–R GSI between pretest and posttherapy; all three clients improved to a clinically significant degree on this scale from pretest to the 1-year follow-up (note that none of the clients received any psychotherapy or made any medication changes in the year between posttherapy and follow-up). Weight remained essentially unchanged for Kate and Samia across time. Jessie gained weight and developed a regular monthly menstrual period during

TABLE 12.2
Change in Symptom Checklist–90—R (SCL-90–R) Global Severity Index
(GSI) *T* Scores and Body Mass Index (BMI)

| | SCL-90–R GSI *T* scores | | |
Assessment	Samia	Kate	Jessie
Pretest	61	60	64[a]
Posttest	46[b]	55[b]	60
1-year follow-up	49[b]	52[b]	58[b]

| | BMI | | |
	Samia	Kate	Jessie
Pretest	19.1	18.6	18.7
Posttest	18.9	18.5	19.4
1-year follow-up	19.3	18.7	19.6

[a]Note that because of an incomplete pretest SCL-90–R, Jessie's pretest scores were obtained, with her permission and institutional review board approval, from treatment archives. Previous treatment as usual for Jessie took place in the same clinic where she was seen for study visits, and as part of treatment as usual, she was regularly assessed using the many of the same measures as were used in the present research. These scores were obtained from her last prestudy-enrollment assessment using the SCL-90–R; there was no break in time between termination of her previous therapy and assessment and her enrollment in the study. [b]Clinically significant change compared with pretest using Schmitz, Hartkamp, and Franke's (2000) cutoffs. All changes represent movement from the "moderately symptomatic" to the "functional" category.

her participation in the study; this weight gain was retained at the 1-year follow-up. Hence, in terms of symptom reduction, treatment was effective for all three cases. In terms of weight gain, treatment was effective for one case (Jessie). In terms of attachment, all three participants were classified as securely attached by the RS measure at all three time points (pretest, posttest, and follow-up).

Postsession Therapist and Client Data

An effect size analysis (difference between means divided by the average standard deviation; effect sizes of .20 are small, .50 are medium, and .80+ are large)[4] was used to determine differences for the therapist's ratings across clients and for each of the clients' ratings on the summed postsession measure. Curve estimation regressions were conducted for all data to determine whether there were systematic changes across treatment; in all cases, the regressions were significant and the linear trend was the best fit for the data.

_____

[4]The highest possible score for each session is 21, and the lowest possible is 3.

Therapist Postsession Data

For the therapist with Samia, the average postsession evaluation score was 15.12 (SD = 11.61); the linear curve estimation regression was significant, $F(1,15)$ = 31.86, $p < .001$, with a relatively steady increase from 11 in Session 1 to 21 in Session 17. For Kate, the average was 15.21 (SD = 3.57); the linear curve estimation regression was significant, $F(1,17)$ = 9.18, $p < .01$, with a relatively steady increase from 15 in Session 1 to 20 in Session 19. For Jessie, the average was 13.42 (SD = 4.86); the linear curve estimation regression revealed no significant trends in the data (lowest score = 4 in Session 17,[5] highest score = 20 in Session 15). Effect size analyses indicated that the therapist on average rated sessions with Samia and Kate as better than those with Jessie (ds = .21 and .42, respectively). Furthermore, the therapist judged that sessions with Samia and Kate became progressively better over time, whereas sessions with Jessie stayed consistently low.

Client Postsession Data

For Samia, the average postsession evaluation score was 16.94 (SD = 2.51). The linear curve estimation regression was significant, $F(1,15)$ = 5.34, $p < .05$, but observation of the graph revealed that the score for Session 1 was very low (9) compared with the rest of the data. When Session 1 was removed from the data, there were no trends in the data (ratings varied between 15 and 20). For Kate, the average was 18.16 (SD = 2.48). The linear curve estimation regression was significant, $F(1,17)$ = 28.77, $p < .001$, with a relatively steady increase in the data from 16 (Session 1) to 21 (Session 19). For Jessie, the average was 9.58 (SD = 3.98). The linear curve estimation regression was significant, $F(1,17)$ = 16.94, $p < .001$, with a steady increase in the data from six (Session 1) to 15 (Session 19). Effect size analyses showed that Kate evaluated the sessions more positively than did either Samia (d = .49) or Jessie (d = 3.23) and that Samia also evaluated sessions more positively than did Jessie (d = 2.27). Hence, of the three clients, Kate evaluated the sessions most positively and progressively rated sessions higher over time. Samia's ratings were consistently high over time. Jessie's ratings were lower overall but did increase over time.

Description of Relational Events in the Three Cases

There were three, six, and eight events, respectively, for Samia, Kate, and Jessie (all of whom had 17 to 19 sessions of therapy). Events were in Sessions 3, 11–12, and 17 for Samia; Sessions 9, 13, 13–14, 15, 16 (two events),

---

[5]This session did not contain an RE. In this session, the client claimed to have "already seen" a therapeutic exercise provided by the therapist that was new to her and also apparently fell asleep during a guided meditation exercise.

and 19 for Kate; and Sessions 3, 10, 11, 16, and 19 for Jessie. The total number of minutes spent in relational work was 13.94 for Samia, 61.88 for Kate, and 51.35 for Jessie. In terms of valence (ratings of how positive or negative the event was), 67% for Samia, 33% for Kate, and 0% for Jessie were coded as *mildly positive*; the remainder were *neutral* or *negative*. The valence of the events did not change systematically across therapy for any of the three cases. Furthermore, in terms of client behavior during these events, 69% of Samia's, 85% of Kate's, and 50% of Jessie's behavior was coded consensually as involving productive exploration; the remainder did not involve productive exploration. The therapist initiated most events: all three events in Samia's case (two by asking for feedback, one by stating her feelings), four of six of Kate's events (all by asking for feedback), and seven of eight of Jessie's events (six by asking for feedback, one by stating feelings).

Thus, although there were not many REs for Samia, the ones that did occur were positive, with good client exploration. REs were prominent for Kate in the latter half of her therapy, with her initiating these events; she explored productively during these events, but outcomes were somewhat mixed. There were several REs for Jessie, but these involved only moderate client exploration and negative outcomes.

Influence of Therapist Interventions

We compared therapist interventions used during REs when the client was judged to be exploring the therapeutic relationship versus those used when the client was judged to be not exploring the relationship (see Table 12.1). There was not sufficient quantitative data for statistical analyses; instead, we a priori considered a difference in overall usage of five interventions during exploration versus nonexploration periods to be large. The two interventions the therapist used more often during exploration than during nonexploration with all three clients were reflecting–validating feelings–supporting, and asking the client to explore. With Kate and Jessie, the therapist used psychoeducation and direct guidance more often during nonexploration than during exploration, and with Kate, the therapist used challenge and interrupts–changes topic, denies feelings–disagrees more during nonexploration than during exploration.

CONCEPTUALIZATION OF RELATIONAL EVENTS FOR SAMIA

Exemplar RE for Samia

The following excerpt is from Sessions 11 and 12. Before Session 11, Samia had written a hierarchy of forbidden foods that listed a Chipotle burrito as one of her most forbidden foods. During Session 11, the therapist brought Chipotle burritos for them to eat together as an acceptance exercise. Samia knew beforehand that the session would involve difficult acceptance exercises but did not know what specifically the session would include in advance.

> *Therapist:* What emotions come up for you?
>
> *Samia:* I'm annoyed. [Laughs.] 'Cause I had already planned out what I was going to have for lunch.
>
> *Therapist:* Mmm hmm. So you're feeling sort of . . .
>
> *Samia:* It bothers me that I have to change that.
>
> *Therapist:* So you're feeling sort of trapped, or caught. [Pauses. Client nods.] What do you notice in terms of sensations, as you eat?
>
> *Samia:* Mmm. I feel anxious. And angry . . . [Discussion of using mindfulness to observe the current emotions and sensations of eating.]
>
> *Therapist:* I notice for you there's some judgments or some feelings that come up, like, you mentioned anger, and I'll bet some feelings of anger at me.
>
> *Samia:* It's not really so much real anger. It's more like anger at the situation, and like . . .
>
> *Therapist:* "Why do I have to do this?"
>
> *Samia:* Yeah, like crap, like yeah, I shouldn't have written that stuff [i.e., identified the feared foods on the worksheet].
>
> *Therapist:* [Laughs.] "Why was I honest?"
>
> *Samia:* So it's like this annoyance at being honest. Even when I did it, I was like, "Oh, I'm probably going to have to do these things, cause why else would . . . "
>
> *Therapist:* "Why else would we be writing it down?"
>
> *Samia:* Yeah.
>
> *Therapist:* Isn't that interesting? All those thoughts that your mind provides you, that "I could get out of this. What the heck was wrong with me that I didn't try and get out of this?" An awareness that, "Well, I sort of knew that I wasn't going to get out of this."
>
> *Samia:* And also it's kind of like, seriously, you're going to have me do all of these hard things. . . . And then it's kind of like, "What else am I going to have to do now? Ooh.

Therapist: [Laughs.] "I did it! I did it!"

Samia: Crap. Yeah. And like, I've done that now, what other things am I going to have to do?

Therapist: You remind me of the centipede phobia lady, after she'd been petting four or five centipedes. "Well, now what?" You know, "Life is finished for me now. Nothing to be afraid of."

Samia: Yeah.

Therapist: Yeah. So some fear, and some pushing yourself.

In Session 12, the therapist inquired about the anger during the previous session again.

Therapist: Were you angry at me? [Laughs.] Or, at least . . .

Samia: No! It actually wasn't. . . . It was not specific . . .

Therapist: Just anger . . .

Samia: It was kind of a nice anger? Like, it felt like . . . an empowering anger. Maybe like when you feel angry, but it's a. . . . You feel angry, like a justifiable . . . I don't know how to exactly describe it. I got in my car and I had music on, and I started like . . . singing really, really loudly! [Laughs.]

Team's Conceptualization of Samia

Context of the Therapy

The overall therapeutic relationship was characterized by mutual warmth, caring, and a lack of conflict. For example, in the first session when Samia dissociated when talking about obsessive symptoms (e.g., fearing dirty silverware), the therapist responded caringly, asking what she could do to help Samia come back into the room with her. The therapist also treated Samia gently when there was a threat of her needing to be hospitalized for weight loss. Samia seemed to value the ACT approach from the outset of therapy, quickly grasping the ACT concepts and finding the mindfulness exercises beneficial.

Patterns During the Relational Events

A pattern of conflict avoidance emerged during the REs. The therapist attempted to explore Samia's anger toward her several times, but Samia denied any anger toward the therapist and indicated instead that she was angry about the therapy situation (e.g., having to eat a feared food). The therapist and Samia developed a complementarity throughout the relational work, such that Samia's compliance and vulnerability were in harmony with the therapist's nurturance and leadership.

Effects of the Relational Work

There were only three relatively brief REs, and their effects were minimal. In response to the therapist's probes, Samia was able to express her feelings, but she typically said her feelings were toward the situation rather than to the therapist. Thus, it appeared the therapist asking Samia about her feelings encouraged Samia to express her feelings, even though she did not explore these feelings in depth.

Client Contributions to the Relational Work

The client's interpersonal ease, intelligence, compliance with the therapy, and deferent presentation likely contributed to the lack of conflict in the sessions. Samia seemed fragile (e.g., dissociating) and had a childlike presence (e.g., sitting with her legs tucked under her) that seemed to elicit caregiving and may have inhibited her exploring negative REs in depth. Samia described herself as a people pleaser but also stated that she was occasionally passive aggressive. Her avoidance of conflict may have been related to her relationship with her mother, whom she described as having a history of emotional lability: Samia indicated that she had not argued with her mother since an incident 5 years earlier when her mother claimed that she would "kill herself" if Samia did not listen to her.

Therapist Contributions to the Relational Work

The therapist appeared natural and comfortable during REs; she was warm, caring, empathic, and maintained an open, accepting stance. She seemed to like Samia as a person.

Therapist's Conceptualization of Samia

REs played a relatively minor role in Samia's treatment. With a history of four inpatient hospitalizations and the threat of another impending at the beginning of therapy, Samia was acutely aware of what AN had cost her, and the urgency and risk of her situation may have enhanced her willingness to undertake the work of therapy and initial agreement about the tasks and goals of therapy. Throughout treatment, Samia expressed minimal negative emotion toward the therapist (the first author), even when probed directly. This lack of negative emotion may have represented genuine willingness to experience difficult situations in therapy, accurate labeling of anger as directed at the situation, or maladaptive conflict avoidance. However, Samia did demonstrate growing ability in ACT to fully experience and acknowledge her negative emotions overall.

CONCEPTUALIZATION OF RELATIONAL EVENTS FOR KATE

Exemplar Relational Event for Kate

The following excerpt was taken from the beginning of Session 9. In a previous session, Kate had reported that she had tried to explain ACT to a friend and wondered whether she had done it "right," as she felt "confused" about some of the aspects of the therapy. The therapist had expressed reservations about explaining the model in more detail.

> *Kate:* The main thing is . . . I felt frustrated because I wanted you to confirm if what I had described was right or not, and you didn't, which is maybe okay. Also . . . I got the feeling you were a little angry or upset, and I felt, I felt bothered because of that . . .

> *Therapist:* . . . I wonder if what's frustrating is that you're being asked to stay with that confusion. . . . this worry that perhaps I was angry with you . . . and it sounds like . . . a lot of things came up for you. You had a sense of frustration, of irritation, of confusion. . . . So I'm curious, when that came up for you, . . . what gave you the sense that I might be angry? . . .

> *Kate:* I guess it was mainly . . . the tone of voice. And anger, as we've just said, you've just said, is really hard for me. I don't want people to be angry at me. I'll do anything so that they're not. That's really, really uncomfortable.

> *Therapist:* Hmm. Well, I don't recall feeling any anger, and I would tell you if I was. It's rare for me to feel angry at my patients. . . . I can tell you the things that do it fairly reliably, if I'm asking a patient to try something and a patient is unwilling. . . . [But] that doesn't fit with you or characterize you very well. . . . You know, you take notes, and you're very, you know, very conscientious. . . . But, you know, you mentioned tone of voice. When did you notice that?

> *Kate:* When I mentioned something about the homework that I had had to finish . . . it seemed like you got a little bit upset then, and then I thought, "Uh oh, I betcha she thinks I'm a smart aleck" . . .

> *Therapist:* Mmm, no. My perception of you is that you try very, very hard to understand things.

Kate: I do, yeah.

Therapist: And you're wonderfully active about it. It's actually very refreshing really that if something isn't clear, or you're confused . . . you're good about stopping me and saying, "Wait a minute, here." You're also good about challenging things that don't fit for you. . . . You're here and you're listening and you're working hard, and I like it. You know, it's assertive. . . . I have a lot of respect for it. I think it's great . . .

Kate: Maybe it was something else going on then, maybe it was something from me, I don't know, but I got, yeah, the sense, not real strong, not like you were just . . .

Therapist: Ready to storm out of the room at you, yeah?

Kate: Yeah, not that, but just a maybe a little bit upset with me, and um, I don't know. Maybe it's because I was feeling and did a little bit of challenge, which I don't always do.

Therapist: Mmm-hmm, and that that's scary.

Kate: So maybe it's something new for me, and maybe my expectation is that the person is gonna get mad. . . . I think I told you when I was growing up, a couple of times I disagreed with my parents and then it was like, "Well, no, you can't do this." So, maybe I imagined or expected that you as the person in authority . . . would get upset with me, for saying, "Well, gee, this looks kind of obvious here." . . . So I did feel like, well, I need to share this. . . . I'm glad that we're talking about it.

Team's Conceptualization of Kate

Context of the Therapy

Overall, the therapeutic relationship was good, with a genuine connection between therapist and client. Kate mentioned in the follow-up interview that she had liked the balance of support and encouragement for action provided by the therapist and that she had benefited from the mindfulness and acceptance exercises. There was some disagreement, however, about the tasks and goals in that Kate wanted to talk more about the therapeutic relationship than the therapist did.

Patterns During the Relational Events

In positive REs, the therapist was typically open and inquisitive; Kate was engaged by the therapist's empathic, inquisitive prompts and assertively shared her thoughts and feelings regarding the relationship and the therapy. In negative events, however, the therapist exhibited more authoritative behavior (interruption, challenge, and psychoeducation), which resulted in disagreements with Kate. These disagreements occurred more often when Kate was exploring non-ACT material or when Kate critically questioned the relevance of ACT exercises. The therapist's directiveness seemed to trigger Kate's transference (i.e., resentment of therapist's control and feeling neglected or disregarded in the therapeutic relationship) and fueled their relational discussions.

Effects of the Relational Work

The overall effects were mildly positive. In terms of positive effects, the therapeutic bond was strengthened, Kate progressively became more assertive about voicing her negative reactions to the therapist and stating her needs, and Kate gained some insight into her relational patterns (that they were from transference from her relationship with her adoptive mother). On the negative side, Kate seemed to feel controlled, confused about when it was okay to share her feelings, and disregarded.

Client Contributions to the Relational Work

Kate's intellect, maturity, previous therapy experience, relational orientation, and insightfulness contributed to the positive effects of the REs and the insight she gained from them. Kate's motivation to change, dedication to the therapy, and strong work ethic were evident in her completion of all homework assignments and engagement in the process. Kate appeared more interested in understanding her role in relationships than in dealing with eating behaviors. She became progressively more assertive in expressing her feelings toward the end of therapy (e.g., initiated discussion of transference issues, noting the parallels between her relationship with the therapist and her adoptive mother), although she was still somewhat tentative in expressing herself.

Therapist Contributions to the Relational Work

The therapist cared deeply about Kate and was empathic when she was in emotional distress. She regularly asked Kate for feedback and reacted nonpunitively (remaining calm and respectful without being angry) when Kate expressed negative reactions. The therapist adhered closely to the ACT protocol and was directive throughout most of the therapy.

Therapist's Conceptualization of Kate

Kate struggled repeatedly with her willingness to engage in ACT; experiencing confusion, anxiety, resentfulness, and anger at the therapist (the first author) (for not alleviating this confusion and anxiety) in the early phases of therapy, and fear and anger at the therapist in the middle phase of therapy, when acceptance exercises began. The therapist, likewise, struggled with uncertainty, a social desire to help control Kate's pain, and feelings of guilt for exposing Kate to the unpleasant experiences she had previously avoided. However, over several sessions, the therapist was able to model, and Kate was able to experience, nonjudgmental, mindful acceptance of these feelings, coupled with movement toward feared experiences and toward a valued life.

CONCEPTUALIZATION OF RELATIONAL EVENTS FOR JESSIE

Exemplar Relational Event for Jessie

The following excerpt was taken from Session 16. In a previous session, the therapist had tried to encourage Jessie to approach a situation she had identified as creating discomfort for her (not exercising at the gym for 1 week) as an acceptance exercise. Jessie had expressed unwillingness to engage in this exercise, and the therapist had pressed her. In this session, they talk about that experience.

> *Jessie:* It's . . . stresses me when I . . . when someone tries to control what I do.
>
> *Therapist:* Okay. So, getting some anger at me about . . . telling you what to do. And of course, I can't control what you do. I'm not sitting in your apartment saying, "Unh uh! You don't get to go out to the gym." But the only reason to come to therapy is because you think it will be helpful. And the only reason to do a therapy homework assignment is to get the benefit out of it. And when you come here and you do, do the homework, presumably, you trust in me that it will be helpful. But if you don't do the homework, there's a couple of reasons. You might logically think it won't be helpful, you might think something else will be more helpful, you might be fearful in doing that. . . . I don't know what . . . comes up for you. I just know you won't benefit if you don't do it. You know, you won't get out of it what there is to get out of it. What you do you think?
>
> *Jessie:* If I never get anything out of it, then . . . which is possible it might be, then . . . it might just be a waste.
>
> *Therapist:* Yeah, yeah. It would be a bummer. It is a lot of time, just like going to the gym is a lot of time. It's a lot of time if you're two

hours a week, on days when you do, doing your homework. And on the other hand, I would bet that even if you don't do your homework, you're thinking about it. In fact, correct me if I'm wrong, did you spend as much time thinking about "I know I'm going to the gym, my therapist is going to be pissed at me," as you would have, kind of, not going to the gym? [Client doesn't respond.] And how long was your workout today?

Jessie: Less than an hour.

Therapist: I mean, do you think you spent, over the last 72 hours, an hour thinking about, "God, what am I going to say to her?" "She's going to be mad," is that right? [Client doesn't respond.] I don't know, something like that, maybe? You know, so that's a lot time. So, what do you think? What would be helpful at this point? [Long pause.] So, say an hour?

Jessie: [Mouths words:] I don't know. [Shakes head.]

Therapist: What thoughts are running through your mind?

Jessie: I shouldn't have had that personal training session, and I should have set that for Monday morning.

Therapist: So you're feeling kind of guilty?

Jessie: And resentful that this is what is expected of me and that if we do this, that's somehow going to make me better.

Therapist: So, it's kind of both. You feel guilty and you also feel kind of resentful and angry that if someone's telling you to not do something you feel like doing. Well, if you leave therapy and it was a big success; you know, "You got to go out and see my therapist. My whole life is improved," what would we have done then? What would have changed about your life that you thought it was such a great success?

Jessie: Just being able to live a normal life . . .

Team's Conceptualization of Jessie

Context of the Therapy

The therapeutic relationship was good enough overall to keep Jessie in therapy for the contracted 19 sessions, but it often seemed rocky, with considerable disagreement between the therapist and Jessie on the goals and tasks of therapy. As Jessie mentioned in the follow-up interview with the therapist, she was disappointed that the focus of therapy was very structured and that she had not been able to discuss the problems she wanted to discuss, although she also felt that some exercises had been helpful.

Patterns During the Relational Events

During the REs, Jessie and the therapist engaged in disagreements that followed a distinct pattern: (a) the therapist requested feedback; (b) Jessie criticized the appropriateness of ACT; (c) the therapist attributed Jessie's negative response to noncommitment or misunderstanding of ACT principles; (d) Jessie acquiesced and then blamed herself; (e) the therapist requested recommitment; and (f) Jessie reluctantly recommitted. In this iterative pattern, Jessie was submissive yet subtly hostile, while the therapist was dominant and critical and demanded compliance.

Effects of the Relational Work

The effects ranged from no effects to very negative effects. After the negative REs, Jessie seemed less open in her expression and seemed to feel controlled, frustrated, and forced to recommit to therapy. For example, when Jessie stated she did not do the homework because she felt it was not helpful and said she felt controlled when given a homework assignment to not go to the gym, the therapist questioned Jessie's commitment to therapy and asked her to recommit herself, which Jessie reluctantly did. Jessie often appeared to be telling the therapist what she thought the therapist wanted to hear rather than genuinely expressing her thoughts and feelings.

Client Contributions to the Relational Work

Jessie was sometimes able to express negative feelings toward the therapist, although she was often resistant in the therapy. She defied the therapist, yet had a childlike, passive part that acquiesced quickly and then blamed herself. Her true voice and opinion rarely seemed to be present in the room. This shutting down and acquiescing may have reflected long-standing relational patterns, such as with her father, who physically abused her.

Therapist Contributions to the Relational Work

The therapist was committed to the therapy and genuinely wanted Jessie to improve. She seemed frustrated with Jessie's lack of commitment and baffled by why Jessie kept coming to their sessions if she was not getting anything out of therapy. During REs, the therapist dismissed Jessie's negative reactions to therapy and attributed them to fear-based avoidance on Jessie's part and persistently requested Jessie's recommitment. The therapist adhered to the protocol more insistently and pushed and confronted Jessie more aggressively than she did the other two clients.

Therapist's Conceptualization of Jessie

The outcome of the relational work for Jessie can be conceptualized in terms of the ACT concept of *pliance*, which is behavior controlled by social consequences rather than by the actual contingencies of the behavior. For example, a client who follows the therapist's rule, "If you do your therapy homework, I will see you are progressing," may be doing so out of pliance (i.e., out of wanting the therapist's social approval). Similarly, not following the rules may be due to counterpliance (i.e., because the therapist's disapproval is reinforcing). Pliance–counterpliance can become generalized such that people are sensitive only to the social whims of others, including therapists, and not at all to direct contingencies. It can also become augmented, becoming a general principle that an individual follows even in the absence of direct social consequences. AN can be conceptualized as a problem of generalized, augmented pliance, where clients follow the *ply* "If I do not eat, I will become thin and attractive to others," while remaining insensitive to the behavior's direct (and ultimately fatal) contingencies. In ACT, the goal is to help clients become sensitive to such direct contingencies, without using the therapeutic relationship to learn new plys.

Jessie began therapy a highly pliant client, who mentioned frequently her own confusion at various rules for living that she had absorbed (e.g., from her therapists, her physician, her personal trainer, magazines, peers). She ended therapy clinically improved, but the relational work with Jessie suggested that she may have improved only by substituting one generalized, augmented ply ("If I do not eat, I will be attractive to others") with another ("If I do not eat, I will have a negative social label, an 'eating disorder'") through developing a ply in her relationship with the therapist ("If I do not eat and overexercise, my therapist will be disappointed in me").

Signs of pliance and counterpliance frequently emerged in the relational work with Jessie. For example, she reported feeling "bad" because the therapist "seemed disappointed" in her when she failed to complete homework; she also reported feeling "resentful" in response to the therapist's disapproval. Similarly, at follow-up, Jessie stated that what helped her was the fact that yet another therapist seemed to think that she was "too thin" and that her eating disorder was serious. Such evidence of pliance and counterpliance in the relational work suggests the therapist's more general failure to help Jessie turn away from maladaptive socially mediated rules for living and instead directly experience how her behavior worked in her own life.

In this sense, despite her clinical improvement, ACT was not effective in helping Jessie make contact with her own experiences. However, one reality of generalized pliance may be that some plys have better contingencies than others, even if clients are insensitive to them. Developing and following a generalized, augmented ply that involves eating for social rewards or because of the demands of a therapeutic relationship, although not an optimal therapy outcome, is still clearly more adaptive than following one which specifies never eating, and may partially account for Jessie's maintenance of her improvement even after the therapeutic relationship had ended.

DISCUSSION

Our goals in this study were to evaluate the process and outcome of REs in manualized ACT for AN and, if possible, to determine their helpful or corrective components. The most obvious overall finding that emerged is that the nature, extent, and outcomes of the relational work differed substantially among the three clients, despite the fact that the same therapist treated all three, using a treatment manual.

Clearly, unique therapist–client relationships emerged in each case, which influenced the REs. For Kate, relational work was a small but significant aspect of her treatment, with generally positive outcomes as she and the therapist navigated struggles with the sometimes counterintuitive experience of ACT. For Samia, relational work played a minor and neutral role against the much larger impact of an ACT experience that was well matched to her needs. For Jessie, despite her therapeutic improvement in the treatment as a whole, the outcomes of the relational work specifically were apparently negative: Although the ruptures that emerged in her work with the therapist did not cause her to terminate from therapy, she did not appear to benefit from discussions of the therapeutic relationship.

Although significant relational work and immediacy discussions emerged for two out of three clients in this case series, it is important to put the results in the context of treatment with ACT, an approach that does not emphasize relational work. ACT therapists, like other effective therapists, work to foster a positive working alliance and demonstrate empathy for their clients. ACT also conceptualizes the therapeutic relationship as an egalitarian one in which both therapists and clients are "in the same soup" and likely to experience similar struggles. Thus, relational work in ACT usually takes the form of therapist self-disclosure and shared engagement in therapeutic processes. However, in ACT, the therapeutic focus is not on how the client relates to others but on how the client relates to his or her own thoughts, emotions, and internal experiences. This discrepancy in theoretical approach may explain why there were three to eight REs in the cases we have described here, as compared with 19 in the case described in Kasper et al. (2008) and 56 in the case described in Hill et al. (2008), both of which involved interpersonal therapists.

In addition, in contrast to the Kasper et al. (2008) and Hill et al. (2008) cases, the treatment examined in the present study was manualized and followed a detailed session-by-session protocol, which may have limited the therapist's ability to respond flexibly to emerging evidence of relationship ruptures. ACT is not typically a manualized treatment; ACT therapists outside of research protocols are encouraged to implement the therapy flexibly, not moving on to a new facet of treatment until clients show clearly specified signs of therapeutic progress. For example, in a nonmanualized ACT with Jessie, the therapist would likely have responded to her pliance by spending more time helping Jessie make contact with her own experiences, in contrast to her rules about desirable behavior. Some of these interventions would likely be relational in character, such as the therapist acting with humility in session, deliberately undermining her own authority and encouraging Jessie not to believe the therapist's claims (Ciarrochi, 2008).

Therapist's Contributions to the Relational Work

For all cases, the therapist contributions that appear to have had the greatest positive impact on relational exploration and rupture resolution were empathy, invitations to explore relational issues and problems, openness to positive and negative feedback, direct requests for feedback, inquiries about the relationship, and a nonjudgmental response to negative affect directed at her. Similar therapist behaviors have also been shown to relate to CREs with therapists-in-training about their own therapy (Chapter 11, this volume). Although these therapist interventions make sense and seem to fit with good therapy, it is important to remember that it can be difficult to be empathic during the tense moments of REs.

One cluster of therapist behaviors that appeared to have failed to foster exploration during REs included behaviors, such as psychoeducation, direct guidance, and challenge, all of which are interventions that may be particularly common in CBT therapies. Although these interventions might be purposeful and useful (e.g., teaching a client to respond mindfully to negative emotions that arise toward the therapist rather than processing the emotions in another fashion), therapists regardless of modality must be careful to attend to markers of relationship rupture and to watch for evidence that their interventions both advance the therapy and the therapeutic alliance. A second cluster of therapist behaviors associated with a lack of client exploration included more obviously unhelpful therapist behaviors, such as interruptions and changing topics. Nevertheless the presence of these behaviors here suggests that they may commonly occur during REs.

Client Contributions to the Relational Work

Productive client behaviors in the REs observed here included client assertion and exploration of feelings about the therapeutic relationship. It is important to note that some of the REs were initiated by clients. Kate, for example, occasionally asserted and explored her own feelings and reactions to the therapy, additional evidence of the important role of client involvement and agency in therapy (Bohart & Tallman, 1999).

Individual differences among these three clients likely contributed directly or indirectly (through their interactions with the therapist) to the differences we observed in REs. In general, it appears that client openness, psychological mindedness, and lack of fear of (or willingness to tolerate) conflict may contribute to the resolution of REs. In addition, client perception of being in a gradually improving therapeutic alliance may be important.

Considering each client specifically, we note that Kate was older and that her eating disorder had had its onset well into adulthood, making her case atypical in a variety of ways. In addition, she had a previous history of interpersonally oriented and dynamic psychotherapy. In the current therapy, she used language, such as the word transference, that suggested that she saw the therapy relationship as a source of insight about other relationships in her life. Her active, assertive stance, her thoughtfulness, and her beliefs about therapy likely contributed to both the number and quality of REs that occurred in her work here.

Samia, in contrast, described herself as a "people pleaser" and appeared reluctant to engage in conflict with the therapist. Instead, she focused on the content and process of ACT therapy itself, with a basically positive but perhaps superficial working relationship with the therapist.

Jessie struggled to engage either with the ACT content of therapy or with the therapist. Unlike Samia, she did not appear to avoid conflict; she had the greatest number of REs of the three clients. However, these relatively frequent relational discussions did not seem helpful: When conflicts emerged, she had difficulty expressing feelings openly, communicating resistance and disagreement in a passive, acquiescent fashion. Although Jessie's REs were never rated as positive, and although her ratings of the therapy itself were never as high as those of the other two clients, she rated the therapy itself as gradually more useful and productive over time, and in fact, her postsession ratings of therapy increased more from Session 1 to her last session than either Kate's or Samia's.

It is particularly intriguing that Jessie improved clinically, remained in therapy, and rated the therapy as increasingly beneficial over time, even though both the therapist (in postsession evaluations) and the research team (in coding REs) acknowledged significant flaws in the therapeutic alliance. Given her relational history (e.g., she reported ongoing and intermittently supportive relationships with both parents, despite substantial conflict with both and a history of physical abuse from her father), she may not have experienced a relationship marked by conflict as unusual or negative. It is possible that simply the experience of expressing dissatisfaction without retribution was helpful for her. Other research has demonstrated that an initially poor but gradually improving therapeutic alliance predicts positive outcome in therapy (Florsheim, Shotorbani, Guest-Warnick, Barratt, & Hwang, 2000; Joyce & Piper, 1998). Jessie's case suggests that client perception that the therapeutic relationship is improving may provide incentive to remain in therapy and resolve even negative REs, allowing the work of therapy to continue.

In terms of attachment orientation, all three of these clients were classified as securely attached from the outset of therapy; their security across a range of relationships may have served as a resource to draw on in navigating the challenges of developing and maintaining a productive therapeutic alliance and may help explain why all three clients were able to benefit from the therapy experience regardless of their REs. However, the lack of variability in terms of attachment orientation in these clients limits our ability to speculate on how the REs may have differed with a client who was preoccupied, dismissive, or fearful–avoidant in attachment style.

Limitations

One important limitation in these case studies was our inability to clearly link the REs we observed with outcome. Although it appears at least that the REs that we observed did not have a large negative outcome on either the therapeutic alliance or on the outcome for these three clients, even when we coded them as negative, we have little data to support the claim that the neutral or positive REs exerted a positive effect at the level of outcome (although we did find certain therapist and client behaviors that appeared to facilitate or impede the therapeutic process).

An additional limitation of these data and results is possible bias on the part of the judges and/or the therapist. Many of the judges on the primary team had an interpersonal and/or psychodynamic theoretical orientation; some were skeptical before analyses that ACT and/or manualized therapies in general could be helpful. The primary team thus may have been biased about the ability of the therapist to use ACT to help clients. The therapist, on the other hand, who was involved primarily in identifying REs, as an auditor, and in providing an alternative perspective and conceptualization of the cases, held an eclectic theoretical orientation but often used CBTs and manualized therapies with clients. She may have been biased to find her own therapeutic work effective and appropriate. Both the primary team and the therapist in their conceptualizations relied on specific session data, including video and verbatim transcripts, to draw conclusions, but clearly the conceptualization by both the primary team and the therapist are subject to some interpretation. Indeed, we have tried to provide a rich dialectic between the primary team's and the therapist's conceptualizations of the REs, to provide a synthesis that will allow the fullest possible depiction of the impact of the REs for these clients.

Finally, although these three case studies build on the work done by Kasper et al. (2008) and Hill et al. (2008) to begin to create a rich picture of how REs occur and are experienced in psychotherapy of various types, we cannot generalize these findings to other cases. It is especially important to be aware that the therapist and all three clients were European American.

Implications for Practice and Research

The results from this study extend the findings of Kasper et al. (2008) and Hill et al. (2008) and suggest that immediacy discussions of the therapeutic relationship can be powerful and helpful interventions, even in noninterpersonally oriented therapy. Therapists, regardless of theoretical orientation, can ask clients for feedback about therapy and the therapeutic relationship. Because clients often do not know that it is appropriate to talk about negative feelings, they might have to be encouraged to reveal such feelings, especially negative feelings about the therapist. These data also suggest that, in common with research on ruptures in psychotherapy (Safran & Muran, 2000), therapists can attend to evidence that clients are dissatisfied or unhappy in the therapeutic relationship and can address these feelings directly with clients using immediacy. This may be especially important in highly structured or manualized therapies, particularly those that include elements clients are likely to find challenging or upsetting, such as exposure work. Therapists should also be aware that clients may not respond openly or positively to immediacy discussions, even (or perhaps especially) when a rupture has occurred; in this case, we agree with other researchers that a nondirective or humble approach by the therapist may be most productive (Beutler, Moleiro, & Talebi, 2002).

These data provide less information addressing the question of when relational exploration by CBT therapists may be actually inappropriate or may represent an unhelpful response by a therapist attempting to manage a difficult client. It is intriguing, but hardly conclusive, that the most REs in this study occurred with the client Jessie, who appeared to benefit least from them, and nearly all of these were initiated by the therapist. However, because Jessie improved gradually over time both in outcome and in her ratings of the therapy process, it is not clear whether these REs were actually unhelpful or whether the opportunity to air her dissatisfaction, however unproductively, played some role in helping her remain in a therapy that was generally beneficial for her. Although we believe that offering clients explicit opportunities to discuss the therapeutic relationship is generally beneficial, more research is needed to identify under what circumstances it may be harmful, particularly in therapies that are not interpersonally focused, and where an unproductive discussion of the therapeutic relationship might serve to increase client negative affect or distract from other potentially beneficial interventions.

Future research is also needed on negative responses to REs, as well as on the impact of relational work in noninterpersonally focused psychotherapies. In addition, research is needed to determine the circumstances under which noninterpersonally focused therapists attend directly to the therapeutic relationship and what the effects are of such interventions in comparison with similar therapist behaviors in dynamic or interpersonal psychotherapy.

Finally, we are excited by the implications of our modifications to the consensual qualitative research method because these modifications make the approach more applicable to studying therapy cases (see also Jackson et al., 2011). Use of the team's collective clinical wisdom to conceptualize cases allows judges to include a greater understanding of the context to explicate the data. The use of multiple perspectives and continual reworking helps to ensure that researchers stay close to the data. This method could be applied to research on the impact of other cognitive behavioral interventions, such as the use of exposure, metaphor, mindfulness techniques, or other events in CBT or ACT.

REFERENCES

American Psychiatric Association. (1994). *Diagnostic and statistical manual of mental disorders* (4th ed). Washington, DC: Author.

Bell, L. (2002). Does concurrent psychopathology at presentation influence response to treatment for bulimia nervosa? *Eating and Weight Disorders, 7*, 168–181.

Beutler, L. E., Moleiro, C. M., & Talebi, H. (2002). Resistance. In J. C. Norcross (Ed.), *Psychotherapy relationships that work* (pp. 129–143). Oxford, England: Oxford University Press.

Bohart, A., & Tallman, K. (1999). *How clients make therapy work: The process of active self-healing.* Washington, DC: American Psychological Association. doi:10.1037/10323-000

Ciarrochi, J. (2008, August). *Supercharging therapy with values.* Keynote address presented at the ACT-Oceana II conference, Christchurch, New Zealand.

Derogatis, L. R. (1994). *Symptom Checklist–90—R (SCL-90–R): Administration, scoring and procedures manual.* Minneapolis, MN: National Computer Systems.

Derogatis, L. R., & Cleary, P. A. (1977). Confirmation of the dimensional structure of the SCL-90: A study in construct validation. *Journal of Clinical Psychology, 33*, 981–989. doi:10.1002/1097-4679(197710)33:4<981::AID-JCLP2270330412>3.0.CO;2-0

Florsheim, P., Shotorbani, S., Guest-Warnick, G., Barratt, T., & Hwang, W. (2000). Role of the working alliance in the treatment of delinquent boys in community-based programs. *Journal of Clinical Child Psychology, 29*, 94–107. doi:10.1207/S15374424jccp2901_10

Fraley, R. C., Niedenthal, P. M., Marks, M. J., Brumbaugh, C. C., & Vicary, A. (2006). Adult attachment and the perception of emotional expressions: Probing the hyperactivating strategies underlying anxious attachment. *Journal of Personality, 74*, 1163–1190. doi:10.1111/j.1467-6494.2006.00406.x

Hayes, S. C., Strosahl, K., & Wilson, K. G. (1999). *Acceptance and commitment therapy: An experiential approach to behavior change.* New York, NY: Guilford Press.

Heffner, M., & Eifert, G. H. (2004). *The anorexia workbook: How to accept yourself, heal your suffering, and reclaim your life.* Oakland, CA: New Harbinger.

Hill, C. E., & Knox, S. (2009). Processing the therapeutic relationship. *Psychotherapy Research, 19*, 13–29. doi:10.1080/10503300802621206

Hill, C. E., Knox, S., Thompson, B. J., Williams, E. N., Hess, S. A., & Ladany, N. (2005). Consensual qualitative research: An update. *Journal of Counseling Psychology, 52*, 196–205. doi:10.1037/0022-0167.52.2.196

Hill, C. E., Sim, W., Spangler, P., Stahl, J., Sullivan, C., & Teyber, E. (2008). Therapist immediacy in brief psychotherapy therapy: Case study II. *Psychotherapy, 45*, 298–315. doi:10.1037/a0013306

Hill, C. E., Thompson, B. J., & Williams, E. N. (1997). A guide to conducting consensual qualitative research. *The Counseling Psychologist, 25*, 517–572. doi:10.1177/0011000097254001

Jackson, J., Chui, H., & Hill, C. E. (2011). The modification of consensual qualitative research for case study research: An introduction to CQR-C. In C. E. Hill (Ed.), *Consensual qualitative research: A practical resource for investigating social science phenomena* (pp. 285–303). Washington, DC: American Psychological Association.

Joyce, A. S., & Piper, W. E. (1998). Expectancy, the therapeutic alliance, and treatment outcome in short-term individual psychotherapy. *Journal of Psychotherapy Practice and Research, 7*, 236–248.

Kasper, L., Hill, C. E., & Kivlighan, D. (2008). Therapist immediacy in brief psychotherapy therapy: Case study I. *Psychotherapy: Theory, Research, & Practice, 45*, 281–297. doi:10.1037/a0013305

Safran, J. D., & Muran, J. C. (2000). *Negotiating the therapeutic alliance: A relational treatment guide.* New York, NY: Guilford Press.

Schielke, H. J., Fishman, J. L., Osatuke, K., & Stiles, W. B. (2009). Creative consensus on interpretations of qualitative data: The Ward method. *Psychotherapy Research, 19*, 558–565. doi:10.1080/10503300802621180

Schmitz, N., Hartkamp, N., & Franke, G. H. (2000). Assessing clinically significant change: Application to the SCL-90–R. *Psychological Reports, 86*, 263–274.

Thompson-Brenner, H. & Westen, D. (2005). Personality subtypes in eating disorders: Validation of a classification in a naturalistic sample. *British Journal of Psychiatry, 186*, 516–524. doi:10.1192/bjp.186.6.516

Welch, R. D., & Houser, M. E. (2010). Extending the four-category model of adult attachment: An interpersonal model of friendship attachment. *Journal of Social and Personal Relationships, 27*, 351–366. doi:10.1177/0265407509349632

13

CORRECTIVE EXPERIENCES IN COGNITIVE BEHAVIOR AND INTERPERSONAL–EMOTIONAL PROCESSING THERAPIES: A QUALITATIVE ANALYSIS OF A SINGLE CASE

LOUIS G. CASTONGUAY, DANA L. NELSON, JAMES F. BOSWELL, SAMUEL S. NORDBERG, ANDREW A. McALEAVEY, MICHELLE G. NEWMAN, AND THOMAS D. BORKOVEC

In a seminal publication, Goldfried (1980) identified a number of principles of change that cut across different forms of psychotherapy, among which was the therapist's facilitation of corrective experiences (CEs). As with all of the other principles he identified, Goldfried asserted that the types of CEs (and/or the procedures to foster them) are likely to differ from one theoretical orientation to another. In humanistic and psychodynamic therapies, for instance, CEs are assumed to take place within the context of the therapeutic relationship (e.g., disconfirmation of transference-related fears). CEs most frequently emphasized in cognitive behavior therapy (CBT), however, are assumed to involve between-sessions activities (e.g., gradual exposure to feared situations).

To our knowledge, no one has directly compared different types of therapy to empirically explore how CEs differ or are similar across orientations. In this chapter, we address this issue by examining CEs in two manualized treatments for generalized anxiety disorder (GAD): CBT and interpersonal–emotional processing therapy (I-EP). Specifically, we present the qualitative analysis of the case of one client who, as part of a randomized clinical trial (RCT), received both of these treatments. Methodologically, this design provides unique conditions to assess similarities and differences in CEs involved

in the therapeutic conditions investigated, as both treatments were conducted by the same therapist, with the same client, and at the same time
(i.e., sessions occurring on the same day).

Adopting the Penn State University conference definition of CEs as
our starting point ("CEs are ones in which a person comes to understand or
experience affectively an event or relationship in a different and unexpected
way"; see Chapter 1, this volume, p. 5), our goal was to shed light on the
nature of CEs, as well as on what facilitates them and what follows them
within and across two different therapeutic approaches.

METHOD

Data for this case study were derived from an RCT for GAD (Newman
et al., 2011) that tested the efficacy of a CBT treatment augmented with
I-EP interventions. In the condition from which this case was drawn, the
therapist provided the client with 50 minutes of CBT followed by 50 minutes
of I-EP, for each of 14 sessions. This case was chosen because it was known
to be a successful case of reduction in GAD symptoms. Within this case,
we conducted intensive analyses of several therapeutic events identified as
containing CEs.

Participants

The client, "Adam," was a 50-year-old, European American, hetero-
sexual man. As a participant in the therapy trial described above, he was seeking treatment to address his GAD symptoms. At the onset of therapy he was
also experiencing marital difficulties and stress at work. He was slightly overweight and typically dressed in business casual attire. He had previously been
divorced and was remarried, living with his second wife at the time of treatment. He had several children from his first marriage as well as several step-
children. He had a doctoral degree and was employed in an applied science
field. The therapist, "Dr. E," was a European American woman in her late
30s. She was thin and dressed in a professional manner. She had a doctoral
degree in clinical psychology and more than 10 years of postdoctoral therapy
experience. Her theoretical orientation was primarily psychodynamic, but
she had been trained in CBT and previously served as a protocol therapist in
a CBT trial for panic disorder. Before the current study, she participated in a
preliminary open trial on the integrative protocol received by the client
(Newman, Castonguay, Borkovec, Fisher, & Nordberg, 2008) and demonstrated both adherence to, and competence in, its CBT and I-EP components.
She believed that CBT and I-EP were both effective treatments for GAD.

Measures

Four instruments assessing anxiety symptoms were used in the RCT as primary outcome measures, each demonstrating good psychometric qualities (see Newman et al., 2011, for a detailed description). Two of these measures were administered and rated by the therapist: The Hamilton Anxiety Rating Scale (HARS; Hamilton, 1959) is a 14-item measure of severity of anxious symptoms, and the Clinician Severity Rating (CSR) for GAD (ranging from 0 = *none* to 8 = *very severely disturbing/disabling*) of the Anxiety Disorders Interview Schedule for *DSM–IV* (ADIS-IV; Brown, Di Nardo, & Barlow, 1994). The other two were self-report measures: The Penn State Worry Questionnaire (PSWQ; Meyer, Miller, Metzger, & Borkovec, 1990) is a 16-item measure of frequency and intensity of worry, and the State–Trait Anxiety Inventory—Trait version (STAI–T; Spielberger, Gorsuch, Lushene, Vagg, & Jacobs, 1983) is a 20-item measure of trait anxiety. Because one of the goals of the RCT was to assess whether the integrative treatment could improve the impact of CBT with regard to interpersonal functioning, the Inventory of Interpersonal Problems–Client (IIP-C; Horowitz, Rosenberg, Baer, Ureño, & Villaseñor, 1988) was also used. The IPP-C is a 64-item measure of distress arising from interpersonal sources.

Treatments

Cognitive Behavior Therapy

Targeting intrapersonal aspects of anxious experience, the CBT protocol included self-monitoring of anxiety cues, relaxation methods (e.g., breathing techniques), cognitive restructuring, and self-controlled desensitization (SCD), which involves the client imagining coping with a stressful situation while being relaxed. Therapists addressed only the learning and application of these methods as they related to intrapersonal anxious experience. For example, when doing cognitive therapy with aspects of client anxiety that related to other people, the therapist and client could work on identifying nonadaptive thoughts and on logical analysis of such cognitions to generate more accurate ways of perceiving. However, the therapist could not work on developmental origins, the deepening of affective experience, analysis of how client behavior may have been contributing to relationship difficulties, and behavioral interpersonal skill training.

Interpersonal–Emotional Processing Therapy

This treatment protocol was informed by Safran and Segal's (1990) interpersonal schema model, which provides a coherent integration of cognitive, interpersonal, and emotional issues in human functioning and therapeutic change. However, in contrast to Safran and Segal's model, our modification was specifically designed to address interpersonal problems and facilitate emotional processing without the direct integration of cognitive techniques. The goals of I-EP were (a) identification of interpersonal needs, past and current patterns of interpersonal behavior that attempt to satisfy those needs, and the underlying emotional experience; (b) generation of more effective interpersonal behavior to better satisfy needs; and (c) identification and processing of avoided emotion. The interventions were based on the principles of an emphasis on phenomenological experience; therapists' use of their own emotional experience to identify interpersonal markers; use of the therapeutic relationship to explore affective processes and interpersonal patterns, with therapists assuming responsibility for their role in the interactions; promotion of generalization through exploration of between-sessions events and provision of homework experiments; detection of alliance ruptures and provision of emotionally CEs in their resolution; processing of patient's affective experiencing in relation to past, current, and in-session interpersonal relationships using emotion-focused techniques; and skill training methods to provide more effective interpersonal behaviors to satisfy identified needs.

Procedures for Coding Corrective Experiences

For the present case study, four researchers (the first four authors) acted as judges in conducting the qualitative analyses. One judge (the first author) was a licensed PhD-level clinician and experienced psychotherapy researcher. The other three judges were advanced doctoral students in clinical psychology, each with a master's degree and between 4 and 7 years of clinical and research training and experience. They were three men and one woman. The three doctoral students were all European American (average age of 30 years); the first author was French Canadian (in his late 40s). The judges were of diverse theoretical orientations (two identified more heavily with CBT and two with combinations of psychodynamic, interpersonal, and humanistic orientations), although all shared an interest in psychotherapy integration and a respect for a variety of theoretical orientations.

Before conducting the analyses, the judges recorded their expectations and biases related to CEs in psychotherapy. All four judges indicated that they believed that CEs in general could be therapeutic. Furthermore, they indicated that different types of CEs would be therapeutic in the two treatment segments. For example:

- In CBT, CEs might be more likely to focus on intrapersonal concerns (e.g., challenging automatic thoughts or core schemas, creating mastery experiences, facing feared situations, or challenging the fear of negative consequences of letting go of worry) (endorsed by all four judges).
- In I-EP, CEs might be more likely to focus on interpersonal concerns (e.g., challenging interpersonal fears as well as beliefs that wishes or needs will not be met) (endorsed by all four judges) or on intrapersonal concerns specifically around the experience of emotions (e.g., allowing oneself to experience or express emotions previously believed to be unacceptable) (endorsed by two judges).
- CEs may be more likely to take place in session within the therapeutic relationship in I-EP, whereas they may be more likely to take place outside of the session (as homework) in CBT (endorsed by two judges).
- Across both treatments, CEs are likely to build on one another—that is, small or mini-CEs may be likely to lay the groundwork for larger, more impactful CEs (endorsed by two judges).

All four judges also indicated that they believed that GAD could be successfully treated using psychotherapy, yet they all also saw it as a relatively difficult problem to treat. All believed that both CBT and I-EP could be potentially effective in treating GAD. None thought that CBT or I-EP would generally be more effective than the other, although two noted that the treatments might be differentially effective for different types of individuals or based on the nature of the presenting concerns (e.g., whether worry focused on primarily intra- vs. interpersonal issues). Two judges also suggested that the combination of the two treatments might be most effective for some individuals. All had some experience treating individuals with GAD (ranging from having treated one client with a primary diagnosis of GAD to substantial experience across a number of years), and all had used several different approaches to treating GAD.

Qualitative Analyses

The qualitative analyses were conducted using Elliott and colleagues' (Elliott, 1994; Elliott et al., 1994) comprehensive process analysis (CPA). One researcher (the second author) had previous experience conducting qualitative research, although the others had no such experience. In preparing to conduct the analyses, the authors read a detailed manual on conducting CPA (Elliott, 1994) and also consulted with Robert Elliott before beginning coding.

After the judges watched all of the taped sessions of the case and took detailed process notes, they individually went back through their notes and identified moments throughout the treatment in which they thought that CEs had occurred. The judges then met to arrive at a consensus regarding CE events in each segment of therapy (CBT and I-EP) on which to focus their analyses. Based on this consensus meeting, two events were identified in each segment. In line with the definition of CEs mentioned above, the primary criterion used to identify a therapeutic event as a CE was that it involved an actual moment of disconfirmation of the client's expectations. Specifically, the events identified as CEs involved the client doing something different or reacting in a way that was inconsistent with his previous maladaptive pattern of reacting to anxiety-provoking situations and experiencing a different outcome. After consensus was reached regarding the identification of CE events, the judges then used session transcripts to identify the speaking turns that marked the beginning and ending of each event, as well as the speaking turns that composed the pivotal moments of each event.

The CPA framework comprises three broad domains: context, key responses, and effects. The domain of *context* includes factors that led up to or impact the manifestation of the event and includes four levels: *background* (relevant features of the client and therapist that preceded the event—including aspects of the client's presenting problems, characteristic coping style, history, and current life situation, as well as therapist personal characteristics and treatment principles); *presession context* (relevant events that have occurred since treatment began, either in or out of session, e.g., previous therapist interventions, experiences between sessions); *session context* (relevant features of the session in which the event occurred, leading up to the event, including aspects of therapeutic tasks and the alliance); and *episode context* (important features of the episode containing the event, i.e., what was being discussed immediately leading up to the event, interventions made, etc.).

The second domain, *key responses,* includes four aspects of client and therapist responses: *action* (e.g., client self-disclosure), *content* (e.g., belief, fear), *style* (e.g., warm, respectful), and *quality or skillfulness* (e.g., well-timed, evocative).

The third domain, *effects,* refers to the consequences of the event over time, including *immediate effects* (e.g., weeping), *within-session effects* (e.g., strengthening of the therapeutic alliance), *postsession effects* (e.g., increased willingness to try something new between sessions, decreased scores on symptom measures at future sessions), and *posttreatment effects* (e.g., increased ability to assert interpersonal needs in relationships). All decisions throughout the process are made by consensus among judges.

In conducting this study, it became clear that the CEs in this case could not be captured by a few discrete interventions by the therapist and one or two specific statements of the client, thus making the domain of key responses less useful for analysis. Because of this, we collapsed the analyses of two of the domains mentioned above—that is key responses and immediate effects—into a broader analysis of *significant events*. In addition, because some of the CEs in this case took place outside of session and were then reported and processed in the therapy, we have modified the format of presentation slightly to improve readability (although it is important to note that the CPA analyses themselves were not modified).

RESULTS

Following Elliott's (1994) guidelines and previously published research using CPA (Elliott et al., 1994), we first provide background information about the client. We then present the analyses in terms of context, the CE, and the effects for the CBT treatment, followed by the same analyses for the I-EP treatment. We also present quantitative analyses based on the outcome measures.

Background

Adam defined himself as a man with integrity (trustworthy, honest) and deep commitment to his religion and the contract of marriage. In terms of coping style, he revealed himself to be a logical and analytical thinker, frequently providing detailed and intellectual responses and at first rarely expressing emotions even when directly prompted. His problem solving style appeared to fit the Type A category, such that in stressful situations he reportedly tended to deny ("stuff away") his painful feelings and act in a manner that was impulsive and hostile.

At the beginning of therapy, Adam reported a high level of GAD symptoms (including worry and somatic distress across a broad range of situations and events). He reported that he was also experiencing stress at work and marital conflict, both other major concerns for which he had sought treatment. He was contemplating divorce because he was tired of feeling torn between his needs and his wife's needs but felt trapped by his religious beliefs, which led him to believe that divorce was unacceptable. The marital conflict had escalated after they moved from a state where his wife had important family ties so that he could take a new job. Because he had previously promised her that they would never make such a move, his wife accused him of being untrustworthy (an accusation that was in conflict with the way he defined himself). She also complained that he did not trust her, a statement that was consistent with the way that he admittedly viewed women.

Throughout the treatment, Adam reported a difficult interpersonal history. His father was authoritarian, distant, and physically abusive. His mother was kind but submissive to his father and did not protect him from the father's abuse. He reported being a rebellious child who had no close friends. His divorce from his first wife was traumatic, and his children were removed from his care. In addition, he reported feeling animosity toward young, attractive, and rich women (a categorization that could fit the therapist).

Corrective Experiences in Cognitive Behavior Therapy Treatment

Presession Context

Early in treatment (Sessions 1–4), Adam had difficulty implementing and benefiting from techniques prescribed in the CBT protocol (e.g., progressive muscle relaxation, deep breathing, cognitive restructuring) in response to the stressful events with which he was confronted. At the end of a guided relaxation exercise in Session 4, however, the client reported a substantial reduction in anxiety and stated to the therapist, "That's the impact you have on me."

In Session 5, Adam reported having experienced a shift in his average mood from anxious to relaxed. He also stated that he was able to make this shift by monitoring his anxiety during the day and challenging the associated thoughts ("Maybe I am not so bad"; "We can work with this"). Perhaps reflecting a small CE, he seemed intrigued by the impact of these techniques, as they had led him to understand (or at least contemplate) events in a different and unexpected way. The therapist reinforced Adam for reacting differently to his internal experience and realizing that he has a choice to evaluate his thoughts rather than engage in all-or-none thinking. The session ended with Dr. E examining the fears associated with a list of worries that Adam developed during the previous week and giving a relaxation exercise for homework.

Dr. E began the subsequent session (Session 6) with a brief relaxation exercise that helped the client "find calmness inside." After this exercise, Adam spontaneously stated, "This stuff is working, shaving off the peak [of the intensity of the anxiety]." This statement led to a discussion of how Adam had discovered that when he catches himself feeling tense (physical sensations), using diaphragmatic breathing helps him reduce his anxiety. Dr. E tried to help Adam learn how to let go of whatever was on his mind when he worried (what he called "mind grinding"). The client stated that the idea of letting go was very threatening, as he worried that he would not be able to pay attention to what was going on and would forget things that he needed to do as part of his daily responsibilities at work. The therapist then focused on these specific thoughts and ended the session with homework to track the worry, generate alternatives to worry, and note how many times Adam catches himself worrying and try to make a shift.

Session Context

The first identified CE in the CBT treatment occurred in Session 7. Dr. E began this session by asking whether Adam had experienced any successful (even if small) shifts in his reactions to anxiety cues, such as breathing more deeply, focusing more on the present moment, or becoming more aware of self-talk. Adam answered generally (without providing any specific examples) that this had happened significantly in different instances during the week and stated that he had experienced an increased impact and accelerated use of the techniques he had learned thus far in treatment. Dr. E reflected and reinforced Adam's increased awareness and repeated practice of what they had been working on. Adam felt supported and then reported being surprised by how the different techniques (cognitive and behavioral) had meshed together. After the therapist validated this experience ("They really do all start out as separate pieces. You learn them separately but then you get to see how they fit together, as you work with them more"), the client stated that this experience in itself had been an unexpected and significant change:

> I'm not a good assembler. I'm a dissembler type of person, where I'll take a big picture and break it apart, and look at it until I can understand. But this whole thing is sort of like an assembly, and that's not a typical way of me thinking. I'm thinking a sort of the reverse. I'm having to shift a paradigm.

Dr. E then asked Adam to talk about a specific occurrence during the past week when he successfully applied something that they had been talking about.

Corrective Experience Episode Context

Adam then described a situation that was typically stressful for him that had recurred in the past week (driving in traffic when late for an appointment), as well as the associated somatic symptoms (sweating) and automatic thoughts. This time, however, he reminded himself of the techniques that were discussed and worked on in therapy. The following is a transcription of the significant event. (At the beginning of treatment, both client and therapist agreed to refer to one another by their first names, and this was consistently done throughout. To avoid potential confusion, however, we refer to the therapist as "Dr. E" and the client by his first name [which we changed here for confidentiality purposes]).

Adam: . . . and that's a good word. I was more aware of my emotional state. And so, I was driving along, and then I suddenly became aware—"I'm really tailgating that guy," I mean, I'm really, I can sense myself . . .

Dr. E: [Laughs.] Oh, good . . .

Adam: . . . doing the typical thing, which is . . .

Dr. E: Good . . .

Adam: . . . pressing, just pressing the issue, driving . . .

Dr. E: Good . . .

Adam: I don't do road rage, but I, uh, but people tend to push . . . and I said, "OK, well, we've been working on this. I can, I can relax." So, sort of like, "Eh, OK, I can slow down here." It, so part of this fitting in says, "Well, OK. Uh, what can I do? Well, I can relax, or I can look at the scenery, or I, this thing about being in the now." . . . So, I, I was driving along, and I thought, "OK, I can settle down here and I'll just look around, and I'll [raises eyebrows] do what I told Dr. E I was doing, and I'll look at the trees, and the flowers . . ."

Dr. E: Yeah.

Adam: And so I found . . . that I was more conscious of . . .

Dr. E: Great!

Adam: . . . of that, and so, I'm not saying I was super good at it, but at least I was conscious of . . .

Dr. E: Absolutely. Yeah.

Adam: . . . the things that we've been talking about . . .

Dr. E: Yeah . . .

Adam: . . . and then, um, usually when I'm uh, in a, in a group of four or five people that are doing sequential presentations, a bunch of [different experts] and all this stuff. So, I, usually I got a little bit tense when [sniffs loudly] this one guy was chopping into my time, you know I drive. It's really costly for me to go out on the road for a 20-minute presentation, [raises eyebrows, laughs] and this guy's cutting into my time, and I, I'm standing there thinking, "Darn, darn, darn, darn, darn." And then I thought,

"So, what? So what can I do here? Well, you know, not lots, just lay back and enjoy it." [Shrugs shoulders.] You know?

Dr. E: [Laughs.]

Adam: So, I, I, I shifted to, "OK, no big deal. They'll get my message. No matter." And, and, so that stuff is meshing in.

Significant Event (Analysis of Corrective Experience)

In this event, Adam related an experience in which he became aware of both somatic symptoms and a maladaptive behavior—tailgating another vehicle—as they were happening. He also noted becoming aware of the situational cues that triggered these internal responses and that were at the core of his GAD symptoms. He then chose to respond differently than usual: He reminded himself of the techniques he had learned in therapy to react in a more adaptive manner and engaged in responses (e.g., relaxation, mindfulness, cognitive reappraisal) that were different from previous cognitive, somatic, and behavioral reactions typically triggered in similar stressful situations. In contrast to his previously held belief that he was helpless to impact his experience in such situations, Adam then felt relief and an increased sense of agency: While he was anxious, hostile, and uncomfortable at the beginning of the experience, he appeared to become confident, forthright, active, and even happy, as it progressed. It is interesting to note that immediately after describing the tailgating event, Adam then reported using the same skills (awareness of anxiety, self-efficacy statements, and behavioral activation) in response to a stressful situation that happened on the next day of the same business trip, as well as other occasions when he used applied relaxation techniques almost automatically ("I am not consciously doing it but it's sort of soaking in"), self-monitoring of anxiety states, and cognitive reappraisal ("What are the alternatives?"). This was in contrast to past responses to situational and internal cues that would typically lead to an anxiety spiral and maladaptive behaviors.

It is important to note that while he was reporting the events just described, Adam seemed aware of his maladaptive responses. Throughout the session, he also appeared to have evidenced an increased sense of control over his habitual reactions, as well as an accurate self-evaluation of the limits of his current change. In response to Dr. E's questions about the effects of his increased awareness of internal and situational anxiety cues and his shift in response to these cues, Adam reported a decrease in overall stress level (experienced specifically in somatic symptoms associated with GAD, i.e., physical tension such as "crunching" his teeth, lower levels of muscle tension and general tension, "brain pressure"). It should also be mentioned that the nature of this CE (and the manner in which it was described by the client in the session that follows it) seemed to indicate a strong therapeutic alliance at this stage of treatment. A high level of agreement on goals and tasks was evidenced by the client's willingness to continue thinking about and practicing concepts and skills learned in treatment outside of session. Furthermore, evidence of a strong bond was manifested in the client's explicit evocation of the therapist during the event.

Within-Session Effect

Although a strong therapeutic alliance appeared to have facilitated this CE, the event itself may have also further enhanced the bond and collaboration between Adam and Dr. E. During the session, the client appeared happy, if not proud of himself, in sharing his success with the therapist. Dr. E also appeared authentic in her support and praise of Adam, and he was genuinely accepting of (and attentive to) her compliments. There was also reciprocity in the explicit affirmation of others, as manifested by the client complimenting the therapist on her skill at capturing his experience. As a whole, a pleasant, mutually attuned, and productive atmosphere emerged from the session. Both of them were fully engaged in the work of therapy, yet there was also laughter (as an expression of delightful surprise and praise for Adam's successful experiences).

Postsession Effect and Second Corrective Experience Presession Context

Subsequent CBT sessions appeared to build on the first CE event through their focus on applying the same skills to conflictual interactions with his wife. Consequently, these sessions were an effect (or consequence) of the first CE, yet also provided context for the second CE event, which occurred in Session 12.

In the sessions leading up to the second CE event, Adam reported an increase in marital tension, including experiencing frequent arguments with his wife. Continuing to become more self-aware, he described what he typically experiences during these interactions, including thoughts (worry, rumination, automatic thoughts such as "I am a failure"), emotional and physical sensations (anxiety, tension), and behaviors (becoming hostile and defensive, withdrawing). Dr. E introduced several interventions to address these experiences and modify Adam's reactions in these situations. For example, she set up and repeated several SCD exercises in which she asked Adam to imagine being in the interaction with his wife he had just described, only this time, to imagine staying in the situation, being honest with her while remaining calm (as opposed to going with his typical thought, "I am a failure"). The therapist also assigned homework exercises designed to practice skills learned in session (e.g., "letting go") and "de-automize" and challenge statements (such as, "This is a test and I will fail") by introducing alternative self-statements (e.g., "I am valuable"), appraisals, and the downward-spiral technique (i.e., "What does it mean when someone is not affirming you?").

Corrective Experience Episode Context

The second CE in the CBT treatment was identified at Session 12. Adam began this session by reporting having engaged in a different and more adaptive reaction during the week. The following is a transcription of the report of the significant event.

Dr. E: . . . you're saying you were able to kind of sit still better through this 2-hour discussion with [your wife] . . .

Adam: Yeah . . .

Dr. E: . . . that you were able to kind of shift a little bit in your head . . .

Adam: Yeah [Nods.] . . .

Dr. E: . . . in terms of . . . not just interpreting everything she was saying as something you need to defend against . . .

Adam: [Nods.]

Dr. E: . . . but, but rather what—what—what might you have been saying to yourself?

Adam: Well, I don't know exactly. I was saying, "Well, OK, I hate this, [rubs forehead] I'm tired, I'm, uh, I can't absorb any more of this conversation; it's been going intensely for two hours, it's exhausting." She said, "Well you talk with Dr. E for two hours." I said, "Yeah, I walk out of there and I'm exhausted too!" [Laughs.] I re—, I mean it, it's really intense. So anyway, but [points finger] to, to do the, to talk about this part, I was better able to listen and try to discern what she was saying. I, I, I'm not, I still felt . . . defensive but . . .

Dr. E: Mm hmm . . .

Adam: I didn't start crashing inside like I used to do . . .

Dr. E: Excellent!

Adam: So, so anyway . . .

Dr. E: Excellent . . .

Adam: Uh . . .

Dr. E: OK, Adam, tell me what . . .

Adam: [Sips beverage.]

Dr. E: Let's go back, um, to that time you were having that discussion with her. What kinds of things . . . were you saying to yourself that helped you stay less defensive, to help you just kind of, you know . . .

Adam: [Nods.]

Dr. E: . . . not crash inside?

Adam: Well I, [sighs] I think a couple things.

Dr. E: OK.

Adam: One is that, something that she said to me. She said, "You know, you have . . ." and we'll get back to this . . .

Dr. E: OK.

Adam: . . . she said, "You have, uh, ceased or, or, or dispensed yourself from almost every other relationship . . .

Dr. E: Hmm . . .

Adam: . . . in, in the family, your father, your mother, your first wife, your kids. You have really just terminated almost . . . all the relationships." But she said, "You know, I'm still here, even though these people hurt you," she said, "I'm still hanging in here, I'm still tenacious; I'm still loving you," and, and she said, "I'm showing you I am interested and tenacious . . .

Dr. E: Mmm . . .

Adam: . . . in hanging in with you." She said, "Most other people would have walked away from you a long time ago." And I agree. They probably would of 'cause I have not been a very nice person [fidgets with mug]. I mean, I'm no lawbreaker and I'm not a rapist, and all that stuff but I, I, I have distanced myself from these people because of hurt [raises eyebrows] and fear of, a fear of hurt.

Dr. E: OK. Alright.

Adam: . . . But anyway, so . . .

Dr. E: You . . .

Adam: I recognized, I recognized that she does love me, and she has a, a, an interest and a tenacity and a love . . .

Dr. E: Boy . . .

Adam: . . . that, that, that, it, she's hanging in there, and so to answer your question, now I recognize that, that she does care and her wisdom is good [licks lips]. And so my shift, my paradigm shift a little bit has been, "I don't have to be defensive about this, but I have to be honest about it." I have to be, to, to not shut up and run away, but I have to be able to say, "OK, let's talk about this." I'm not good at that, but I'm getting better at it.

Dr. E: Ah, Adam, you're doing great!

Adam: Well . . .

Dr. E: If you're saying . . .

Adam: . . . thank you [sips beverage.].

Dr. E: . . . these things to yourself, you're doing great! That's . . .

Adam: Yeah, pretty much, I'm, I mean, I'm . . .

Dr. E: [Laughs.]

Adam: I'm beginning to say, "OK, maybe we can make this work here."

Dr. E: [Sighs.] That's huge!

Significant Event (Analysis of Corrective Experience)

Although he reported signs of being defensive and argumentative early in this event, Adam remained in a stressful and emotionally difficult situation for nearly 2 hours, during which his wife told him both painful and nurturing things. He appeared at first to be emotionally vulnerable, anxious, depressed, hurt, bitter, physically uncomfortable (tired), and uncertain and then showed himself to be active, effortful, expressive, assertive, introspective, respectful, and collaborative. This shift apparently occurred when he made a conscious effort not to interpret what she was saying as something that he had to defend himself against, as he typically had interpreted these discussions in the past. Instead, he told himself not to be defensive and to stay present in the situation, while listening to and being honest with his wife. Adam also stated that he was becoming better at handling this discussion. This conveyed not only a shift in his appraisal of his wife's intentions toward him and his new intentions toward her but also a change in the self that involved increased confidence, assertiveness, and a sense of mastery or efficacy. He agreed with his wife that he had contributed to the difficulty he experiences in their relationship, as well as his past relationships. He also explicitly and fully recognized that his wife loves him and that, in contrast with other people in his life, she has not given up on their relationship. As a result, he did not "crash inside" (grow angry, feel overwhelmed, and withdraw) as he had in the past. After having reported the event that took place with his wife, Adam stated that from this new experience, he was beginning to have a sense of hope and self-efficacy about improving his marital relationship, as conveyed by his comment "OK, maybe we can make this work here."

It should be noted that throughout the examination of the event, Dr. E facilitated Adam's awareness of important changes in his pattern of appraisal, attitude toward himself and others, intentions, and behavior related to his relationship with his wife. The therapist also praised him for being able to make these changes. This praise appeared to enhance the alliance, as shown by Adam's expression of gratitude. In addition to letting her know that her feedback was important to him, Adam's acceptance of the therapist's positive view of his change may have facilitated the processing and integration of the new experience.

Within-Session Effect

This event had a direct impact on what took place for the rest of the session. Specifically, after a discussion about Adam's internal reactions in interactions with his wife, Dr. E set up an SCD with the goal to cement his new and adaptive reaction. She asked him to visualize the very event that he reported, followed by a different internal reaction. Specifically, she instructed him to "imagine saying to yourself, as you did, 'Here is a woman who loves me, who cares. . . . Let's see if I can stay here, not being defensive. . . . I can do this.'" After the SCD was completed, the therapist told Adam that if he does what he just imagined when he is afraid, he will have more choice. Adam then reported that he feels threatened by people and that he gets scared when he becomes attached. He also stated that he gives control to others and then resents it. When Dr. E asked about his fear with his wife, Adam replied that she might prevent him from accomplishing his personal goals. The exploration and challenging of this fear then led to the uncovering of what appeared to be a core belief: "Every time I've cared about someone, I've lost something of myself. Therefore, it is dangerous to get close." The session ended with Adam remarking that he has never had a good relationship. Dr. E asked him to examine the meaning of this statement: "Does this mean that you cannot have a good relationship?"

Postsession Effect

The CE that was reported in Session 12 also had a direct impact on the remaining CBT sessions, which focused on further integration of learned concepts and skills, as well as relapse prevention. Specifically, Dr. E continued to assign homework targeted at practicing and reinforcing new and more adaptive behaviors in potentially stressful situations, particularly while communicating with his wife. In the penultimate session, Adam described his ability to see that not everything is a threat and not all criticism is a challenge. Following an SCD exercise similar to the one that took place in Session 12 (which he reported finding helpful), Adam gained the following insight: "She, my wife, is more threatened than I am . . . and if I can keep this in mind, I will be less defensive." In the final CBT session, Dr. E asked Adam what he would take with him. He answered, "Shifting focus." He then provided two examples: (a) doing deep breathing or increasing his awareness of his surroundings when he is in stressful situations, such as when driving in the car (clearly referring to the event described in Session 7); and (b) changing his view—"I don't have to feel attacked; I can negotiate" (clearly referring to the event described in Session 12).

Summary

Two CE events were identified in Adam's CBT treatment. The first took place between Sessions 6 and 7, and the second took place between Sessions 11 and 12. The first event involved the client's successful implementation of the techniques learned thus far in therapy in a stressful situation (caught in traffic while being late for a job-related meeting), leading to a more positive, and disconfirming, outcome (e.g., reduced tension, allowing him to stay in the present moment). The second event also involved implementing skills learned in therapy and trying something different, this time in the context of an emotionally charged interaction with his wife. Although both of these events occurred outside of sessions with Dr. E., they were clearly linked with the work being done in treatment and the use of between-sessions homework, a core component of CBT. Furthermore, the disclosure and processing of the events with Dr. E appeared to be essential to the absorption of the CE event. Finally, a strong therapeutic alliance appeared to be both a facilitator and an effect of these CEs.

Corrective Experiences in I-EP Treatment

Presession Context

Immediately after Dr. E described the rationale and procedures involved in I-EP in Session 1, Adam expressed his apprehensions about relating with her in a nonchoreographed way (i.e., in a personal, spontaneous way). Throughout the initial I-EP sessions, when asked to talk about his emotions, Adam described thoughts and engaged in long storytelling. However, even early on, he was able to recognize that talking a lot allowed him to put a shield up, especially to prevent women (including Dr. E) from getting close. He wondered aloud what would happen if he let go of this shield and reported being concerned about experiencing and expressing sexual feelings toward Dr. E. He also reported being concerned about the therapist investigating his emotional experience while adopting a distant, objective attitude of a doctor. He stated that showing emotion would be painful to him because of being hurt in the past. The therapist validated and normalized Adam's experience, then reassured him about the balance that she would maintain in terms of facilitating emotional experience (not being cold and distant) while maintaining boundaries (not being an intimate friend). When she asked, at the end of the session, how he felt, Adam reported finding himself "weepy, but also being calm and relieved."

An apparent alliance rupture occurred in Session 2 when Dr. E attempted to facilitate Adam's expression of feelings toward his wife. When he described thoughts, she focused him back on emotion. He then became noticeably irritated with Dr. E, yet resisted talking about his irritation by speaking about his thoughts rather than feelings. Adam then expressed significant distress, stating that he had had "two weeks from hell" in his relationship with his wife and felt trapped: "If I could figure out a way to kill myself without pissing off Jesus . . ." He also disclosed examples of significant animosity toward unmarried women, expressing his frustration with "the young coed in a new car." The session ended with Dr. E asking him (as homework) to think about what he wanted from his wife, suggesting that failing to consider his needs may contribute to his marital problems. The following week, Adam reported that he wanted acceptance and affirmation. He was, however, unwilling to answer the therapist's questions about his feelings toward his wife. Adam acknowledged that he did not trust that the therapist would accept him if he were to reveal himself. The therapist responded that she had observed that when Adam had been willing to take risks (rather than worrying about what to say and how to say it), she had felt that he was more real and was able to feel more compassionate toward him. Adam acknowledged his awareness of the distance he puts between himself and others out of defensiveness: "I'll divest myself of everything before I let people take them from me."

Similar issues were reenacted in subsequent sessions when Dr. E tried to focus on Adam's feelings and needs with regard to his wife. He had difficulty connecting with his feelings, which he avoided by intellectualizing (providing "why" responses to emotional questions), a dynamic that was pointed out by the therapist. Adam admitted that he was afraid of sharing his feelings with others, including Dr. E, for fear of being criticized, but he also recognized that he was sad for hurting Dr. E by rejecting her efforts to have him connect to his feelings. He also recognized he was missing something in relationships, that he is "numbed" when he is with others and that he wanted to experience more emotional intensity. In the following session (Session 6), Dr. E pointed out that in the previous session Adam appeared to be working harder not to intellectualize.

Adam recognized that this was difficult, yet there was also a sense of a "new adventure," in which Dr. E was challenging him, while in the context of asking him to trust her. The therapist wondered about her own contribution to their lack of task agreement (she asked about emotion, and he went into his head). In response to this, Adam described his conflict in their relationship: He wanted a deep connection but did not know how (and was afraid) to have an intimate yet nonsexual relationship with a woman. Exploration of this conflict led Adam to express his frustration at not being able to break out of his shell. Despite this, in the following session, he reported needing to keep his emotions "in the box" when talking about his painful relationship with his children. Dr. E's attempts to explore his feelings about his children only led to more long-winded intellectual discourse. Dr. E stated that she had tried to get close to Adam's hurt, yet he responded by talking about something else, which made her feel pushed away.

Session Context

The first identified CE in the I-EP treatment occurred in Session 8. With the intention of helping Adam improve his relationship with his daughter, Dr. E began the session by asking him what he wanted from the relationship. After showing signs of anxiety (shifting body position, smirking, rubbing hand around mouth, sighing), Adam went into a long intellectual discourse about the time course of this relationship. After Dr. E reiterated the original question, Adam stated, "The bottom line is I don't want a relationship with her because it would just bring up more hurt than it's worth."

Corrective Experience Episode Context

After this comment, Dr. E asked Adam to put aside what is possible or not with his daughter and to describe his feelings and needs. Rather than answering the question, Adam asked Dr. E whether she had a child and went on to describe, in a very intellectual and global way, how his daughter was taken out of his life and he had become used to it. The therapist pointed out that Adam answered her question with a thought and asked whether he was aware of his feelings toward his daughter, to which he replied that he did not know what feelings he had toward her. Dr. E then pointed out Adam's pattern of failing to directly answer her questions and the distancing impact this has on her. Adam reacted by acknowledging that he provides an intellectual answer to an emotional question: "I am a scientist . . . I'm giving you a rational response to an emotional question." The following is a transcription of the significant event that followed.

> Dr. E: This is even before I asked about your feeling, I think. It can be almost anything that I ask. It doesn't have to be just in regard

to emotion. So, and, and that was something I was watching because I thought, "Well, maybe it is just an issue of feelings, and if they're not that accessible to you, and you go around and figure out how to respond." And that's fine, that's, I, um, I appreciate that, but it's not just about feelings. It seems as though nearly any question that I might ask you to try to help, further us, further your work . . . your response [sighs] . . . I guess the impression is, it comes back based on how you want it . . . how you want to answer and what information you want to provide as opposed to what I'm asking for . . .

Adam: [Raises eyebrows.] Hmmm. [Looks up; rubs mouth.] So, it's a control issue . . .

Dr. E: I think so . . .

Adam: [Has a 6-second pause; appears to be thinking.]

Dr. E: Mm hmm.

Adam: I, I would agree that it's a control issue [nods head]. I . . . all right, let's leave it at that.

Dr. E: OK.

Adam: I, I realize that it's a control issue . . .

Dr. E: OK.

Adam: . . . and by doing that kind of stuff, um, I control the quality and content of the information that I give you.

Dr. E: Yeah, and you have every right to do that, but you need to know the impact it has on me.

Adam: [Smiles during therapist's pause.]

Dr. E: [Has a 7-second pause.] You could, you could tell me if there's something you don't know, or you don't want me to know, or just don't feel comfortable talking about. You could tell me that, but that would have a different impact on me. You have every right to control the information you give me, and what you share. Absolutely. And I don't want, I have no need to take that away from you . . . but like I said, you just need to know by doing it in the way you're doing it has . . .

Adam: I would be a good politician because I could give you spiel [laughs] . . .

Dr. E: Yeah.

Adam: . . . and, and uh, not answer it at the same time.

Dr. E: Absolutely, and you can do it. You, you have a gift of being able to do it a way that I think many people would find smooth and congenial. But, if there's anyone . . .

Adam: [Laughs.]

Dr. E: . . . who is intent on wanting to know you . . .

Adam: [Raises eyebrows and sighs.]

Dr. E: . . . or wanting to share with you, um, it's going to be frustrating.

Adam: I'm sure it is.

Dr. E: Yeah.

Adam: [Smiling.] Thank you for your honesty. Yeah, that's a good observation, I . . . I don't, I, I, I, emotionally, I work, maybe what I do is, that I don't want to hurt people. That's a feeling, I guess that that's a feeling that I have, is that I don't want to hurt people.

Dr. E: But you do. So, your intent is gonna be quite different than your impact.

Adam: [Nods.] Having said that, I also don't want to be criticized by people [slight smile]. And so, I suppose what I might do, thinking about it, is that I give people some palatable words and some palatable thoughts so that they can find something positive to say even if they didn't wanna say or had criticisms of me . . .

Dr. E: Wait a minute; I'm not sure I understand that. Let's try that again. You don't want to be criticized. But, wait. Maybe you misunderstood when I say how do you try to avoid criticism, you say you like to present certain palliative persona . . . in an effort to avoid criticism. So, that, is that, what are you doing in here exactly to try to . . . avoid being criticized by me?

Adam: Putting on a good front in an effort to control, in an effort to avoid . . . being hurt by perhaps bringing up emotions or feelings that are hurtful or painful to me . . .

Dr. E: OK, so, so you mean really, it would be hurtful or painful to be criticized if you put a part of your core out there, whether it's real feelings or whatever . . .

Adam: Yeah, and . . .

Dr. E: And?

Adam: . . . so I smoke screen it . . .

Dr. E: Ah, you know what? [Laughs.] OK. That seems obvious that that's what you're doing . . .

Significant Event (Analysis of Corrective Experience)

In this event, the therapist confronted Adam about his pattern of react-ing defensively toward her questions and interventions. Adam recognized the way he interacts with her and, after Dr. E communicated her acceptance and support, he further specified his interaction pattern in therapy (avoiding responding to her questions as a way to "control the quality and content of the information" he gives her). Dr. E validated Adam's right to choose how he interacts with her, but she also disclosed the impact that this has on her and informed him that he would have a different impact on her if he would tell her why he does not answer her questions. Adam further self-disclosed about his way of interacting with the therapist, yet in a sarcastic, defensive manner. Dr. E reiterated Adam's right to choose (and complimented him on) how he interacts with others but also further specified the frustrating impact this may have on people who really want to know him, including her. This intervention seemed to positively impact the alliance (with Adam thanking Dr. E for her honesty) as well as foster the client's awareness and insight. Adam recognized the negative impact he has on others and then disclosed conflicting fears of, on the one hand, hurting people, and on the other, being criticized. He also recognized that the latter fear is a motivating factor to deceive or manipulate people. Dr. E reflected Adam's disclosure and then asked whether he was also manipulating her, to avoid being criti-cized. He acknowledged this. Using the evocative term *smoke screen*, Adam symbolized why and how he is evasive and manipulative with the therapist, a disclosure that she validated and supported. Throughout the event, Dr. E used (in a focused, persistent, gentle, warm, nonjudgmental, and tactful way) a number of interventions (interpretation, confrontation, self-disclosure, reformulation, validation) primarily aimed at fostering a process of meta-communication. She also simultaneously drew links between how the client was interacting with her and how he interacts with others. Dr. E did so by demonstrating a skillful balance of challenge and support (as described by Linehan, 1993), most likely providing a CE by exploring (in an emotionally immediate way) his fear of being criticized and his need for control, while neither controlling nor criticizing him—and in fact, doing quite the opposite.

Issues related to the working alliance before and during the event also seem noteworthy. There was disagreement on the tasks of therapy early in the session, as Adam did not answer Dr. E's questions, engaged in emotional avoidance, and thereby controlled the content and process of their inter-action. Despite this, however, the bond appeared to be strong, as he clearly respected the therapist and kept track of what she was asking him. In addi-tion, the bond was strong enough for Dr. E to interrupt Adam when he was avoiding and to explicitly challenge him about his way of reacting to her.

When the metacommunication took place during the event, the agreement on the task was high, as shown by Adam's willingness to engage in difficult work. As noted above, the bond also appeared to increase during the event, as Adam expressed his gratitude for the therapist's self-disclosure.

Within-Session Effect

The above CE directly influenced the rest of the session, both in terms of content and process. Having agreed on Adam's tendency to smoke screen, Dr. E asked him whether smoke screening works in his relationships with others and whether this allows him to avoid getting hurt and to get what he wants. Adam replied that the answer to both of these questions was no. A few minutes later, when talking about what he wants in his relationship with his wife, Dr. E pointed out that Adam was again smoke screening and asked whether he was aware of this. Dr. E asked him how he can find what he wants (to be accepted for who he is) with his wife if he smoke screens her. In response to this, Adam exclaimed, "This is an 'aha' moment for you and me." When Dr. E asked how this realization felt, Adam again began to smoke screen, and the therapist noted this. Adam then reported this in the moment processing of their experience was threatening in one way, yet exciting in another, adding that if he could get past the perceived threat, he could find in Dr. E someone who could bring "clarity with care." After Dr. E replied that "this sounds to me like trust," Adam mentioned that he does not know what trust is but that perhaps things can be different with her. In turn, Dr. E suggested that their relationship might be worth Adam taking a chance to be hurt. While continuing to process what happened between them, the therapist summarized that Adam wants someone to help him without criticizing him, and this led him to recognize that he was afraid that she would criticize him. When asked how he had been feeling for the past 30 minutes, Adam said "relieved"—a clear description of disconfirmation of his expectations and fear. The therapist ended the session by asking whether Adam could try to generalize what he learned in the session (what he feared, what he did, what happened, and what he got) to relationships outside therapy.

Postsession Effect and Second Corrective Experience Presession Context

The CE that took place in Session 8 of I-EP seemed to have a major impact on all of the following sessions of I-EP treatment as well as on events that emerged between sessions. In the following session, Adam and Dr. E processed the new way of relating that the last session represented. They further explored Adam's difficulty and unwillingness to share his emotion with the therapist (partially based on his belief that engaging in any type of intimacy with another woman would be dishonest to his wife) and the impact this has on Dr. E (e.g., feeling frustrated and discounted) and other people in his life (e.g., his wife). They explored his sadness at not being able to establish the type of relationship he wants with others, beginning with his wife. In Session 10, Dr. E complimented Adam for not having smoke screened in the previous session while they were exploring his smoke screening. In fact, she apologized for not appreciating this as it was happening. This exchange represented a new experience for Adam, as being open and expressing his feelings led not only to the opposite of what he feared but also to what he actually wanted (to be accepted and validated rather than criticized by the therapist). They explored what this meant to him (insight that he can trust and let his guard down with a woman), what he has done to make this happen (taking a chance in opening up), and the control that he has in choosing which relationships are worthy and safe enough to do this. They then worked on generalizing this new way of relating, including conducting a role play in which Dr. E played Adam's son, who recently hurt his feelings.

In Session 11, Dr. E remarked that Adam had changed and that she much preferred sitting with him now because he seemed more genuine, and this also allowed her to be more herself. Adam stated that very few people see his "real self," as he does not share his feelings with them (including his wife). Dr. E replied that she found this sad because he is a "wonderful person to be with." They then explored what prevented him from being himself, as opposed to being angry, which he felt he was most of the time and expected from others (including his wife and father). However, a subsequent two-chair exercise led Adam to recognize that one of his wife's expectations was for him to be more connected with her. After Adam voiced a need to be affirmed by his wife, Dr. E drew a parallel with the therapy by asking Adam to accept and process it ("let it sink in") when his wife affirms him. In the following session (Session 12), Adam recognized the impact of his anger and his deception on others and its contribution to unsatisfying dynamics in his relationships, to which Dr. E further disclosed the impact of his deception on her. This openness on the part of the therapist led Adam to share something very important about his anger: that he destroys precious possessions, the way that his father previously destroyed a precious toy. Adam then voiced that he was embarrassed about telling her this story, leading Dr. E to reassure him that there was no need to be embarrassed and to express sadness at hearing the story. When Adam said that he did not want her to feel for him, Dr. E replied, "I care about you because you bothered to show yourself to me." At the end of the session, the client stated that all of the six important people in his life had hurt him. Dr. E then provided Adam with advice about getting what he wants from relationships, especially with his wife (specifically, she recommended that he not cave in, not give up on getting what he needs, and not "trash" parts of himself). Adam then stated that, unlike in the past, he now has some control over his reactions to others.

Session Context

Dr. E began Session 13 by asking how Adam was doing with not smoke screening (i.e., being more genuine and real) with people outside of therapy. After reminding the therapist that he destroys possessions that he prizes, Adam disclosed that it occurred to him that he does the same thing to relationships—he trashes people by rejecting or walking away from them when there is a conflict.

Corrective Experience Episode Context

Adam then described an event that took place during the past week with a mentor and close friend of his, in which he felt rejected. After sharing his feelings and processing the event with his wife, he decided to disclose his feelings to this friend, rather than "trashing" the relationship (his initial impulse). Although we viewed this event (and the fact that he shared his feelings with his wife) as an effect of the CE that took place in Session 8, it also appeared to be a significant CE on its own. The following is a transcription of the event.

> *Adam:* I shared with him my feelings and how I reacted to that conversation we had [licks lips] and I said, "This is really tough for me to talk about because [looks upward, shakes head] it, it sounds so irrational [raises eyebrows] that I, I just, I really . . .
>
> *Dr. E:* Mm hmm . . .
>
> *Adam:* . . . felt rejected [nods]. He says, "Well, that's good, you're sharing." [Looks to side, laughs.] I thought, [laughs] "Right." [Laughs.] And so he said, "Well I real—, I really appre—" but there was [motions outward with hands] some chitchat, some talk. He said, "Well, I wanna tell you something." He said, [shrugs shoulders] "I really value your relationship and I, and I, I'm not gonna run away from you." He said, "I have many new friends but," he says, "You're a real special friend to me." And, and so . . . and then he explained [nods] to me [motions toward self with right hand] why he had to meet with another person he was mentoring and [licks lips] he said, "But I . . . but I'm not gonna" he said, "I'm not gonna run away from you. I'm not gonna leave you." [Nods.] Like, and part of this, part of this thread [throws hands up slightly] is like [covers left side of face], "This is really strange, it sounds like this is two lovers talking" [laughs] . . . and it wasn't . . .

Significant Event (Analysis of Corrective Experience)

In this event, Adam disclosed his feelings of rejection to his mentor after realizing that he was once again "trashing the relationship." Rather than moving away from his mentor, he took the risk and disclosed his feelings. In doing so, he behaved differently from what was typical for him (he did not avoid or smoke screen), and he took the risk of being criticized or rejected by revealing his true, negative, and painful feelings. When his mentor complimented Adam for sharing his feelings, he had doubts about his mentor's reaction. However, as the mentor described how he valued their friendship and that he did not want to reject him, Adam appeared to process this unexpected and positive experience, including the fact that such intimacy between two men made him uncomfortable. Throughout the event, Adam appeared anxious and uncertain (he at first dismissed the veracity of his mentor's reaction). However, by disclosing his feelings directly, appropriately, nonjudgmentally, and in an emotionally present way (by metacommunicating), as well as by letting his mentor express his own reactions more fully, Adam showed himself to be introspective, respectful, gentle, active, expressive, and collaborative.

Within-Session Effect

As with all of the CEs described here, this event directly influenced the rest of the session within which it occurred (or was reported). It impacted the content and process of the interaction, as well as the homework prescribed at the end of the session. Immediately after reporting the event, Adam acknowledged that this was a new experience for him. Although he had previously expressed anger and frustration to other male friends, this was the first time that he had expressed feelings of rejection. Dr. E reinforced this experience and highlighted the short- and long-term consequences of behaving differently. She also highlighted the energy cost of keeping a façade (a comment that the client described as a "tremendous insight"), using a personal story in her life to make this point. Dr. E then disclosed how much more enjoyable it has been for her since Adam stopped keeping that façade (or the smoke screen) and asked him what he thought made the difference. Adam replied that it was her challenging of his smoke screening (the CE in Session 8 described above). Later in the session, Adam stated that he views others as the enemy and if he stops seeing them as a threat, he would not need to smoke screen. The therapist then set up a homework assignment for him to behave differently with his wife in the middle of an argument (reminding himself that she is not a threat and that he has to be assertive in expressing his needs, rather than walk away or cave in).

Postsession Effect

Building on his interactions with the therapist and the recent event with this mentor and friend, the final I-EP session (Session 14) focused on how Adam could improve his relationship with his wife. Several role plays with feedback led to a greater understanding of how Adam could get what he wants with his wife and have a more harmonious relationship (e.g., taking more initiative rather than waiting for his wife to complain about not doing things together), as well as skill acquisition regarding how he could relate better (be more empathic, recognize his contribution to their marital problems). Dr. E shared that she very much appreciated working with Adam. She pointed out the changes that he had made in therapy and how hard he had worked to make a shift in their relationship. Adam recognized that no longer smoke screening with Dr. E and his attempts at clarifying their relationship led to tremendous change in other domains, such as work and dealing with depression, further stating, "I got the 'aha' here and then I had to do the work. . . . It has been a life changing experience."

Summary

Like in the CBT treatment, two CE events were identified in Adam's I-EP treatment. The first took place within Session 8, and the second took place between Sessions 12 and 13. The first event involved in-the-moment processing of the therapeutic relationship in an emotionally immediate way, which was facilitated by the use of metacommunication. This communication was corrective in that it involved the exploration of Adam's fear of being criticized and his need for control, while Dr. E was neither controlling nor criticizing him. The second event also involved emotional processing and metacommunication; however, in this case, the client was the one to generate the CE with an important other outside of the therapy context. This event was disconfirming in that the client was able to communicate his fears and needs in an emotionally immediate way, and not only was he not met with anger or criticism, but the relationship was strengthened. Once again, a strong relationship appeared to be both a facilitator and an effect of these CEs.

Quantitative Analysis

Using the same composite outcome variable derived by Newman et al. (2011), we examined the relative course of the client's GAD symptoms from intake to posttreatment, and at six-, 12-, and 24-month follow-up. The composite score was composed of the anxiety scale from the STAI–T, the HARS, PSWQ, and the GAD CSR from the ADIS-IV. These ratings were converted to standardized scores and averaged for the client, which provided a composite measure of his anxiety symptoms. On the basis of this composite measure, the client's GAD symptoms, which were significantly elevated above the study sample mean ($z = 1.07$), had fallen meaningfully by the end of treatment ($z = -0.47$) and improvement was maintained throughout the follow-up period ($z = -0.22$ at 6 months, $z = -0.56$ at 1 year, $z = -0.43$ at 2 years). Analysis of this client's IIP-C indicated that the interpersonal distress scale, although high at the start of treatment, fell significantly (as determined by the reliable change index [RCI]) by the end of treatment, and fell further (another RCI increment) by 6-month follow-up, passing below the clinical cutoff during this time. These gains were maintained at 2-year follow-up.

DISCUSSION

The qualitative analyses revealed both similarities and differences across treatment modalities with regard to the nature of CEs, the factors that may foster them, and their consequences. The findings also suggest ways in which the combination of different approaches can have a synergistic impact on the facilitation and realization of a core principle of change that can involve many dimensions of human functioning and change.

What Is the Nature of a Corrective Experience?

CEs in both approaches were characterized by the client deliberately and consciously engaging in responses that were different from, or opposite to, those that were typically triggered by feared situations in the past. Also in both treatments, Adam's reaction (surprise, relief, and pride) to his new responses reflected disconfirmation of his previous expectations and fears (consistent with the Penn State definition of CEs).

In addition, however, we found differences in the way that CEs manifested across treatments. In CBT, Adam learned that when confronted with stressful situations, he was capable of shifting his thoughts and intentions, reducing his somatic reactions, and modifying his behavioral responses. In I-EP, the client learned that when he was with significant people in his life, he was capable of being in touch with his emotions and interacting in a genuine, open, and nonmanipulative way. Although CEs that took place in CBT also involved interpersonal change, the client acquired intrapersonal skills that were different from the skills he learned in I-EP. For CBT, in contrast to I-EP, when being confronted by his wife, the focus was not on disclosing his emotions but on resisting his urges to avoid or escape, challenging his automatic thoughts that she was a source of threat, and paying attention to what she was saying. Although CBT and I-EP used different pathways toward new experiences (e.g., intra- vs. interpersonal), the client clearly exhibited gains in both domains.

What Facilitates Corrective Experiences?

Our findings suggest that CEs, within and across the two treatments, were facilitated, at least in part, by several factors related to the therapist, client, relationship, and external events. We present these variables as separate categories, while fully recognizing that they interact dynamically and are interdependent (at a conceptual and clinical level).

Therapist Technique Factors

CEs seemed to be facilitated by the persistent, systematic, and competent use of interventions prescribed by (and at the core of) the treatments. For example, in CBT, these include helping the client face anxiety-provoking situations through self-monitoring, the teaching and repeated practice of breathing and relaxation exercises, cognitive restructuring, and exposure techniques. In I-EP, these include exploring emotional and interpersonal needs, exploring the client's maladaptive behaviors as they happen in the here and now, using metacommunication skills, and training in specific interpersonal skills. Although these sets of interventions underscore important differences between these treatments in the procedures used and the focus of interventions (e.g., reducing tension vs. emotional deepening), a number of common, underlying change processes are apparent. Examples include increasing client awareness, helping the client to tolerate stressful or difficult situations and experiences, the processing of new experiences, and the generalization of learning outside of therapy.

Therapist Relationship Skills

In both CBT and I-EP treatments, the therapist's empathy, warmth, and openness likely provided facilitative conditions for the client's deliberate and successful engagement in new responses to threatening situations. The therapist's normalizing, support, and validation of the client's difficulties, as well as her reinforcement of new adaptive responses are also likely to have facilitated CEs. While working with different clinical material between the therapy segments, Dr. E showed a great sense of timing (e.g., when she swiftly moved from the client's mastery of anxiety-provoking situations in the session [e.g., by means of SCD] to the prescription of relevant homework) and tact (as exemplified by her nonjudgmental attentiveness to and reflection of emotionally sensitive issues that were unfolding in therapeutic relationship).

In terms of personal style, or the interpersonal manner with which she implemented the interventions that contributed to CEs in both treatments, the therapist was involved, collaborative, respectful, and gentle but also confident (enacting her role as an expert in dealing with difficult and/or delicate issues in a warm and professional way) and instructive (providing the client with direct and explicit guidance and feedback related to events in and between sessions). Using Linehan's (1993) metaphor, the therapist's style could be described as reflecting a skillful balance of support and challenge.

Client Factors

Considerable evidence pointed to the crucial role of the client in facilitating and achieving CEs. Perhaps speaking to client motivation and engagement, our observations suggest that it is important for the client to be willing to repeatedly face difficult situations and experiences, in and outside of the therapy session, that will allow maladaptive responses to be systematically triggered. In other words, the client must be willing to take risks and be open to the tasks of treatment. Adam's fear, for example, was activated when he was asked to imagine stressful scenes in CBT or to explore his emotions in I-EP, leading him to respond defensively by keeping information from the therapist and controlling the course of the conversation. Both of these client-generated situations set the stage for CEs.

In addition to anxiety, other negative emotions experienced by the client may have facilitated CEs, such as hurt, hostility, and vulnerability associated with the experience of being rejected and criticized, or depression and physical discomfort triggered by stress. Psychological distress and pain, in other words, may have motivated the client to take risks rather than continuing to respond (intra- and interpersonally) in ways that were not working for him. Adam's awareness of, and insight into, his maladaptive patterns of reacting (e.g., realizing in I-EP that he destroys relationships when hurt by others, recognizing avoidance in CBT) may also have contributed to his willingness to engage in new ways of behaving and relating, both within and outside of sessions.

Beyond these important motivating factors, transformative experiences appear to have necessitated the client's willingness and ability to learn, practice, and/or implement adaptive responses in sessions. This included, for example, Adam's use of breathing and relaxation techniques in reaction to early anxiety cues during CBT, as well as answering the therapist's questions without smoke screening and learning how to metacommunicate in I-EP (self-disclosing his defensiveness and owning the conflict over his wish and fear with the therapist). Thus, compliance and diligence on the part of the client appeared to be crucial (using a pharmacotherapy metaphor, for interventions to be effective, they not only need to be prescribed—they also need to be absorbed).

Also reflecting the agentic role of the client, the occurrence of CEs outside of therapy sessions seemed to have been facilitated by the client reminding himself of the techniques learned in therapy to help him react differently in these situations. Adam explicitly mentioned using these techniques in the first CE event reported in the CBT treatment, and a similar process can easily be inferred from what took place in the sessions preceding the second CE in the I-EP treatment. It is important to note, however, that these between-sessions CEs were contingent on the client's access to, and willingness to engage in, meaningful activities (e.g., having a job) and relationships (e.g., being in a committed relationship). As obvious as it may seem, one not only needs to learn and remember new ways of functioning but also needs opportunities to use and/or consolidate them. Our results also suggest that Adam's ability to recognize and willingness to report (in session) between-sessions CEs may have helped him process and integrate their therapeutic impact.

In both treatments, two CEs were identified, and in each case the first one appears to have facilitated the second. It may be that clients who possess characteristics that are facilitative of one CE may also be predisposed to experiencing multiple CEs throughout the course of treatment. Alternatively, CEs may sometimes build on each other relatively independent of client factors, and the client's first successful experiment with a new way of reacting, being, or relating can serve as a stepping stone or springboard for additional transformative experiences. In line with this, although ultimately representing an interaction between intervention and client factors, clients may possess certain characteristics that increase their probability of experiencing a CE in particular treatment approaches, as opposed to others. In the present case, Adam's logical, analytical coping style may have made him particularly suited to the rationale underlying and procedures prescribed in CBT. This suitability may in turn enhance engagement, which may increase a client's willingness to take the sorts of risks that underlie CEs. Interestingly, additional evidence from this same case addresses the converse argument (low suitability would result in limited engagement). Although Adam initially expressed confusion and defensiveness related to the tasks and goals of the I-EP treatment, his ability to trust the therapist and stay with it eventually led to multiple CEs.

Relationship Variables

Reflecting the collaborative nature of a positive working alliance, the transformational experiences observed in both CBT and I-EP required that the client be open to Dr. E's interventions and willing to take risks. Within the holding environment provided by the therapist, Adam showed courage and persistence in working beyond his anxiety, defensiveness, and mistrust. Throughout his efforts to change, he remained extremely collaborative and respectful toward Dr. E. The interpersonal style of both the client and therapist (before, during, and after the CEs) displayed a reciprocal level of engagement, as well as a mutual attunement to each other's efforts and reactions. In addition to being facilitated by a strong alliance, the transformative experiences observed in both CBT and I-EP also appeared to have led to the increase in agreement on the various therapeutic tasks and goals, as well as a strong bond (as manifested, e.g., by the therapist acknowledging that she liked Adam and Adam explicitly recognizing and appreciating Dr. E's support and honesty). While resting on a solid foundation, ruptures in the alliance were observed in the I-EP treatment (e.g., when Dr. E attempted to explore Adam's emotions and needs toward others). As noted, such ruptures may have been due, in part, to a clash between some of the interventions prescribed in I-EP and the personal characteristics of the client mentioned above (i.e., his logical, analytic style). What clearly emerged from our qualitative analyses, however, is that these ruptures set the stage for the two CEs in I-EP.

External Variables

An example of a facilitative external event observed in this study was the encouragement the client received from his wife before he took the risk of calling his mentor and the alternative view that this mentor provided to the client's perception of having been rejected. Another example was his wife's expression of her love, while confronting him about important (positive and negative) issues in their relationship.

What Were the Consequences of Corrective Experiences?

Adam's shift from habitual maladaptive reactions to new, difficult, but also rewarding (personally and interpersonally) adaptive reactions appeared to have had a number of therapeutic consequences that were observed in both treatments. First, CEs seem to have facilitated symptomatic improvement. This is illustrated, for example, in the decrease in anxiety reported in CBT sessions and the reduction of depression that the client attributed to his more genuine way of interacting with others during I-EP. Although we cannot infer that CEs were solely or mostly responsible for the client's symptomatic (and interpersonal) improvement, our qualitative observations are very much in line with the quantitative changes that we found in the outcome measures. Second, a sense of self-efficacy also appeared to build progressively, as the client faced and successfully dealt with threatening and/or previously avoided situations and experiences. As explicitly stated by the therapist, the client's willingness and effort to engage in situations and new experiences allowed him to experience a disconfirmation. These disconfirmations, characterized by the integration of new information (that was counter to previous experience and expectations), helped Adam to become more flexible— cognitively, emotionally, and interpersonally.

All of these findings suggest that the factors that appear to facilitate CEs (therapist and client variables, as well as relationship factors) interact dynamically as therapy unfolds. For example, the first CE event in each treatment allowed Dr. E to further identify and understand Adam's maladaptive patterns of response and also helped Adam to increase his own awareness and insight regarding these processes. Dr. E was then better able to teach and reinforce new and more adaptive response patterns. CEs not only appeared to be facilitated by several relationship variables, but they also seemed to enhance the alliance and deepen the therapeutic relationship. Initial CEs, and their processing in each treatment, also seemed to facilitate generalization (and automatization, consolidation, integration) of therapeutic learning outside session.

Convergences, Divergences, and Integration of Therapeutic Interventions

The findings discussed here highlight several common factors of CBT and I-EP, especially with regard to the effect of CEs and the variables that appear to facilitate them. Common client factors that facilitated CEs appeared to be motivation, treatment engagement and compliance, and an ability to trust in the therapist and the treatment. Common relationship factors included a strong bond and (at least eventual) agreement on tasks and goals. Common effects included future CEs; decreased tension and anxiety; and increased cognitive, emotional, and interpersonal flexibility. In addition, CEs in both treatments appeared to instill a sense of mastery and hope in the client.

Our analyses also revealed important differences, primarily with regard to the type (or nature) of CEs that took place in these treatments (e.g., intra- vs. interpersonal, reduction of arousal vs. emotional evocation and deepening) and the techniques that were used to foster them (e.g., breathing training vs. identification of interpersonal needs). These differences, however, are far from irreconcilable and can be viewed as complementary. For example, a therapist could, with a similar client, use CBT interventions that focus on specific internal issues (e.g., somatic markers, cognitions) to help the client cope with particular stressful situations (e.g., to reduce anxiety, worry, and anger when stuck in traffic) and humanistically based interventions (e.g., exploration of emotion) to help the client become more aware of his interpersonal needs.

The focus on different dimensions of functioning can also allow the client to acquire and simultaneously use a variety of skills to handle complex situations. There are several potential skills following from CBT and I-EP that are likely to help clients resolve interpersonal conflicts. For example, learning to reduce anxiety cues as they emerge; paying attention to and evaluating negative thoughts; resisting urges to avoid or escape; focusing on what another person is saying; being aware of one's emotions, needs, and impact on the other; and genuinely and openly metacommunicating are all skills that are likely to help clients resolve interpersonal conflicts. In addition, several of the techniques used in the two treatments are procedurally different yet are aimed at facilitating the same process of change—these are, one might say, different means to the same end (e.g., facilitating awareness of maladaptive patterns, exposure, processing of new experiences, reality testing). Furthermore, these techniques are likely to have a synergic impact, working together to promote even greater change. For instance, learning strategies for more effectively managing his own emotional reactions likely helped Adam to be more present in his interactions with others and respond more adaptively to them, thus leading to more satisfying interactions and further reducing his distress. Technical commonalities between these two treatments should also be mentioned. For example, both therapies are directive (i.e., requiring the therapist to frequently and explicitly direct the focus of treatment) and use homework. These similarities may also have had a synergic effect.

Our analyses also suggest that some client characteristics might fit more easily within some treatments than others (e.g., those who are more problem-focused and logical or analytical might be inclined toward CBT). However, this does not mean that other treatments are incompatible with some clients. In fact, although this client's logical and analytical style may have been one of the reasons why he was initially reluctant to accept the rationale of and engage in the tasks prescribed in I-EP, his eventual involvement in this treatment appears to have led to a significant and gratifying transformation.

Limitations

Limitations of this study include the reliance on a single case that came from the controlled setting of an RCT. In addition, many of the findings confirmed expectations of the research team regarding differences between the two approaches, leaving open the possibility that confirmation biases contributed to the analysis. It should also be noted that although the members of the research team each had different beliefs and expectations, many of them had also discussed other clients in supervision together, which may have led to the judges mutually influencing one another. Another important limitation is that three of four identified CEs in this case occurred outside of sessions and that therefore the researchers had to rely on only the client's report in their analyses of these events. Therefore, future studies (in naturalistic and controlled settings), with therapists using different treatments, with different clients, and different researchers are needed before more confident assertions can be made about the convergence and complementary processes that were observed in this study about CEs.

REFERENCES

Brown, T. A., Di Nardo, P. A., & Barlow, D. H. (1994). *Anxiety Disorders Interview Schedule for DSM–IV*. New York, NY: Oxford University Press.

Elliott, R. (1994). *Understanding the change process in psychotherapy: Comprehensive process analysis*. Unpublished manual, Toledo, OH.

Elliott, R., Shapiro, D. A., Firth-Cozens, J., Stiles, W. B., Hardy, G. E., Llewelyn, S. P., & Margison, F. (1994). Comprehensive process analysis of insight events in cognitive–behavioral and psychodynamic–interpersonal psychotherapy. *Journal of Counseling Psychology, 41*, 449–463. doi:10.1037/0022-0167.41.4.449

Goldfried, M. R. (1980). Toward the delineation of therapeutic change principles. *American Psychologist, 35*, 991–999. doi:10.1037/0003-066X.35.11.991

Hamilton, M. (1959). The assessment of anxiety states by rating. *The British Journal of Medical Psychology, 32*, 50–55. doi:10.1111/j.2044-8341.1959.tb00467.x

Horowitz, L. M., Rosenberg, S. E., Baer, B. A., Ureño, G., & Villaseñor, V. S. (1988). Inventory of interpersonal problems: Psychometric properties and clinical applications. *Journal of Consulting and Clinical Psychology, 56*, 885–892. doi:10.1037/0022-006X.56.6.885

Linehan, M. M. (1993). *Cognitive behavioral treatment for borderline personality disorder*. New York, NY: Guilford Press.

Meyer, T. J., Miller, M. L., Metzger, R. L., & Borkovec, T. D. (1990). Development and validation of the Penn State Worry Questionnaire. *Behaviour Research and Therapy, 28*, 487–495. doi:10.1016/0005-7967(90)90135-6

Newman, M. G., Castonguay, L. G., Borkovec, T. D., Fisher, A. J., Boswell, J. F., Szkodny, L., & Nordberg, S. (2011). A randomized controlled trial of cognitive–behavioral therapy for generalized anxiety disorder with integrated techniques from emotion-focused and interpersonal therapies. *Journal of Consulting and Clinical Psychology, 79*, 171–181. doi:10.1037/a0022489

Newman, M. G., Castonguay, L. G., Borkovec, T. D., Fisher, A. J., & Nordberg, S. (2008). An open trial of integrative therapy for generalized anxiety disorder. *Psychotherapy: Theory, Research, & Practice, 45*, 135–147. doi:10.1037/0033-3204.45.2.135

Safran, J. D., & Segal, Z. V. (1990). *Interpersonal process in cognitive therapy*. New York, NY: Basic Books.

Spielberger, C. D., Gorsuch, R. L., Lushene, R., Vagg, P. R., & Jacobs, G. A. (1983). *Manual for the State–Trait Anxiety Inventory: STAI (Form Y)*. Palo Alto, CA: Mind Garden.

14

VARIETIES OF CORRECTIVE EXPERIENCING IN CONTEXT: A STUDY OF CONTRASTS

TIMOTHY ANDERSON, BENJAMIN M. OGLES,
BERNADETTE D. HECKMAN, AND PETER MacFARLANE

Consistent with Goldfried's (1980; see also Chapter 2, this volume) description of *corrective experiences* (CEs) as principles of change, we argue that CEs may be best understood as operating within the broader context of a person's cultural, interpersonal, and intrapersonal experiences. Goldfried suggested that *clinical strategies* or *principles of change* might be useful clinical heuristics that fall between abstract theoretical frameworks (with their associated philosophical stances) and therapeutic techniques and procedures. As one of these "essential ingredients of change," CEs integrate various common psychotherapy factors for the purpose of helping the client replace old experiences and patterns with new emotional and psychological experiences. We also argue that Goldfried's notion can be extended to aid in understanding the interplay between other common factors within the contextual (Frank & Frank, 1991) and generic (Orlinsky & Howard, 1986) models of psychotherapy.

We further define CEs operationally as including a new experience or experiences in which there is significant contrast to the client's set of prior

We are thankful to Grace Jameson, Xiaoxia Song, and Andrew McClintock for their contributions in conducting this study.

experiences. To establish this argument, we define corrective experiencing in relationship to its placement within these models of psychotherapy and derive some basic propositions for investigating CEs. We then report on a qualitative study designed to provide initial data on the varieties of CE in different types of therapy.

INTEGRATED CONTEXTUAL MODEL

Our conceptualization of CE within the generic and contextual models of psychotherapy is depicted in Figure 14.1. Before describing such conceptualization, we hasten to say that the integration of these models offers nothing dramatically new from the original contributions of these landmark publications and only claims some original reorganization of the factors and how they operate (Anderson, Lunnen, & Ogles, 2010).

The generic model of psychotherapy (Orlinsky & Howard, 1986) describes psychotherapy using a flowchart in which cultural inputs shape the therapeutic processes, which then influences the individual in the form of outputs, including client outcome. The model is generic because it is broad enough to encompass all therapeutic orientations. Inputs include environmental and societal influences and patterns along with the individual characteristics and qualities of the client and therapist that affect the treatment. Processes of treatment include the therapeutic contract, operations, and bond along with in-session impacts that are affected by client and therapist self-relatedness and the temporal patterns of interaction that develop. Outputs include the effects of the process on daily social and other events, changes in therapist and client, and of course functional and symptomatic client outcomes.

The generic model emphasizes the context of treatment and the influence of culture, society, and all that clients and therapists bring with them to treatment. Client inputs, especially previous interpersonal relationships, are the fodder that creates the contrasting experiences that are part of our working definition of a CE (see below). For example, therapist inputs provide the relationship and interactions that contrast with the client's earlier experiences. Other therapist inputs from Orlinsky and Howard's (1986) model (characteristics and patterns) may hinder the development of these relationships. The processes of therapy include the opportunity for contrasting experiences that bring about expected changes (outputs) that influence both client and therapist and produce other associated outcomes.

Frank and Frank's (1991) contextual model of psychotherapy proposes that all therapies (and other healing rituals) are effective as a result of four essential and common elements. These elements are (a) "an emotionally

282   ANDERSON ET AL.

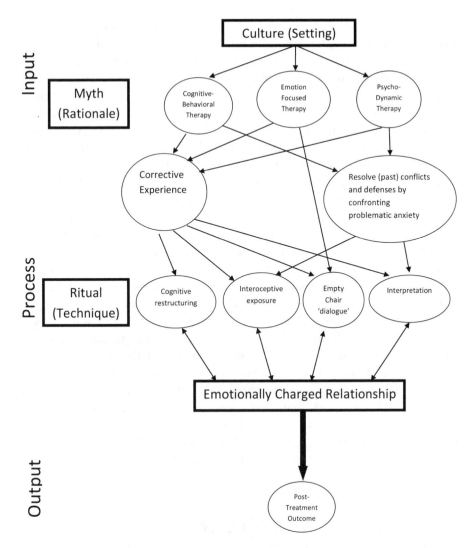

Figure 14.1. The corrective experience as a principle within the integrated contextual model. Reprinted From *The Heart and Soul of Change: Delivering What Works in Therapy, Second Edition* (p. 147), edited by B. L. Duncan, S. D. Miller, B. E. Wampold, and M. A. Hubble, 2010, Washington DC: American Psychological Association. Copyright 2010 by the American Psychological Association.

charged, confiding relationship with a helping person" (p. 40); (b) "a healing setting" (p. 41); (c) "a rationale, conceptual scheme, or myth that provides a plausible explanation for the patient's symptoms and prescribes a ritual or procedure for resolving them" (p. 42); and (d) "a ritual or procedure that requires the active participation of both patient and therapist and that is believed by both to be the means of restoring the patient's health" (p. 43)

CEs can be viewed to be part of the contextual model through their explicit inclusion in the rationale for treatment. As part of a treatment ritual, the CE was first conceptualized by Alexander and French (1946) as a major shift from insight to action within psychodynamic treatment. In addition to continuing to be a major influence in psychodynamic treatment (Chapters 3 and 4, this volume), the understanding of how CEs contribute to client improvement have been construed flexibly across orientations. We believe that the pantheoretical nature of the CE construct is one indication that it operates through common components of treatments (Weinberger, 1993). Specifically, within our integrated contextual model of psychotherapy, we believe that CEs operate at the principle level of change (Chapter 2, this volume). As can be seen in Figure 14.1, therapy principles may operate both within orientations that explicitly incorporate CEs as part of the treatment rationale and within orientations that use a different approach and vocabulary. Arrows noting the paths of change might cross over even in unexpected directions (that is, incorporating principles from different orientations). We assume that Goldfried's (1980) notion of *principle*, then, can be used for intermediate levels other than the space between techniques and orientations, including the contextual model space between culture and therapeutic orientation. In addition, we believe it is consistent with the above models to place psychotherapy principles as the metaphoric hub of the contextual wheel. Thus, the potential power of a CE is that it may integrate, connect, or otherwise buttress any number of contextual factors and influences. The implication of this slight extension of the use of psychotherapy principles is that the "culture or (setting)" contextual factor can often be meaningfully integrated with psychotherapy orientations, techniques, and emotionally charged relationships.

SOME PROPOSITIONS

We began our work on CEs using the Penn State University conference definition: "CEs are ones in which a person comes to understand or experience affectively an event or relationship in a different and unexpected way" (Chapter 1, this volume, p. 5). Based on our integration of the contextual and generic models of psychotherapy, we elaborated on this definition by delineating a set of theoretical propositions to provide greater precision in our qualitative work. We relied on the "different and unexpected" aspect of the Penn State definition by operationally defining CEs to include a recognizable contrast with the client's prior experiences. In the psychodynamic literature, this phenomenon has been referred to as the *principle of contrast* (Knight, 2005) and is derived from Alexander and French's (1946) original theorizing that CEs develop from the therapist's attempts to prompt new experiences within the client and thereby counteract a tendency for the therapy experience from becoming overly routine. We propose the following implications of this definition.

1. Corrective experiencing operates at the principle level and may become evident in the rationale for, or the procedures of, both treatments that explicitly identify it as a change mechanism and treatments that identify different change mechanisms.
2. Corrective experiencing is most frequently an interpersonal phenomenon and can occur within the healing setting and the therapeutic relationship, or "parallel with the treatment in the daily life of the patient" (Alexander & French, 1946, p. 66). Some aspect of the therapist's behavior contrasts with client relational expectations and usual patterns of relationships (Knight, 2005), which facilitates or promotes the opportunities for the client to actually have a new experience and a CE.
3. Corrective experiencing is not necessary for change in treatment but is often a component of successful treatment.
4. What a client experiences as new may not be consistent with the main theme, contents, and techniques of therapy. Thus, CEs may be independent of what observers of the treatment (including the therapist) might predict.
5. The client's experience of contrast and then eventual explanation for change may appear to be unrelated to the path predicted by the therapeutic model.

We do not assume that this list is exhaustive, yet we contend that these propositions warrant investigation and may lead to a more rich and complete description of the role of CEs in successful therapy.

In the present study, we use qualitative methods to begin the process of describing corrective experiencing in successful cases across a variety of therapist orientations and experiences. Successful cases from two psychotherapy studies were identified to provide a heterogeneous sampling of therapists, modalities, and contexts for the purpose of building a contextual understanding of CEs. We use these qualitative data to investigate the following questions:

1. In the termination interviews, do clients identify CEs contrast experiences as important contributors to positive improvement?
2. What are the types and varieties of contrast experiences? Can researchers learn something about CEs by categorizing or grouping them together?

3. To what extent do contrast experiences occur across different therapeutic orientations and therapists with various backgrounds and training?
4. By linking contrast experiences described by clients in termination interviews with observations of therapist–client interactions during therapy sessions, how does the context of therapy, such as the setting, rationale for treatment, the therapeutic relationship, and rituals and procedures facilitate and promote the emergence of corrective experiences?

METHOD

Participants

Clients

We chose two databases for case selection because part of our aim was to apply the contextual model to a variety of cases and situations. First, we drew on the Vanderbilt II Psychotherapy Training Study (Vanderbilt II; Strupp, 1993), in which highly experienced therapists practiced their treatment as usual (TAU) for one cohort and then were trained for a year in time-limited dynamic psychotherapy (TLDP), a manualized treatment that aimed to use the therapeutic relationship in ways that promoted the traditional and historic definition of a CE (Alexander & French, 1946). In fact, a CE is so central to TLDP that Levenson's (1995) adaptation of the adherence measure includes an item rating the trainee's ability to promote a CE within the client. Clients were recruited through mass media advertisements in the community, were screened to ensure suitability for psychotherapy, and were diagnostically heterogeneous. Clients were offered a maximum of 25 sessions and most attended all the sessions ($M = 22$ sessions).

Second, we included cases from the Ohio University Helping Relationships Study (OUHRS), a recently completed study in common factors, in which half of the clients were treated by therapists-in-training (therapists had 2 years of didactic and 1 year of clinical practicum). The other half of the sample were treated by doctoral students from nonclinical fields of study (e.g., chemistry) and had no didactic or clinical training experiences. Because of the unique nature of the sample, client participants were recruited using a symptom screener followed by a clinical interview to verify that they had clinical levels of distress. Each client was offered a maximum of seven sessions and offered a genuine psychotherapy experience on completion of the study.

Case Selection

Cases that reflected the most positive outcomes on the basis of a self-report measure of global symptoms and a global clinician rating were selected from the larger Vanderbilt II and OUHRS samples. For the self-reported symptoms, the Symptom Checklist–90—R (SCL-90–R; Derogatis, 1983) was used from the Vanderbilt II sample and the Outcome Questionnaire–45 (OQ-45; Lamert, Lunnen, Umphres, Hansen, & Burlingame, 1994) was used from the OUHRS sample. In addition, both samples used the global clinician ratings from the Global Assessment Scale (GAS; Endicott, Spitzer, Fleiss, & Cohen, 1976), a one-item rating from 0 to 100 that is made by independent clinicians approximately one week before and one week after meeting with their clients. Regression analysis was conducted using each pretreatment and termination measure to generate unstandardized residual change scores (i.e., removing the pretreatment score from the termination score). These global symptom and GAS change scores were examined within each sample to select those clients with the greatest amount of improvement within their respective samples. Specifically, the global symptom and GAS change score had to fall above the median within each sample to be retained.

Using the above criteria, 20 (31.3% of the available cases) were selected from the Vanderbilt II sample and seven (15.5 % of the available cases) were selected from the OUHRS sample, for a total of 27 cases. Two of the cases could not be analyzed further because of recording failures of the termination interviews. In terms of training and type of therapy, the majority of these good outcome cases were treated by therapists from the Vanderbilt study who were conducting TAU ($n = 12$), followed by TLDP ($n = 8$), and untrained doctoral students from other disciplines ($n = 6$). Only one case had a therapist who was in-training within the OUHRS sample.

Researchers

The research team consisted of a White male professor, a White male associate professor, an Asian American female assistant professor, and a White male advanced doctoral student. Researchers ranged from 42 to 51 years in age. All of the authors were adherents of the contextual model, one with more cognitive behavioral roots (Ogles) and another with psychodynamic–interpersonal roots (Anderson). One member of our team brought a multi-cultural studies lens from her work in social justice and health disparities research (Heckman). MacFarlane was influenced mostly by psychodynamic and experiential approaches. The team shared similar biases, although the differences noted above also influenced our interpretations. We started with a clear expectation that the CEs would be located within the therapeutic relationship and assumed that CEs would appear along the lines of traditional dynamic constructions of CEs (Alexander & French, 1946; Strupp & Binder, 1984). However, we also expected that the appearance of CEs might appear differently for different types of theoretical orientations or levels of training but that CEs should nonetheless manifest among a range of theoretical contexts.

Procedures

Corrective Experience Selection

CEs from therapy sessions were described retrospectively by clients during the termination interviews, which were conducted by independent clinicians. In addition to asking about various facets of the client's experience of change, clinicians also asked the client to identify whether there was anything that happened during the therapy and especially in the relationship with the therapist that was novel and might have contributed to the changes they had experienced.

To provide a more specific and systematic method for identifying CEs, only those change experiences that included an allusion to a contrast with the client's prior experiences were considered to be a CE. Operationally, a CE contrast was identified when clients described (a) a change that (b) was linked to an event or set of events, which were (c) specifically identified by the client as contrasting with their typical experiences from the past (i.e., "new"). Using this definition, a client who reported feeling less anxious than they felt at the beginning of therapy would not be considered to have had a CE. However, a client reporting feeling less anxious and calmer than ever before after the therapist encouraged her to look in the mirror and pinch her cheeks would fit this operational definition of having a CE.

All termination sessions were screened for CEs by the first author, last author, and three clinical psychology graduate students. The locations within these termination sessions for all possible contrast experiences were noted by each observer for later evaluation. Each potential CE was then reviewed by a second member of the research team to determine whether it met the above criteria of a CE. Mostly, the CE was in the same location of the semistructured termination interview and tended to occur when the assessing clinician asked the aforementioned question about new experiences or events that might have contributed to their improvements. Typically, one CE was identified, but when there was more than one CE, the CE that best fit the definition was selected.

Next, we searched the therapy session recordings to identify these CEs (identified from the termination sessions) for the location within the therapy sessions in which the CE occurred. If the CE occurred outside of the session, the first discussion of the CE event was located. Identifying the CE event was facilitated by allusions to time or other contextual cues that the client spontaneously provided while describing the CE contrast in the termination interview. Once located, both the actual CE from therapy and the retrospective description from the termination interview were examined using qualitative analysis. Having both the retrospective recall of the experience and the actual event from the therapy was useful for categorizing the CEs but was especially useful for identifying the contextual aspects of the CE.

Qualitative Procedures

Qualitative methods (Glaser & Strauss, 1967; Strauss & Corbin, 1990) in this project were broken into two phases. Phase I involved building meaningful categories of CEs that could aid our understanding of CEs and the contexts in which they occur. Initially, we attempted to understand the meaning of each individual self-reported CE from the termination interviews, along with the actual CE events from the therapy sessions. Then, by comparing and contrasting each individual case example with all other cases, we began to build meaningful groupings that were both practical and closely grounded in the data. At this point, each of the CEs and our initial impression of them were compared with all other cases using the constant comparative method (Glaser & Strauss, 1967; Strauss & Corbin, 1990). From these iterations of comparisons, meaningful groupings of practical, but higher order, categories emerged from the data. To keep the groupings closely grounded in the data, we again compared the original client reports of the CEs with the categories as a final step in creating the Phase I categories. This coding process continued in an iterative fashion until no additional coding yielded additional understanding of the model of clients' CEs.

This process allowed the researchers to maximize their understanding through a deep engagement with the material while following a rigorous and predetermined methodology. Through the coding procedure, the researchers' preexisting theoretical assumptions were critically questioned and evaluated in the light of the actual data to minimize the risk of using the data to confirm those preexisting assumptions. Detailed record keeping of the process allowed for reduced subjectivity and transparency in reporting the results.

Phase II built further on this Phase I analysis by conducting individual case study analyses. We examined each of the cases for which we identified the CE within the therapy sessions. The purpose of this additional analysis was to understand how the contextual model might enrich the theoretical understanding of how CEs emerged and operated in the therapeutic settings.

RESULTS

Phase I: Description of Corrective Experiences Using the Principle of Contrast

The standardized outcome scores did not significantly vary by therapist training status or by type of therapy (e.g., TLDP vs. TAU) on either the self-report symptom measure or GAS ratings. A total of 14 cases had CEs associated with specific events, 12 of which occurred within the therapy sessions. For the two CEs that occurred outside of therapy, we located the specific session in which the event was communicated in therapy. The mean session number in which the CE was located was the 11.9th session, and there was considerable variation ($SD = 9.6$ sessions, ranging from the 1st to the 25th and last session). The mean session for the CE was the 13.5th session in the Vanderbilt II sample (which had a 25-session limit) and only the 3.5th session for the OUHRS sample (which had only a seven-session limit). Table 14.1 provides an overview of the taxonomy derived through qualitative analysis of the CEs, including basic definition.

Relational Enactment With Therapist

These CEs were attributed to, and/or arose as a result of, interacting with a therapist who played a direct and often central role in enacting an interpersonal narrative with the client. The actual CE therapy events for this category appeared more manifestly dramatic compared with other instances of CEs from the other CE categories. Characteristics of the client's presenting problem could often be located within the CE event, but a defining characteristic of this category was that important elements were unique and fit the notion of a contrast principle insofar as they were new and different from prior interpersonal pattern or from the identified source of the client's distress.

This first CE category matched most closely to the Alexander and French (1946) prototype for a corrective emotional experience in that the therapist appeared to be enacting a unique relational drama with the client. These cases included enactments of specific events in which the therapist's actions were unique and often outside of what might be considered ordinary therapeutic practice and hence provided clients with a novel experience. At times, the idiosyncratic qualities of the client–therapist relationship were emphasized in the termination interviews. When we observed the contrast experiences to which the clients' referred, we found that these therapists were highly expressive, charismatic, and sometimes even bizarre in their methods. Some of these therapists appeared to talk as much or more than their clients, and the high level of spontaneity in emotional expression and behavior was

TABLE 14.1

Categories of Corrective Experiences (CEs)

Category/client interpersonal focus	Definition	Type of therapy and no. of clients				
		FT TLDP	FT TAU	PT TAU	Untrained	Total
	CEs that occurred in therapy sessions					
1. *Relational enactment with therapist/other*	Therapists play a direct and often central role in enacting an interpersonal narrative with the client. Contrast may appear more exaggerated and surprising when compared with other types of CEs.	1	2		1	4
2. *Client discovery of new experience/self*	The therapeutic relationship provides a supportive base for the client to discover new experiences. Although the therapist may play an important facilitative role in the discovery, the focus remains on the client's emerging new experience itself.	1	2			3
2a. *Client discovery of corrective anger/self*	In this subcategory, client anger had been forbidden or blocked from expression in their day-to-day lives. Therapists were supportive and warm in the service of encouraging the client to take risks to access and express anger.	1	3			4
2b. *Client experiences therapist-offered warmth/self*	The client experiences the therapist's warmth, empathy, and other positive relational experiences. The CE contrast is to other relationships and thus the therapist warmth fulfills unmet personal and relational needs in and of itself.	2	2		1	5

(*continues*)

TABLE 14.1
Categories of Corrective Experiences (CEs) (Continued)

Category/client interpersonal focus	Definition	Type of therapy and no. of clients				
		FT TLDP	FT TAU	PT TAU	Untrained	Total
3. *Therapeutic framework or structure facilitated CE/—*	The structure of the therapeutic framework itself provides a new experience. Knowledge of confidentiality, session length, regularity of therapist response modes provide the client with a contrast to ways of relating outside of therapy.	1			1	2
	CEs that occurred outside therapy sessions					
4. *Relational enactment outside of therapy/other*	A person outside of the therapeutic relationship plays a direct and often central role in enacting an interpersonal narrative with the client. Contrasts may appear more manifestly exaggerated and dramatic than other types of CEs.	1			1	2
5. *Self-directed CEs outside of therapy/self*	The client engages in self-reflection of emotional and psychological experiences and induces a mostly self-directed correction of their future experiences. The client may observe himself or herself behaving differently outside of therapy and incorporate that insight into future experiences.	2		1		3
6. *No contrast or environmental change/ other*	Although change is noted, there are no identified contrast experiences that are part of these changes. A contrast experience may be noted but linked only to an environmental change that is independent of changes in the client's experience.	1	2		1	4
Recording failures (missing)						2
Grand total						27

Note. FT TLDP = Fully trained, doctoral-level therapists practicing time-limited dynamic psychotherapy; FT TAU = Fully trained, doctoral-level therapist practicing treatment as usual; PT TAU = Partially trained, clinical psychology doctoral students practicing treatment as usual; untrained = untrained doctoral student in disciplines other than psychology or related mental health discipline. The first part of the table includes CEs in which the timing of the CE occurred within the therapy session and in the presence of the therapist (19 clients). The second part of the table contains categories where the CE occurred outside of the therapy session, including two clients who reported environmental change. These two groupings were further divided on the basis of the relational focus of the client toward others persons during the CE which were relatively more Other focused (i.e., Categories 1 and 4) versus those which were more self-focused (Categories 2 and 5). A dash indicates no determined interpersonal focus for that category.

noteworthy. Two of these therapists laughed loudly and heartily in response to their clients' disclosure of emotionally painful experiences. The specific contrast events observed in these cases often were highly idiosyncratic and diverged from ordinary therapeutic norms of practice.

Case examples from this category manifest these dramatic qualities. One of the cases (Anderson & Strupp, 2000) was previously studied in depth. That case was notable because the therapist, "Dr. C," made several provocative, often blatantly sexual comments to "Nancy" (the client) that were upsetting to her. She often responded by withdrawing and becoming quiet. However, Nancy agreed with the therapist's assessment (shared by Dr. C during the first two sessions) that she needed to become angry and battle with the therapist. In the termination interview, Nancy reported agreement with that initial assessment and that the experience of battling with Dr. C was contrasted with her typical interactions with her father. Specifically, she said that her father would "dissolve" in the face of her anger. However, Dr. C responded differently to the client's anger because "he got mad and said that I was wrong." The client reported that the therapist was not only frustrated with her but importantly that "he cared and really was involved after all."

Another example involved the same therapist with a different client. In her termination interview, the client reported that the therapist "would ask me to do different things, and I often had difficulty doing them." These requests for this socially inhibited client sharply contrasted with anything else she had ever done or could imagine. The specific example that she noted in the termination interview was that

> he told me to look in the mirror, and I thought he had someone behind the mirror. He told me to pinch my cheeks, and tell myself what I liked about myself. Vanity is a bad thing in my household. . . . It was very embarrassing.

However, the client found that, although discomforting, the somewhat paradoxical and exaggerated acts were a "revelation" and diffused the power of her concerns about vanity. Our general impression of the sessions was that the therapist appeared disinterested and bored when the client would report about her life in a somewhat dry and monotone manner. However, at various times he would inject himself into the session in dramatic ways, as described above.

Client Discovery of New Experience

The largest number of cases were categorized as *client discovery of new experience*. *Discovery* is meant to connote the clients' relatively more active role in the emergence and uncovering of the new experience, especially when compared with the manner in which clients were prompted or provoked in the *relational enactment with therapist* category. However, we found that the therapists played a significant role in these cases as well, although less manifestly demonstrative. In fact, the more we observed of these cases, the more we found ways in which the therapist played a significant role in the discovery of the new experience and may even have become the object of those expressed emotions. The therapist sometimes even seemed to be cheering the client on to take a risk and welcome the new experience. We identified two subcategories for client-supported discovery of new experiences.

Client Experiences Therapist Offered Warmth

Four of the cases appeared to be examples in which a generally positive, warm, and friendly therapeutic relationship provided a unique contrast to their prior experiences in which those positive qualities were absent or neglected. These general relational qualities were apparently difficult for many clients to pinpoint with examples of specific events. Three of the four clients in this category provided generic descriptions of the CE. However, the contrasts to prior unmet relational needs were clearly identified. For example, one client had previously found it difficult to be liked and accepted by others and very generically contrasted this with the warm relationship with the therapist. A different client said that she was able to open up around men because the therapist had simply paid a lot of attention to her.

There was some indication that the positive relational bond in therapy may have inherently fulfilled unmet personal and relational needs. In addition, some of these CE contrasts included a sense of surprise in discovering that the therapeutic relationship had become so important to them. One client described noticing the affective involvement of the therapist earlier in therapy, although he mentioned that he was "just doing his job." It was not until the last four sessions that the client realized that the therapist "really cared for me. This was confirmation that I had value. I never expected that he cared about me, until the very end." This client wonderfully described how basic warmth and caring translated into a CE:

> In fact it was the day that I left that he made some matter-of-fact statements that he had enjoyed himself. It was pretty clear that he had a personal viewpoint of me, and it was very nice. It's not the kind of impression that you have of people involved in that kind of role—to maintain complete objectivity as opposed to a level of involvement. That was very important and had a lot to do with why I felt better. [Nods head.] What I needed or had lost was that sense of value and sense of commitment about things. And with someone else having commitment, it made it easier for me to recommit to myself, my own basic values, which are not so bad. And I think that's pretty much all that I needed.

Client Discovery of Corrective Anger

Three of the clients had identified CE contrasts as the expression of angry experience. We found it interesting that each of these clients had noted that they had been the object of angry, dominant authority figures in their youth, and at least two of the three had attributed their own inability to express anger as being related to childhood experiences. These clients had previously forbidden or blocked anger in their day-to-day lives and the emergence of anger was often a theme within the therapies. For example, one client had always made herself available to others and had difficulty expressing her dissatisfaction when her needs were not met. The client's CE was located in the 16th session; the client was able to truly express strong anger and frustration at the therapist when he came late for the session. Unlike with Dr. C, these therapists did not overtly provoke the client's anger; they tended to provide more of a steady, supportive role for the emergence of new states of anger.

For example, in one case the client reported the therapist "all but begged me to be angry with her. She made it almost normal and said 'You *will* be angry with me.'" That same client noted that part of her struggle in expressing anger was that she could not express her anger in the moment and the therapist's encouragement helped her to express it, even though it had compounded over time. This encouragement was clear in part of her description of her CE:

> I was just very angry by the time I got around to telling her that I was angry. . . . But by the time I could tell her about that, I was angry about three things. . . . I mean, she was the first person, and believe me, that felt good. I was not going to do it even then. . . . And so I told her about it, and we talked, and talked and talked. And I was so glad. She was the *first* authority figure that I *successfully* dealt with my anger.

Finally, these clients' therapists were supportive and warm in the service of encouraging the clients to take risks to admit and experience feelings of anger. It is interesting to note that the contrast markers of the angry experience were sometimes not manifested noticeably in the sessions. For example, in the case example for this category (described below in Phase II), the client admitted to angry feelings with the therapist, but this did not emerge until several sessions following the original incident and after considerable encouragement by the therapist. This case had qualities of enactment (Category 1) in that the client's experience was related to the therapist having to miss sessions with the client. However, what placed the client's CE in the *client discovery of corrective anger* category was the fact that the therapist did not appear (and was not described by the client) to be prompting these feelings in the client in any sort of dramatic or provocative manner. Instead, the therapist was gently following and exploring the unfolding of this new experience, and both therapist and client seemed to be aware that the client needed to lead in this experiential journey.

Therapeutic Framework or Structure Facilitate a Corrective Experience

The CEs in this category focused on the basic rules and structure of the therapeutic framework, which appeared to provide these clients with assurance and safety. Knowledge of confidentiality, session length, regularity of therapist modes of responding, therapist expertise, and defined client and therapist roles are included in this category. For example, one client did not refer to the therapist directly but stated that she had not released much information in situations in which she did not feel protected and that rules around confidentiality was what allowed her to "let it out." Another client referred to how she was surprised by inaccurate expectations about her role in that she was pleasantly surprised that as the client, she directed the course of conversation in therapy.

Clearly, framework issues are not independent of the therapeutic relationship, and references to the conditions of therapy are often an allusion to the relational qualities of the therapist. For example, a client identified her CE as occurring in the first session of therapy when she felt that a big load had been lifted from her shoulders. She described the basic framework of therapy as providing her the safety to share issues around her sexuality. Having felt safe because of the therapeutic framework, she told the therapist her background history of having been rejected and humiliated by her family and church community after disclosing to them that she was a lesbian. The client commented on it directly in the first session, "My God, I have not talked about things that I have had in my head since I was 3 or 4 years old, things that I've seen and heard. And it's very, very difficult to articulate nondescript things." Certainly this client would not have felt safe to discuss her story with a therapist who did not demonstrate positive rapport skills. For example, in that first session the client said, "I'm very comfortable. And I feel a lot of warmth from you. I feel trusting ..." And then later, "I am not society's 'normal' example of what lesbian is, and I think you probably enjoy talking with me."

Relational Enactments Outside of Therapy

It is interesting that a number of CE contrasts were identified as occurring outside of therapy. Thus, we identified two cases in which a person outside of the therapeutic relationship played a direct role in enacting an interpersonal CE contrast experience with the client. Similar to the in-therapy version, these moments of contrast experience appeared more manifestly sharp and dramatic than other types of CEs. Also similar was that important elements of the contrast experience were new and different from prior interpersonal patterns and lent the possibility for experiencing the problem in a new way, which may or may not have been accompanied by insight or a new perspective.

In many of these cases in which the client's identification of the CE occurred outside of therapy, the relationship of the therapeutic work to the CE event was apparent to us. For example, one client had developed a very positive therapeutic bond and had numerous insights inside of the therapy sessions about how she would not stand up for herself and allowed others to take advantage of her. The therapist was practicing TLDP, and there were relatively frequent attempts to explore the therapeutic relationship. However, the CE contrast identified by the client occurred in a specific event in which she was able to express her anger at her father. She described how her father would come over to her house and would use her tools without asking for permission. She described being able to stand up to him by being able to turn off the electricity to her workshop area while he was using her tools. What this client found corrective about this experience was that she described her experience shifting from one of anxiety to one of a new and direct expression of anger.

Self-Directed Corrective Experience Outside of Therapy

This category of client CEs was analogous to the second within-therapy category in that the CEs involved a new and emerging internal experience. For these CEs, clients engaged in emotional and psychological self-reflection and as a result were able to induce a mostly self-directed correction of their future experiences. These CEs are noteworthy in that clients identified them as occurring outside of the therapeutic setting and dialog, even though we often could find a meaningful relationship to the within-therapy work and the CE that occurred outside of the therapy session.

For example, one client who was highly self-conscious described a CE when hosting an out-of-town guest and was concerned about the negative judgments that her guest would make about her. The CE contrast occurred when she recognized an emergent internal voice:

> And then I thought "I suppose he never has flaws, and I suppose . . ."
> And I just straightened that thing out. It was the one voice speaking to
> the other voice. And previously, I don't think I would have ever heard
> that second voice. All I had heard was the first voice. And I think that
> was an automatic kind of thing that I wasn't aware of.

This client observed her critical internal voice outside of therapy and was able to discover a new experiencer voice that went on to shape future experiences. Recognition of the new voice was consistent with the themes of therapeutic work, but the emergence of the new experience occurred outside of therapy.

Another client, treated by an untrained therapist, had a similar experience of being able to identify and correct obsessive and compulsive behaviors. It is interesting to note that this client made it clear that, even though she found the therapy experience generally helpful, her self-directed CE was almost entirely independent of the therapy experience.

> And then there's habits, like doing things in a specific order. And I just felt like if I didn't do it, there's going to be *problems*, you know. . . . And then a couple of times I would not do them and then I would stop for a minute and think, "No, I have to fix it," you know. And that's how it started off *not* doing it.

Noteworthy about this client's self-directed CE was that insight developed after her behavior. Thus, she became aware that she had been able to briefly perform tasks without obsessing and used her insight to reciprocally expand on the gains of her corrections.

Phase II: Adding Case Context to Understand Corrective Experiences as a Working Principle

We selected two cases for further examination of the CEs to understand the processes through which CEs emerged in treatment as well as to inform the clinical theory of CEs using the contextual model. The first case is from the *relational enactment with therapist* category and the second is from the *client discovery of new experience* category. To anticipate our conclusion, we believe that both cases illustrate how the CE may become a significant marker for the client because it occurs at a point in which a wide variety of contextual elements are meaningfully integrated for the client.

A Case of "Complexia": Relational Enactment With an Untrained "Therapist"

"Kathy," a 20-year-old university student with generalized anxiety disorder, reported feeling like "a worry wart" from constant anxiety that interrupted her sleep or her ability to find any moments of enjoyment. She also reported feelings of perfectionism and guilt for several unnamed sins, which were too numerous for her to list. She tended to feel more anxious when alone and lacked confidence and esteem in herself. Kathy wanted friends but had difficulty forming friendships because others did not share her values. She felt highly sensitive to the judgments of others. This feeling had been exacerbated at the beginning of treatment by a roommate who took pleasure in teasing and making fun of her. Her therapist, "Mr. Green," was in his mid-20s and working on his dissertation in history. Mr. Green was notably similar to Dr. C. (see Relational Enactment With Therapist section) because of his spontaneity, numerous self-disclosures, and other somewhat charismatic characteristics.

The CE contrast for Kathy was that Mr. Green differed from other relationships because he did not judge her or make fun of her for her fears, as did others in her social network. In fact, she noted in the termination interview that she had become able to laugh about her own fears in the presence of an understanding person. Mr. Green had a lighthearted approach and the interpersonal ability to laugh at her problems and at himself without laughing at her as a person. She noted, "He never made judgments, like 'Oh, you shouldn't have done that.' He was always like, 'That's a situation. Now, let's talk about what you can do now.'"

The therapeutic relationship appeared to be the primary source for her CE because the therapist normalized her problems through self-disclosure and laughter. Again, in the termination interview, she explained,

> He would tell me about things from his life that would help me illustrate my point a little more, and to help me through. I liked that aspect of it a lot. It was more like talking to a friend, but he didn't make it seem like I was telling someone all about my problems.

In our search for links to this CE within the therapy sessions, we found numerous examples of the generally positive ways that her relational experience with Mr. Green was different from her relationships with friends. However, one segment from the third session provides the best example. The client had exhausted her list of fears for the week, and she was not only engaged but even gleefully participating in making light of her own anxieties.

Kathy: Well, I was watching TV, and they were talking about if you pick your skin it is a huge sign of "complexity disorder." I don't even know what that is and I was just wondering if you knew what it was. And I don't think I have this complexity disorder, I just think I like picking my skin, and I am bored and I have done it ever since I was little.

Mr. Green: Exactly. Freud said . . . [Therapist is smiling as he seems to pretend taking an expert role.]

Kathy: I was just wondering what it was.

Mr. Green: Freud said sometimes a cigar is just a cigar. There is a point at which there is all these sorts of pop psychology—that might be a sign for people who have this disorder—it might be one of the things that they do.

Kathy: Right.

Mr. Green:	But it doesn't mean that everybody who does it has this disorder.
Kathy:	Exactly.
Mr. Green:	And yeah, otherwise, I probably have more disorders and neurosis, and I mean I am sure the guys in the white suits could come and throw me into the straitjacket and carry me away based on my problems. But in terms of what is it called? [Smiling widely.]
Kathy:	Complexity disorder?
Mr. Green:	Remember, I am not a psychologist, I just play one on TV. [Hamming it up, he turns to the camera recording the session.] So I have no idea. [There is more laughter.]
Kathy:	I know it is okay.
Mr. Green:	So I have no idea what that means or what it is. It sounds like to me it could either (a) be a concocted thing or (b) just you know someone grasped onto this and thought hey, we at *Nightline, Dateline* . . . whatever. Um, get it on there and let's make lots of remotely neurotic people do more neurotic things they have been doing their entire lives without realizing it was a problem.
Kathy:	Exactly. Let's set "Kathy" back a few more—a few more years.

At this point in the session the client reflected on her experience and described her CE in a clear and defined manner:

Kathy:	But it helps just to talk about it in my opinion. It doesn't matter that anybody—that anybody does anything bad or that you totally change your behavior based on it—but it helps me just to know that I can tell you almost anything, and I can tell you anything, and you won't tell anybody, and you won't think any less of me because I told you, and then I go out of here just feeling like this huge weight has been lifted off and for about 2 hours I am totally stress free.
Mr. Green:	And then it all starts over again. [Smiling.]
Kathy:	And then I am like can't wait until next Wednesday, got to go.
Mr. Green:	So if you had the time if you could go to therapy once every 4 hours, it would be very good. [Laughing.]
Kathy:	It would be really good. [Laughing.]

How might the contextual model aid in our understanding of how common factors coalesced into Kathy's CE? Most notable in the client's description of her CE was a strong, emotionally charged relationship. We saw Mr. Green as being unflappable in the face of the client's recounting of numerous fears, and he actually steered the discussion toward these fears. His approach tended to link the client's fearful content with the most warm and interpersonally engaging aspects of their relationship. Although he did not engage in a close, empathic tracking of the client's experience, such as would be expected from expert reflection and acceptance of feelings, Mr. Green nonetheless demonstrated a highly attuned awareness for when it was permissible for him to engage the client with humor-filled bantering about the client's fears. There were moments when the client gave signals that some fears were too great to approach, at which time the therapist would approach the topic more gingerly.

This sensitive modulation of his humor was also linked to the ritual (technique) of this untrained therapist. Mr. Green conducted the sessions systematically by opening a notebook and reviewing the client's primary fears and anxieties from previous sessions, as well as asking her to identify any fears and anxieties that were not on his list. When the client was in the midst of a story about how her life had been interrupted by a fear or phobia, the therapist would interject his own form of the client's fear in his own life (although we thought that he did not appear to be anxious about much of anything). At these points, he would expand and disclose about his own life and conclude with suggestions for how he had coped (or dismissed) the fear.

The myth (theory and rationale) of these segments seemed to be that fears should be approached and discussed in a fun, good-humored manner and that many fears could be dismissed but that other fears were legitimate, although they did not have to control one's life. This form of untrained exposure therapy can be explained through the integrative conceptualization of Wachtel (2007), even though Mr. Green had no training and was not conducting any recognizable form of therapy.

The combined culture (setting) and myth (theory and rationale) of the treatment was a significant aspect of the treatment as well. Mr. Green turned expectations on their heads and used his lack of expertise to the client's advantage (because he "just play[s] [a psychologist] on TV"). Fitting into his rationale that most fears and anxieties are overblown, he questioned aspects of the culturally derived profession of therapy as being part of the client's problem (by making "lots of remotely neurotic people do more neurotic things"). Perhaps with as much skill as a social constructivist, Mr. Green challenged the culture (setting) of the very chair from which he was sitting. In a delightfully mischievous manner, the entire discussion focuses on a faux disorder ("complexia"), and the Freud quote is used to make the point that worries and concerns are frequently not as substantial as they may first appear. These cultural (setting) elements of the segment are integrated with the myth (theory and rationale), ritual (technique), and emotionally charged relationship to form the CE.

A Case of Rational Anger: Client Discovery of Anger

"Claire," a 28-year-old woman in a highly paid profession, presented to therapy, stating that she had long-standing problems forming close and stable relationships, had a habit of focusing on others' needs often at the expense of her own needs, and suffered from recurrent bulimia. For Claire, the experiences of anger and hurt were difficult, and as such, she was often unable to express her dissatisfaction with others when her needs were not met. Claire was very self-conscious at the onset of treatment and often apologized for being tearful. However, as the alliance developed, Claire became more open, verbal, and animated in session, stating that her therapist (a psychodynamic therapist in the Vanderbilt II TAU group) was not as judgmental as her previous therapist and that she felt more comfortable confiding in the therapist.

The CE contrast in this case involved Claire's acknowledgement of anger toward the therapist and the unexpected experience of being validated for those feelings. The empathy and validation she received from the therapist countered feelings of guilt and beliefs that her anger must be stifled or "rational." The critical event for the CE occurred when the therapist had been ill and called to cancel their appointment for later that day. Claire had felt angry but did not disclose her feelings because she concluded that her anger was not rational. Initially, Claire stated that she had little reaction to the cancellation.

> Claire: I felt very comfortable that you would see me just as soon as you could and I also felt like I could have, if something really bad happened, and I couldn't handle it, that you would do everything that you could to accommodate me. I was not ever fearful that you would not accommodate me . . . I still never questioned that you were really sick. There was no way that you could see me. Yeah, I never questioned that, and I, ah, and feel that I still could have told you that I was having this awful, terrible time.

> Therapist: Except the one time that I called you and I was sick . . .

> Claire: Yeah.

> Therapist: Remember I could barely talk, and I had a real high fever. Was that the day you called?

> Claire: Yup.

> Therapist: Was that the day that you were going to put yourself in the eating disorders unit?

Claire: Yeah, that was the same day. And, but, I still never questioned that you were really sick. There was no way that you could see me. Yeah, I never questioned that, and I, ah, and feel that I still could have told you that I was having this awful, terrible time.

Therapist: That's what I wonder, the fear. If you feared telling me, if that's similar to, if you would have felt . . . because I couldn't have responded by coming into the office.

Claire: Yeah, there was no way you could.

Therapist: So you didn't even want to have the option of being rejected?

Claire: [Voice softens.] Now that may be true. There could probably be a lot of that, because I *knew* that you couldn't and so I . . . and that was the one time that I really . . . God, that was a horrible day. It was the third day of a three day. Oh, God! That was just horrible and the only way that I made it through Saturday and Sunday was because I knew that I was going to be in here on Monday. Now I say that it was the only way, but I'm sure that I would have made it through, because for years I made it through.

Therapist: But at least you stopped, because you knew that you were coming in. Didn't you stop?

Claire: Mm hm. Mm hm. And um, that was a real hard, that was just uhh!

Therapist: Did any, did it connect, after we talked, did you feel any differently?

Claire: I felt a little anger . . . because, I was like . . . which is, in one sense anger, and in another sense . . . irrationally, I felt anger. Rationally . . .

Therapist: Forget rationally. Anger is not rational. Anger is a feeling.

Claire: But how can you rationally be angry at someone when there's no thought? I mean, I was like, anger is usually directed at someone because they did something wrong. And if it's properly directed . . .

Therapist: Well . . . no, you know that you had a feeling and maybe there wasn't logic that I deserved your wrath, because I was sick. But your feeling was . . .

Claire: My feeling was "Darn, she picked a hell of a day to get sick!" [Claire and therapist laugh.]

Therapist: Yeah.

Claire:	Wooo! [There is lots of shared laughter.]
Therapist:	And there's *nothing* wrong with feeling that way! You don't have to negate that feeling. That it's perfectly okay.
Claire:	That's how I felt. There's just no other way to put it. That is exactly how I felt [laughing].
Therapist:	I'm sure you did and you needed to come in and talk about what was going on that day.
Claire:	And I felt so guilty about feeling that way . . . because it wasn't your fault. But I felt angry too. "Why today?" "Why me?" You know, but in a way, everything has good things that come out of it. And it forced me, it probably made me realize how important my therapy was to me. See, up until then it was one of my flaky deals that I do, you know [laughs]. Every once in a while I do something different to make a statement to myself, not really to anyone else but to make a statement to myself. And um, I realized that this is very important to me. So good things come out of it.
Therapist:	The people that you can feel angry at and then you feel guilty, that you feel angry at them, are the people that you're closest to.

At this point, the conversation shifted to discussing her guilt over becoming angry at her mother. She had repeatedly apologized to her mother for having become angry and to the point that her mother told her to quit apologizing. Even though the experience of anger was not detectible to us within the therapy session, this admission of anger constituted a new experience for Claire, who typically avoided expressing her emotions and needs. For Claire, such expressions were dangerous because she believed that they would lead to rejection by others. However, the therapist forced her to admit to her anger in the final sessions, and it was this admission by Claire, coupled with an accepting and validating response by the therapist, that led Claire to the CE. As reported by Claire in her termination interview, the CE was admitting to her anger and the experience

> that it was okay not to be perfect. She was the first person that I let see
> that [I] wasn't perfect, and she didn't reject me. She didn't reprimand me.
> She helped me feel that it's okay to not be perfect.

When we linked the CE contrast to the therapy sessions, the most striking discovery was that we could not find any overt displays of anger by Claire. Many of the therapist's interventions (myths and rituals) appeared focused to address Claire's inability to be genuine and spontaneous when around other people. The CE of admitting to her genuine feelings of anger was directly associated with the majority of the therapist's interventions, which highlighted Claire's tendency to (a) control her relationships (Therapist: "Were you invested in changing him?"), (b) have a low sense of self-worth underlying her constant need for external approval and validation (Therapist: "If you like yourself more, you may be more comfortable receiving it [e.g. praise, love]"), (c) be passive in expressing emotions and needs and sacrifice own emotional needs in romantic relationships, and (d) overidentify with her mother and behave with helplessness and passivity. In treatment, the therapist often related the client's thoughts, feelings, expectations and behaviors to those of her mother. Through questions and interpretations, he drew connections between Claire's choices and their uncanny similarity to her mother's choices. For example, the therapist frequently pointed out that, like her mother, she dealt with conflict and difficulties by denying her emotions and ignoring her needs.

Caretaking was a primary way for both mother and daughter to justify ignoring their own needs. For example, when discussing the mother's desire for Claire to have children so that the mother could take care of them, the therapist stated that for Claire's mother, "if you are taking care of other people, you don't have to be responsible for yourself." Thus, from the therapist's dynamic framework, the therapist's less reactive and somewhat neutral stance and interpretations about denial of her own needs provided an important link to the CE contrast of Claire's acknowledgement and admission to her anger toward her therapist.

The experience of acceptance and validation by the therapist was in sharp contrast to previously painful experiences of rejection in response to her expression of her needs that was ultimately corrective for Claire. In fact, the emotionally charged relationship is directly referred to in Claire's description of the CE contrast and slowly engendered trust in sharing her experiences with the therapist. The dynamic approach was also linked to how the therapeutic relationship fulfilled unmet emotional needs. The therapist avoided praising Claire in spite of her obvious attempts to earn admiration and approval for her therapeutic accomplishments. This neutral stance appeared paradoxically empowering for Claire by demonstrating to her that she was fully accepted, regardless of her progress in therapy or accomplishments. However, the therapist's warm tone of voice and obvious interest in the client's experiences conveyed warmth and acceptance and were obviously contributing to an emotionally charged relationship.

The CE was also infused with strong cultural factors that influenced her identity and the ways in which she experienced permission to acknowledge certain feelings express and embrace power in society. Claire's interpersonal relationships were strongly influenced by childhood interactions, especially an overidentification with her mother and the idealization of her father. In terms of her cultural background, Claire was raised in a largely patriarchal, German immigrant family that held traditional beliefs about the roles of the mother and father in the family. Thus, despite the fact that Claire's mother had a marketable skill with computers, which at the time was a potentially profitable career, Claire's mother assumed the role of homemaker and relinquished her career goals in support of her husband's education and career development. According to Claire, her mother made major self-sacrifices in her life and was very unhappy with her life circumstances. Her father, on the other hand, was the traditional breadwinner of the family and was withdrawn and emotionally unavailable in his daughter's life. For Claire, the only time her father noticed her was when she achieved.

Claire's cultural identity emerged in significant ways in the sessions leading up to the CE. One main topic that was discussed following the therapist's maternity leave pertained to Claire's own strong desire to have children, but how, as a young professional woman, she felt stifled from expressing those desires in both professional and personal relationships. Claire said that she felt "physically sick" when thinking about how companies for which she interviewed would find ways to ask about her desire to have children. In addition, she also felt uncomfortable with her desire for children because she had just ended a love relationship in which the man had had no desire for children. In the following two sessions, just before the CE, Claire elaborated on this failed relationship as well as other close relationships in which she felt unable to express herself. With her former boyfriend, she was "terrified" that if she expressed her needs that the man would see the "real me," and she would be rejected. Using the contextual model, the cultural representation of Claire's female identity in both her personal and professional life appears to be largely influenced and reinforced by a patriarchal value system that viewed children as a hindrance to career development. For Claire, this was psychologically oppressing, undermined her needs in romantic relationships, and stifled her ability to acknowledge and express needs to both self and others.

This case illustrates how the CE was influenced by numerous contextual factors. The integration of these factors of the therapeutic relationship, cultural influences, and the treatment factors were all significant influences in the emergence of the CE experience. Figure 14.2 provides a graphical depiction of how the CE contrast (splash in the figure) served an integrative function for these themes drawn from various contextual locations from within the contextual model (for convenience, we rotated the relationship factor to have each contextual factor equally spaced). We believe that the therapist's having given birth may have been a strong influence for the client to disclose feelings and desires that had been suppressed around her cultural self. The psychodynamic treatment rationale

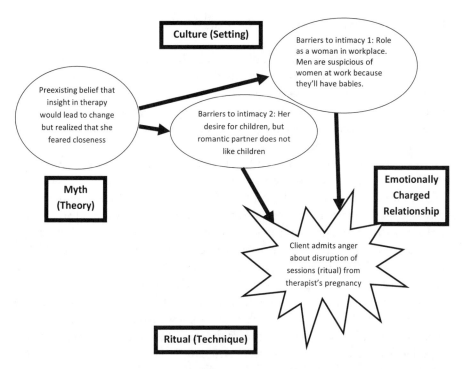

Figure 14.2. Illustrative contextual map for Claire's corrective experience.

and interventions, expressed through a warm, emotionally charged relationship with the therapist, was consistent with the cultural and psychological needs of the client. Issues described above in the session leading up to the CE also coordinate to contribute to the CE, metaphorically sparked by the confluence of contextual factors that likely lend meaning to the CE moment of contrast.

DISCUSSION

This study began with an operational definition of CEs as contrast experiences. We felt it important to have a clear-cut, although admittedly somewhat arbitrary, definitional anchor because of the relatively sparse amount of empirical work on CEs. Perhaps most noteworthy of our findings is that CEs occur in highly variable situations, settings, and relationships. We also propose that CEs might best be understood within the integrated contextual model. To discuss and explore these findings, we now return to address the four questions that framed our investigation.

Type of Corrective Experience Contrasts

First, we found from Phase I of our study that clients easily identified CE contrast experiences as important contributors to improvements in therapy. In fact, most clients described contrast experiences of one sort or another that exceeded our expectations. Of course, reporting an experience that describes some contrast from earlier experiences is not sufficient on its own to substantiate our propositions.

Second, we were impressed (and somewhat surprised by) the variety of CE contrasts, as well as the variety of contexts in which they occurred. CEs occurred both inside and outside of therapy, some included the therapist, but others appeared to be intrapersonal experiences. We found some CEs included a direct and dramatic enactment with the therapist (i.e., the *relational enactment with therapist* category), but these were a minority of cases. Other clients described CEs as developing through the therapy process as the therapist provided the openness and warmth that facilitated the client's discovery of emerging, new experiences that had not been previously available (*client discovery of new experience*). We were somewhat surprised that a number of clients identified the basic structure of therapy as the source for their contrast experiences (*therapeutic framework or structure facilitated CE*). We were also somewhat surprised by clients who described their CE as occurring outside of the therapy sessions, some of which were prompted by another person (*relational enactment outside of therapy*), as well as CEs that developed through the client's internal awareness and processing of their own experiences (*self-directed CEs outside of therapy*). In sum, the variety of contexts and relationships in which CEs occurred is one of the main findings of this study.

Many aspects of these categories can be found within Alexander and French's (1946) original theorizing. We originally thought of the *relational enactment with therapist*–type of CE as fitting most closely with the Alexander and French definition of a corrective emotional experience. However, we subsequently found that many aspects of Alexander and French's writing speak to several of the other varieties of CEs that we identified in the present study. Upon reinspection, we found it notable that Alexander and French's notion of a CE as a contrast is described as a something of dialectic between experiences inside versus outside of therapy. They further emphasized other contextual elements of the therapeutic setting and framework as one of many (contextual) tools for provoking new, corrective emotional experiences within the client:

> [It] is important to remember that the patient's new emotional experiences are not confined to the therapeutic situation; outside the treatment he has emotional experiences which profoundly influence him. The corrective emotional experiences within the transference situation enable the

patient to endure or to meet successfully life experiences which he had been unable to face before, and the influence of the treatment is itself reinforced by each such success. A proper coordination of life and therapeutic experiences is the basis for determining when a change in the frequency of the interviews or an interruption of treatment is necessary. (Alexander & French, 1946, p. 339)

We were also surprised by the great variety of relational targets in the CEs in this study. The nature and structure of the treatments offered in these two data sets likely enhanced the possibility that the therapist would be included in part of the CE with the client. For example, in TLDP a primary objective of the treatment is to create in-session corrective emotional experiences with the client through early and frequent exploration of transference. However, the TLDP-based CEs were not exclusively interpersonal. In CEs that were categorized as noninterpersonal, clients experienced the CE as more self-directed and at times independent of therapy. In CEs that are relational and occur in therapy, the categories identified suggests that the therapist's role in promoting the CE can vary from direct to indirect facilitation of the CE.

The CE categories also varied by their apparent location within the contextual model. Some of the categories were determined to be more closely related to specific contextual factors than others. For example, *relational enactment with therapist* seemed most closely aligned with Frank and Frank's (1991) emotionally charged relationship factor and closely akin to the interpersonal qualities of Alexander and French's (1946) corrective emotional experience. In contrast, the *therapeutic structure or framework facilitated CE* seemed more closely aligned with the culture (setting) factor in the contextual model. The importance of the setting was stressed by Frank and Frank and by Orlinsky and Howard (1986). The importance of frame and the ground rules of therapy are also stressed in many works on therapy application, such as Langs's (1989) mammoth two-volume guide on conducting psychoanalytic psychotherapy. However, we were surprised that several clients had stressed the simple structure and framework of therapy as being a major aspect of their CE.

Although we believe the categories of CE identified in this study add a richer understanding of CEs, we recognize the limitations of our method. The categories appear to be theoretically meaningful, but they are not mutually exclusive or final. There may be overlap among the categories, and certainly a larger sample of clients may result in types of CE that we did not identify. However, we sorted each client into the categories as if they were mutually exclusive. When adding context to the CEs in Phase II of this study, it was easy to see how most of the CEs in our study would touch on other categories. This was likely because the CEs seemed central to the client's issues and rooted in the overall therapeutic experience.

Our method provided some safeguards in applying the contextual model to these cases. It is noteworthy that the CEs identified as being due to environmental changes in the client's life from Phase I were strikingly unidimensional in nature. What likely distinguished these change events was that the corrective action was not meaningfully incorporated into the client's experience. Hence, the client's emotional and psychological experiences were not altered, except in the most superficial and reactive manner. That is, the correction had little or no influence on how the client routinely interpreted her world, and hence there was little opportunity for new meaning. It is true that these clients likely experienced a change in mood from the external event, but the event was not sufficient to catalyze shifts within psychological and emotional experience. The fact that these external events were not integrated with the client's experience is good reason to question whether such a change event should be classified as a CE at all. The external event appeared to be correcting a problematic mood, superficial as it might be, but the change was more of a reaction to the external event and not a meaningful correction of experience. Perhaps some other term, such as *corrective reaction*, might better describe these types of change experiences.

Third, CE contrast experiences in this sample occurred in therapies conducted by trained therapists, untrained individuals, and graduate student therapists. These therapists varied in orientation, background, and training. For those therapists in the Vanderbilt II study, many of the contrast experiences occurred with cases conducted in the TAU condition, before therapists received the TLDP-specific training. Finding contrast experiences across the wide range of individuals provides some initial evidence of the generic application and contextual nature of corrective experiencing. At the same time, behavioral and cognitive behavioral approaches were underrepresented in the sample, and additional work would be need to better substantiate our proposition that corrective experiencing is a principle of change that crosses orientations, training, and experiencing.

Placing Corrective Experiences Within an Integrated Contextual Model

Our fourth question asked whether using the contextual model would facilitate understanding how the contrast experience might combine with the contextual factors of therapy to produce a CE. We had theorized that CE contrast experiences would function at an intermediate level of abstraction within the integrated contextual model. The more limited scope of Phase I did not allow for the contextual elaboration and understanding necessary for understanding CEs within the integrated contextual model. At a descriptive level, the clients' recollections of their contrast experiences, mostly during the termination interviews, varied widely in terms of their level of abstraction.

Some of these contrast experiences were remembered as specific events at the level of momentary experience, whereas others were recalled as a more abstract and generalized experience or collection of experiences (e.g., general relational qualities with the therapist). However, our interest in understanding CEs as a psychotherapy principle was less about these stylized differences in recollection and more about how these CE contrast experiences might serve an organizing, integrative function of various contextual elements of the treatment. Thus, Phase II of our study was needed to evaluate whether CEs operated at this principle level of abstraction within the contextual model because the more careful evaluation of cases from Phase II provided the opportunity to place these contrast experiences alongside of other contextual factors (i.e., culture, orientation, techniques, relationship).

Contrast Experience as a Marker

Because the operational definition of a contrast experience was designed as a method for studying CEs, we tended to use these terms synonymously during our analysis. Understanding the relationship between these identified contrast experiences, the CEs, and the eventual therapeutic outcome is an area for future study. There are some reasons for keeping contrast experiences and CEs conceptually distinct. A contrast experience often was reported as a specific event that was momentary in nature, often required links to other experiences and context in order to reach a principle level of abstraction. We suggest that there is much to be learned about CEs through understanding the layers of meaning that surround the moment of contrast and how such moments may develop and mature into an identifiable CE. Thus, if a specific contrast experience can be located within a therapy session, it may become a significant marker (e.g., Greenberg, Rice, & Elliott, 1993), a directional signpost, of the larger change processes occurring within the treatment. Identifying the CE contrast as a marker might facilitate future research in locating more significant aspects and mechanisms within the change process. In the current study, we referred to the CE contrast moments in the termination interviews as markers of therapeutic tasks already completed (e.g., Claire's disclosure that she had been angry). The marker often pointed to the completion of a process that had been initiated much earlier (e.g., Claire's moment of experiencing anger) and became meaningful only when adding the contextual elements of the case. Thus, the markers or contrast experiences facilitated our identifying CEs and their variety of expressions (Phase I of our study), but these contrast experiences needed to be contextualized to locate them at a principle level of abstraction and to understand their significance within the client's life (Phase II).

It is unclear how much the client's recollection of a contrast experience, which is a marker or signpost in its own right, represents the location where change takes place. The purpose and method of the present study could not address the extent (or whether) the CEs and contrast experiences contributed to the overall change for this group of successful outcome cases. However, we found several of these contrast experiences to be moving and convincing. If the client-identified CE was not the actual point of change, it seemed plausible to propose that the actual mechanism or catalyst for change might be located proximally nearby in time (within the session) or linked to the content of the CE.

Contextual Integration

When we examined cases more carefully, the layers of contextual factors surrounding the CE immediately became more apparent and meaningful. These cases demonstrated how the linking of contextual factors, like the spokes of a wheel, may have strengthened the meaningfulness of these CE moments for clients. In fact, we suspect that the more that the CE can encompass multiple layers of context, the more likely it is to leave a lasting impression on the client. For example, in the case of Kathy, we began by identifying Kathy's CE contrast as being attributed to an emotionally charged relationship with the therapist. Upon closer examination, it was clear that many of the positive emotions shared between Mr. Green and Kathy were linked to his status as a faux therapist, which itself was skillfully used as an analogous representation of Kathy's worries as faux problems. Yet, Mr. Green tried to follow a style in which he played the role of therapist, or some shared representation of a therapist, by methodically asking her to identify and making a written record of her every worry. What was corrective, then, was not the simple replacement of an idea with a new idea, an act for an act, an emotional shift, or cultural awareness and acceptance; rather, the experience was the meaningful integration of all of these. For some reason unknown to us, the discussion around the faux disorder of complexia provided the platform through which all of these contextual elements could shape a new meaning within the client's life narrative around worries and anxieties.

Similarly, in the second case example, Claire was able to admit and own her anger and benefit from a contrast response in which the therapist reacted with genuine acceptance, an attitude that differed greatly from Claire's early experiences with her parents. However, this CE emerged at the end of treatment and within a context of therapy in which the setting was neutral and nonjudgmental, allowing Claire to explore and acknowledge the family, cultural, and sociopolitical roots of her poor self-esteem and lack of assertiveness in her relationships. As in the case example with Kathy, there was not one element but, instead, the meaningful integration of all these contextual elements in Claire's therapy that promoted the emergence of a CE.

Consistent with Frank and Frank's (1991) notion of culture, a Western-based individual psychotherapy setting and framework thus appeared significant to both cases. In addition, the use of the contextual model facilitated the identification of important cultural and sociopolitical factors that were deeply embedded in the clients' life narratives. For example, Claire was raised in a largely patriarchal family environment that held traditional cultural beliefs about the roles of men and women in the family. These cultural beliefs framed many of her struggles and, on the basis of the therapist's rationale and procedures in treatment, influenced the therapeutic process and dynamic. In both case examples, the contextual model enabled the evaluation of the CE from not only a person-centered perspective but also from a culture-centered approach that emphasized the importance of family, sociopolitical factors, and the extent to which these cultural factors guide all other contextual elements of therapy. According to Parham (1999) and Taub-Bynum (1984), this "collective cultural unconscious" develops from the cumulative experiences that individuals encounter in the overarching cultural context within which they and their families are situated and that both the therapist and the client bring to all psychotherapeutic settings.

Corrective Experiences Are Uniquely Calibrated to Clients Within a Context

We found it noteworthy that the overall thresholds for contrast experiences were highly individual and uniquely calibrated for each individual client. What becomes a corrective contrast for one individual may not be corrective to another person. Again, the notion of the contrast experience as a marker for the CE is useful here as well because the meaningfulness of the marker was not always clear when we observed these therapy segments in isolation from the larger context or narrative in which they occurred. In Chapter 2 of this volume, Goldfried notes that often initial reports of CEs are reported by clients as casual and seemingly nonconsequential events (e.g., passing observations at the end of the session). Goldfried explains this phenomenon as being due to the fact that clients have yet to integrate genuine change experiences into a self-schema. It would be understandable if therapists spend a significant amount of time guessing and trying to understand how ready a client might be to integrate new experiences. On the basis of our findings, it might also be asked whether therapists might calibrate expectations and understandings of clients to better identify client CEs within sessions or perhaps to earlier recognize what might potentially become a CE. Although we would like to believe that therapists can predict and deliberately introduce new experiences, our findings suggest that this did not appear to happen in several cases. It is possible that a therapist might improve in calibrating when a client might be ready for a new experience by increasing his or her sensitivity to the threshold at which new experience confronts a client's pre-existing expectations—too little new information and the client is unaware, whereas too much may be overwhelming and equally ineffective. Therapists cannot know the just-noticeable difference that will prompt a CE without having an intimate awareness of the client's experiential world. An example of this unique calibration was seen in Claire's disclosure of anger, which was barely identifiable to our observations but was highly meaningful and corrective from her point of view. However, even when finding the correct level of calibration, it is often necessary for further developments of the contrast experience before it fully blossoms into a CE. As noted, a significant lesson from this study was that contrast experiences and CEs were not simultaneous events. In the case of Claire, accepting irrational anger within herself was not apparent to Claire at the time in which she had identified her experience of angry feelings when the therapist called to cancel their appointment. The CE of disclosing that previously forbidden experience to an important person (the therapist) occurred weeks later. The contextual model provided a lens for understanding how the contrast experience served as a marker in which numerous other important experiences had become attached, evolving into a context-rich cluster of experiences (the CE). Our understand was that it was this synthesizing and organizing of experiences that gave the CE enough power to become a meaningful moment of change. Thus, Claire illustrates that the linking of experiences after the initial contrast experience often requires an incubation period, perhaps time for additional experiences to be shaped and assimilated for that initial contrast to become truly corrective. This aspect of Claire is similar to the CE in Victor Hugo's *Les Miserables*, originally described by Alexander and French (1946) when introducing the corrective emotional experience construct. In the novel, Jean Valjean's contrast experience of being exonerated by a bishop was initially not a positive influence but instead unleashed a destructive rampage. It was not until many significant events had transpired that this contrast developed into a full CE. Only years later, after maliciously stepping on the hand of a child and robbing him of his coin, insight emerged from the bishop's simple act of grace, transforming the contrast experience into a CE. Similarly, Claire had experienced anger toward her therapist much earlier when the therapist had cancelled her appointment, and she found the experience to be corrective only later through links to a wider context of experiences. For Jean Valjean, the CE may have needed to be integrated with stark interpersonal interactions and widespread social changes (the French Revolution), but fortunately psychotherapy does not require such dramatic events to inspire CEs for most clients. We suspect that the internal dramas of clients who experience CEs, although not always apparent to initial observation, frequently are no less dramatic and consequential to their lives.

Although the construct of the CE has long been used in clinical practice and theory to describe the most significant points of client change, the scientific understanding has lagged far behind. Similarly, CEs have been frustratingly elusive as an empirical research topic. The present study provided a basic descriptive framework for CEs that began with a theoretically grounded operational definition of the contrast experience. That CEs occur both inside and outside of therapy, as well as through both interpersonal and intrapersonal processes, was not expected at the outset of this study. We conclude that CEs are a wide-ranging phenomenon that at this point can best be described by their variety of manifestations. Because of this variation in how CEs appear, future research might be advanced through a more specific approach to studying subclasses or the therapeutic processes that relate to the emergence of CEs. For example, what therapist interpersonal behaviors are most likely to occur for clients who experience a CE in which there is a relational enactment with the therapist? Are there traces of failed CEs for clients who have outcomes that are negligible, and why do these contrast experiences not develop into full-fledged CEs? Further, if CEs serve as a principle of change, integrating contextual information from the client's culture along with treatment techniques, orientation, and the therapy relationship, then it might also be useful to identify broader client outcomes in therapy through these same factors. Clearly, considerable research will be needed to understand the conditions under which clients are capable of integrating new experiences within a wide range of prior experiencing.

REFERENCES

Alexander, F., & French, T. M. (1946). *Psychoanalytic therapy: Principles and applications.* New York, NY: Ronald Press.

Anderson, T., Lunnen, K. M., & Ogles, B. M. (2010). Putting models and techniques in context. In B. Duncan, S. Miller, & B. Wampold (Eds.), *The heart and soul of change* (2nd ed., pp. 143–166). Washington, DC: American Psychological Association.

Anderson, T., & Strupp, H. H. (2000). *Training in time-limited dynamic psychotherapy: A systematic comparison of pre- and posttraining cases treated by a single therapist.* Unpublished manuscript, Ohio University, Athens.

Derogatis, L. R. (1983). *SCL-90–R: Administration, scoring, and procedures manual for the revised version.* Baltimore, MD: Clinical Psychometric Research.

Endicott, J., Spitzer, R. L., Fleiss, J. L., & Cohen, J. (1976). The Global Assessment Scale: A procedure for measuring overall severity of psychiatric disturbance. *Archives of General Psychiatry, 33,* 776–771.

Frank, J. D., & Frank, J. B. (1991). *Persuasion and healing: A comparative study of psychotherapy.* Baltimore, MD: The Johns Hopkins University Press.

Glaser, B., & Strauss, A. (1967). *The discovery of grounded theory: Strategies for qualitative research*. Chicago, IL: Aldine.

Goldfried, M. R. (1980). Toward the delineation of therapeutic change principles. *American Psychologist, 35,* 991–999. doi:10.1037/0003-066X.35.11.991

Greenberg, L. R., Rice, L. N., & Elliott, R. (1995). *Facilitating emotional change: The moment-by-moment process*. New York, NY: Guilford Press.

Knight, Z. G. (2005). The use of the "corrective emotional experience" and the search for the bad object in psychotherapy. *American Journal of Psychotherapy, 59,* 30–41.

Lamert, M. J., Lunnen, K., Umphres, V., Hansen, N. B., & Burlingame, G. (1994). *Administration and scoring manual for the Outcome Questionnaire (OQ-45.1)*. Salt Lake City, UT: IHC Center for Behavioral Healthcare Efficacy.

Langs, R. (1989). *The technique of psychoanalytic psychotherapy: Technique of psychoanalytic psychotherapy*. New York, NY: Aronson.

Levenson, H. (1995). *Time-limited dynamic psychotherapy: A guide to clinical practice*. New York, NY. Basic Books.

Newman, M. G., Stiles. W. B., Janeck, A., & Woody, S. R. (2006). Integration of therapeutic factors in anxiety disorders. In L. G. Castonguay & L. E. Beutler (Eds.) *Principles of therapeutic change that work* (pp. 187–200). Oxford, England: Oxford University Press.

Orlinsky, D. E., & Howard, K. I. (1986). Process and outcome in psychotherapy. In S. L. Garfield & A. E. Bergin (Eds.), *Handbook of psychotherapy and behavior change* (3rd ed., pp. 311–381). New York, NY: Wiley.

Parham, T. A. (1999). Invisibility syndrome in African descent people: Understanding cultural manifestations of the struggle for self-affirmation. *The Counseling Psychologist, 27,* 794–801. doi:10.1077/0011000099276003

Strauss, A., & Corbin, J. (1990). *Basics of qualitative research: Grounded theory procedures and techniques*. Thousand Oaks, CA: Sage.

Strupp, H. H. (1993). The Vanderbilt psychotherapy studies: Synopsis. *Journal of Consulting and Clinical Psychology, 61,* 431–433. doi:10.1037/0022-006X.61.3.431

Strupp, H. H., & Binder, J. L. (1984). *Psychotherapy in a new key: A guide to time-limited dynamic psychotherapy*. New York, NY: Basic Books.

Taub-Bynum, E. B. (1984). *The family unconscious*. Wheaton, IL: Quest.

Weinberger, J. (1993). Common factors in psychotherapy. In G. Stricker & J. R. Gold (Eds.), *Comprehensive handbook of psychotherapy integration* (pp. 43–56). New York, NY: Plenum Press.

15

THE STREAM OF CORRECTIVE EXPERIENCES IN ACTION: BIG BANG AND CONSTANT DRIPPING

MARTIN GROSSE HOLTFORTH AND
CHRISTOPH FLÜCKIGER

Other chapters in this book have described or investigated corrective experiences (CEs) in a variety of contexts. Some of them, for example, have presented how CEs are understood within particular theoretical orientations, and others have studied how they manifested themselves in the different treatment (or training) settings. In contrast, this chapter investigates a specific issue about CEs, but one that is likely to cut across different orientations, settings, and patient populations. The issue investigated is related to the way that CEs might take place in therapy: Do they manifest themselves primarily as single and events, and/or do they tend to build themselves gradually, as accumulations of smaller but incremental therapeutic episodes?

Specifically, the chapter describes the results of a study investigating these two indicators of psychotherapy trajectories (i.e., "big bang" and "constant

We are very grateful to Hansjörg Znoj for providing the patient data of the Bern Outpatient Clinic from 2000 to 2008. Both authors were actively engaged at the Bern Outpatient Clinic during the period of data collection. We are also grateful for the valuable conceptual and practical inputs of the research and therapy teams of the clinical psychology and psychotherapy section at the department of psychology at the University of Bern. This study was supported by Grants P00P1_123377/1 and PA00P1_124102.

dripping") of CE, and their relationship with outcome. Before presenting this study, however, we briefly describe the theoretical context we have adopted for our investigation (i.e., Grawe's, 2006, consistency theory). In this model, CE can be facilitated by two mechanisms of change (the clarification of patient's motivation and the patient's mastery of his or her problem), both of them assumed to contribute to favorable therapy outcomes.

GENERAL CHANGE MECHANISMS AND CORRECTIVE EXPERIENCES

According to consistency theory, the therapy process frequently involves a number of tasks or goals. Although many tasks or goals may be shared by various approaches, the interventions used to achieve them can vary from one orientation to another. On the basis of an extensive study of the findings of controlled therapy studies and naturalistic process-outcome studies (Grawe, Donati, & Bernauer, 1994; Orlinsky, Grawe, & Parks, 1994), Grawe (1997) summarized psychotherapeutic interventions by four general change mechanisms: (a) resource activation, (b) problem activation, (c) motivational clarification, and (d) mastery–coping.

The mechanism of *resource activation* is realized in interventions that focus on the sound and healthy parts of the patient's personality rather than on the patient's problems (de Shazer, 1988; Erickson & Rossi, 1979; Flückiger, Caspar, Grosse Holtforth, & Willutzki, 2009; Gassmann & Grawe, 2006; Wood & Tarrier, 2010). Working with activated strengths is assumed to initiate and maintain positive feedback circuits, foster the therapeutic relationship, reinforce patients' positive expectations for change, and increase patients' openness to therapeutic interventions (Flückiger, Wüsten, Zinbarg, & Wampold, 2010). The change mechanism *problem activation* refers to the assumption that a patient needs to come into direct contact with painful emotions to overcome his or her problems (Gassmann & Grawe, 2006). Exposing the patient to previously avoided stimuli in behavior therapy, focusing on the emotional core themes in emotion-focused therapy, and addressing the patient's problematic transferences in psychodynamic therapies are all instances of problem activation.

Whereas resource activation and problem activation are considered catalysts for change, motivational clarification and problem mastery are assumed to involve specific types of CEs by the patient (Alexander & French, 1946; Goldfried, 1980; London, 1969). *Motivational clarification* involves becoming aware of the motivational determinants of one's unpleasant emotions (e.g., wishes, fears, expectations, standards); reevaluating one's negative primary appraisals (Lazarus, 1991) of situations and events (Grosse Holtforth, Grawe, & Castonguay, 2006); and changing one's intentions in clarity, direction, or strength. Such motivational clarification can facilitate CEs, as it can lead a person (to use the Penn State University [PSU] definition of this construct; see Chapter 1, this volume) to "understand or experience affectively an event or relationship in a different and unexpected way" (p. 5). Motivational clarification experiences may occur in the context of a variety of interventions, such as classical psychoanalysis, other psychodynamic therapies, gestalt therapy, emotion-focused therapy, or schema therapy.

For Grawe (2006), however, a CE is not restricted to experiencing a new understanding (clarification) but can also lead to the experience of new behaviors (i.e., new ways of coping and/or a greater sense of self-efficacy—mastery experiences). The experience of mastering one's problems and/or better coping with them represents a change in the patient's secondary appraisal of situations (Lazarus, 1991). *Mastery–coping* experiences are assumed to relate to events that confer a better sense of self-efficacy (Bandura, 1977), as well as a change in one's coping strategies and behaviors. Classical behavior therapy represents the prototype of a therapy approach that predominantly aims at mastery–coping experiences (Grosse Holtforth et al., 2006). In single therapy sessions, CEs are assumed to be generated by first triggering the cognitive–emotional schemata underlying the patient's problematic experiences and behaviors and then by overlaying them with new ones (Grawe, 2006; Greenberg & Safran, 1987; Grosse Holtforth et al., 2006).

To clarify the synergistic interplay of the general change mechanisms according to consistency theory, consider the following clinical example:

> Mr. C was diagnosed with social phobia. The first sessions of his therapy focused on understanding the difficulty of getting in contact with other people. Following general psychoeducation, he linked his avoidance of certain social situations to a feeling of inferiority when being exposed to such situations. These feelings reminded him of many very painful situations of his school days, when he was frequently ridiculed by classmates. Based on a better understanding of his current negative self-esteem (a clarification experience), he was able to better understand his irritation in a recent phone call with his best friend, when the latter made fun of him (problem activation). He remembered that he previously succeeded in managing comparable situations within a group of colleagues. Based on these memories, he was able to capitalize on his preexisting abilities (resource activation). He learned to be more relaxed during phone conversations with his friend, take his jokes more lightly, and respond also with jokes (mastery experience). Along with being more relaxed, he experienced that his fears of being ridiculed did not materialize (another clarification experience).

BIG BANG AND CONSTANT DRIPPING

The potentially corrective information, as well as the associated experiences, may take the form of singular macroevents (big bang) and/or may present as cumulative microevents (constant dripping [wearing away the stone]). The micro–macro distinction relates closely to the concepts of first- and second-order changes by Watzlawick, Weakland, and Fisch (1974) or to the concepts of assimilation and accommodation by Piaget (1977). However, for the current purposes, it is important to note that according to Piaget (1977), assimilation and accommodation are two inseparable processes that are in permanent interaction. For example, in cognitive behavior therapy (CBT), psychoeducation and the fostering of change expectations (assimilation) may prepare the ground for cognitive restructuring as a result of exposure (accommodation). In this sense, smaller assimilations may pave most of the way to a big accommodation (Kanfer & Schefft, 1988).

AN EMPIRICAL ANALYSIS OF CHANGE EXPERIENCES OVER THE COURSE OF PSYCHOTHERAPY

In our previous research, the clarification and mastery measures have demonstrated their potential to explain the therapy process and predict outcome (Flückiger, Regli, Zwahlen, Hostettler, & Caspar, 2010; Grosse Holtforth et al., 2006). With the present study, we expand this line of research by examining the trajectories of change experiences to clarify the related processes of change further.

We model the change process as apparent in experiences of clarification and mastery in a naturalistic sample of psychotherapy patients and relate parameters describing the trajectories of these experiences to the therapy outcome. It is important to note that the PSU consensus definition of CEs implicitly favors singular and identifiable events over a corrective accumulation of smaller miniexperiences. Thus, our main research question is whether treatment outcome is a question of big-bang change experiences (big C) or a constant dripping of smaller change experiences (small cs). We hypothesize that the overall level of change experiences reported by patients after each session is a better predictor of positive outcomes than extraordinarily strong change experiences in single sessions. If the big bang model described the data well, positive peaks should be most predictive of positive outcomes. If the constant dripping model described the data well, the estimated intercepts of the individual trajectories should predict positive outcomes. We examine the other estimates of the shapes of change experiences over time and their relationships with outcome for descriptive and exploratory purposes.

METHOD

The study uses naturalistic patient data that were collected at the psychotherapy outpatient clinic of the University of Bern, Switzerland, between 2000 and 2008.

Patients and Therapists

From a total of 429 patients who started psychotherapy and provided postsession reports, 223 patients returned outcome questionnaires at post assessment. On average, patients were 36 years old (SD = 12.5), and 53% were women. Principal diagnoses at intake were: 36%, affective disorder; 36%, anxiety disorder; 11%, adjustment disorder; and 17%, other disorders according to the Structured Clinical Interview for *DSM–IV* (SKID; Wittchen, Zaudig, & Fydrich, 1997). Patients were treated by 108 therapists (mean age = 34.9 years, SD = 6.4; 64 % were women). The majority of these master's level psychologists (87 %) had a minimum of 2 years of postmaster psychotherapy training. The therapists were supervised biweekly in small groups.

Treatment

The therapists practiced general psychotherapy (Caspar & Grosse Holtforth, 2010; Grawe, 1997, 2004). *General psychotherapy* is an integrative form of CBT that differentially combines specific empirically supported interventions from cognitive–behavioral, process–experiential, and interpersonal interventions with therapeutic strategies for fostering a custom-tailored therapeutic relationship, as well as capitalizing on the patient's strengths. In general psychotherapy, the change targets are the identified sources of insufficient need satisfaction, assuming that the better satisfaction of associated goals is the mediator leading to symptom reduction and better well-being. Specific interventions included interventions aiming at mastery experiences (e.g., learning problem-solving strategies), as well as clarification-oriented interventions aimed at resolving motivational conflicts (e.g., two-chair exercises). In an individual case formulation, the therapist identifies the overall level of need satisfaction in the patient's life, specific unsatisfied goals, and the sources of this dissatisfaction. The individual therapy sessions typically lasted 50 minutes.

Measures

After each session, change experiences were assessed using the Bern Post-Session Report for patients (BPSR-P; Flückiger, Regli, et al., 2010).

This 22-item self-report scale was developed based on the model of general change mechanisms by Grawe (1997), as well as previous versions of the measure (Grawe & Braun, 1994). Its scales represent four mechanisms of change, that is, problem activation, resource activation, clarification, and mastery–coping, plus a scale for the therapeutic relationship. For this analysis, we used the Clarification subscale (three items; item example: "I understand myself and my problems better now"; Cronbach's α = .80) and the Mastery–Coping subscale (three items; item example: "Now I feel better prepared for situations I could not handle before"; Cronbach's α = .85) of the BPSR-P. The items are answered on 7-point Likert scales ranging from −3 (*not at all*) to 3 (*yes, exactly*). The BPSR-P has shown a satisfactory factor structure, $\chi^2(428) = 576$, comparative fit index = .94, root-mean-square error of approximation = .057, standardized root-mean-square residual = .052, as well as evidence of validity in a larger sample of the same clinic (Flückiger, Regli, et al., 2010). By taking whole sessions as units of analysis, postsession BPSR-P ratings can be seen as patient reports on experiential results of in-session processes.

Three self-report scales assessed therapy outcome. The summary score of the revised Goal Attainment Scaling (GAS; Kiresuk & Lund, 1979; Willutzki, 1999) indicates how patients evaluate their improvement regarding therapy goals being individually specified at the outset of therapy. The German version of the Global Severity Index (GSI) represents the overall severity of various psychological symptoms as measured by the Brief Symptom Inventory (BSI; Franke, 2000; Cronbach's α = .94). The global score of the Inventory of Interpersonal Problems (German version, IIP-64-D; Horowitz, Strauß, & Kordy, 2000; Cronbach's α = .81) measures the general distress that patients experience in interpersonal relationships (Flückiger, Regli, Grawe, & Lutz, 2007). The versions of IIP-64-D, BSI, and GAS that we used are widely utilized in German-language psychotherapy research (Grosse Holtforth, Grawe, & Lutz, 2009).

Procedures

At intake, patients participated in an interview with an experienced psychotherapist, a separate standardized interview for *DSM–IV* classification (SKID) with a master's level psychologist in postgraduate psychotherapy training, a session for the completion of standardized questionnaires (including BSI and IIP-64-D) supervised by a bachelor's level clinical psychology student, and an optional interview together with a significant other of the patient's choice. There was no standardized assessment of personality disorders. After treatment, patients completed the same battery of standardized questionnaires, together with retrospective outcome measures including the

GAS. A reduced number of questionnaires was completed by patients every 10 sessions, and the BPSR-P was completed after each session (Grosse Holtforth et al., 2009). Patients gave their informed consent to the procedures before the intake interview.

RESULTS

In our empirical analysis, we first describe the shape of trajectories of change experiences, then examine the associations between single parameters of change estimates, and finally relate the change estimates to therapy outcome.

Indicators of Individual Change: The Shape of Trajectories of Clarification and Mastery Experiences

Using hierarchical linear modeling (Bryk, & Raudenbush, 1992; Raudenbush, Bryk, Cheong, & Congdon, 2004), four estimates or indicators were calculated to describe individual trajectories (see Figure 15.1):

1. *Intercept:* The intercept that is centered to Session 3 is an indicator of the early processes in therapy.
2. *Slope:* The slopes describing the log-linear increase of intensity of experiences over the whole course of therapy.

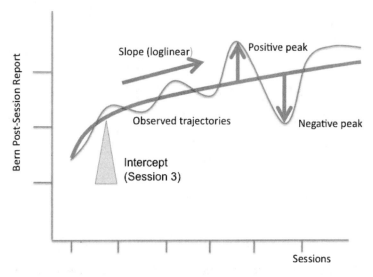

Figure 15.1. Descriptive dimensions of individual trajectories.

TABLE 15.1
TABLE 15.1
Descriptives of the Trajectories of Corrective Experiences
(Mastery and Clarification)

| | BPSR-P | | | | | | | |
| | Mastery | | | | Clarification | | | |
Indicator	*M*	*SD*	Max.	Min.	*M*	*SD*	Max.	Min.
Intercept$_{Session 3}$	.57	.052	2.7	−1.8	.90	.044	2.7	−.1
Slope$_{log 10}$	.82	.037	3.2	−1.2	.50	.030	2.7	−.7
Positive peak	.96	.030	2.2	−.5	.95	.028	2.0	−.3
Negative peak	−1.28	.058	.3	−4.8	−1.17	.045	.7	−3.2

Note. BPSR-P = Bern Post-Session Report for patients; Max. = maximum; Min. = minimum.

3. *Positive peak:* Representing the highest divergence between the estimated and the observed values on the postsession reports after Session 3 in the positive direction.
4. *Negative peak:* Representing the highest divergence between the estimated and the observed values on the postsession reports after Session 3 in the negative direction.

Descriptive information about the shapes of the trajectories of clarification and mastery experiences is given in Table 15.1. Figure 15.2 depicts the log-linear trajectories over 20 sessions of therapy. We intercorrelated the four indicators (intercepts, slopes, positive peaks, and negative peaks) between

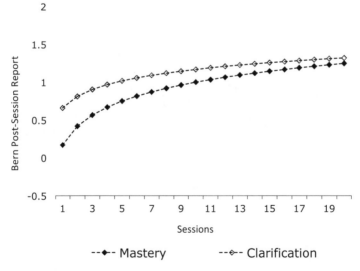

Figure 15.2. General trajectories of mastery and clarification over the course of 20 sessions.

TABLE 15.2

Correlations Between the Process Estimates

Process Estimate	1	2	3	4
Mastery				
1. Intercept	—			
2. Slope	−.44***	—		
3. Positive peak	−.38***	.11	—	
4. Negative peak	−.29***	.04	.60***	—
Clarification				
1. Intercept	—			
2. Slope	−.41***	—		
3. Positive peak	−.31***	.10	—	
4. Negative peak	−.41***	.22**	.62***	—

Note. **$p < .01$. ***$p < .001$.

mastery and clarification, respectively. The intercepts of mastery and clarification experiences are intercorrelated at .78, their slopes at .57, the positive peaks at .65, and the negative peaks at .54. Note that these indicators refer to hierarchical linear modeling estimates (one intercept and one slope by each patient). At the level of single sessions (raw data with repeated session-by-session assessments of each patient), mastery and clarification experiences correlated at .62. The correlations between the different process estimates are presented in Table 15.2. Intercepts and slopes are negatively correlated with each other. This indicates that in those cases in which there are lower scores at the beginning, the patients have a higher chance to improve their scores over the course of therapy. It is interesting that both peaks are negatively associated with intercept and slope. This means that those cases with generally positive early process evaluations show less distinctive amplitudes in both directions.

Associations Between Process and Outcome

We correlated the estimates of the early therapy process (intercept), the trajectories over therapy (slopes), and the intensity of the highest and lowest ratings (positive and negative peaks) with outcome (see Table 15.3). To control for intake characteristics and total standard deviations of mastery and clarification experiences, partial correlations are reported. Confirming our hypothesis, intercepts generally showed the highest correlations with therapy outcome in comparison with the other process estimates. Generally, among the outcome measures, goal attainment showed the strongest associations with the process estimates. It is surprising that negative and positive peaks were negatively associated with outcome, that is, patients demonstrating extremely positive or extremely negative amplitudes regarding

TABLE 15.3

Partial Correlations Between the Process Estimates and Outcome

Process estimate	GAS post	GSI post	IIP-64-D post
Mastery			
Intercept mastery	.46***	.30***	.29***
Slope mastery	.10	.17*	.09
Positive peak mastery	−.42***	−.18*	−.10
Negative peak master	−.28***	−.15*	−.03
Clarification			
Intercept clarification	.36***	.22**	.25**
Slope clarification	−.01	.20**	.20**
Positive peak clarification	−.34***	−.11	−.02
Negative peak clarification	−.35***	−.08	.06

Note. Controlled for Global Severity Index (GSI) intake, Inventory of Interpersonal Problems (German version; IIP-64-D), and standard deviations of mastery and clarification experiences. High scores for Goal Attainment Scaling (GAS) indicate successful outcomes. Low scores for GSI and IIP-64-D indicate successful outcomes. Post = assessment at posttherapy outcome.
*$p < .05$. **$p < .01$. ***$p < .001$.

clarification and mastery experiences in both directions (positive and negative) generally showed worse outcomes than those patients with moderate amplitudes.

DISCUSSION

In this chapter, we have outlined the principles of consistency theory as a general model of psychological functioning and change (Grawe, 1997, 2004). According to consistency theory, the central change experiences are motivational clarification and problem mastery. In the empirical part of this chapter, our main objective was to gain evidence for deciding whether singular, extreme change experiences (big bang), continuous change experiences of lower intensities (constant dripping), or both predict positive outcomes. In accordance with our hypotheses, our results indicated that the average level of change experiences predicted positive outcome most strongly and consistently. In contrast, extremely intense change experiences (high and low) even predicted worse outcomes.

Despite the naturalistic nature of the present study and the reasonable sample size ($N = 223$), the partly surprising results need to be replicated to further increase confidence in their validity. The results trigger various future research questions, for example, addressing the nature of the overall level of change experiences, potentially adverse components of strong singular change experiences, and the distinctness of clarification and mastery experiences.

The overall level of mastery and clarification experiences was more predictive of positive outcome than were single extreme sessions. This result fit well with findings that suggest that general, rather than highly specific, processes of change are predictive of improvement (Crits-Christoph, Connolly Gibbons, Hamilton, Ring-Kurtz, & Gallop, 2011; Hoyt & Melby, 1999). The microstructure of such generalized processes of change may best be described as a stream of various kinds of interrelated patient and therapist in-session and out-of-session processes that add up to therapy success. Most likely, many change processes are not limited to particular situations or experiences, whether it is a specific kind of generalized healer-and-patient interaction (e.g., Type I and II alliance; Luborsky, 1976), a unique explanation that imparts to a specific change model, or the implementation of a particular treatment in which the patient undertakes specifically prescribed tasks that might reduce the problem (Frank & Frank, 1991). Considering the complexity of psychotherapy, not one specific event is likely to be uniquely impactful. Rather, the patient's improvement may well be best explained by the interaction of many processes, including those mentioned above and the change of expectations being generated in the overall healing process (Grawe, 2004; Wampold, 2001, 2007).

The following example with Mr. C might illustrate the interdependent streams contributing to the change experiences represented in single-session experiences:

> During one session, Mr. C role-played a difficult conversation with his superior. He intended to take a vacation at the end of May. In the first role play, Mr. C showed assertive behavior, which however, appeared too aggressive to the other group members. They proposed showing more friendly and affiliative behavior (i.e., let the boss finish his sentences, or maintain eye-contact with the boss). In the second role play, the person acting as the superior had a hard time declining Mr. C's request, even though the timing of the vacation did not fit perfectly with the team's work schedule. In this role play, Mr. C succeeded in showing behavior that was assertive as well as friendly. At the end of the session, all group members and the therapists provided positive feedback. Subsequently, Mr. C was very happy, proud, and relieved. In the standardized post-session questionnaire, Mr. C reported strong mastery experiences.

When recounting the sequence of events in this passage, what influenced Mr. C's mastery experiences? Was it the positive feedback at the end of the session? Was it the experience of self-efficacy in the role plays during the session? Was it the supportive climate among group members? Was it the courage Mr. C had gained by raising the topic of a vacation with the superior in the week before the session? Was it a role play by another group member during the last therapy session that encouraged him to make this big step to raise the topic in conversation with the boss? Was it the psychoeducation in the first sessions? Was it seeing that the other group members have similar and even worse problems? Was it the courage to call a professional therapist after a long time of suffering from his lacking assertiveness? Or was it the courage to admit to himself that he needs help for his problems? Even in its brevity, this example helps to illustrate how multidimensional and complex change processes in psychotherapy are, and how hard it is to pinpoint singular events and experiences that may have been corrective.

The negative correlation of the big bangs with outcome was surprising. If replicable, why should extremely positive and extremely negative change experiences be associated with worse outcomes? In other words, why should grand insights and big steps in solving one's problems be bad? Possible explanations may concern patient personality, suboptimal intensity of change experiences, or the timing of the experience. It might be that reporting very intense experiences in postsession reports is an indicator of a trait-level tendency to experience events very intensely, as it would be the case with high levels of neuroticism. It might also be that there are optimal levels of change experiences, be they positive or negative. In other words, there might be too much or too little of insight or of mastery, and individuals might differ in how much insight they can take at a time or regarding how many new ways to act they can deal with at a time. Accordingly, positive and negative peaks would represent too little or too much of these experiences. A possible example for too little of these experiences are too hesitant and cautious exposure exercises in anxiety therapies that trigger only very low levels of emotional arousal that are not sufficient for productive emotional processing. In contrast, an example of too much of these experiences may be premature exposure exercises in trauma therapy. Premature exposure interventions may solely arouse high levels of anxiety without habituation and/or processing of the experience. It might also be that patients report change experiences at the end of sessions but that such insights fade away quickly or represent premature illusions of mastery, which may prove wrong over time.

Although conceptually, clarification and mastery are clearly distinct change experiences that are both grounded in a wealth of empirical findings (Grawe, 1997; Grawe et al., 1994; Orlinsky et al., 1994), correlations between clarification and mastery experiences were generally found to be high. Methodologically, the high correlations might be attributable to similar response biases in both ratings or to implicit ratings of patient satisfaction overriding the explicit rating of change experiences. Such potential artifacts notwithstanding, the strong association between experiences of clarification and mastery might also be indicative of a high interconnectedness of these two change processes, so that the interpretation of an experience as either clarification or mastery may rather be a matter of attentional focus at the time of rating. These questions are important challenges for future research using self-reported change experiences.

Our study has several limitations. With regard to the concept of CEs, the major limitation is that the BPSR-P was not designed to assess CE according to the PSU definition but was devised previously to assess change experiences as defined by consistency theory (Grawe, 1997, 2004). Postsession patient ratings of change experiences using the BPSR-P were seen as report on the experiential result of all CEs made during the session. However, an assessment of single CEs within a session through self-report would need to ask the person to recall components of single CEs within a session, that is, at least the potentially corrective information (the trigger), and subsequent change experiences. An assessment of CEs in this sense, through retrospective self-report, would require a high level of awareness and high levels of memory capacity. Therefore, it is doubtful whether a postsession self-report measure would be the most adequate instrument for the assessment of single CEs occurring within sessions. To better capture CEs within sessions, future studies could use a combination of self-report and video-rating methods. Whereas external raters could rate interactional sequences between patient and therapist, as well as patient verbal and non-verbal behaviors being indicative of CEs, interviewers could assess patients' recalled CEs when watching videos of sequences within single sessions of their therapies (Elliott & Shapiro, 1988).

Other limitations of the current study are patients being treated according to one specific therapy approach (general psychotherapy) at only one outpatient clinic by rather inexperienced therapists. Furthermore, the presented results are rather experience distant and therefore hard to grab onto for clinical purposes. Future case studies using observer report, as well as process recall methods, will help to bring the rather abstract findings to life.

Overall, our theoretical considerations, as well as our empirical results, cast a grain of doubt on the therapeutic value of singular and intense change experiences in the sense of "aha" experiences or instances of cutting the Gordian knot. We would rather assume that the change process in psychotherapy is a self-organizing sequence of finer grained assimilations paving the way to bigger accommodations (Kanfer & Schefft, 1988). If our findings can be replicated, they are validating news for clinicians who are somewhat hesitant to push patients toward single big-bang experiences and believe that the balanced stream of concerted change experiences is more likely to be associated with positive outcomes. The results would speak for somewhat humble therapists that recognize the need for a working through (or consolidating) therapeutic process (e.g., Linehan. 1997). In addition, the findings would also have implications for treatment planning as well as training. If an accumulation of many smaller change experiences is more important than singular big change events, treatment and therapist training will need to emphasize the repetition of change experiences more strongly in service of the patient consolidating newly gained insights or changed behaviors. Along these lines, therapeutic change may be seen as a learning process that inherently contains progress and reversals (Dilk & Bond, 1996). Under this perspective, psychotherapy represents a reasoned, smooth, and continuous process of fading in adaptive behaviors and fading out problematic behaviors, and therapists would be called to take a persistent, calm, and determined stance, as opposed to an either too cautious or too adventurous approach.

REFERENCES

Alexander, F., & French, T. (1946). *Psychoanalytic therapy: Principles and application.* New York, NY: Ronald Press.

Bandura, A. (1977). Self-efficacy: Toward a unifying theory of behavioral change. *Psychological Review, 84,* 191–215. doi:10.1037/0033-295X.84.2.191

Bryk, A. S., & Raudenbush, S. W. (1992). *Hierarchical linear models.* Newbury, CA: Sage.

Caspar, F., & Grosse Holtforth, M. (2010). Klaus Grawe: On a constant quest for a truly integrative and research-based psychotherapy. In L. G. Castonguay, J. C. Muran, L. Angus, J. A. Hayes, N. Ladany, & T. Anderson (Eds.), *Bringing psychotherapy research to life: Understanding change through the work of leading clinical researchers* (pp. 113–123). Washington, DC: American Psychological Association. doi:10.1037/12137-010

Crits-Christoph, P., Connolly Gibbons, M. B., Hamilton, J., Ring-Kurtz, S., & Gallop, R. (2011). The dependability of alliance assessments: The alliance–outcome correlation is larger than you might think. *Journal of Consulting and Clinical Psychology, 79,* 267–278. doi:10.1037/a0023668

De Shazer, S. (1988). *Clues: Investigation solutions in brief therapy.* New York, NY: Norton.

Dilk, M. N., & Bond, G. R. (1996). Meta-analytic evaluation of skills training research for individuals with severe mental illness. *Journal of Consulting and Clinical Psychology, 64,* 1337–1346. doi:10.1037/0022-006X.64.6.1337

Elliott, R., & Shapiro, D. A. (1988). Brief structured recall: A more efficient method for studying significant therapy events. *British Journal of Medical Psychology, 61,* 141–153. doi:10.1111/j.2044-8341.1988.tb02773.x

Erickson, M. H., & Rossi, E. (1979). *Hypnotherapy: An exploratory casebook.* New York, NY: Irvington.

Flückiger, C., Caspar, F., Grosse Holtforth, M., & Willutzki, U. (2009). Working with the client's strengths—A microprocess approach. *Psychotherapy Research, 19*, 213–223. doi:10.1080/10503300902755300

Flückiger, C., Regli, D., Grawe, K., & Lutz, W. (2007). Similarities and differences between retrospective and pre–post measurements of outcome. *Psychotherapy Research, 17*, 371–377. doi:10.1080/10503300600830728

Flückiger, C., Regli, D., Zwahlen, D., Hostettler, S., & Caspar, F. (2010). Der Berner Therapeuten und Patientenstundenbogen 2000. Ein Instrument zur Erfassung von Therapieprozessen. [Berne postsession reports for patients and therapists]. *Zeitschrift für Klinische Psychologie und Psychotherapie, 39*, 71–79. doi:10.1026/1616-3443/a000015

Flückiger, C., Wüsten, G., Zinbarg, R. E., & Wampold, B. E. (2010). *Resource activation—Using the client's own strengths in psychotherapy and counseling.* Cambridge, MA: Hogrefe.

Frank, J. D., & Frank, J. B. (1991). *Persuasion and healing: A comparative study of psychotherapy* (3rd ed.). Baltimore, MD: Johns Hopkins University Press.

Franke, G. (2000). *Brief Symptom Inventory von L. R. Derogatis—Kurzform der SCL-90–R, Deutsche Version* [Brief Symptom Inventory by L. R. Derogatis—Short form of the SCL-90–R, German version]. Göttingen, Germany: Beltz Test.

Gassmann, D., & Grawe, K. (2006). General change mechanisms. The relation between problem activation and resource activation in successful and unsuccessful therapeutic interactions. *Clinical Psychology and Psychotherapy, 13*, 1–11. doi:10.1002/cpp.442

Goldfried, M. R. (1980). Toward the delineation of therapeutic change principles. *American Psychologist, 35*, 991–999. doi:10.1037/0003-066X.35.11.991

Grawe, K. (1997). Research-informed psychotherapy. *Psychotherapy Research, 7*, 1–19. doi:10.1080/10503309712331331843

Grawe, K. (2004). *Psychological therapy.* Cambridge, MA: Hogrefe & Huber.

Grawe, K. (2006). *Neuropsychotherapy.* Mahwah, NJ: Erlbaum.

Grawe, K., & Braun, U. (1994). Qualitätskontrolle in der Psychotherapie [Quality management in psychotherapy]. *Zeitschrift für Klinische Psychologie und Psychotherapie, 23*, 242–267.

Grawe, K., Donati, R., & Bernauer, F. (1994). *Psychotherapie im Wandel: Von der Konfession zur Profession* [Psychotherapy in transition: From confession to profession]. Göttingen, Germany: Hogrefe.

Greenberg, L. S., & Safran, J. D. (1987). *Emotion in psychotherapy: Affect, cognition, and the process of change.* New York, NY: Guilford Press.

Grosse Holtforth, M., Grawe, K., & Castonguay, L. G. (2006). Predicting a reduction of avoidance motivation in psychotherapy: Toward the delineation of differential processes of change operating at different phases of treatment. *Psychotherapy Research, 16*, 626–630. doi:10.1080/10503300600608215

Grosse Holtforth, M., Grawe, K., & Lutz, W. (2009). Interventionsbezogene Diagnostik. [Assessment in psychotherapy]. In M. Hautzinger & P. Pauli (Eds.). *Enzyklopädie der Psychologie, Bd. 2 Psychotherapeutische Methoden* (pp. 1–74). Göttingen, Germany: Hogrefe.

Horowitz, L. M., Strauß, B., & Kordy, H. (2000). *Das Inventar zur Erfassung interpersonaler Probleme (IIP-64-D)* [Inventory of interpersonal problems, German version]. Weinheim, Germany: Beltz.

Hoyt, W. T., & Melby, J. N. (1999). Dependability of measurement in counseling psychology: An introduction to generalizability theory. *The Counseling Psychologist, 27,* 325–352. doi:10.1177/0011000099273003

Kanfer, F. H., & Schefft, B. K. (1988). *Guiding the process of therapeutic change.* Champaign, IL: Research Press.

Karoly, P., & Anderson, C. W. (2000). The long and short psychological change: Toward a goal-centered understanding of treatment durability and adaptive success. In C. R. Snyder & R. E. Ingram (Eds.), *Handbook of psychological change* (pp. 154–176). New York, NY: Wiley.

Kiresuk, T., & Lund, S. (1979). Goal attainment scaling: Research, evaluation, and utilization. In H. C. Schulberg & F. Parker (Eds.), *Program evaluation in health fields* (Vol. 2, pp. 214–237). New York, NY: Human Science Press.

Lauterbach, W. (1996). The measurement of personal conflict. *Psychotherapy Research, 6,* 213–225. doi:10.1080/10503309612331331718

Lazarus, R. S. (1991). *Emotion and adaptation.* London, England: Oxford University Press.

Linehan, M. M. (1997). Validation and psychotherapy. In A. C. Bohart & L. S. Greenberg (Eds.), *Empathy reconsidered: New directions* (pp. 353–392). Washington, DC: American Psychological Association. doi:10.1037/10226-016

London, P. (1969). *Behavior control* (1st ed.). New York, NY: Harper & Row.

Luborsky, L. (1976). Helping alliances in psychotherapy. In J. L. Cleghhorn (Ed.), *Successful psychotherapy* (pp. 92–116). New York, NY: Brunner/Mazel.

Orlinsky, D., Grawe, K., & Parks, B. (1994). Process and outcome in psychotherapy: Noch einmal. In A. E. Bergin & S. L. Garfield (Eds.), *Handbook of psychotherapy and behavior change* (4th ed., pp. 270–376). New York, NY: Wiley.

Piaget, J. (1977). *The development of thought: Equilibration of cognitive structures.* Oxford, England: Viking.

Raudenbush, S., Bryk, A., Cheong, Y. F., & Congdon, R. (2004). *HLM 6: Hierarchical linear and nonlinear modeling.* Lincolnwood, IL: Scientific Software International.

Wampold, B. E. (2001). *The great psychotherapy debate: Models, methods, and findings.* Mahwah, NJ: Erlbaum.

Wampold, B. E. (2007). Psychotherapy: The humanistic (and effective) treatment. *American Psychologist, 62,* 855–873. doi:10.1037/0003-066X.62.8.857

Watzlawick, P., Weakland, R., & Fisch, R. (1974). *Change*. New York, NY: Norton.

Willutzki, U. (1999). *VEV-VW: Neue Version des Veränderungsfragebogens des Erlebens und Verhaltens von Zielen [VEV-VW. A revised version of the questionnaire to assess changes in experiencing and behavior]*. Unpublished manuscript, Department of Psychology, University of Ruhr, Bochum, Germany.

Wittchen, H.-J., Zaudig, M., & Fydrich, T. (1997). *SKID- Strukturiertes Klinisches Interview für DSM–IV Achse I und II* [Structured clinical interview for DSM–IV Axis I and II]. Göttingen, Germany: Hogrefe.

Wood, A. M., & Tarrier, N. (2010). Positive clinical psychology: A new vision and strategy for integrated research and practice. *Clinical Psychology Review, 30,* 819–829. doi:10.1016/j.cpr.2010.06.003

16

CORRECTIVE RELATIONAL EXPERIENCES IN SUPERVISION

NICHOLAS LADANY, ARPANA G. INMAN, CLARA E. HILL,
SARAH KNOX, RACHEL E. CROOK-LYON, BARBARA J. THOMPSON,
ALAN W. BURKARD, SHIRLEY A. HESS, ELIZABETH NUTT WILLIAMS,
AND JESSICA A. WALKER

> For not only does the student manage to use supervision to acquire skills,
> but the recurrent crises—the learning blocks, the problems in learning
> and in teaching that arise—are themselves an essential part of the total
> process that must be worked through in order to make the most fruitful
> headway in acquisition of experience and skill.
> —Ekstein & Wallerstein, *The Teaching and Learning of Psychotherapy*

Supervision, like psychotherapy, is arguably a place where corrective relational experiences (CREs) occur. Specifically, it is hoped that trainees, like clients, develop and grow through supervisory experiences that create a novel and meaningful change in how trainees view themselves, their supervisors, and their clients.

Consistent with the definition put forth by the Penn State University conference (see Chapter 1, this volume) we define a CRE in supervision as occurring when a trainee feels a distinct shift, such that he or she comes to understand or experience affectively the relationship with the supervisor in a different and unexpected way and is thereby transformed in some manner. We recognize that although all of supervision might be a learning or transformative experience, a CRE can be classified as a specific event (within or across sessions) within the supervisory relationship. Because we were most interested in the transformation that occurred within the supervisory relationship, we

We thank Kristin Bertsch and Sepideh Soheilian for their assistance with the participant interviews.
We also thank Natasha Taban for her assistance in relation to summarizing the participant data. The
fourth and fifth authors contributed equally to the project and are listed in alphabetical order. Likewise,
the seventh through 10th authors contributed equally and are listed in alphabetical order.

bounded our definition more than previous definitions of corrective experiences (e.g., Penn State conference).

CREs have been discussed only briefly in the supervision literature. Ladany, Friedlander, and Nelson (2005) provided an example of how a male supervisor could offer a female trainee a corrective experience whereby she changes her negative expectations of working with men on the basis of their interpersonal interactions in supervision. Similar to research on CREs, empirical work on CREs in supervision has been lacking. Instead, supervision research has largely focused on corrective changes in the ability to use clinical skills (Alssid & Hutchinson, 1977; Borzumato-Gainey, 2005; Komiskey, 2004) as a means of looking at corrective experiences in supervision rather than transformative relational changes.

Given the lack of theoretical and empirical work on CREs in supervision, we looked to the psychotherapy literature to ground the current study and offer perspectives on the potential manner in which CREs may present themselves in supervision (e.g., Alexander & French, 1946; Goldfried, 1980; Levenson, 2003; Strupp, 1986; Teyber, 2006). Thus, we believe that CREs in supervision (a) occur, (b) can be quite meaningful, and (c) occur regardless of the theoretical orientation of supervisor and supervisee.

Because of the limited literature and our desire to capture an in-depth narrative analysis of trainees' subjective experience with CREs, we conducted a qualitative investigation of CREs from the perspective of doctoral students involved in supervision. Data were analyzed using the consensual qualitative research (CQR) methodology (Hill, 2011; Hill et al., 2005; Hill, Thompson, & Williams, 1997). Our research questions were: (a) What kinds of CREs do trainees report? and (b) What impact do CREs have on the supervision, on the trainees, and on clients? A novel feature of this study was the use of two different CQR teams to analyze the data. In response to repeated questions about the trustworthiness of qualitative research (Williams & Morrow, 2009), we sought to assess the extent to which two distinct research teams would reach similar findings when analyzing exactly the same data. Completion of this study, then, not only illuminated supervisees' experiences of CREs but also shed light on the data analysis process at the heart of CQR.

METHOD

Participants

Trainees

Fifteen doctoral psychology students (11 White, one Indian American, one Asian American, one Hispanic/White, one African American; 10 women, five men; 10 clinical, five counseling) who ranged in age from 24 to 52 years ($M = 32.06$, $SD = 8.46$) participated in this study. Participants had conducted between 11 and 60 months of supervised psychotherapy ($M = 33.40$, $SD = 14.53$) and had worked with a median of 125 clients (range = 17–500 clients). The number of weeks of supervision with the current supervisor ranged from four to 116 weeks ($M = 27.33$, $SD = 27.29$) for an average of 1.43 hours per week ($SD = 0.56$). In terms of theoretical orientation, nine trainees indicated that their approach was integrative; three, cognitive–behavioral; two, psychodynamic; and one, systems.

Supervisors

Participants reported that they were receiving supervision from 15 (11 White, two African American, one Pacific Islander/White, one Hispanic/White; nine women, six men) supervisors who ranged in age from about 35 to 63 years old ($M = 46.00$, $SD = 9.05$). Supervisors ranged in education (10 PhD counseling psychologists, two PsyD psychologists, one EdD psychologist, one MSW licensed clinical social worker, and one MA clinical therapist).

Interviewers

Two female doctoral students in counseling psychology conducted the interviews. Both were in their 20s; one was White European American, and the other was Middle Eastern American. They were trained by one of the authors to conduct CQR interviews.

Judges

Ten (all had doctoral degrees in counseling psychology or counselor education, eight women, two men; nine White European American, one South Asian American, ranging in age from early 30s to early 60s) judges completed the data analyses. Each of the 10 judges was randomly assigned to one of two teams, each with three primary team members and two auditors. Before the investigation, all of the researchers indicated their biases and expectations in relation to the analytic procedures and anticipated findings. Knowledge of these biases and expectations was used by each team to increase self-awareness during the analysis process. Most of the team members believed that CREs emerge from ruptures or impasses in the supervisory work, that the supervisory relationship needs to be positive for CREs to emerge, and that CREs typically have positive outcomes. Most also reported having had negative supervisory experiences that made them aware of the negative aspects of supervision. Finally, all researchers indicated that they anticipated only small differences in findings between the two teams, mostly focused on labels for the categories.

Interview Protocol

Based on the existing literature and the clinical experience of the researchers, a set of interview questions was developed to explore CREs in supervision (see Appendix 16.1). These questions were divided into 10 areas: (a) the general supervisory relationship, (b) general supervisor approach, (c) description of the most significant CRE that occurred in supervision, (d) what occurred to make the CRE corrective, (e) how the CRE influenced supervision, (f) how the CRE affected the supervisory relationship, (g) how the CRE affected trainee evaluation, (h) parallels between supervision and therapy, (i) reactions to the research, and (j) demographics. The interview was semistructured, with specific questions asked of all participants, and additional probes used to capture more detail where appropriate.

Procedures

Recruitment and Interviews

Participants were solicited through e-mail mailing lists (e.g., Division 17 [Society of Counseling Psychology], American Psychological Association; Asian American Psychological Association; Association of Women in Psychology) and academic contacts. Potential participants replied directly to the researchers about their interest, and they were then contacted to set up a phone interview date. As an incentive, those who agreed to participate were given a pound of gourmet coffee or hot chocolate as a token of appreciation. Before the interview, participants were provided with the definition of CREs and the interview protocol. Ranging from 30 minutes to 1.5 hours in length, interviews were recorded, transcribed verbatim, and checked for accuracy.

Consensual Qualitative Research Data Analysis Process

CQR (Hill, 2011; Hill et al., 1997, 2005) was used to analyze the data. In sum, the data analysis process consisted of coding into domains (i.e., moving the raw data into content-similar areas), abstracting the core ideas (i.e., summarizing the raw data within domains into more succinct statements), auditing the domains and core ideas, conducting cross-analyses (i.e., identifying patterns of responses across participants within domains and then coding the core ideas into these categories), and auditing the cross-analysis. Each of the two teams consensually completed these steps independent of the other team (i.e., there was no discussion of the data between teams throughout the process).

Once the data had been completely analyzed by each team, one person from each team reviewed both teams' separate cross-analyses (including the categories and core ideas) and identified similarities and differences in the cross-analysis categories. This process resulted in a table of matched (close in content regardless of the exact wording used) and mismatched categories. These same two researchers then created a new table that combined the most common elements of both cross-analyses (in some cases, the categories overlapped enough to support a collapse or division of categories, depending on their judgments of which team's analysis seemed to best reflect the meaning of the data). We also indicated in this new table the number of cases from each team that applied to each given category, and then we determined whether the category was general, typical, or variant (rare was dropped as an option, as it would have resulted in too many subcategories that would have more likely confounded than enriched the findings). As an example, one team reported 10 cases for *supervisor approach: supportive*, whereas the other team reported 13 cases for *supervisor approach: supportive, open*. The final category, integrating the team's initially separate cross-analyses, was titled *supervisor approach: supportive* (10 to 13 cases) and was considered typical because it applied to more than half of the sample. This process involved multiple discussions about how the results from both teams fit or did not fit until consensus was reached. Following the reviews by the two team members, an additional person for each of the two teams reviewed the table and provided additional feedback, which was then used to revise the table. The final merged table was then distributed to all team members for review and comment.

Results

Exhibit 16.1 provides the results of the combined cross-analysis. Categories were designated on the basis of the number of cases that they contained. Categories containing 14 to 15 cases were deemed *general*, those containing eight to 13 cases were considered *typical*, and those containing four to seven cases were labeled *variant*. The categories are reviewed in the subsequent sections and illustrated by case data.

Supervisory Interactions Before Event

Quality of Relationship

Typically, participants reported that the relationship with their supervisor was positive, most often using the word *good* to make this point. One trainee stated that he "admired and respected" his supervisor and that they both "liked" one another. At the same time, participants also typically reported having some negative feelings about the supervisory relationship (e.g., supervisors were described as occasionally "off task," "too formal," or

EXHIBIT 16.1
Final Domain List

I. Supervisory interactions before event
  A. Quality of relationship
    1. Good relationship (typical)
    2. Negative feelings about relationship (typical)
  B. Supervisor approach
    1. Instructional (typical)
    2. Supportive (typical)
    3. Mentor (variant)
    4. Consultant (variant)
    5. Flexible (variant)
    6. Self-disclosing (variant)
    7. Interpersonal, psychodynamic (variant)

II. Antecedent
  A. Trainee had concerns about supervision or supervisor (typical)
  B. Trainee had concerns about challenging clinical situation (variant)
  C. Trainee had concerns related to self (variant)

III. Description of Event
  A. Supervisor interventions
    1. Supported, normalized, validated (typical)
    2. Open (typical)
    3. Processed the supervisory relationship (typical)
    4. Parallel process (typical)
    5. Focused on feelings about clinical situation (typical)
    6. Encouraged trainee to trust instincts or find own answers (variant)
  B. Trainee actions and experiences
    1. Trainee disclosed, open, vulnerable (typical)
    2. Didn't like supervisor's intervention (variant)

IV. Consequences of event
  A. Improvements in supervision
    1. Strengthened or transformed the supervisory relationship (general)
    2. Trainee felt more comfortable disclosing (typical)
    3. Supervisor more available and responsive (variant)
    4. More able to discuss the supervisory relationship (variant)
  B. Improvements in trainee
    1. Positive impact on work with clients (typical)
    2. Increased self-efficacy as a professional (typical)
  C. Supervisor evaluated trainee more positively (typical)

V. What trainee wishes had been done differently
  A. No changes (typical)
  B. Wishes supervisor had been more sensitive to trainee's needs (variant)
  C. Wishes trainee had been more open or assertive with supervisor (variant)
  D. Wishes concern had been addressed earlier (variant)

VI. Reactions to interview: Stimulated reflection (typical)

Note. General = 14–15 cases; typical = 8–13 cases; variant = 4–7 cases.

"competitive"). These results suggest that no relationship is perfect and all relationships have both positive and negative aspects.

Supervisor Approach

Typically, supervisors were described as instructional and supportive in their approach to supervision (e.g., the supervisor preferred the "teacher role"). In addition, variant forms of supervision included the supervisor being viewed as a mentor or consultant, as flexible, self-disclosing, or interpersonal–psychodynamic.

Antecedent

Trainee Had Concerns About Supervision or Supervisor

Typically, participants reported having had concerns about their supervisors immediately before the CRE. One participant talked about how his supervisor seemed hurried, stressed, and distracted in supervision, which in turn made the trainee feel "unsafe." Another participant was "frustrated" by the supervisor's sole focus on offering suggestions about what to try in psychotherapy.

Trainee Had Concerns About a Challenging Clinical Situation

Trainees also typically had concerns about a challenging clinical case. One trainee reported working with a client who had "a lot of anxiety and getting pulled into the client's anxiety," leading this trainee to start into the supervision session "going a mile a minute" wanting to know what to do. Another trainee reported feeling concerned about a client who talked about "death at a very deep level." In yet another case, the trainee was overwhelmed with the severity of a client's disturbance and needed to talk with the supervisor about it.

Trainee Had Concerns Related to Self

Trainees variantly reported concerns about themselves. For example, one trainee was aware that he was being "dismissive" of a client, which was uncharacteristic of him. Another trainee was aware of how she wanted to make a good impression with her supervisor.

Summary of Antecedents

These data suggest that there was some turbulence before the emergence of the CRE. This turbulence was often related to the supervisory relationship itself but was also often related to the clinical work or the personal issues of the supervisee.

Description of Event

Supervisor Interventions

During the event, supervisors typically used five types of interventions. First, they supported, normalized, or validated the trainees. For example, one participant indicated that his supervisor "really went to bat" for him by "normalizing" his experience. Another supervisor encouraged a trainee to trust that the concern about evaluation was "normal" for interns and if not dealt with would create "barriers" in supervision.

Second, supervisors were open or self-disclosing. For example, one supervisor self-disclosed about her personal experiences and negative reactions to clients.

Third, supervisors processed the supervisory relationship, that is, used immediacy to talk about the here-and-now interaction). For example, trainees and supervisors talked about their hopes and intentions for supervision. In addition, they discussed trainees' concerns about disappointing supervisors.

Fourth, supervisors attended to parallel process. As an illustration, one trainee saw parallels between the CRE discussion of gender and race with his supervisor, subsequent diversity discussions with clients, and later supervisory discussions of diversity issues. Another trainee noted that his interactions with clients using an interpersonal approach were more solidified after the supervisor's modeling of processing the relationship during the CRE.

Fifth, supervisors focused on feelings about a clinical situation reported by the trainee. One supervisor explored with his trainee what it was like to push himself to be such a "stellar intern" and wanted to know what was going on for the trainee.

Variantly, supervisors intervened by encouraging trainees to trust their instincts or find their own answers to problems. For example, one supervisor engaged in a Socratic process with the trainee; another explicitly stated that the trainee should listen to her own instincts.

Trainee Actions and Experiences

Typically, trainees responded to the supervisors' interventions used during the CRE event by disclosing openly and becoming vulnerable. A poignant illustration occurred in a case in which a trainee was for the first time able to say the words "I don't know," which ran against her idea of what would be "professional" in supervision. This leap of faith on the part of the trainee led to what she described as a "new transparency" in supervision.

At times, even though the CRE was transformative in a positive direction, trainees did not like some of their supervisor's interventions. For example, one trainee felt her supervisor become distant; another supervisor's negative feedback and criticisms created self-doubt in the trainee. In the end, though, these negative reactions led to a positive transformation.

Timing and Length of Corrective Relational Experience

Typically, the CRE occurred early in the relationship (i.e., 4 months or less). The CRE also typically lasted for more than one session.

Consequences of the Corrective Relational Experience

Improvements in Supervision

As a result of the CREs, trainees noted a variety of ways in which supervision improved. Generally, they recognized that the supervisory relationship was strengthened, transformed, or deepened after the CRE. As an example, one trainee indicated that the CRE "opened the door" in supervision for affect and not just cerebral or technical discussions. Another person noted that the CRE helped solidify the supervisory working alliance. Typically, trainees who also felt more comfortable disclosing were more likely to bring up personal issues or risky clinical issues (e.g., sexual attraction) after the CRE than before. In addition, trainees variantly noted that they became more available and responsive in supervision (e.g., more invested in training) and recognized that they were more able to discuss the supervisory relationship (e.g., more able to bring things up in the moment) after as compared with before the CRE.

Improvements in the Trainee

CREs also led to improvements in trainee development. Specifically, trainees typically indicated a positive impact on their clinical work. Examples include a trainee believing that she "could sit with clients and not worry how this would be brought up in supervision" and another trainee believing that she was "more empathic with clients." Trainees also typically reported increased professional self-efficacy (e.g., one trainee saw himself as "less of a burden" on the supervisor, given that he perceived himself to be less of a "student" in relation to the supervisor; other trainees felt more stable and confident; and others came to realize that they did not need to know all the answers).

Supervisors Evaluated Trainees More Positively

Typically, trainees believed that they were evaluated more positively by their supervisors after the CRE. One trainee indicated that his supervisor evaluated him higher because he was able to let go and share emotions, as well as do insight work about his own personal experiences with clients.

Another trainee mentioned that her supervisor saw her as "ballsy" by raising here-and-now concerns.

What the Trainee Wishes Had Been Done Differently

Looking back, trainees did not typically wish anything had been done differently regarding the CRE. Variantly, however, trainees wished that their supervisors had been more sensitive to their needs (e.g., responded sooner to trainee as a colleague), that they had been more open or assertive with their supervisor (e.g., trainee would have liked to have been more open at an earlier time), or wished the concern had been addressed by the supervisor sooner.

Reactions to the Interview

Trainees typically believed that their participation in the research stimulated reflections about CREs in supervision. One trainee identified how the discussion highlighted the fact that the CRE was a pivotal point in supervision, and another trainee indicated that the research brought forward a concept that he had never thought much about before.

Illustrative Case: The Returning Veteran

"Miguel," a Latino American doctoral student in his late 20s, had been working with clients for about 3 years when he was called into military service from the Reserves. After interrupting his doctoral program to serve a tour of duty, he returned to school and encountered some difficulty adjusting to civilian life and the stressors of his graduate program. In addition, his wife was pregnant at the time of his return, and they had just learned that she had to be on hospital bed rest for the entire pregnancy. Because a previous pregnancy had miscarried, they were quite anxious about this pregnancy. Miguel was thus rushing between home, the hospital, and graduate work, all the while trying to internally work through his recent experiences in active duty.

Miguel's CRE occurred when he was completing an assistantship at a university counseling center. He found himself increasingly frustrated with his clients, who were struggling with "trivial" issues such as homesickness, being away from boyfriends and girlfriends, or getting into sororities and fraternities. His relationship with his supervisor, "Ann" (a White European American woman in her late 50s with a feminist orientation), before the CRE was described as professional but also a bit cold and by the book. However, Miguel respected Ann and found her to be supportive and knowledgeable. As a supervisor, Ann was open to hearing about anything in relation to clients or how personal issues may be affecting Miguel. She was supportive and challenging, and she treated Miguel like a colleague-in-training. Consistent with her feminist orientation, she frequently talked about the multicultural dynamics between them as supervisor and supervisee (e.g., gender, race, sexual orientation). In addition, they often discussed their mutually agreed-upon goals in supervision.

Immediately before the CRE, and about a month into the semester, Miguel was providing Ann with a status report and notes about his clients and caseload. He found himself being dismissive of some of his clients' concerns, particularly a client who was upset because she could not get into a sorority. He recalled how Ann had previously indicated that supervision, in addition to talking about clients, was a place he could bring up his reactions to clients, as well as personal issues that may be related to his clinical work. In the moment of discussing his cases, he decided to take her up on this offer and shared his current personal struggles, about which he felt embarrassed and worried that they would affect his evaluation. He was also concerned that Ann would be critical of him. However, exactly the opposite happened. Miguel stated that "the floodgates of support opened" and that Ann offered support and encouragement to him to feel his emotions. Specifically, she helped him realize that his anger and dislike for the client were likely hindering the therapeutic process, enabling Miguel to open up further and become more vulnerable with Ann about his reactions. Ann also was Socratic in her supervisory approach and focused on the supervisory alliance. In addition, she helped normalize Miguel's struggle with his client by disclosing how she had managed her own negative reactions to clients. Although the initial CRE event occurred during the 4th week, the CRE lingered and lasted and reemerged multiple times throughout the semester.

As an outcome of the CRE, Miguel indicated that the supervisory relationship opened wide: Whereas initially his flow of communication had been a trickle, now it allowed him to talk about anything without a filter, feeling hugely supported by Ann, and he felt that he could trust her with anything. Moreover, Miguel noted that the CRE led him to be more comfortable as a therapist and separate out his personal stressors from his therapy work. Furthermore, he no longer felt that he had to do therapy perfectly. In the end, he believed that Ann evaluated him more positively because he was able to do better work in supervision.

DISCUSSION

Overall, the findings of this study indicate that CREs do indeed occur in supervision and are meaningful to trainees. In addition, because CREs were reported for trainees and supervisors from a variety of psychotherapy theoretical backgrounds, it appears that CREs are pantheoretical (i.e., not restricted to one theoretical approach). The supervisory relationships in which CREs occurred tended to be rather positive. Furthermore, although distinctive types of CREs could not be determined (i.e., categories of types of CREs), supervisors tended to respond in a similar fashion during the varied CREs identified. In addition, the CREs led the trainee to feel better about the supervisory experience, themselves as professionals, and their work with clients.

In Chapter 11 of this volume, a research investigation on client perspectives on CREs was described. Recognizing the sample differences, tentative and suggested patterns seemed to emerge in comparing these samples. Similar to CREs in therapy, CREs in supervision often resulted from a rupture or negative experience between the dyad. For both sets of participants, the therapist–supervisor explored feelings, normalized the experience, and validated or accepted the client–trainee, and ultimately, the CRE led to a transformation of the relationship. Of course, supervision can be characterized as consisting of three dynamics that the therapy relationship does not include, that is, its involuntary nature, its educative goals, and its evaluation component (Ladany, 2005). In contrast to the CREs found in therapy, the CREs in supervision had an educative component (i.e., impact on client care), and the involuntary and evaluative aspects of supervision often led to a hesitation for the trainee before the event and added to the transformative aspects following the event.

Because supervision is a process in and of itself, related to but distinct from psychotherapy, it behooves theoreticians to consider constructs that are relevant to supervision proper. To that end, the next section integrates the findings into an existing theoretical model of supervision.

Locating Corrective Relational Experiences Within Theories About Supervision

The process of working through a CRE in supervision directly links to supervision theory and practice (e.g., Bernard, 1997). In particular, the findings offer evidence in support of a new type of critical event that fits within the critical events in supervision model (Ladany et al., 2005), a pantheoretical model of supervision that posits that the most meaningful aspects of supervision can be defined by critical events that occur. These critical events typically have a beginning, middle, and end and can exist within a session or across supervisory sessions. The most common critical events that have been identified include remediating skill difficulties and deficits, heightening multicultural awareness, negotiating role conflicts, working through countertransference, managing sexual attraction, repairing gender-related conflicts, addressing problematic supervisee emotions and behaviors, facilitating supervisee insight, and working through therapist shame.

Ladany et al. (2005) described four components of critical events: the supervisory working alliance (the bond and agreement on tasks and goals, based on Bordin's, 1983 model); a marker (initiates the event and can be something as simple as a statement or something the supervisor observes such as a dynamic in the trainee's behavior); the task environment (a series of supervisor-initiated interaction sequences, such as focusing on the supervisory working alliance, the therapeutic process, supervisee feelings, counter-transference, parallel process, supervisee self-efficacy, supervisee's experience, therapy skills, knowledge, multicultural awareness, evaluation, and case review); and the resolution (which can range from successful to unsuccessful in changing the supervisory alliance, and/or the trainee's knowledge, self-awareness, and therapy skills).

Our findings offer an additional critical event: providing a CRE. In addition, the findings suggest ways in which each component of the model occurs. First, a common marker for a CRE event may be that there is some conflict between the trainee and supervisor in which the trainee is not feeling good about the process of supervision. Second, the task environment that seems to offer the best opportunity for a successful resolution consists of (a) normalizing the trainee's experience, (b) the supervisor self-disclosing or becoming open about one's own experience (new interaction sequence), (c) focusing on the supervisory alliance, (d) attending to parallel process, and (e) exploring the trainee's feelings. Third, as a result of these interaction sequences, the likely resolution is that the supervisory alliance is strengthened (i.e., transformation of the supervisory relationship, the trainee had increased comfort in disclosing), the trainee becomes more self-efficacious, and the trainee's skills with clients and client work are enhanced. In sum, the results point to ways in which a model for providing a CRE can be used by practitioners to facilitate successful outcomes in supervision (see Figure 16.1).

Limitations

Perhaps because our study was a first to look at CREs in supervision, a variety of limitations are evident. First, the findings for our study are limited, in part, to how the interviews were conducted. In previous qualitative investigations, the interviews seemed to cover more ground and offered more depth of findings. Our results may also have been limited by the ambiguity of the construct itself (e.g., CREs are not well defined), or the interviews themselves did not facilitate the kinds of depth that would be expected (e.g., the training of the interviewers was inadequate). Second, participant self-selection clearly occurred, and hence it is unclear how frequently CREs actually happen in supervision. Finally, two teams reviewed the same data, and although there was much overlap, there were also unique differences between

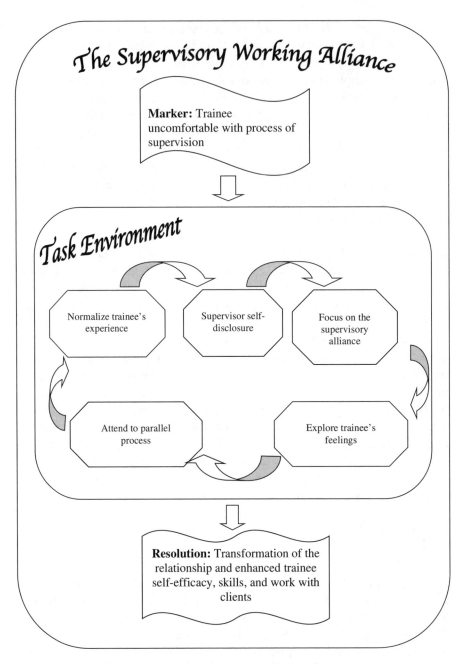

The Supervisory Working Alliance

Marker: Trainee uncomfortable with process of supervision

Task Environment

Normalize trainee's experience

Supervisor self-disclosure

Focus on the supervisory alliance

Attend to parallel process

Explore trainee's feelings

Resolution: Transformation of the relationship and enhanced trainee self-efficacy, skills, and work with clients

Figure 16.1. Providing a corrective relational experience. The arrows are not intended to indicate that the interaction sequences occur in any particular order, or are unilateral or sequential as shown, but rather are represented pictorially as heuristic device to represent one way they may occur.

the teams in how the data were interpreted, particularly in relation to some of the identified categories. It seems likely that although we attempted to guard against personal biases and expectations, each team may have exhibited a drift toward some of the members' preconceived ideas. For example, one team found parallel process to be an important category, whereas the other team included those data more in relation to supervisory interventions in the context of the CRE. To be sure, both teams included the data; however, the reason one team highlighted these data more may have to do with work some of the researchers on that team had done in the area of parallel process. Similarly, one team had highlighted concepts related to immediacy more than the other team, perhaps again in part because that team had people on it who had a unique interest in immediacy as an intervention. It is interesting that neither parallel process nor immediacy was noted as potential bias or expectation of the respective teams. In the end, further exploration into this methodological phenomenon seems warranted.

FUTURE RESEARCH DIRECTIONS

Additional testing of the critical events model related to CREs through qualitative (e.g., replication) and quantitative methods would add to our understanding. For example, applying a common task analysis paradigm, researchers could identify supervisory sessions in which a CRE had occurred versus sessions in which a CRE did not occur, then work backward to see what types of interactions took place that led or did not lead to CREs. In addition, our data suggest that client care may have been enhanced as a result of CREs. If that is indeed the case, then it would behoove researchers to examine the extent to which such enhancement actually occurs. Moreover, CREs have been examined primarily from the lens of something the supervisor provides. Additional study is warranted to determine how much of it is in the province of the supervisor, supervisee, or both.

Finally, it would be useful to study more about the prevalence of CREs, when and where they tend to occur. Although in this study CREs tended to occur early in the supervisory relationship, we wonder if that is typical. Even though our research points to the potential meaningfulness of such events, it is unclear if these events are a typical occurrence in supervision or if they are few and far between.

APPENDIX 16.1: CORRECTIVE RELATIONAL EXPERIENCE INTERVIEW PROTOCOL

Thank you very much for you participation in this research on corrective relational experiences (CREs) in supervision. We are most grateful for your willingness to discuss your experiences as a trainee in supervision.

We define *corrective relational experiences* as specific times in supervision when the supervisee feels a distinct shift, such that he or she comes to understand or experience affectively the relationship with the supervisor in a different and unexpected way, and is thereby transformed in some manner. Note that although the entire relationship might be a learning or transformative experience, we are most interested in examining here a specific event in supervision that you consider to be corrective in relation to you and your supervisor. This event may have occurred within a single session or may have occurred over the course of multiple sessions. Please review the questions below when reflecting on your experience.

1. Reflect back on your supervision experiences over the course of the current semester. Please describe the most significant CRE that occurred in supervision.
    a. What was going on in supervision prior to event?
    b. What was the marker/trigger/initial behavior that started the event?
    c. When in the supervisory relationship did the CRE occur?
    d. How long was the CRE?
2. What occurred to make it corrective—that is, How did your supervisor respond to the issue? Probes: To what extent did your supervisor:
    a. Focus on the supervisory working alliance
    b. Focus on the therapeutic process
    c. Explore your feelings
    d. Focus on countertransference
    e. Attend to parallel process
    f. Focus on your self-efficacy
    g. Normalize your experience
    h. Focus on your skill(s)
    i. Assess your knowledge
    j. Focus on your multicultural awareness
    k. Focus on evaluation
3. What was the extent to which the CRE was resolved/unresolved or was a positive/negative outcome?
4. Describe how the CRE impacted the relationship with your supervisor.

a. How did this event affect your work with your supervisor?
b. How did you look at your supervisor after the event? OR how did this experience transform your supervision with your supervisor?
c. Describe how you wished your supervisor would have responded differently.
d. Describe what you would wished you would have done differently and why.
5. Describe any parallels between the CRE and your work with any of your clients (before or after the event; supervisor to client or client to supervisor).
6. In general, how would you describe your relationship with your supervisor (positive and negative aspects)?
7. To what extent do you believe this CRE affected how your supervisor evaluated you?
8. Describe your supervisor's approach to supervision (counselor, consultant, teacher; goals of supervision, countertransference, gender dynamics, multicultural issues, etc.).
9. What additional thoughts do you have about CREs?
10. Biographical data questions
a. Trainee demographic information (gender, race, age, months of supervised counseling experience, total number of clients seen in your lifetime, field of graduate study, theoretical orientation, how many weeks you have met with your supervisor, how many hours per week you meet with your supervisor)
b. Supervisor demographic information (gender, race, approximate age, field, degree, theoretical orientation)
11. Please describe any reactions you have based on your participation in this research study.

Do you have any thoughts or feelings about this interview that you would like to discuss before we conclude?

REFERENCES

Alexander, F., & French, T. M. (1946). *Psychoanalytic therapy: Principles and applications*. New York, NY: Ronald Press.

Alssid, L. L., & Hutchison, W. R. (1977). Comparison of modeling techniques in counselor training. *Counselor Education and Supervision, 17*, 36–41.

Bernard, J. M. (1997). The discrimination model. In C. E. Watkins (Ed.), *Handbook of psychotherapy supervision* (pp. 310–327). New York, NY: Wiley.

Bordin, E. S. (1983). Supervision in counseling: II. Contemporary models of supervision: A working alliance based model of supervision. *Counseling Psychologist*, *11*, 35–42.

Borzumato-Gainey, C. (2005). An examination of factors affecting peer feedback in group supervision. *Dissertation Abstracts International: Section A. Humanities and Social Sciences*, *65(12)*, 4471.

Ekstein, R. & Wallerstein, R. S. (1958). *The teaching of psychotherapy*. New York, NY: Basic books.

Goldfried, M. R. (1980). Toward the delineation of therapeutic change principles. *American Psychologist*, *35*, 991–999. doi:10.1037/0003-066X.35.11.991

Hill, C. E. (Ed.). (2011). *Consensual qualitative research: A practical resource for investigating social science phenomena*. Washington, DC: American Psychological Association.

Hill, C. E., Knox, S., Thompson, B. J., Williams, E. N., Hess, S. A., & Ladany, N. (2005). Consensual qualitative research: An update. *Journal of Counseling Psychology*, *52*, 196–205. doi:10.1037/0022-0167.52.2.196

Hill, C. E., Thompson, B. J., & Williams, E. N. (1997). A guide to conducting consensual qualitative research. *The Counseling Psychologist*, *25*, 517–572. doi:10.1177/0011000097254001

Komiskey, C. A. (2004). Supervisors' perceptions about giving and receiving corrective feedback: Implications for counselor education and supervision. *Dissertation Abstracts International: Section A. Humanities and Social Sciences*, *65(4)*, 1264.

Ladany, N. (2005). Conducting effective clinical supervision. In G. P. Koocher, J. C. Norcross, & S. S. Hill. *Psychologists' desk reference* (2nd ed., pp. 682–685). New York, NY: Oxford University Press.

Ladany, N., Friedlander, M. L., & Nelson, M. L. (2005). *Critical events in psychotherapy supervision: An interpersonal approach*. Washington, DC: American Psychological Association. doi:10.1037/10958-000

Levenson, H. (2003). Time-limited dynamic psychotherapy: An integrationist perspective. *Journal of Psychotherapy Integration*, *13*, 300–333. doi:10.1037/1053-0479.13.3-4.300

Strupp, H. H. (1986). Psychotherapy: Research, practice, and public policy. How to avoid dead ends. *American Psychologist*, *41*, 120–130. doi:10.1037/0003-066X.41.2.120

Teyber, E. (2006). *Interpersonal process in therapy: An integrative method* (5th ed.). Belmont, CA: Brooks/Cole.

Williams, E. N., & Morrow, S. L. (2009). Achieving trustworthiness in qualitative research: A pan-paradigmatic perspective. *Psychotherapy Research*, *19*, 576–582. doi:10.1080/10503300802702113

III

CONCLUSIONS

17

CORRECTIVE EXPERIENCES IN PSYCHOTHERAPY: DEFINITIONS, PROCESSES, CONSEQUENCES, AND RESEARCH DIRECTIONS

CLARA E. HILL, LOUIS G. CASTONGUAY, BARRY A. FARBER,
SARAH KNOX, WILLIAM B. STILES, TIMOTHY ANDERSON,
LYNNE E. ANGUS, JACQUES P. BARBER, J. GAYLE BECK,
ARTHUR C. BOHART, FRANZ CASPAR, MICHAEL J. CONSTANTINO,
ROBERT ELLIOTT, MYRNA L. FRIEDLANDER, MARVIN R. GOLDFRIED,
LESLIE S. GREENBERG, MARTIN GROSSE HOLTFORTH,
ADELE M. HAYES, JEFFREY A. HAYES, LAURIE HEATHERINGTON,
NICHOLAS LADANY, KENNETH N. LEVY, STANLEY B. MESSER,
J. CHRISTOPHER MURAN, MICHELLE G. NEWMAN,
JEREMY D. SAFRAN, AND BRIAN A. SHARPLESS

After 5 years of conceptualizing, investigating, and writing about corrective experiences (CEs), we (the authors of this chapter) met to talk about what we learned. In this chapter, we summarize our joint understanding of (a) the definition of CEs; (b) the contexts in which CEs occur; (c) client, therapist, and external factors that facilitate CEs; (d) the consequences of CEs; and (e) ideas for future theoretical, clinical, empirical, and training directions. As will become evident, the authors of this chapter, who represent a range of theoretical orientations, reached consensus on some CE-related topics but encountered controversy and lively debate about other topics.

WHAT ARE CORRECTIVE EXPERIENCES?

Although we based our discussions, as well as the chapters in this book, on the definition presented in Chapter 1, additional thoughts emerged from considering and investigating this construct. Currently, we understand CEs in psychotherapy to involve a disconfirmation of a client's conscious or unconscious expectations (see Chapters 3 and 4) as well as an emotional, interpersonal, cognitive, and/or behavioral shift. In CEs, clients typically reencounter previously unresolved conflicts (see the Alexander & French, 1946, definition) or previously feared situations (whether internal or external) but reach a new outcome in terms of their own responses, the reactions of others, or new ways of interacting with others.

Despite consensus on this broad definition of CEs, we debated the details. Some authors argued that the correction needs to include new behaviors, whereas others argued that the correction may consist solely of new internal experiences. We finally agreed to distinguish two types of CEs. *Type 1 CEs* are new or unexpected thoughts, emotions, sensations, behaviors, or feelings about one's self that result from the client encountering an event that is different from (and thus disconfirming of) his or her frame of reference. In Chapter 10, for example, Heatherington et al. reported that 30% to 40% of clients identified this type of "new experiential awareness" as a salient change event. In such events, it could be that the client behaves as he or she always has but the therapist responds differently than have other influential people in the client's life, which leads the client to experience differently, and perhaps reevaluate, self and/or others. Relatedly, Farber, Bohart, and Stiles, in Chapter 7, noted that Gloria (in the *Three Approaches to Psychotherapy* videos; Shostrom, 1965) appeared to feel close to Carl Rogers when she disclosed that she would have welcomed him as her father. He responded that she "would make a pretty good daughter." This moment seemed very meaningful for Gloria, disconfirming her expectations of men.

In *Type 2 CEs*, the client actively does something different in situations that typically have triggered apprehension and negative emotion, leading to a new outcome. In support of this type of CE, Heatherington et al. (Chapter 10) reported that 41% to 48% of clients undergoing primarily cognitive behavior therapy (CBT) and combined CBT and integrative therapy identified a change in behavior as a significant shift event. Although both CE subtypes involve outcomes that challenge previously negative expectations, Type 2 CEs involve clients taking action and trying out new behaviors outside of the therapeutic relationship. Type 2 CEs can occur with others outside of therapy and can involve situations in which individuals face their fears (e.g., in exposure) and learn that nothing bad happens. They learn that they can handle the feared situation and are thus more likely to approach such situations in the future.

The two types of CEs can certainly be interrelated. Type 1 CEs may have a motivating effect that allows clients to try out new behaviors, as the therapist's reactions result in a greater sense of trust. In an analogous manner, the ongoing experiencing of Type 2 CEs, either repeated in a single context or across a broad range of interpersonal relationships, may catalyze significant emotional or cognitive shifts. Behaving differently thus disconfirms a client's previously held negative expectations of self and others. This disconfirmation of negative self–other expectations, as well as positive shifts in emotion and self-concept, contributes to what is corrective in a CE event. In short, CEs can lead to behavioral changes, and behavioral changes can lead to significant shifts in cognition and emotion.

We also discussed the potency of CEs. Whereas the classic characterization views CEs as sudden and immediately life changing, some of us thought that CEs result in lasting change only if repeated or only if one CE leads to other CEs in a synergistic way. For example, an in-session CE may be followed by the client trying out new behaviors outside the session, which then might result in another CE, and so forth, promoting an eventual consolidation of changes (e.g., the case presented by Berman et al. in Chapter 12, in which "Kate" became progressively more assertive in confronting relationship issues). There may thus be a tipping point at which CEs result in lasting change.

Some of us were also mindful that the change evoked through CEs is not always linear, given that clients often take one step back after taking two steps forward. As Caspar and Berger noted in Chapter 9, clients have a tendency to return to familiar ways of reacting and behaving, which impedes change and requires therapists to recreate favorable conditions under which clients can again seek to tolerate previously intolerable experiences. Therapists often have to follow up and help clients identify the personal impacts and meanings of their CE experiences to help them consolidate their gains and articulate or solidify their new views of self (Chapter 2, by Goldfried), which could increase their hopes and expectations for positive future outcomes (White, 2007).

We did not reach consensus as to whether a CE is a discrete event or an accretion based on an overall therapeutic relationship. Some empirical evidence that a majority of CEs are discrete events comes from Anderson, Ogles, Heckman, and MacFarlane (Chapter 14), who found that 14 of 21 (66%) clients identified a CE that was a discrete enough event that it could be located in a session (or in a distinct moment if it occurred outside of therapy). Castonguay et al. (Chapter 13) also identified four specific CE events, two in each of the treatments (CBT and interpersonal–emotional processing) conducted by the same therapist with the same client. In contrast, Knox et al. (Chapter 11) found several events that were very broad and transpired across multiple sessions (with one taking place over 2 years).

We also debated how to distinguish CEs from insight or awareness. Many of us believed that insight can precede, be part of, or follow CEs but that there could also be CEs without awareness or insight into the new reactions to previously feared or apprehended situations. Similarly, we debated and then concluded that CEs could be an outcome of therapy, a mechanism of change leading to an outcome, or simply the process of successful treatment, such that good therapy is a succession of CEs.

Thus, although we reached some shared understanding of the nature of CEs, we by no means came to a clear consensus, reflecting the complexity of this construct and the heterogeneity of our theoretical perspectives. For the remainder of this chapter, however, we continue to define CEs as events or experiences that are unexpected and result in a major shift of some kind.

IN WHAT CONTEXTS DO CORRECTIVE EXPERIENCES OCCUR?

We agreed that for CEs to occur, there generally needs to be a well-established therapeutic alliance that provides safety and trust. At times, a positive alliance is established rapidly, and CEs occur even during the first therapy session; at other times, they may take longer to happen. There may even be instances in which a CE occurs in the context of an initially poor alliance and then facilitates the development of a better alliance (see Christian, Safran, & Muran, Chapter 4). In addition, most of us believe that CEs also occur in contexts other than the therapeutic relationship. For example, CEs often occur in relationships with friends, family, and significant others, and sometimes people can have CEs based on their own internal experiences.

WHICH CLIENT FACTORS CONTRIBUTE TO CORRECTIVE EXPERIENCES?

Berman et al., in Chapter 12, provided evidence that three different clients seen by the same therapist had very different amounts and types of CEs. This finding suggests that client variables need to be considered when we think about CEs.

We all strongly believed that clients are active agents in the generation of CEs. Therapists may set the stage for CEs (by providing the facilitative conditions, challenging, interpreting, providing necessary information), but they do not provide the experiential changes associated with a CE. Clients must be motivated to change; willing to face difficult situations; and willing to take risks to overcome avoidance, ambivalence, or reluctance. In addition, clients must be actively engaged in the therapeutic interaction; attend to their own and their therapist's reactions; and be willing to learn and practice new, more adaptive responses to previously avoided experiences. Of course, clients' active involvement in activities outside of sessions could also promote CEs and help them apply what they learned in therapy to their lives.

Some of us also thought that for CEs to take place, clients' fears, expectations, and maladaptive emotional responses must be activated and challenged in some way. Such a process is often associated with a period of disjunction, turbulence, anxiety, or other negative emotions (see Hayes, Beck, & Yasinski, Chapter 5; and Caspar & Berger, Chapter 9). The turbulence could arise either inside or outside of session, setting the stage for the occurrence of a CE. On the other hand, the level of arousal should probably not be too high, so as not to exceed what clients can currently tolerate. Relatedly, some authors argued that clients' awareness of, and insight related to, their maladaptive expectations, emotions, and/or patterns of reacting could facilitate their willingness to take risks and engage in new and corrective experiences.

We debated how much clients must verbalize and overtly make sense of CEs (including CEs that happen outside of sessions) for such experiences to have lasting impact. As mentioned earlier, we speculated that some CEs happen outside of client awareness (as in latent learning) and yet could still be manifested through behavioral change. This reasoning suggests that some CEs may become fodder for therapy discussions, whereas others may not, yet both types potentially can be therapeutic for clients.

WHICH THERAPIST VARIABLES SET THE STAGE FOR CORRECTIVE EXPERIENCES?

Therapists can set the stage for CEs by providing facilitative conditions (e.g., acceptance, empathy, genuineness, openness, willingness to engage with the client) and by implementing specific interventions (e.g., reflections of feeling, self-disclosure, support, normalizing fears, reinforcing change, two-chair role plays, educating clients about the therapy process and their contribution to their difficulties, interpretation, immediacy, exposure exercises, modeling, skill training, cognitive restructuring). We all agreed, however, that there are no particular therapist behaviors that inevitably lead to CEs.

Some authors thought that CEs are particularly likely to occur when the therapist takes a risk to do something unusual, bold, or perhaps even benevolently shocking, such as using reframing interventions or giving personal disclosures that convey emotionally immediate and empathic attunement to the client's present need (e.g., when the therapist said "Let me" to a client when she wanted the therapist to take care of her; Knox et al., Chapter 11). In contrast, some authors argued that therapists might facilitate a CE simply by being different from important others in clients' lives or by behaving differently from what clients expect (e.g., using supportive rather than con-frontational interventions early in treatment). Similarly, the CE taxonomy presented by Anderson et al. in Chapter 14 included categories of CEs prompted externally by dramatic therapist behaviors or by therapists who, in a variety of more benign behaviors, facilitated the unfolding of the client's internal discovery. Whether by using disarming interventions or by enacting a general way of being and relating, therapists may introduce a sense of uncertainty, dissonance, or the unexpected, and thus foster CEs. The overarching notion, then, is that therapists pose an alternative, a disconfirmation, a challenge, or an unexpected frame of reference to the client's personal understanding of self and other that within the context of the healing therapy relationship enables the client to change to resolve the dissonance.

In addition, some authors emphasized the importance of therapist persistence. Because CEs require that clients face a situation from which they expect a painful and/or threatening outcome, resistance or defensiveness is to be expected. Thus, therapists need not retreat from clients' initial hesitance. Extremely important, however, is that therapists show tact and timing, remaining responsive and attuned to the client's immediate needs. To paraphrase Geller (2005), *therapeutic tact* is the capacity to tell clients something they do not want to hear in a manner in which they can hear it. Sometimes the combination of therapist persistence, tact, and attunement can also lead clients to recognize and voice maladaptive patterns that they have perpetuated out of fear; if such client recognition is acknowledged with support and empathy by the therapist, that in and of itself can be a powerful and potentially corrective experience. This effect was illustrated by Castonguay et al. in Chapter 13 when a therapist noted the impact of the client's repeated refusal to answer the therapist's questions. This challenge led the client to acknowledge that his controlling of the content and quality of what he revealed in therapy ("smoke screening") was his way of avoiding being criticized by the therapist. Compassionate persistence on the therapist's part was needed to help the client begin to approach a painful topic.

We also agreed that therapists need to responsively tailor their interventions to the client's needs, which may change over the course of therapy or even within a specific episode during treatment. For example, therapists may need to understand and validate a client's negative expectations before attempting to disconfirm these expectations (Constantino & Westra, Chapter 8). A therapist might, for instance, see potential in a client and be optimistic about treatment, but such hope may not necessarily resonate with the client; the therapist's positive view of the client might be too discrepant with the client's view of self, leading the client to refute, distort, and misinterpret the therapist's message. As suggested above, then, it may be that only after the client feels validated and understood that the therapist can be experienced as credible enough to provide a meaningful foundation for the occurrence of a CE.

HOW DO EXTERNAL FACTORS CONTRIBUTE
TO CORRECTIVE EXPERIENCES?

We discussed the role of support networks in enabling clients to engage in and/or make use of CEs. Some authors thought, for instance, that the attachment to and support from significant others could be facilitative. In addition, for clients who lack good interpersonal relationships, a CE that involves changing maladaptive ways of being with and relating to others may help the client obtain a more adaptive social network.

External factors might also, however, restrict clients from making full use of CEs. For example, a client may have a CE in a treatment session but might not have the opportunity to generalize, elaborate, or consolidate the CE outside therapy. In addition, family structure, cultural traditions, and economic considerations may all impede the full realization of CEs (e.g., significant others might actively oppose the change or tacitly sabotage it). Thus, the input of others might undermine the therapist's input, and unless these powerful influences are addressed, the client's typical ways of relating to and experiencing self and other might remain intact despite the therapist's best efforts. Such stagnation may be particularly likely for clients whose difficulties are situated within the context of a strongly entrenched family system. From the perspective of the models proposed by Caspar and Berger in Chapter 9, the environment has a crucial impact on the chance that new patterns will have a lasting corrective effect.

On the other hand, some of us have observed that CEs in therapy often interact positively with clients' external life events or relationships with important others. For example, a CE involving greater awareness of primary emotions, such as sadness, love, or curiosity, can help a client open up to previously overlooked possibilities for deeper, more authentic relationships offered by significant others (Greenberg & Elliott, Chapter 6). Similarly, others may react positively to and thus reinforce tentative signs of client change emerging out of CEs. Indeed, Heatherington et al. (Chapter 10) found that clients spontaneously described external contributors to CEs about 5% of the time.

WHAT ARE THE CONSEQUENCES OF CORRECTIVE EXPERIENCES?

We had fairly good consensus that the changes that clients make as a result of CEs include the full range of changes seen in successful therapy. One way of summarizing such changes is to note that clients often move from a position of being (a) unconsciously incompetent to (b) consciously incompetent to (c) consciously competent to (d) unconsciously competent

(Bateson, 1973; see also Goldfried, Chapter 2, this volume). Similarly, Caspar and Berger, in Chapter 9, proposed that the change process involves a deautomatization, followed by an increased awareness and conscious functioning, and then a reautomatization in a more adaptive way.

Many CE-related changes are intrapersonal. Some of these changes are immediate, such as a client gaining a sense of relief or acquiring sudden insight. Yet CEs may also lead to more gradual internal changes, such as greater self-control, increased sense of agency and choice, increased willingness to take risks, empowerment, and hopefulness. These changes may involve acceptance (e.g., when circumstances cannot be changed or one cannot repair a relationship). Such acceptance could correct the client's illusion that the world inevitably thwarts what he or she seeks, that a person can be happy all of the time (i.e., never feel anxious or sad), or that a person can have complete control over his or her life. There are also likely to be longer term intrapersonal changes, such as symptom reduction, especially when reduction of anxiety and avoidance occur after CEs. A new view of self, increased cognitive and emotional flexibility, and personality change may also emerge. As part of such longer term changes, clients may learn to tolerate mistakes and accept that not only do they not need to be perfect but that life itself is inherently imperfect. They may also allow themselves to experience previously disavowed affects, have greater tolerance of unacceptable thoughts, be more able to self-soothe, and accept themselves in appropriate ways (Greenberg & Elliott, Chapter 6; and Farber et al., Chapter 7).

Another set of consequences associated with CEs involves positive changes in the therapeutic relationship and therapy process. CEs may lead to increased client confidence in the therapeutic relationship and a deepening of the bond and greater intimacy, which then allow the therapist and client to work together in more profound ways. In addition, CEs may lower client anxiety and heighten client self-efficacy in session, which may enhance the client's willingness to disclose and communicate, as well as decrease the likelihood of terminating prematurely.

Relatedly, client CEs may affect the therapist by providing a better understanding of the client's internal world and interactions with others (Sharpless & Barber, Chapter 3). In addition, CEs can help the therapist become more responsive to clients, better identify and process client maladaptive patterns, and more effectively teach and/or reinforce adaptive patterns of client behavior. Furthermore, the awareness of a client's CE may feel personally and professionally affirming, providing a powerful reinforcer of the therapist's efforts.

In addition, CEs can lead to adaptive client changes in relationships with others. Clients may modify their expectations of others and revise their self–other models, enabling them to be more adaptive and flexible in relationships, which may increase the likelihood that others will respond to them in ways that reinforce these new behaviors. CEs might also afford clients an improved ability to receive and initiate a range of relationship overtures without a significant threat to self. And, for clients who are therapists-in-training, CEs may help them empathize more and be more able to facilitate CEs in their role as therapists with their own clients.

With regard to long-term consequences of CEs, we believed that CEs can build on each other but that it may take a while for a client to have the opportunity (or the willingness) to make use of a CE. Furthermore, small or preliminary experiences that are inconsistent with previous ways of reacting to threatening or difficult events can set the stage for later and more dramatic, explicit, and enduring shifts in being or relating with others. Conversely, CEs may fade if clients do not use and elaborate upon them. Even emotionally powerful epiphanies tend not to be lasting unless they are consolidated. In addition, for CEs to be consolidated or generalized, not only do clients have to react differently (cognitively, emotionally, and/or behaviorally), but others (including the therapist) may need to consistently respond differently to clients' new behaviors, and clients may need to realize that others have indeed changed in how they respond.

IMPLICATIONS FOR DEFINITION, RESEARCH, PRACTICE, AND TRAINING

Implications for the Definition of Corrective Experiences

The chapters in this book represent a considerable range of alternative conceptualizations of CEs. Unsurprisingly, then, our discussions left us with many questions regarding the definition and theoretical understanding of CEs. For example, how do CEs differ from insight, perceived helpfulness, good therapy, or mastery? Are most CEs observable, or do many of them develop more covertly over time? What is the threshold for considering an event to be a CE? That is, when does an in-session event rise to the level of a CE? What intensity is needed to be considered a CE? What are the necessary components of CEs, and do these differ for Type 1 CEs (resulting from encountering an event that disconfirms one's expectations or fears) and Type 2 CEs (resulting from doing something that disconfirms one's expectations or fears)? In other words, what are the outer boundaries of CEs?

We also wondered about good-enough moments that might produce CEs, when CEs may generalize to life outside of therapy, and what maintains a CE or makes it enduring. Is affect needed for a CE to occur or endure? How might CEs occur differently in diverse therapeutic orientations (e.g., psychodynamic, cognitive–behavioral, experiential) or different modalities (e.g., group therapy, conjoint family therapy, child therapy)? Can we predict when CEs will occur? How does the therapeutic relationship interact with CEs? Do CEs need to occur rarely to have power, or can "good therapy" simply be understood as a continuous CE?

Ladany et al., in Chapter 16, offered perspectives on how CEs are manifested within the supervisory process. It is interesting to note that many of the aforementioned process variables identified (e.g., members in the dyad, outcomes) were evident in the supervision CEs, although the content of CEs in supervision seemed different from those in therapy. Hence, further exploration of how CEs differ in psychotherapy and supervision is warranted.

Implications for Research on Training

Methodological Challenges

A major methodological issue is the perspective from which the data are gathered. Would we obtain different results if CEs were assessed by clients, therapists, and observers? It was also suggested that when we ask clients about CEs could make a difference (i.e., the longer after the event the questioning occurs, the more likely that the client's memory would be a reconstruction of events rather than a recall of the experience).

Several of us conducted studies in which clients were asked about their CEs; however, specific procedures varied across studies, so results also likewise varied. For example, Heatherington et al. (Chapter 10) used an open-ended self-report questionnaire to ask clients the following:

> Have there been any times since you started the present therapy that you have become aware of an important or meaningful change (or changes) in your thinking, feeling, behavior, or relationships? . . . If yes, what do you believe took place during or between your therapy sessions that led to such change (or changes)?

In contrast, Knox et al., in Chapter 11, used a semistructured interview to ask clients to reflect retrospectively about CEs after therapy was over; similarly, in Chapter 16, Ladany et al. used a semistructured interview to ask supervisees about their experiences of CEs in supervision. In Chapter 14, Anderson et al. combined these methods by interviewing clients posttherapy and then having judges search through sessions to find the CEs. Finally, Berman et al. and Castonguay et al. (Chapters 12 and 13, respectively) had observers examine sessions to identify and analyze CE or corrective relational experiences.

Obviously, these different methods yield different types of results. We acknowledged the possible impact of differing demand characteristics posed by the study questions and procedures and noted that simply asking about CEs may bring them into awareness for clients in a way that might not otherwise occur. At the same time, we wondered to what extent the researchers' and the clients' understanding of the term CE was similar.

We also wondered whether the best way to investigate CEs is by having trained judges observe live or videotaped sessions. Farber et al. (Chapter 7) suggested that one could tell that Gloria had a CE by a change in her eyes and tears welling up, but we cannot count on similar evidence arising across all clients. Furthermore, trained judges may not be able to observe all the CEs that take place in the treatments and are undoubtedly biased by their own personal reactions as to what a CE would be like for them.

One suggestion to address some of these methodological concerns was to use interpersonal process recall (Kagan, 1975) or brief structured recall (Elliott & Shapiro, 1988) to help clients describe what occurred for them at the time of the CE. Thus, for example, researchers could use the Helpful Aspects of Therapy Form (Llewelyn, 1988) to identify sessions in which CEs are likely to have happened and then interview clients and therapists using interpersonal process recall about the CE precipitants and consequences. As one possible multiperspective design, researchers could videotape sessions and have clients observe the video and recall their CE-related experiences, have trained judges code those events, and have therapists recall them as well. Likewise, researchers could use consensual qualitative research for cases (Jackson, Chui, & Hill, 2012) to analyze the richness of event-based data. Task analysis (see Greenberg, 2007) is also likely to be a good approach for developing, refining, and testing theories about the developmental process of CEs. In addition, observer-based coding systems that explicitly focus on the emergence of unexpected outcome narratives (White, 2007) in videotaped therapy sessions (Boritz, Angus, & Bryntwick, 2010; Gonçalves, Matos, & Santos, 2009) might also provide a promising research strategy for identifying what contributes to CEs.

Research Ideas

The following listing describes a few of the many research ideas we generated.

1. Researchers could assess whether hope is both a crucial indicator and an outcome of CEs.
2. Researchers could assess to what extent CEs relate to therapy outcome. For example, are CEs necessary and sufficient for change or improvement at termination and follow-up evaluations? What is the relative contribution of singular CEs, the number of CEs, and the timing of CEs in predicting outcome?

What are the mechanisms or pathways by which CEs lead to positive outcomes?

3. Rates of occurrence of Type 1 CEs versus Type 2 CEs could be compared, along with any differences in impact over time. Researchers could also compare rates of Type 1 and Type 2 CEs in different theoretical approaches to therapy. Do Type 1 and Type 2 CEs build on one another in a continuous and linear fashion? Do clients develop a new view of self and others as a consequence of experiencing either a Type 1 or Type 2 CE in therapy?

4. Are there other types of CEs? Can these types be distinguished empirically?

5. Researchers could assess the relationship between insight and CEs.

6. The sequence of steps leading to CEs could be examined to construct models of the process of CEs. Researchers could investigate which client and therapist characteristics are most predictive of CEs, as well as whether there are interactions among client, therapist, technique, and relationship variables that foster CEs (i.e., aptitude–treatment interactions).

7. Researchers could interview people who had successful therapy but who identify no CEs to determine what occurred in therapy that was helpful in the absence of CEs.

8. Researchers could test the assumption that CEs must involve new and unexpected reactions, perhaps by having judges observe nonverbal or verbal indicators of surprise as markers (e.g., "feels strange") or through client reports of surprise or newness.

9. Researchers could examine the relationship of the occurrence of CEs inside and outside of sessions. The nature, frequency, and impact of CEs occurring inside and outside therapy settings could be compared.

10. The effects of clients' CEs on friends and family members could be studied.

11. Researchers could investigate the impact of discussing CEs. Do clients need to explicitly process CEs to consolidate them? Are there individual differences in the impact of focusing attention on CEs? For example, some clients may feel that the therapist is taking the experience away if CEs are discussed too much, whereas other clients may need to process CEs to consolidate them or to help them happen again.

12. Researchers could search for a tipping point in the accumulation of CEs: How many CEs are needed, and does subtype

matter (Type 1 and/or Type 2)? Do CEs involving a small accretion or a "big bang" have different effects (see Chapter 15)?

13. Researchers could look for associations between CEs and other productive process variables, such as good moments (Mahrer, Dessaulles, Nadler, Gervaize, & Sterner, 1987), helpful significant events (Elliott, 2010), innovative moments (Gonçalves et al., 2009), unexpected outcome stories (Angus & Greenberg, 2011), rupture resolution (Safran & Muran, 1996), or relational depth events (Wiggins, Elliott, & Cooper, in press). Findings would provide evidence of construct validity for CEs.

Implications for Practice

Therapists across many approaches view CEs as desirable events to be encouraged or facilitated. Not all of the consequences of CEs, however, are positive, and thus therapists need to be aware that they may need to help clients manage the powerful experiences evoked by CEs.

Furthermore, the notion that CEs are client experiences that are often cocreated by the client and therapist has implications for practice. Given that these events are not something a therapist does to a client (i.e., metaphorically, therapists are midwives of CEs, not surgeons), the therapist works to set a favorable atmosphere in which CEs might take hold. The therapist's objective is thus to create favorable conditions (e.g., a safe relationship, implementation of specific techniques) for effective work to take place, and then to validate and encourage the client to grow and change. In such fertile soil, CEs may grow.

Once these favorable conditions are in place, however, there may still be times when the therapist needs to intervene to destabilize the client in order to facilitate the occurrence of CEs. How might this be done? Therapists might, for instance, facilitate CEs by providing clients with a rationale for intervening in a way that may be incongruent with the client's expectation for how people typically react to him or her. Furthermore, it may be useful to process CEs with clients (Hill & Knox, 2009).

Some of us thought it would be useful to develop manuals for facilitating CEs, although more research is certainly needed before doing so. Such manuals would describe the facilitative conditions and processes that nurture CEs. For example, specific CE-fostering interventions could be delineated and integrated into treatment manuals for different approaches with different types of clients. Of course, we acknowledge that such manuals involve generalizing and the uniqueness of CEs may well argue against such generalization.

Implications for Training

A good first step in teaching beginning therapists about CEs is to ask them to reflect on moments in their own experiences, whether as clients in therapy or in their lives outside of therapy, when they felt that something significant, even momentous, occurred for them. They could then try to reconstruct the antecedents and consequences of these CEs, including their own and their therapists' feelings, thoughts, and behaviors. It might also be helpful for trainees to remember or imagine not only in-session changes but also whether these identified CEs had intrapersonal or interpersonal ramifications outside the therapy room. It is important, too, that trainees could be asked to consider whether their experiences of CEs led to a desire or need for more CEs, or alternatively, the feeling that therapy has reached a desired consequence and that termination should now be considered. Trainees who have never experienced CEs might think about whether they are in some way envious of those who have had such experiences. An inspirational short story on this theme of envying those who have had CEs is Friedman's (1997) "Mr. Prinzo's Breakthrough."

A good follow-up exercise would be for students to learn to identify CEs, perhaps by viewing tapes of expert therapists (e.g., the American Psychological Association series of psychotherapy sessions; http://www.apa.org/pubs/videos/about-videos.aspx) or therapists in commercial movies (e.g., *Good Will Hunting*, *Ordinary People*). It is important, as part of such exercises, to emphasize to students that CEs typically occur organically in the context of good-enough conditions rather than being engineered or manipulated.

Reading about and watching videos of CEs may help students learn about CEs, but experiential learning (including role-playing attempts at facilitating CEs) is likely to be of even greater value. In this regard, we thought that students' knowledge of therapeutic CEs would be enhanced by having them compare such experiences with those of CEs that might happen outside of therapeutic settings. Included, for example, might be CEs that occur during the course of friendships and other intimate relationships or while listening to music or engaging in some artistic or spiritual activity.

Another key point related to training is that trainees need to learn to tolerate the client's potential strong reactions before, during, and after significant CEs. The therapist's ability to tolerate clients' uncertainty and distressing reactions may help clients stay with their new emerging experiences. Conversely, we thought that trainees also need to understand and accept that not all clients experience CEs, that not all effective therapies include CEs, and thus that trainees are not failing in their role if their clients do not experience CEs.

An additional way in which trainees might learn about CEs is through experiencing CEs in the context of supervision (Ladany et al., Chapter 16). In this case, the supervisor becomes a model of how one can facilitate a CE.

The trainee, in turn, learns how a CE may be experienced and can benefit a client. Making this learning explicit could help trainees understand the CE process more deeply. Similarly, and hopefully, trainees also themselves experience CEs in their role as supervisees and therapists. In this regard, Stahl et al. (2009) explored how therapists experience significant and dramatic learning from interactions with their clients.

Another CE-based possibility for training is simply to suggest that trainees monitor their clients' CEs by asking about them in session (see also Hill & Knox, 2009). Therapists could also ask clients to complete postsession questionnaires such as those used in the study discussed by Heatherington et al. in Chapter 10, thus raising trainees' awareness and appreciation of the CE phenomenon.

A final point is that training in case conceptualization is vital. Trainees need to be able to formulate good case conceptualizations, so that they can understand how a CE would be useful for the client and are able to recognize what facilitates and prevents the clients in having CEs.

CONCLUSION

In sum, there has been a broad consensus across therapists and therapy researchers of different theoretical orientations and generations that CEs are a central part of the therapy change process. At the same time, it is clear that much work remains to be done to better understand CEs. Although more than 60 years have passed since Alexander and French (1946) proposed CEs as a key change process in psychoanalysis and psychotherapy, this construct has failed to receive detailed conceptual and empirical scrutiny. We hope that we have sparked the imagination and curiosity of psychotherapy researchers and scholars to build on what we have examined here, and we urge them to continue these efforts to enhance our understanding and appreciation of CEs.

REFERENCES

Angus, L. E., & Greenberg, L. S. (2011). *Working with narrative in emotion-focused therapy: Changing stories, healing lives.* Washington, DC: American Psychological Association. doi:10.1037/12325-000

Alexander, F., & French, F. (1946). *Psychoanalytic therapy: Principles and application.* New York, NY: Ronald Press.

Bateson, G. (1973). *Steps to an ecology of mind: Collected essays in anthropology, psychiatry, evolution, and epistemology.* London, England: Paladin, Granada.

Boritz, T., Angus, L., & Bryntwick, E. (2010, June). *Development of the Narrative and Emotion Processes Integration Scale.* Paper presented at the annual meeting of the Society for Psychotherapy Research, Asilomar, CA.

Elliott, R. (2010). Psychotherapy change process research: Realizing the promise. *Psychotherapy Research, 20,* 123–135. doi:10.1080/10503300903470743

Elliott, R., & Shapiro, D. A. (1988). Brief structured recall: A more efficient method for identifying and describing significant therapy events. *The British Journal of Medical Psychology, 61,* 141–153. doi:10.1111/j.2044-8341.1988.tb02773.x

Friedman, B. J. (1997). Mr. Prinzo's breakthrough. In B. J. Friedman (Ed.), *The collected short fiction of Bruce Jay Friedman* (pp. 198–208). New York, NY: Grove.

Geller, J. D. (2005). Style and its contributions to a patient-specific model of therapeutic technique. *Psychotherapy: Theory, Research, & Practice, 42,* 469–482. doi:10.1037/0033-3204.42.4.469

Gonçalves, M. M., Matos, M., & Santos, A. (2009). Narrative therapy and the nature of "innovative moments" in the construction of change. *Journal of Constructivist Psychology, 22,* 1–23. doi:10.1080/10720530802500748

Greenberg, L. S. (2007). A guide to conducting a task analysis of psychotherapeutic change. *Psychotherapy Research, 17,* 15–30. doi:10.1080/10503300600720390

Hill, C. E., & Knox, S. (2009). Processing the therapeutic relationship. *Psychotherapy Research, 19,* 13–29. doi:10.1080/10503300802621206

Jackson, J., Chui, H., & Hill, C. E. (2011). The modification of CQR for case study research: An introduction to CQR-C. In C. E. Hill (Ed.), *Consensual qualitative research: A practical resource for investigating social science phenomena* (pp. 285–303). Washington, DC: American Psychological Association.

Kagan, N. (1975). *Interpersonal process recall: A method of influencing human interaction.* Houston, TX: University of Houston.

Llewelyn, S. (1988). Psychological therapy as viewed by clients and therapists. *British Journal of Clinical Psychology, 27,* 223–237. doi:10.1111/j.2044-8260.1988.tb00779.x

Mahrer, A. R., Dessaulles, A., Nadler, W. P., Gervaize, P. A., & Sterner, I. (1987). Good and very good moments in psychotherapy: Content, distribution, and facilitation. *Psychotherapy: Theory, Research, & Practice, 24,* 7–14. doi:10.1037/h0085693

Safran, J. D., & Muran, J. C. (1996). The resolution of ruptures in the therapeutic alliance. *Journal of Consulting and Clinical Psychology, 64,* 447–458. doi:10.1037/0022-006X.64.3.447

Shostrom, E. L. (Producer). (1965). *Three approaches to psychotherapy* [Film]. Orange, CA: Psychological Films.

Stahl, J. V., Hill, C. E., Jacobs, T., Kleinman, S., Isenberg, D., & Stern, A. (2009). When the shoe is on the other foot: A qualitative study of intern-level trainees' perceived learning from clients. *Psychotherapy: Theory, Research, & Practice, 46,* 376–389. doi:10.1037/a0017000

White, M. (2007). *Maps of narrative practice.* New York, NY: Norton.

Wiggins, S., Elliott, R., & Cooper, M. (in press). The prevalence and characteristics of relational depth events in psychotherapy. *Psychotherapy Research.*

INDEX

Beneficial uncertainty, 130
Berger, T., 142
Bernier, A., 132
Bern Post-Session Report for patients
    (BPSR-P), 321–322, 329
Between-sessions experiences
    corrective, 44, 357
    and in-session experience, 261
    instigations in, 27
    positive experiences in, 21
    relational enactments, 296–297
    self-directed, 297–298
Bibring, E., 35
"Big bang" trajectory, 317–318, 320
Blake, E., 163
Blocking, 108
Blum, H. P., 54
Bodily experiences, 87–88, 96
Body mass index (BMI), 218n1
Bohart, A. C., 113
Bordin, E. S., 347
BPSR-P (Bern Post-Session Report for
    patients), 321–322, 329
Brady, J. P., 15
Brain structures, 142
Branigan, C., 92
Bridges of meaning, 113–115
Brumbaugh, C. C., 220
Bunge, M., 152

Carver, C. S., 148–151
Caspar, F., 142
Castonguay, L. G., 3–4, 27, 72, 135
CBT. *See* Cognitive behavior therapy
CE. *See* Corrective experience
CEE. *See* Corrective emotional
    experience
Chamodraka, M., 163
Chance, 45–46
Change. *See also* Therapeutic change
    acceptance of, 362
    ambivalence about, 132–133
    big bang trajectory of, 320
    client concerns about, 127
    client perspectives on, 180–181
    coding of, 171–175
    consistency theory of, 318–318
    corrective emotional experiences
        in, 89

emotions in, 92–93
exposure techniques for, 70–72,
    74–78
indicators of, 323–325
influences on, 147
and in-session experiences, 116–117
lasting, 154–155
as learning process, 330
of patterns, 78–79
positive interpersonal, 46
preparation for, 71–72
principles of, 245, 281
process of, 72–75, 146–147, 328–330
range of, 361–362
in self-concept, 133
in therapeutic relationship, 182, 362
in Type 2 corrective experiences,
    356–357
Change mechanisms, 317–330
    big bang trajectory, 320
    in consistency theory, 318–318
    constant dripping trajectory, 320
    over course of psychotherapy,
        320–326
    in psychoanalytic literature, 31–32
    results from study of, 326–330
Characteristics, personality, 275
Chicago Institute for Psychoanalysis, 52
Cislo, D., 162
Clarification
    and mastery, 328–329
    motivational, 318–319
    and positive outcome, 327
    trajectories of, 323–325
Client(s). *See also* Client perspectives
        on corrective experience study;
        Client perspectives on corrective
        relational experiences study
    actions of, 200, 358
    context of, 313–315
    emotional discoveries made by,
        293–296, 302–307
    expectations of, 43, 122–123
    in facilitation of corrective emo-
        tional experience, 274–275
    in facilitation of corrective
        experience, 44
    frame of reference of, 128–129
    increasing awareness in, 20

Cognitive behavior therapy, *continued*
and interpersonal–emotional
processing therapies,
277–278
and new awareness in client,
183–184, 187–188
in qualitative analyses, 249–251
relational exploration in, 241, 242
relationship variables with, 275–276
and therapist relationships skills,
273–274
Type 2 corrective experiences in,
356
Cognitive–emotional–behavioral
patterns, 17–18
Cognitive–emotional functioning
models, 141–152
combined regulation, 147–152
connectionist, 142–147
Cognitive–emotional processing, 73, 80
Cognitive models, 141–142
Cognitive therapy (CT), 134
Cohen, J. N., 206
Collective cultural unconscious, 313
Combined regulation models, 147–152
Community mental health clinic
(CMHC), 165, 168
Competence
conscious, 18, 151
patterns of, 144
therapist level of, 45
unconscious, 18, 26, 151
Complementarity, 135
Complementary responses, 131
"Complexia," 298–302
Compliance, 274–275
Comprehensive process analysis (CPA),
248–249, 251
Conceptualizations
in anorexia nervosa case studies,
229–237
of corrective emotional experience,
40, 42–43
of corrective experience, 363–364
of psychotherapy, 19
of relational events, 226–237
Conditions of worth, 105–106, 114–115
Conference on the Process of Change,
125, 164

Conflict
in acceptance and commitment
therapy, 217
in corrective experience, 103
repetition of, 34
schemas of, 150–151, 154
in therapeutic relationship, 239–240
Confrontation, 62
Connectionist models, 142–147,
152–153
Conscious competence, 18, 26, 151
Conscious incompetence, 18, 26
Consensual qualitative research (CQR),
195, 338–339
Consequences
alignment of, 25–26
coding of, 250–251
in cognitive behavioral approach,
78–79
of corrective emotional experiences,
46
of corrective relational experiences,
343–344
in expectancy-based approach, 134
in GAD case study, 276–277
in implications for practice, 367
long-term, 363
postsession, 256–257, 260–261,
267–269, 271
in STAIRCaSE metaphor, 16
within-session, 256, 260, 267, 270
Consistency theory, 318–319, 326
Constant comparison method, 169
"Constant dripping" trajectory, 317–
318, 320
Constantino, M. J., 127, 134
Constructs, 107
Contact, initial, 126–128
Context
of CE episode, 250, 253–255, 257–
259, 263–265, 269, 358
learning as dependent on, 74–75
presession, 250, 252–253, 256–257,
261–263, 267–269
session, 250, 253, 263, 269
of therapeutic relationship, 191
of therapy, 228, 231, 234–235
of treatment, 282
Contextual integration, 312–313

postsession evaluation of, 220
relational enactments of, 290, 293,
    294, 298–302, 308–309
relational work of, 229, 232, 235, 238
relationship skills of, 273–274
responses of, 124–125, 131, 192, 250
warmth of, 294
Therapists-in-training
    actions of, 342–343
    in case study, 344–345
    in client perspectives study, 164–165
    as clients, 192
    concerns of, 341
    dual awarenesses of, 209–210
    improvements in, 343
    needs of, 344
    research on, 364–367
    in supervision study, 336–337
Therapy
    client deeply involved in, 198
    client realizations about, 204
    concerns addressed in, 198
    context of, 228, 231, 234–235
    duration of, 52
    favorable conditions in, 124, 129
    means vs. ends of, 37
    positive outcomes of, 197
    relational enactments outside of,
        296–297
Thought (in STAIRCaSE), 16
Threat, 127
Three Approaches to Psychotherapy (E. L.
    Shostrom), 104–105
Time-limited dynamic psychotherapy
    (TLDP), 286, 291–292, 309, 310
Timing, 343
Timulak, L., 162
TLDP. *See* Time-limited dynamic
    psychotherapy
Tomlinson, T. M., 107
Traditional models, 141–142
Training. *See also* Therapists-in-training
    in corrective relational
        experiences, 208
    emotional, 52
    implications of CEs for, 368–369
Transference
    and corrective emotional experience,
        41–42

dependence, 40–41
manipulation of, 35–36
positive dependence, 40–41
role of, 52–54
Transformation
    with corrective relational experience,
        206–207
    process of, 91–96
    and supervisory relationship,
        335–336, 346
Traumatic experiences, 34, 96
Treatment. *See also* Interventions
    for anorexia nervosa, 221
    in change experiences over course of
        therapy study, 321
    client expectations in, 122–123
    early phase of, 128–130
    for generalized anxiety disorder,
        246–248, 261–272
    initial contact for, 126–128
    late phase of, 133
    manualized, 237–238, 245, 286
    means vs. ends of, 37
    middle phase of, 130–133
    myth and setting of, 301–302
Treatment as usual (TAU), 286,
    291–292, 310
Treatment expectations, 122–123,
    127–128
Truax, C. B., 107
Truthfulness, 188
Tugade, M. M., 92
Type 1 and Type 2 corrective
    experiences, 356, 363, 366, 367

Unblocking
    in case example, 111–112
    focusing as, 88
    in person-centered therapy, 108
Unconditional positive regard,
    105–106, 111
Unconscious, collective cultural, 313
Unconscious competence, 18,
    26, 151
Unconscious incompetence, 17–18
Understanding, 117
Units of meaning, 171–173
University training clinic (UTC),
    164–165

ABOUT THE EDITORS

Louis G. Castonguay, PhD, completed his doctorate in clinical psychology at the State University of New York–Stony Brook; a clinical internship at University of California, Berkeley; and a postdoctorate at Stanford University. He is currently a professor in the Department of Psychology at Penn State University. With more than 120 publications (including four coedited books), his scholarly work and research focus on different aspects of the process of change and training, especially within the context of psychotherapy integration. He is also involved in the investigation of the efficacy of new integrative treatments for generalized anxiety disorder and depression, and the development of practice research networks aimed at facilitating the collaboration between clinicians and researchers. He has received several awards, including the Early Career Contribution Award from the Society of Psychotherapy Research and the David Shakow Award from Division 12 (Society of Clinical Psychology) of the American Psychological Association (APA). He has received four recognitions from APA Division 29 (Division of Psychotherapy): the Jack D. Krasner Memorial Award, the Award for Distinguished Contributions to Teaching and Mentoring, the Distinguished Research Publications Award, and the Distinguished Psychologist Award for his lifetime contributions to the field of psychotherapy. He also served as president of the North American Society for Psychotherapy Research and the International Society for Psychotherapy Research.

Clara E. Hill, PhD, completed her doctorate in counseling psychology at Southern Illinois University and a clinical internship at the University of Florida. She is currently a professor in the Department of Psychology at the University of Maryland, College Park. With more than 250 publications (including 10 books), her scholarly work and research focus on psychotherapy process, therapist interventions, therapist training, dream work, and qualitative research methods. She has received several awards, including the Leona Tyler Award from Division 17 (Society of Counseling Psychology) of the American Psychological Association (APA), the Distinguished Psychologist Award from APA Division 29 (Psychotherapy), the Outstanding Lifetime Achievement Award from the Section of Counseling and Psychotherapy Process and Outcome Research of the Society for Counseling Psychology, and the Distinguished Research Career Award, Society for Psychotherapy Research. She served as editor of the *Journal of Counseling Psychology* and *Psychotherapy Research*, and also served as president of the North American Society for Psychotherapy Research and the International Society for Psychotherapy Research.